Vedic and Sanskrit Historical Linguistics

PAPERS OF THE 13TH WORLD SANSKRIT CONFERENCE

Edinburg, Scotland (UK) [10-14 July 2006]

General Editors

Peter Bisschop

Paul Dundas

ISBN: 978-81-208-3529-0(Set)

Vol. I. **Scientific Literature in Sanskrit :**
Ed. by S.R. Sarma, Gyula Wojtilla

Vol. II. **Battle, Bards and Brahmins :**
Ed. By John Brockington *(In the Press)*

Vol. III. **Vedic and Sanskrit Historical Linguistics**
Ed. by Jared S. Klein, Elizabeth Tucker]

Vol. IV. **[Āgamas and Tantras :**
Ed. by Bruno Dagens, Gavin Flood]

Vol. V. **[Veda :**
Ed. by Joel Brereton, Theodore Proferes]

Vol. VI. **[Poetry, Drama and Aesthetics :**
Ed. by Mandakranta Bose, David Gitomes, David Smith]

Vol. VII. **[Philosophy :**
Ed. by Jonardon Ganeri]

PAPERS OF THE 13TH WORLD SANSKRIT CONFERENCE
Vol. 3

Vedic and Sanskrit Historical Linguistics

Edited by

JARED KLEIN
ELIZABETH TUCKER

MOTILAL BANARSIDASS PUBLISHERS
PRIVATE LIMITED • DELHI

PAPERS OF THE 13TH WORLD SANSKRIT CONFERENCE HELD IN Edinburg, Scotland, 10-14 JULY 2006

VOL. 3

General Editors:

Paul Dundas and Peter Bisschop

*First Edition : Delhi, **2014***

ISBN: 978-81-208-3632-7

MOTILAL BANARSIDASS

41 U.A. Bungalow Road, Jawahar Nagar, Delhi 110 007
8 Mahalaxmi Chamber, 22 Bhulabhai Desai Road, Mumbai 400 026
203 Royapettah High Road, Mylapore, Chennai 600 004
236, 9th Main III Block, Jayanagar, Bangaluru 560 011
Sanas Plaza, 1302 Baji Rao Road, Pune 411 002
8 Camac Street, Kolkata 700 017
Ashok Rajpath, Patna 800 004
Chowk, Varanasi 221 001

Printed in India

by RP Jain at NAB Printing Unit,
A-44, Naraina Industrial Area, Phase I, New Delhi–110028
and published by JP Jain for Motilal Banarsidass Publishers (P) Ltd,
41 U.A. Bungalow Road, Jawahar Nagar, Delhi-110007

General Preface

The Thirteenth World Sanskrit Conference was held in Edinburgh, Scotland on the 10th–14th July 2006. To the delight of the organisers it was attended by a record number of participants from all parts of the world. At a time when the study of Sanskrit and related Indological subjects is becoming increasingly embattled in certain countries, such regular gatherings assume a particular importance in confirming scholarly solidarity as well as disseminating the most recent fruits of research.

The conference was divided into fourteen subject sections, each chaired by two scholars: 1. Veda; 2. Epics; 3. Purāṇas; 4. Āgamas and Tantra; 5. Vyākaraṇa; 6. Linguistics; 7. Poetry, Drama and Aesthetics; 8. Scientific Literature; 9. Buddhist Literature; 10. Jaina Studies; 11. Philosophy; 12. History, Epigraphy and the Arts; 13. Law and Society; and 14. Culture and Society.

As now customary, arrangements for the publication of the proceedings became the responsibility of the conference organisers. To this end, the various section chairs were requested to edit the proceedings volume of their subject after inviting the submission of papers from participants and then submit a manuscript to the general editors for inspection and final formatting. It should be noted that the chairs of two thematic subpanels of the Philosophy section ('Śāstrārambha-Philosophical Introduction' and 'New Directions in the Study of Yoga'), of History, Epigraphy and the Arts, and of Law and Society, wished to make their own arrangements for publication elsewhere. In addition, it was decided that papers in the Culture and Tradition section which had been invited for publication should be placed in appropriate volumes of the proceedings.

The general editors would like to thank Petteri Koskikallio and Lumi Sammallahti for taking expert control of the final formatting and technical production of the proceedings. It is anticipated that these Proceedings of the Thirteenth World Sanskrit Conference will reveal the impressive breadth and depth of Indological research at the present time and gain the appreciation of the interested scholarly world.

PETER BISSCHOP
PAUL DUNDAS
General Editors,
Proceedings of the 13th World Sanskrit Conference

Introduction

The present volume contains the published versions of 10 of the 17 papers presented at the Linguistics sessions of the 13th World Sanskrit Conference held on July 13–14, 2006 in Edinburgh, Scotland and dedicated to the memory of Murray B. Emeneau, the doyen of American Indologists.

The contributions[1] include two on phonology (Kobayashi and Kümmel), two on morphology (García Ramón and Tucker), three on syntax (Bubenik, Hettrich, and Hock), one on the semantics of tense and aspect (Dahl), one on lexicography (Krisch), and one on stylistics (Klein). In several instances these papers fit integrally into the research agendas of their authors, representing parts of

---

[1] Not included here are the following papers: Mārcis Gasūns, 'Approaches to the Sanskrit root', Gary Holland, 'Indo-European laryngeals and Vedic meter: Evidence, counter evidence, and a rhythmic rule', Boris Oguibenine, 'Spoken Sanskrit and Buddhist Sanskrit', Georges-Jean Pinault, 'About the "double possessive" compounds in the Vedic language', and Sabine Ziegler, 'The nomina converbalia in the *Ṛgveda*: Towards a syntactic hierarchy of participles, gerunds, verbal nouns and agent nouns'. Two other papers not included here have now appeared in print: Alexander Lubotsky, 'Vedic *puroḍā́ś-* "sacrificial cake", *anaḍúh-* "ox" and the problem of nom. sg. *víṭ*' has appeared under the title 'Vedic "ox" and "sacrificial cake"' in A. Lubotsky, J. Schaeken & A. Wiedenhof (eds.), *Evidence and Counter-Evidence. Essays in Honour of Frederik Kortlandt*, I: *Balto-Slavic and Indo-European Linguistics*. (Studies in Slavic and General Linguistics, 32.) Amsterdam: Rodopi, 2008: 351–360; and Calvert Watkins, 'Two tokens of Indo-Iranian Hieratic Language', has appeared in G. Schweiger (ed.), *Indogermanica. Festschrift Gert Klingenschmitt*. Taimering: Schweiger VWT-Verlag, 2005: 681–687. In addition, Jared Klein's paper, 'Sequential Negation in the *Ṛgveda*' has been replaced by 'Conjunctive Sequences in the *Ṛgveda*'. Klein's original paper has appeared in Alan J. Nussbaum (ed.), *Verba Docenti. Studies in Historical and Indo-European Linguistics Presented to Jay H. Jasanoff by Students, Colleagues, and Friends*. Ann Arbor: Beech Stave Press, 2007: 213–229.

larger projects reflected in recent publications (Bubenik, Dahl, García Ramón, Hettrich, Klein, Kobayashi) or deal with issues touched on repeatedly by their authors over a number of years (Hock). In one case (Krisch), the work announced has in the interim begun to appear in print.[2] It can therefore be said that the papers included here represent a broad reflection of research projects currently underway in Sanskrit Linguistics. That all but one of the papers focus exclusively on Vedic is simply a reflection of the reality that in Western countries the study of Sanskrit has frequently been treated as an entrée to Indo-European linguistics, and it is especially the oldest texts that have been mined for whatever nuggets they can yield relative to our understanding of the proto-language.

The editors are grateful that Motilal Banarsidass, which over the years has made so many important works of Indology and especially Vedic studies available to scholars everywhere, has agreed to publish these proceedings.

JARED S. KLEIN
ELIZABETH TUCKER

Athens, Georgia, 29.11.2009

---

[2] *Rivelex: Rigveda-Lexikon*, I: *Wörter beginnend mit "a"*. By Thomas Krisch with Christina Katsikadeli, Stefan Niederreiter & Thomas Kaltenbacher. (Grazer Vergleichende Arbeiten, 20). Graz: Leykam, 2006. *Rivelex: Rigveda-Lexikon*, II: *Wörter beginnend mit anderen Vokalen als "a"*. Unter Mitarbeit von Christina Katsikadeli, Stefan Niederreiter, Konstantinos Sampanis & Sabine Ziegler. (Grazer Vergleichende Arbeiten, 26.) Graz: Leykam, 2012. For E-book versions, see Krisch's bibliography (p. 262).

Contents

General Preface v

Introduction vii

MASATO KOBAYASHI
Origin and Development of Sanskrit *yy* 1

MARTIN JOACHIM KÜMMEL
Laryngeal Traces without Laryngeals in Vedic Metre? 25

J. L. GARCÍA RAMÓN
On Polymorphic Presents in the *Ṛgveda*: Reduplication and 'Aktionsart' 45

ELIZABETH TUCKER
The 'Competition' in the RV and AV between Stems in *-ín* and Stems in *-vant* Derived from Thematic Nouns 79

VIT BUBENIK
On the Rise and Remaking of the Middle Voice in Anatolian and Indo-Iranian 103

HEINRICH HETTRICH
Some Remarks on the Adverbal Genitive in Ṛgvedic Sanskrit 129

HANS HENRICH HOCK
Vedic Verb Accent Revisited 153

EYSTEIN DAHL
The Development of the Vedic Perfect: from Anterior Present to Inferential Past 179

THOMAS KRISCH
RIVELEX – Presenting the First Volume of a New Dictionary of the *Ṛgveda* 243

JARED S. KLEIN
Conjunctive Sequences in the *Ṛgveda* 265

Contributors 293

General Index 295

Origin and Development of Sanskrit *yy*[*]

MASATO KOBAYASHI

1. INTRODUCTION

In *Aṣṭādhyāyī* 6.1.81–83, Pāṇini teaches exceptional *-ya-* gerundive forms of roots ending in *-ĭ*. The root vowel *-ĭ*, which is in the guṇa grade (*-e*) by Aṣṭ. 7.3.84 *sārvad*^{h}*ātukārd*^{h}*ad*^{h}*ātukayoḥ* (82 *guṇaḥ*), is replaced with *-ay* before the *y-* of an affix only in the words listed there.

> Aṣṭ. 6.1.81 *kṣayya-jayyau śakyārt*^{h}*e* 'In *kṣayya* und *jayya* findet die Substitution von *ay* für *e* statt in der Bedeutung "zu – möglich"' (Böhtlingk 1887: 293). Examples: *kṣayya-* 'destructible': TB 3.11.7.4 *kṣayyá-*,[1] JB 1.241 *kṣayya-*, MS 1.8.6:124.4, KS 31.15:18.8, ŚB, TB, JB etc. *a-kṣayyá-*. *jayya-* 'conquerable': ŚB 1.6.2.3; 11.2.7.9, 13–20, 28, 29, 31; 14.4.3.24 (K 2.5.4.2; 3.2.8.2) *ja̱yya-* /jáyya-/, MS 3.2.1:15.8, 10, TS 1.7.5.4; 5.2.1.1 *an-apa-jayyá-* :: JB 1.326_2 *jeya-*.

> Aṣṭ. 6.1.82 *krayyas tadart*^{h}*e* 'In *krayya-* in der Bedeutung "zum Kauf ausgestellt, verkäuflich"' (Böhtlingk). For example, *krayya-* 'for sale, available for purchasing': MS 3.7.4:78.14 *ékahāyanyā kráyyā* (Mss.

---

[*] I wish to express my sincere gratitude to George Cardona for his advice on native grammar, Werner Knobl for reading the drafts of this paper painstakingly and for giving me many helpful suggestions, especially on the interpretation of the cited texts, and to Alexander Lubotsky for his advice on the historical phonology of Indo-Aryan. The errors and mistakes are mine alone, of course.

[1] The oxytone of TB *kṣayyá-* instead of expected **kṣáyya-* is probably based on that of *a-kṣayyá-* which follows it in the same section (Knobl, personal communication).

ékahāyavyā-),[2] 3.7.4:79.1 *apsú kráyyā* [*-aḥ*] *óṣadʰayo vái sómā* [*-aḥ*] (Mss *krayyā́*), MS 3.7.7:85.10 *vatsataréṇa sā́ṇḍena kráyyasyéndram áhaḥ krīṇāti*, ŚB 3.3.3.1₂ (K 4.3.3.1₂) *so̱mavikrayin kra̱yyas te so̱mo rājā3 i̱ti kra̱yya i̱ty āha*.

Aṣṭ. 6.1.83 *bʰayya-pravayye ca ccʰandasi* (Vārttika *+hradayyā*) 'Hierher gehören auch die vedischen *bʰayya* und *pravayyā*' (Böhtlingk). Examples: *bʰayya-* 'that which is feared': KS 33.4:30.7; PB 10.5.16, 23.6.6. *pra-vayyā-* 'to be impregnated' or 'to be driven': not attested.

These forms are of special interest for the phonology of Sanskrit, firstly because Pāṇini teaches them in *Aṣṭādhyāyī* 6.1, which is a section mainly on phonology (exceptional alternation, sandhi and word accent), and not in 3.1, a section on verbal morphology where exceptional gerundive forms in *-āyya-* such as *ā-nāyya-* (a name of the ritual fire *anvāhāryapacana*) are taught (Aṣṭ. 3.1.127–131); and secondly, because the alternation *-i-* : *-ay-* is taught here as special compared to the regular pattern *-i-* : *-e-* as in √*jay* / *ji* 'win, conquer' : *jeya-* 'to be conquered', etc. In other words, the forms *jayya-*, *krayya-*, *bʰayya-* etc. with /yy/ stand in contrast with regular *jeya-*, *kreya-* 'to be bought', *bʰeya-* 'to be feared', forming minimal pairs[3] belonging to the same grammatical category.

From a diachronic point of view, the forms in *-ayya-* are actually no mystery. Whitney (1889: 345 §963a) already mentions rightly that '[t]he original value of the suffix is *ia*, and as such it has to be read in the very great majority of its Vedic occurrences.' Based on the metrical scansion of *-ya-* gerundives in the *Ṛgveda*, Seebold (1972: 221) demonstrates that the suffix is actually *-iya-* in simplex forms even after a light syllable, while monosyllabic *-ya-* is found in its place when compounded. Since Sievers' Law is

---

[2] Since *kráyyā* here is not followed by an udātta vowel, it should be emended to *kráyyo* (Knobl, personal communication).

[3] Assuming that *e* is phonemically /ai/.

not evoked after a light syllable, it can safely be argued that gerundive forms like *jayya-* were originally formed with the suffix *-iya-*. This suffix is attached to the full-grade roots ending in *-ay*, and *-y-iya-* is then shortened to *-yya-* in a syncope process *i* > Ø / V̆C__*i̯* (Edgerton 1943: 87 'the converse of Sievers' Law').[4] Verbal adjectives in **-i̯o-* or traces of them are found in other branches of Indo-European, for example in Avestan (YAv. *zaoiia-*, OAv. *zəuuīm* acc.sg. 'to be called'), Latin (*eximius* 'distinguished', *genius* 'tutelary deity') and Greek (*hágios* 'holy'). This suffix is reconstructed either as **-iHo-* or **-i-i̯o-*, as the origin of the **i̯* in it cannot be uniquely determined (Schindler 1977: 58; Lubotsky 1997: 142).[5]

An important fact to be noted in this connection is that a geminate *-yy-* is in theory impossible in Sanskrit, for, if there is a Proto-Indo-Iranian sequence like **-aiia-* (the nucleus status of **i* is left unspecified), the first **i* is annexed to the **a* to its left and forms a diphthong */ai/ while the second **i* becomes an onset of the following syllable (*/i̯a/), creating the final output *-eya-*. However, *-yy-* is an acceptable and not uncommon sequence in Pāṇini's grammar. Firstly, Pāṇini teaches forms which contain /yy/ both by derivational rules and by direct listing (*nipātana*). For example, causative stems form compounded absolutives in *-ayya* according to Aṣṭ. 6.4.56 *lyapi lagʰu-pūrvasya* (51 *ṇer*, 55 *ay*), and /yy/ here seems to make position because this suffix occurs only when preceded by a light syllable (*lagʰu-pūrvasya*) and is apparently conditioned by some rhythmic factor as in the case of the reduplicated aorist; forms with the sequence *yy* are explicitly given in many sūtras, such as Aṣṭ. 6.1.81 *kṣayya-jayyau*

---

[4] In the *R̥gveda*, I could not find any unproblematic example where what is written *iy* should actually be read /y/ (cf. Edgerton 1943: 89), but there are cases where *y*, whose underlying form is /iy/, is metrically to be read /y/, as we will see in section **2**.

[5] According to Mayrhofer (1986: 165f.), the sequences **-i̯o-* and **-i(i̯)o-* are reconstructed as distinct morphemes already in PIE, for example in the delocative suffix.

śakyārt^he, etc. mentioned above. Secondly, *-ayy-* and *-aiy-* must have been distinct, as vṛddhi forms like *vaiyākaraṇa-* 'grammarian' from *vyākaraṇa-* 'grammar' are provided for by Aṣṭ. 7.3.3 *na yvāb^hyām padāntāb^hyām pūrvau tu tāb^hyām aic.*[6] Finally, the optional doubling of consonants including semivowels after /r/ or /h/ and before a vowel, taught in Aṣṭ. 8.4.46 *aco rahāb^hyān dve* (45 *yaraḥ, vā*), e.g. *aryyá-* for *aryá-* m. 'lord', shows that the gemination of /y/ is a synchronically active phonological process. Based on these grounds, Pāṇini must have conceived of *yy* as a genuine geminate, and there was a change in the phonological status of /y/ between Proto-Indo-Iranian and Pāṇini.

This paper addresses the question how /yy/ emerged, and how it was incorporated into Sanskrit phonology as an acceptable geminate, from the viewpoint of historical and synchronic phonology.

2. OCCURRENCES OF *yy* IN VEDIC

We will first take a brief overview of the forms containing *yy*, their first occurrence, and which of them are not /yiy/ but real /yy/ on metrical or etymological grounds.

a. [*Ṛgveda*]: Gerundives in *-ā́yya-* (Bartholomae 1907: 321ff., AiG II.2, 285 §173). Metrically *-āyiya-* except RV 1.129.2b *dakṣā́yya-* 'who has to be pleased' (*-ā́yiya-* in the other five occurrences of the word), 6.18.6d *vitantasā́yya-* 'to be contended for' (*-ā́yiya-* in the other three occurrences), 10.122.7c *mahayā́yya-* 'aggrandizement'.

b. [*Ṛgveda*] Gerundives of roots ending in *-ā́*. PB 9.1.21–22 *a-saṃ-hāyya-* 'not to be collected [again]' vs. JB, JUB *a-saṃ-heya-* from √*hā* : *jíhīte* 'start up'. TS 2.2.10.2 *d^hāyyā́-* (Aṣṭ. 3.1.129) 'supplementary verse'. RV 4.29.5d *ā-kāyyà-* 'to be wished for'.

---

[6] The *Ṛgveda* already has one form with *-aiy-*, i.e. the patronymic *vái-yaśva-* from the proper name *vyàśva-*, but as there are only a few cases of *-ayy-* there (see section 2), *-aiy-* hardly makes a phonemic contrast with *-ayy-*.

c. [*Ṛgveda+*]: *-ya-* derivatives in *-āyya-* (AiG II.2, 794 §642ef, 795 §643bα, 286 §173c). While *-ya-* forms of roots in *-ā* usually end in *-eya-*, there are also forms in *-āyya-* (*-ā́yya-* /-ā́yiya-/ or *-āyyà-* /-āyíya-/). RV *nṛ-pā́yya-* 'protecting men', RV 5.66.6c and 8.27.22b *bahu-pā́yya-* 'protecting many'. RV 8.34.5b *pūrva-pā́yya-* 'first drink' (vs. RV 1.135.4e, 7.92.1d *pūrva-péya-*), RV 8.17.13c *kuṇḍa-pā́yya-* name of a ritual (Aṣṭ. 3.1.130).

d. [*Atharvaveda+*]: *-āyya-* gerundives of roots ending in *-ī̆* or derivatives thereof (AiG II.2, 793 §642d, 796 §643bβ). AVŚ 15.3.10 *pra-hāyyà-* 'messenger' from √*hay/hi* 'drive, impel' (vs. AVŚ, ŚB *pra-héya-* 'to be dispatched' in **e** below), AVŚ 6.105.1d *pra-vāyyà-* 'forth-driving' (Whitney). Pāṇini teaches such forms in Aṣṭ. 3.1.123 and 127–131, i.e. Aṣṭ. 3.1.123 *upa-cāyya-* 'to be piled' (?) (*c^handasi*), Aṣṭ. 3.1.127 *ā-nāyya-* a name of the ritual fire Anvāhāryapacana, Aṣṭ. 3.1.128 *pra-ṇāyya-* 'thief' (?) (cf. ChU 3.11.5 *prāṇāyya-* 'trustworthy', a variant for *praṇāya-*), Aṣṭ. 3.1.129 *sāṃnāyya-* a kind of dairy offering (TS 2.5.3.3 *sāṃnāyyá-*), Aṣṭ. 3.1.130 *saṃ-cāyyà-* a kind of Soma ritual, Aṣṭ. 3.1.131 *pari-cāyya-* 'sacrificial fire piled in circle' (TS 5.4.11.3 *pari-cāyyà-*, KS 21.4:42.7 *pari-cāyya-*), *upa-cāyya-* a kind of ritual fire (cf. Agrawala 1953: 370ff.).

e. [*Yajurveda+*]: Above-mentioned *-ăyya-* gerundives of roots ending in *-ī̆* (Aṣṭ. 6.1.81–83, AiG II.2, 791 §642cα, 796 §643bβ). *kráyya-* (for MS *ā-kráyya-* , see section **1**, fn. 2), *b^háyya-* , *jáyya-* , *a-kṣayyá-* (see section 1 for reference). Of the types *jáyya-* 'conquerable' and *jeya-* 'to be conquered', the former is generally older, for it is attested in the Brāhmaṇas and the Brāhmaṇa portions of the Black Yajurveda Saṃhitās. But there is also an old *-eya-* form from a root ending in *-i*, i.e. AVŚ 5.17.3c, ŚB 5.3.1.11 (ŚBK 7.1.4.12) *pra-héya-* 'to be dispatched' (Bartholomae 1907: 322) vs. AVŚ 15.3.10 *pra-hāyyà-* in **d** above.

f. [*Ṛgveda, Atharvaveda*]: Derivatives in *-éyya-* (Bartholomae 1907: 320; AiG II.2, 512 §344). RV 10.10.7b *saha-śéy(i)ya-* 'lying together' (= AVŚ 18.1.8b), *stuṣéy(i)ya-* 'worthy of praise' in RV 10.120.6a *stuṣéyyam puruvárpasam ŕ̥b^hvam* (triṣṭubh), and AVŚ 5.31.12b *śapat^hey(i)yà-* /-yíya-/ 'worthy of cursing' (Whitney).

g. [*Ṛgveda+*]: When taddhita *-ya-* is attached to a stem ending in *-ya*, *-yya-* is the outcome in older texts (AiG II.2, 807 §651a). RV

10.151.4c *hṛdayyà-* 'cordial' (3σ) from *hṛ́daya-* n. 'heart'. TS 4.5.9.1g *niveṣyyà-* 'belonging to the whirlpool' from *niveṣyá-* m. 'whirlpool', and possibly TS 4.5.9.1g *hradayyà-* 'belonging to the lake' as if from an unattested (and unlikely) *hradaya-* n. 'lake'.

h. [*Ṛgveda+*]: Compounded absolutive of causative and other stems (AiG II.2, 781 §635a). RV 1.105.18c, 3.26.1a *ni-cā́yiyā*. Cf. ŚB *paly-áyya, ā-kramáyya, palā́yya, anu-gamáyya, pra-janáyya, uj-jvaláyya* (AiG II.2, 785 §638a).

i. [Brāhmaṇa+]: *śayyā-* f. 'bed' (Aṣṭ. 3.3.99 *saṃjñāyām ... śīn-b^hṛñiṇaḥ*, AiG II.2, 247 §142b), (-)*śayya-* absolutive, etc. (Aṣṭ. 7.4.22 *ayaṅ yi kṅiti* [21 *śīṅaḥ*], AiG II.2, 785 §638a), from √*śay*^(i) / *śi* (*śī*) 'be lying'.

j. [*Ṛgveda*]: Patronymics of unclear etymology. *vayyà-*, always (6×) occurring after caesura and to be read *vayiyà-* /vayíya-/ (another form in *-ayyà-* is g. *hṛdayyà-*). RV 8.68.10d *puru-mā́yiya-*.

k. [*Ṛgveda+*]: Irregular inflectional forms of *rayí-* m. 'wealth' (AiG III, 215 §120aβ; Lubotsky 1995). RV 10.19.7d (2σ), AVŚ$_2$, MS, TS *rayyā́* inst.sg., TS *rayyā́m* loc.sg., ŚB *rayyái* dat.sg. These forms were created secondarily from nom.sg. *rayíḥ* after the model of feminine *-i-*stems like *matí-* : inst.sg. *matyā́* and *puṣṭí-* : dat.sg. *puṣṭyái*.

l. [*Ṛgveda+*]: Inflectional forms of *vṛkī́* stems in *-yī*. RV 2.37.5a *yayiyàm* /-yíyam/ acc. of *yayī́-* 'running', RV 10.155.2c *arāyyàm* acc.sg. of *arāyī́-* 'blackguard woman'. Cf. RV 10.78.7c *yayíy[aḥ* nom.pl.

m. [*Ṛgveda+*]: *-yy* resulting from external sandhi. Always to be read /-yi V-/ in the *Ṛgveda* and the *Atharvaveda* except in RV 10.128.3b *máyy āśī́r astu máyi deváhūtiḥ* and AVŚ 1.1.2d, 1.1.3d *máyy evā́stu máyi śrutám* and 4.25.3b *tváyy údite prérate citrabhāno*.

In most cases of *yy* in the *Ṛgveda*, it is metrically /yiy/, but real /yy/ also occurs at least four times in the tenth book of the *Ṛgveda*, (namely 10.19.7d *rayyā́*, 10.122.7c *mahayā́yyāya*, 10.128.3b *máyy āśī́r astu* and 10.151.4c *hṛdayyàyā*), once in the first book (namely 1.129.2b *dakṣā́yyaḥ*), and also once in the sixth book (6.18.6d *vitantasā́yyaḥ*). Since book 10, and partly also book 1, belongs to newer layers of the *Ṛgveda* text corpus, we can argue that there was no real *yy* in the oldest stage of the Vedic language, except in *vitantasā́yya-* of the sixth book, which, however, is likely to be one of the younger family books. Although real *yy* started to occur only in newer layers of the *Ṛgveda*, Śākalya's redaction generalized *yy* to the older books and changed all /yiy/ to *yy*.

In the Śaunakasaṃhitā of the *Atharvaveda*, *yy* is usually to be read /yiy/, except in a few forms such as *mayy* V-, *tvayy* V- or *rayyā́*, and the geminate status of /yy/ does not seem to be established yet. In the Black Yajurveda Saṃhitās and the Brāhmaṇas, which do not contain many metrical mantras, it is difficult to judge whether /yy/ is a geminate or not.

3. DEVELOPMENT OF *-*ai̯i*- AND RELATIVE CHRONOLOGY

In order to understand how the gemination of /y/, which cannot be of Proto-Indo-Iranian origin, arose in Sanskrit phonology, it will be useful to review the origins of Sanskrit intervocalic /y/. Here I list a few examples of /y/ of laryngeal or glide origin in a postvocalic context, especially before **i*.

i. Non-laryngeal offglide (*Ø > *y* / *i*__V):

**ia* > *iya*?: **i-á-d*^{h}*i̯ai̯* > RV 6.20.8d *iyá-d*^{h}*yai* dat.inf. of √*ay* / *i* 'go'. This form probably does not serve as an example, for **a* of the suffix *-*ád*^{h}*yai* is later than Proto-Indo-Iranian, and also, something irregular seems to have taken place in the reflection of the initial **i* as a syllable nucleus.

The non-laryngeal *y* in *īyivā́ṃs-* (RV 3.9.4a *īyivā́ṃsam*, 10.14.1a *pareyivā́ṃsam*), pf.ppl. of the same root, is not usable either, for connective *-i-* just seems to be added to the weak stem *īy-*.

ii. Laryngeal offglide before **i* (**H* > *y* / V__*i*):

**iHi* > *iyi*: nil.

**iHi* > *ī*: **Hi-Hij-ái̯* > RV *ījé* pf.1, 3sg.mid. of √*yaj* / *ij* 'offer, worship'.

iii. Laryngeal offglide before vowels other than *i (*H > y / i__$V_{\neg i}$):

**iHa > iya*: **Hí-Har-ti > íyarti* pres.ind.3sg.act. of √*ar* / *ṛ* 'start moving'. **Hi-Hā́y-a > iyāya* pf.3sg.act. of √*ay* / *i* 'go'. PIIr. **priH-á- > priyá-* 'dear'.

Aside from **i̯*, a laryngeal offglide as in **iii**. *íyarti* is a source of Sanskrit intervocalic *y*.

iv. Laryngeal onglide between a vowel other than **i* and **i* (**H > y* / $V_{\neg i}$_*i*):

Lubotsky (1995: 214ff.) discusses the development of **aHi* in great detail. According to him, the laryngeal in this context is usually lost and contraction of **a* and **i* to *e* takes place subsequently, unless morphological pressure causes the laryngeal to be restored.

**aHi > ai* ?: In augmented forms like **á-Hisć-a-s* > RV *áicc*^{h}*aḥ* ipf.2sg.act. of √*eṣ* / *iṣ* 'seek' (trisyllabic in RV 10.108.5a), the augment is restored according to Lubotsky (1995: 223).

**aHi > ayi*: **raHí-s > rayíḥ* nom.sg. of *rayí-* m. 'wealth'. Restitution of **H* by analogy is unlikely according to Lubotsky (1995: 222), and so this is probably the only example of uncontracted **aHí*.

**āHi > āyi*: **á-d*^{h}*āH-i > ád*^{h}*āyi* aor.pass.3sg. of √*d*^{h}*ā* 'put'. It is possible that *y* was inserted as a result of analogy to other aorist passive forms, like *ákāri* from √*kar* / *kṛ* 'do' (Lubotsky 1995: 220).

v. PIIr. **i̯* before **i* (**i̯ > y* / V__*i*):

**á-ćrāi̯-i > áśrāyi* aor.pass.3sg. of √*śray* / *śri* 'lean'. Here also, **i̯* might have been restored by analogy to other aorist passive forms.

**ai̯i > ayi*: This is the usual outcome when a suffix beginning with **i* is attached to a causative stem, e.g. RV 7.81.6c *codayitrī́* f. 'inciter', 9.101.1b *mādayitnú-* 'intoxicating', 10.162.6b *mohayitvā́* absol. 'having befuddled', etc. Contraction no longer applies to productive formation patterns like these (Lubotsky 1995: 219).

vi. PIIr. **i̯H* after **ă*:

**ai̯Ha > aya*: **ai̯H-as- > váyas-* n. 'vigor'.

**ai̯Ha > eya*?: them.pres.opt.1sg.mid. such as **sač-ai̯H-a* > RV *saceya* of √*sac* 'accompany'. Optative forms of a thematic stem have *e* throughout the paradigm, and *e* in the first singular might be a result of leveling.

**ai̯Hi* > *e* /aï/: **ćrái̯H-išt^ha-* > **ćrái̯Ø-išt^ha-* > *śréṣṭ^ha-* 'most splendid' (3σ in 8 out of 31 simplex occurrences in the *Ṛgveda* according to Lubotsky (1995: 217). Cf. *śréyas-* 2σ).

**ai̯Hi* > *e* /ai̯/?: **a-nai̯H-iš-n̥ta* > *aneṣata* aor.3pl.mid. (RV 10.155.5a, 4σ). As we have only one occurrence of this form in the tenth book of the *Ṛgveda*, the possibility to scan *e* in this form as disyllabic remains open.

**ai̯Hi* > *ayi* ?: **krai̯H-ii̯a-* > **krai̯Øii̯a-* > MS+ *kráyiya-*; **nái̯H-išt^ha-* > RV 10.126.3c *náyiṣṭ^ha-*. *áyi* in the latter form might be due to analogy to other superlative forms like *jáviṣṭ^ha-* 'quickest' from √*javⁱ* / *jū* 'be quick'.

**ai̯Hi̯* > *ey*: **ćrái̯H-i̯as-* > **ćrái̯Ø-i̯as-* > *śréyas-* 'more splendid' (2σ. See below).

**ai̯HC* > *e*C /aïC/: **nái̯H-tar-* > *nétar-* 'leader' (possibly 3σ in 4 out of 18 occurrences in the *Ṛgveda*), **prai̯H-tár-* > *pretár-* 'friend, lover' (possibly 3σ in RV 1.148.5d, 2σ in RV 4.41.5b). It is not clear whether the disyllabic scansion of *e* reflects vocalization of the **H* (Lubotsky 1995: 218; Tichy 1995: 36).

**ai̯HC* > *ayi* ?: **nái̯H-tum* > AB, TB *-náyitum* inf. of √*nayⁱ*/*nī* 'lead' (Werba 1997: 300). This is a late form and may not represent the original development of the sequence **ai̯HC*.

**āi̯HC* > *ai*C: **(a-)nāi̯H-s-ta* > *naiṣṭa iṣ*-aorist of √*nayⁱ*/*nī* (RV 8.30.3d, 2σ. Narten 1964: 169. Cf. Narten 1964: 52: 'ist die Gruppe *-āi̯i-š-* vielleicht schon vorindisch zu *-āiš-* kontrahiert worden').

What happened to **i̯* (< PIIr. **i̯* or **H*) between **ă* and **i* in pre-Vedic Indo-Aryan is not an easy question, for we need to understand the relative chronology of the developments of laryngeals and intervocalic **i̯* at the same time. Although we could not find any good example of non-laryngeal **ăi̯i* free from morphological pressure, regular developments of **aHi* and **ai̯Hi* (and possibly **ăi̯HC* as well) seem to be *e* /ai̯/ and *e* /aï/, as we see in **daH-iya-* > *-aeya-* 'giving' as in *vasudéya-* n. 'treasure-giving' (Lubotsky 1995: 215), and **ćrái̯H-išt^ha-* > **ćrái̯Ø-išt^ha-* > *śréṣṭ^ha-*

(3σ), respectively. Only *rayíḥ* < **raHí-s*, for which no form seems to serve as a model of analogy[7], shows *ayí* instead of expected *e*.

The chronological order of the sound changes involving Proto-Indo-Iranian non-nucleus **i̯* can be summarized as follows. In pre-Vedic Indo-Aryan, non-nucleus **i̯* was lost between **a* and **i*, including **i* of laryngeal origin (if a laryngeal ever becomes **i* between **i̯* and a consonant, cf. Lubotsky 1995: 218f.). Since diaeresis is strongly disfavored, resulting /aï/ was then contracted to *e*. This change was still going on at the time of the *Ṛgveda* poets, and we have cases of disyllabic scansion of *e* as in *śréṣṭ*^{h}*a-* or *préṣṭ*^{h}*a-*. On the other hand, gerundive forms like *kráyya-* came into the derivational cycle rather late, when the loss of non-nucleus **i̯* between vowels and subsequent contraction was already complete. So it was subject only to *i*-syncope, and resulted in *kráyya-*.

PIIr.		**ćrái̯H-išt*^{h}*a-*
post-PIIr.	dissolution of **H*	**ćrái̯Ø-išt*^{h}*a-*
post-PIIr.	**i̯*-loss before **i*	**ćráØišt*^{h}*a-*
up to RV	contraction of **aï* to *e*	> *śréṣṭ*^{h}*a-*
		**kráy(H)-iya-*
post-RV	*i/u*-syncope	> *kráyya-*

Other forms with underlying or surface /yy/ are explainable within, or at least are not in conflict with, the framework of this relative chronology:

[7] Analogy with the oblique cases (*rāyā́*, etc.) does not provide an explanation for the short *-ă-* of *rayíḥ*. Hence it is possible that *rayíḥ* is a result of regular sound change, at least in part, with the restoration of *-y-* through paradigmatic pressure (Lubotsky 1995: 222f.).

- *śréyas-*, comparative of *śrī́-* f. 'splendor', was discussed by Pinault (1982: 268), who proposes a rule of laryngeal loss before **i̯*. If **-ai̯H-* becomes disyllabic *e* /aï/ before a consonant as the *e* in *nétar-* < **nái̯H-tar-* possibly did, we would expect to see a disyllabic scansion of the *e* in *śréyas-* too. However, the first syllable *śré-* of this word is monosyllabic in all of its four occurrences in the *R̥gveda* (3.8.4b, 5.60.4c, 6.41.4b, 10.31.2d). This fact is more naturally explained by assuming a loss of the laryngeal that would otherwise become a vowel **i*.
- *pra-héya-* (AVŚ+) in section **2e** might be a form old enough to undergo **i̯*-loss and crasis, but it is also possible that it was formed with **-̀i̯a-* instead of **-ii̯a-* (Seebold 1972: 222).
- *-pā́yya-* and *dʰāyyà-* in section **2b**: We do not know what exactly these forms are, but if they come from **-āH-ii̯a-* and if **āHi* > *āyi* is a regular sound change, they can be explained by *i*-syncope.
- *-nāyya-* and *-cāyya-* in section **2d**: These formations are not clear either, and if they come from **-āi̯H-ii̯a-*, we are not sure what would be the regular outcome. As they are not attested in old literature, they might also have been formed after **i̯*-loss and contraction were complete.
- Productive gerundive forms such as *kreya-* in section **1** are formed in a new, remodeled derivational pattern with the suffix *-ya-*.

4. CHANGE IN THE PRONUNCIATION OF **i̯ ~y*

**i̯* is a conditioned allophone of **i* in Proto-Indo-Iranian, and it was probably not distinct from **i* except in the nucleus status. The fact that *y* appears after **i* as a Hiatustilger in the place of a disappeared laryngeal, as in Sanskrit *priyá-* or Avestan *friia-* < PIIr. **priH-á-*, supports the view that **i̯* was originally a glide equivalent of **i*.

The current text of the *Ṛgveda*, which was orthoepically normalized by the redactor Śākalya, does not give any direct evidence for the change in the pronunciation of /y/ (**i̯*), except that it is reported to have been weak at the end of a word: According to Pāṇini, Aṣṭ. 8.3.19 *lopaḥ śākalyasya* (17 *apūrvasya aśi*, 18 *vyoḥ*), word-final /y/ and /v/ are lost before a word beginning with a vowel in Śākalya's view ({y, v} > Ø /-{a, ā}__ $]_{wd}$ $X_{[voiced]}$-/), e.g. /yásmāy arkám/ → *yásmāØ arkám*.[8] While no other major phonetic change is visible, the phonemic status of /y/ (**i̯*) might have started changing by Śākalya's time. Medial *-yi-* is already common in productive formations such as *māday-itnú-* (section **3v**) or *paṭay-iṣṇú-* 'flying', and *yy* has multiplied in his edition of the *Ṛgveda* by syncope and sandhi (section **2m**), suggesting that /y/ can stand on its own independent of and unaffected by adjacent /i/ or /y/. Phonemicization of /y/ seems to be complete by the time when minimal pair morphemes of *i-* vs. *yi-*, as the reduplicants of *iyāya* pf.3sg.act. of √*ay/i* 'go' (RV+) vs. *a-yiyaṁsaṁs* desid.impf. 3pl. of √*yam* 'hold' (KS 23.5:80.16), start to appear in later Vedic texts.

As to Pāṇini, we saw in section **1** that *yy* occurs in forms taught in his grammar and that consonants including /y/ are optionally geminated after /r/ and /h/ according to Aṣṭ. 8.4.46, whereas /y/ after other consonants is not (Aṣṭ. 8.4.47). We argued that his *yy* should be taken at face value, namely as a real geminate with no epenthetic vowel in between. According to Vennemann and Murray (1983: 520f.), a similar gemination found in West Germanic, such as Old Saxon *settian* vs. Gothic *satjan* 'to set' or Old Saxon *kunnies* vs. Gothic *kunjis* 'race' (gen.sg.), occurred as a repair process when the segment on the left of a syllable boundary has lower sonority than the one on the right of the boundary (*sat.jan* and *kun.jis* in this case), the sonority scale

[8] Also in TPr. 10.19 *lupyete tv avarṇapūrvau yavakārau*, VPr. 4.127 *yavayoḥ padāntayoḥ svaramad^{h}ye lopaḥ*.

being glides >> liquids >> nasals >> voiced fricatives >> voiceless fricatives and voiced stops >> voiceless stops. If the same argument can be applied to our case of /-ry-, -hy-/ > *-ryy-*, *-hyy-*, the sonority of Sanskrit /y/ would be placed between /r, h/ and /l, nasals, obstruents/. It suggests that some speakers contemporary with Pāṇini pronounced /y/ with considerably stronger constriction than that of a glide, possibly something close to the IPA palatal approximant [j] or palatal voiced fricative [ʝ].

In the Prātiśākhyas, ŚCĀ 3.2.8 *rep^{h}ahakārau paraṃ tāb^{h}yām* and VPr. 4.102 *paraṃ tu rep^{h}ahakārāb^{h}yām* provide gemination of consonants including /y/ in the same context as in Aṣṭ. 8.4.46. Mention in the *Vājasaneyiprātiśākhya* is especially interesting from a dialectal point of view, because the *Pratijñāsūtra*, a text associated with it, teaches that word-initial /y/ and /v/ and those in the context of gemination are pronounced with occlusion.[9] It might be a precursor of the fortition of Old Indo-Aryan initial /y/ to /j/ in later Indo-Aryan (cf. Varma 1929: 127f.). Furthermore, the Prātiśākhyas describe semivowels as *īṣat-spṛṣṭa-* 'slightly contacted' (ŚCĀ 1.1.30) or *duḥ-spṛṣṭa-* 'poorly contacted' (ṚPr. 13.10), whereas ŚCĀ 1.1.31 *ūṣmāṇām vivṛtaṃ ca*, although interpreted in various ways (cf. Deshpande 1997: 148f.), refers to fricatives as open. If those terms are to be taken literally, occlusion of /y/ might have already been under way when those texts were composed.

[9] *Pratijñāsūtra* 9–10. *at^{h}ānta(ḥ)st^{h}ānām ādyasya padādiṣṭ^{h}asyānyahalasaṃyuktasya, saṃyuktasyāpi rep^{h}oṣmāntyāb^{h}yām, ṛkāreṇa cāviśeṣeṇādimad^{h}yāvasāneṣūccāraṇe jakāroccāraṇam* । *dvirb^{h}āve 'py evam* । 'Der erste der Halbvokale, d.i. *y*, ist in folgenden Fällen als *j* zu sprechen: *a*. initiales *y*, welches nicht mit einem andern Consonanten verbunden ist (...); *b*. jegliches *y*, das mit *r*, *h* oder *ṛi* direkt verbunden ist (...) *c*. wenn es doppelt steht' (Weber 1872: 78f.).

5. DISCUSSION

5.1. Asymmetrical developments of *i̯ and *u̯ in Indo-Aryan

In Sanskrit, /y/ and /v/ are grouped as semivowels (*antaḥstʰā-*) together with /r/ and /l/, and it has been argued that Sanskrit /v/ was originally a bilabial glide just as /y/ was a palatal glide.[10] On the other hand, the *Taittirīyaprātiśākhya* and the *Vājasaneyiprātiśākhya* describe that the teeth are involved in the articulation of /v/,[11] so Sanskrit /v/ has become a labiodental fricative by the late Vedic period, at least for some speakers. Furthermore, there is significant asymmetry between the phonological alternations of /y/ and /v/ even in earliest Sanskrit, and it makes us suspect that Proto-Indo-Iranian non-nucleus *u̯ was strengthened from very early times on:

a. Phonotactically, *vy* is a common sequence, while there is no *yv* in early Vedic texts.

b. /y/ can be geminated in Sanskrit while /v/ cannot, except in the postlexical gemination (section **5.2**).

c. There is no *v* originating from a laryngeal onglide (*V₋ᵤ*Hu*) while *y* in *rayíḥ* might be a phonological development of **raHí-s* (section **3.iv**).

d. The first *h_2 in PIE **pl̥th₂u̯ih₂* develops into Sanskrit *i* in *pr̥tʰivī́-* f. 'earth' as a laryngeal trapped between two consonants normally does, whereas *h_2 between a consonant and *i̯ is lost as in PIE **-dh₂i̯é-ti* > *(ava-)dyáti* pres.3sg.act. of √*dā* 'divide' (Pinault 1982: 266ff.).

---

10 Whitney (1889: 75): 'its original sound was that of our *w*'. Allen (1953: 57): 'its earlier pronunciation was doubtless as a bilabial [w]'.

11 TPr. 2.43 *oṣṭʰāntābʰyāṃ dantair vakāre*, VPr. 1.81 *vo dantāgraiḥ*.

e. We discussed in section **3** above that PIIr. **i̯* between **ă* and **H(i)* is lost and contraction takes place subsequently,[12] while **u̯* is retained as *v* in the same environment.

**u̯ái̯H-ti* > *véti* 'seeks for' vs. **mlau̯H-ti* > *brávīti* 'says'
**nai̯H-tar-* > *nétar-* vs. **tau̯H-s-iH* > *táviṣī-* f. 'power'
**(a-)nāi̯H-išta* > *naiṣṭa* vs. **á-pāu̯H-iš-ṛs* > *apāviṣur*[13]
**bʰā́u̯H-uka-* > *bʰā́vuka-* 'becoming' (YV)

a and **b** might be cases of accidental gap, and there are only single examples (*rayíḥ* and *pṛtʰivī́-*) each for **c** and **d**; but the asymmetry in the development of a laryngeal after a glide in **e**) is hard to understand unless we consider that **u̯* had stronger constriction than **i̯* already in pre-Vedic Indo-Aryan.

Another fact possibly relevant to the asymmetrical fortition of **i̯* and **u̯* is the complete absence of voiced coronal (including palatal) fricative phonemes such as [z] [ʐ(ẓ)] [ʒ] [ʑ] or [ʝ] in Sanskrit phonology. Even where voiced coronal fricatives are posited in intermediate forms in words like *rīḍʰá-* vbl.adj. of √*reh* / *rih* 'lick' < **riẓʰ-ḍʰá-* < PIIr. **liȷ́ʰ-tá-* or *mīḍʰá-* n. 'prize' < **miẓḍʰá-* < PIIr. **misdʰá-*, or in the sandhi /s/ →[ẓ]→ *r* / -$V_{\neg a}$_$X_{\{[\text{voiced}], \neg r\}}$-, they are systematically eliminated in the surface representation, while there is no known restriction against the spirantization of /v/. In Middle Indo-Aryan, /j/ starts appearing in the place of Old Indo-Aryan /y/ as in Ardhamāgadhī *jakkʰa-* corresponding to Skt *yakṣa-* (Pischel 1900, §252), but we do not see any gradual fortition of /y/ going on in Sanskrit, let alone an explicit indication of occlusion as in Holtzmann's Law in Germanic (section **5.3**), according to which intervocalic **i̯* is doubled and then strengthened to a palatal stop in Gothic and Old Norse. Just as *rīḍʰá-* or *mīḍʰá-* can be explained by positing voiced coronal fricatives in intermediate stages, the development of /y/ to /j/ would also be

---

[12] In the case of **ai̯H*, it might be the laryngeal that is lost (see section **3.vi**).

[13] Narten 1964: 169, 52.

better understood if we consider that Sanskrit /y/ was actually undergoing fortition, but due to the gap in the phonemic system of Sanskrit, it remained subphonemic until it has completely become the stop /j/.

5.2. Change in preferred syllable structure

Syllabification is a term covering both assignment of nucleus status to an underlying string and adjustment processes; however, these processes are motivated by different principles sometimes contradicting each other, for example Sievers' Law which eliminates overlength vs. postlexical gemination like *-ry-* > *-ryy-* which creates clusters at the coda. In our understanding, syllabification of Sanskrit involves the following three processes. They partly correspond to chronological layers, but can also be viewed as a synchronic set of rules whose priority may vary in different periods (cf. Kobayashi 2004: 27).

- **Process 1**. Nucleus placement (Kobayashi 2004: 21ff.): In Indo-European languages, high vowels and sonorants (and sometimes even laryngeals) can equally become a syllable nucleus. When there are one or more such segments in a row unsyllabified, the nucleus is assigned iteratively from right to left, e.g. **im-tá-* 'reined' > **i̯m̥-tá-* > *yatá-*, **HiuHn-ás* gen.sg. of m. 'youth' > **Hi̯uHn-ás* > *yūnáḥ*, **HiuHn-tí-* f. > **Hi̯uHn̥-tí-* > *yuvatí-* (Meillet 1934: 134–136; Schindler 1977: 56). This process, by which the rightmost segment becomes nucleus first, reflects a preference that the coda of the syllable should be as small as possible. This rule applied cyclically in Proto-Indo-Iranian, as *śúnaḥ* < **ćún-as* gen.sg. vs. *śvabʰiḥ* (*śvábʰiḥ* in RV Khila 5.15.7b) < **ću̯n̥-bʰis* inst.pl. of *śván-* m. 'dog' shows, but it is grammaticalized and is no longer an active phonological process in Sanskrit.
- **Process 2**. Prosodic well-formedness and repair rules: When strings, including the output of Process 1, are prosodically

parsed, ill-formed syllables or sequences of syllables are dissolved. **Process 2a**: According to the metrical scansion of the *Ṛgveda*, superheavy syllable rhymes are avoided and dissolved by Sievers' Law, e.g. *sū́rya-* /sū́riya-/. **Process 2b**: Also in the *Ṛgveda*, light syllables with /i/ or /u/ followed by /y/ or /v/ respectively are sometimes dissolved by syncope (Seebold 1972: 218ff.). E.g. *hávya-* /háviya-/ 'to be called' in RV 3.49.3c *b^hágo ná kāré háv.yo matīnā́m* vs. 5.33.5d *b^hágo ná hávyaḥ prab^hṛt^héṣu cā́ruḥ*, or *anu-mā́dya-* /anu-mā́diya-/ 'to be acclaimed' in RV 9.24.4c *sásnir yó anumā́d.yaḥ* vs 9.107.11c *anumā́dyaḥ pávamāno manīṣíb^hiḥ*. Such syncope is contradictory to Process 2a, for superheavy syllables, like /mā́d/ in the latter case, are created. In Śākalya's orthoepic normalization of the *Ṛgveda*, Process 2b is generalized. Note that Germanic also shows syncope of **-iji-/-ija-* to **-ji-/-ja-* after light syllables in Class I weak presents such as Gothic *satjan*, Old Saxon *seṭṭian* 'set' from PIE **sed-éi̯e-* (Jasanoff 1994: 275).

Process 3. Syllable boundary rule: In Indo-Aryan geminates or clusters of consonants of the same aperture are preferred across a syllable boundary. An example from an old period is the verbal adjective *vittá-* 'found' vs. Avestan *vista-* < **u̯id-s-tá-*, where interconsonantal **s* is deleted (Mayrhofer 1986: 111; Kobayashi 2004: 37). In the times of Pāṇini and the Prātiśākhyas, postlexical gemination occurs in consonant clusters, e.g. *mád^hya-*, *márta-* → *mádd^hya-*, *mártta-*. This is the newest of the rules mentioned here, for Pāṇini reports in Aṣṭ. 8.4.51 *sarvatra śākalyasya* that Śākalya does not accept such gemination in any context, and it is only optional for Pāṇini himself (Aṣṭ. 8.4.46–47).

If we take *hávya-* /háviya-/ as an example, the Proto-Indo-Iranian string **ȷ́^háuH-iia-* is syllabified as **ȷ́^há. u̯i. i̯a-* by Process 1. Although it passes the check for superheavy rhymes, the sequence /iy/ is not favored in Śākalya's language and partly in the *Ṛgveda* itself, so it becomes /háv.ya-/ by Process 2b. Finally, the /v/ in the cluster is geminated as /háv.vya-/ according to some grammarians by Process 3.

Of these processes, syncope takes place in 2b, and that is where the geminate *yy* is created. Since 2b was already active in Śākalya's days when the pronunciation of /y/ was presumably still not so different from a glide (section **4**), fortition of /y/ started only after the syncope of /i/ and /u/ before /y/ and /v/ had taken place.

5.3. Polarized developments of *-*i*- outside Sanskrit

In Avestan, Proto-Indo-Iranian glide *u̯ remained as such longer than in Indo-Aryan (section **5.1**), at least medially, e.g. Av. *gaoiia-* vs. Skt *gávya-* (Meillet 1950: 71ff.), and there was no need for resyllabification as in Sanskrit, where *u̯ did not form a diphthong with the preceding *a (**góya-*) but made a cluster with the following *i̯.[14]

It is difficult to identify double glide *i̯i̯ in Avestan, mainly because both single and double glides are written *ii* or *uu* in the 'Sasanian archetype' spelling (Hoffmann & Narten 1989: 43ff.). And even where double glide *i̯ is expected, Avestan simplifies almost all gemination, and there seems to be no doubtless case of geminated glide *i̯ there. So for example, *sraiiah-* < **ćrái̯H-i̯as-* might represent double glide *i̯, but it might also have undergone degemination in Iranian (Hoffmann 1976: 615).[15]

[14] In other words, sonority ranking was different: Indo-Aryan *y* > {v, r} vs. Avestan {y, v} > *r*. Note that a semivowel sequence is also dissolved by anaptyxis as in *daēuuaiiå* for **daēuuiiå* (Reichelt 1909: 72; Skjærvø 1997: 117f.; de Vaan 2003: 541).

[15] Pinault (1982) considers that PIIr. **ćrái̯H-i̯as-*, after loss of the laryngeal, was degeminated already in PIIr., and became **śráyas-* in Indo-Aryan, and that *e* was then reintroduced into the first syllable from other forms like *śréṣṭʰa-*. Positing degemination in PIIr. would be unnecessary if **śráyas-*, which must have served as the basis of the *vṛddhi* form *śrāyasa-* taught by Pāṇini in Aṣṭ. 7.3.1 (Wackernagel 1955: 504) could be explained otherwise,

Outside Indo-Iranian, single intervocalic **i̯* is lost (as it is when the following vowel was **i* in pre-Vedic Indo-Aryan) while **i* that ended up between vowels is pronounced as ambisyllabic /yy/ in Attic Greek, e.g. *treîs* 'three', *āeí* 'always', *pleîston* 'most' vs. *At^hēnaíos* 'Athenian' (Allen 1987: 81f.), and Latin, e.g. *trēs* < **tréi̯es* vs. *Pompeiānus* /ĕyy/ < **-ai̯i̯ā-* (Sommer & Pfister 1977: 87; Allen 1978: 38f.). However, there is a cross-linguistic tendency that geminates are more resistant to changes (Kenstowicz & Pyle 1973), and ambisyllabic development of /i/ to /yy/ between vowels might not be limited to Indo-European languages. In Germanic, intervocalic **i̯* is often lost as in Greek or Latin, but **i̯* after a short vowel is geminated in several words by Holtzmann's Law, and further undergoes fortition in Gothic and Old Norse, e.g. Gothic *twaddjē* gen.pl. 'two', Old High German *zweiio* (Krahe 1948: 87f.). Although the principle behind the gemination is not clear, it can be compared to Indo-Aryan developments such as OIA *-aya-* > MIA *-e-* vs. OIA *-īya-* > MIA *-ijja-* (Pischel 1900, §153, §91).

6. SUMMARY

In this paper, we have discussed the origin of the sequence *yy* in Sanskrit, viewing problems such as intervocalic loss of **i̯* and subsequent contraction, syllable-related alternations of semivowels, and pronunciation of **i̯*~/y/. We have argued that **i̯* was originally a glide, which was at first lost between **a* and **i*; but it was gradually phonemicized, underwent fortition, and became an approximant or possibly a voiced fricative in its development in Indo-Aryan.

It is not fortition or phonemicization of /y/ but syncope that is directly responsible for the creation of Sanskrit /yy/. When syncope of /i/ before /y/ first occurred in the *Ṛgveda*, Sanskrit /y/ was

---

for example as a neuter *-as-* stem from the root *śrī́* (Knobl, personal communication).

in the process of acquiring phonemic status, and /yy/ resulting from syncope survived without being resyllabified and dissolved. The syncope of /i/ in turn resulted from a change in prosodic preference that started in the *Ṛgveda* period and was complete by the time of Śākalya's redaction. Originally, superheavy syllables tended to be avoided as Sievers' Law indicates; but when $\bar{\sigma}\sigma_{(y\text{-}/v\text{-})}$ came to be preferred to $\breve{\sigma}\breve{\sigma}_{(i/u)}\sigma_{(y\text{-}/v\text{-})}$, and $\bar{\sigma}\sigma_{(y\text{-}/v\text{-})}$ to $\bar{\sigma}\breve{\sigma}_{(i/u)}\sigma_{(y\text{-}/v\text{-})}$ even if the first syllable would end up superheavy, syncope of the medial /i/ and /u/ occurred and created many new clusters with semivowels, including /yy/. /yy/ was initially a concomitant of syncope, but it became a real geminate as /y/ underwent fortition and became first an approximant, and possibly a more constrictive consonant such as a voiced fricative. In that sense, Sanskrit *yy* is a co-product of change in prosodic preference and fortition of /y/. Śākalya's time is when word-final /y/ was lost between vowels while syncope created *yy*; a comparable situation is found in Germanic, where loss of intervocalic **i̯*, syncope of **i* before **i̯* and (spontaneous) gemination of intervocalic **i̯* took place.

ABBREVIATIONS AND NOTATION

AB	*Aitareyabrāhmaṇa*
Aṣṭ.	*Aṣṭādhyāyī*
AVŚ	*Atharvaveda*, Śaunaka recension
ChU	*Chāndogya-Upaniṣad*
JB	*Jaiminīyabrāhmaṇa*
JUB	*Jaiminīya-Upaniṣad-Brāhmaṇa*
KS	*Kaṭhasaṃhitā*
MIA	Middle Indo-Aryan
MS	*Maitrāyaṇīsaṃhitā*
OAv.	Old Avestan
OIA	Old Indo-Aryan
PB	*Pañcaviṃśabrāhmaṇa*
PIE	Proto-Indo-European
PIIr.	Proto-Indo-Iranian
RV	*Ṛgveda*

ṚPr.	*Ṛkprātiśākhya*
ŚB	*Śatapathabrāhmaṇa*
ŚBK	*Śatapathabrāhmaṇa*, Kāṇva recension
ŚCĀ	*Śaunakīyācaturādhyāyikā*
Skt	Sanskrit
TB	*Taittirīyabrāhmaṇa*
TPr.	*Taittirīyaprātiśākhya*
TS	*Taittirīyasaṃhitā*
VPr.	*Vājasaneyiprātiśākhya*
VS	*Vājasaneyisaṃhitā*
YAv.	Younger Avestan
YV	*Yajurveda* (comprising KS, MS, TS and VS)

*: Reconstructed form (Proto-Indo-Iranian unless otherwise specified)

ˣ: Not attested

>>: higher than

σ: syllable(s)

yiy etc.: Spelled *yy* but pronounced *yiy* according to metrical scansion

REFERENCES

AGRAWALA, Vasudeva Sharana 1953. *India as Known to Pāṇini.* Lucknow: University of Lucknow.

AiG = Jacob Wackernagel & Albert Debrunner, *Altindische Grammatik.* Göttingen: Vandenhoeck und Ruprecht, 1896–1930.

ALLEN, William Sidney 1953. *Phonetics in Ancient India.* (London Oriental Series, 1.) London: Oxford University Press.

——— 1978. *Vox Latina.* 2nd edition. Cambridge: Cambridge University Press.

——— 1987. *Vox Graeca.* 3rd edition. Cambridge: Cambridge University Press.

BARTHOLOMAE, Christian 1907. Zur Gerundivbildung im Arischen. *Zeitschrift für vergleichende Sprachforschung* 41: 319–335.

BÖHTLINGK, Otto 1887. *Pāṇini's Grammatik.* Leipzig: Verlag von H. Haessel. [Reprint: Hildesheim: Olms, 1977.]

DESHPANDE, Madhav M. 1997. *Śaunakīyā-Caturādhyāyikā.* (Harvard Oriental Series, 52.) Cambridge, Mass.: Department of Sanskrit and Indian Studies.

EDGERTON, Franklin 1943. The Indo-European semivowels. *Language* 19: 83–124.

HOFFMANN, Karl 1976. *Aufsätze zur Indoiranistik*, II. Wiesbaden: Reichert.

HOFFMANN, Karl & Johanna NARTEN 1989. *Der sasanidische Archetypus*. Wiesbaden: Reichert.

JASANOFF, Jay 1994. Germanic. In: Françoise Bader (ed.), *Langues indo-européennes*: 251–280. Paris: CNRS Editions.

KENSTOWICZ, Michael & Charles PYLE 1973. On the phonological integrity of geminate clusters. In: Michael Kenstowicz & Charles Kisseberth (eds.), *Issues in Phonological Theory*: 27–43. The Hague: Mouton.

KOBAYASHI, Masato 2004. *Historical Phonology of Old Indo-Aryan Consonants*. Tokyo: ILCAA, Tokyo University of Foreign Studies.

KRAHE, Hans 1948. *Germanische Sprachwissenschaft*. Berlin: De Gruyter.

LUBOTSKY, Alexander 1995. Reflexes of intervocalic laryngeals in Sanskrit. In: Wojciech Smoczyński (ed.), *Kuryłowicz Memorial Volume*, I: 213–233. Cracow: Universitas.

——— 1997. The Indo-Iranian reflexes of PIE *CRHUV. In: A. Lubotsky (ed.), *Sound Law and Sound Law and Analogy. Papers in Honour of Robert S. P. Beekes*: 139–154. Amsterdam: Rodopi.

MAYRHOFER, Manfred 1986. *Indogermanische Grammatik*, I.2: *Lautlehre*. Heidelberg: Winter.

MEILLET, Antoine 1934. *Introduction à l'étude comparative des langues indo-européennes*. 7th edition. Paris: Hachette.

——— 1950. *Les dialectes indo-européens*. Paris: Champion.

NARTEN, Johanna 1964. *Die sigmatischen Aoriste im Veda*. Wiesbaden: Harrassowitz.

PINAULT, Georges-Jean 1982. A neglected phonetic law: the reduction of the Indo-European laryngeals in internal syllables before yod. In: Anders Ahlqvist (ed.), *Papers from the 5th International Conference on Historical Linguistics*: 265–272. Amsterdam: John Benjamins.

PISCHEL, Richard 1900. *Grammatik der Prakrit-Sprachen*. (Grundriss der Indo-Arischen Philologie und Altertumskunde, I.8.) Strassburg: Trübner, 1900. (English translation by Subhadra Jha, *A Grammar of the Prākrit Languages*, Varanasi: Motilal Banarsidass, 1957.)

REICHELT, Hans 1909. *Awestisches Elementarbuch*. Heidelberg: Winter.

SCHINDLER, Jochem 1977. Notizen zum Sieverschen Gesetz. *Die Sprache* 23: 56–65.

SEEBOLD, Elmar 1972. *Das System der indogermanischen Halbvokale.* Heidelberg: Winter.

SKJÆRVØ, Prods Oktor 1997. Avestica II: yokes and spades and remnants of the 'tripartite ideology'. *Münchener Studien zur Sprachwissenschaft* 57: 115–128.

SOMMER, Ferdinand & Raïmund PFISTER 1977. *Handbuch der lateinischen Laut- und Formenlehre*, I: *Einleitung und Lautlehre.* Heidelberg: Winter.

TICHY, Eva 1995. *Die nomina agentis auf -tar- im Vedischen.* Heidelberg: Winter.

VAAN, Michiel de 2003. *The Avestan Vowels.* Amsterdam: Rodopi.

VARMA, Siddheshwar 1929. *Critical Studies in the Phonetic Observations of Indian Grammarians.* London: Royal Asiatic Society.

VENNEMANN, Theo & Robert W. MURRAY 1983. Sound change and syllable structure in Germanic phonology. *Language* 59: 514–528.

WACKERNAGEL, Jacob 1955. *Kleine Schriften*, I–II. Göttingen: Vandenhoeck und Ruprecht.

WEBER, Albrecht 1872. *Über ein zum weissen Yajus gehöriges phonetisches Compendium: Das Pratijnâsûtra.* Berlin: Königliche Akademie der Wissenschaften.

WERBA, Chlodwig H. 1997. *Verba Indoarica. Die primären und sekundären Wurzeln der Sanskrit-Sprache*, I: *Radices Primariae.* Wien: Verlag der Österreichischen Akademie der Wissenschaften.

WHITNEY, William Dwight 1889. *Sanskrit Grammar.* 2nd edition. Leipzig: Breitkopf und Härtel.

Laryngeal Traces without Laryngeals in Vedic Metre?

MARTIN JOACHIM KÜMMEL

1. THE THEORY OF LARYNGEALS 'MAKING POSITION'

Already in 1927, 'the young Kuryłowicz' made the observation that in some words the presence of the newly found Indo-European 'laryngeal' consonants still seemed to have a consonantal effect causing metrical irregularities in Vedic (see also Kuryłowicz 1928). But his idea remained largely unnoticed until the late Jochem Schindler revived it (in lectures), and, lately, the problem was mentioned in the metrical edition of Van Nooten and Holland (1994: vi) and made the object of two papers by Jost Gippert (1997; 1999), and of several by Gary Holland (most recently, at our conference).

What is this impact of Pre-Vedic 'laryngeal' consonants on Vedic metre? It is clear that a Pre-Vedic, Early Proto-Indo-Iranian structure **VC.HV* = – × lost its laryngeal without a trace, leading to a Common Indo-Iranian and Vedic structure **V.CV* = ◡ ×. But the earlier scansion – × could have survived as a metrical licence (lexically or 'phrasally' conditioned, not general): a synchronically light syllable may appear in the place of a heavy syllable (*brevis in longo* scansion for which I will use the abbreviation BIL and the symbol ◠).

NB: This allegedly includes cases of the Indo-Iranian 'Vocalization' *CHC > *CHьC (> *C(ʰ)ьC > Vedic CiC) – a fact that has been used as an argument to show that a svarabhakti vowel developed following the consonantal laryngeal.

Gippert (1997: 78) claims that 'at least' 100 out of 215 cases of irregular triṣṭubh cadences can be explained by laryngeal effects. However, in this counting he explicitly included other laryngeal effects as well as doubtful cases where the laryngeal could only be reconstructed circularly because of the metrical data (e.g., for *áhan-* 'day'). If we subtract these, the number is reduced to 76 out of 215, i.e., about 35%. Now it is crucial to compare this to the general frequency of such syllables containing a laryngeal following a short vowel and a single consonant – which Gippert did not do (though he was aware of the problem, 1999: 125). To get an idea, I simply counted the verbal roots with a synchronic structure °*aC-* in the RV, and thus I arrived at approximately 80 seṭ roots vs. 120 aniṭ roots, i.e., roughly 40%. Since this is the same percentage as for '*brevis in longo*', we may conclude that there is no significantly heightened frequency of seṭ cases showing *brevis in longo* when compared to their general frequency. But in fact, the *locus classicus* of the problem has never been the triṣṭubh cadence alone.

1.1. Suggestive data present themselves when we have a look at the words and verses collected by Oldenberg (1888: 11–12, 64) and Arnold (1905, §190 ii & §220 ii) for purely metrical reasons: A laryngealist's eyes will soon recognize many 'laryngeal' cases, like *savitā́* at the end of the gāyatrī or jagatī cadence, standing in the place of – ◡ ×, as a preform **sau̯Hь-tā́* would have counted, e.g., RV 5.82.9c *prá ca suvā́ti savitā́* ◡ ◡ ◡ – | ◡ ^ ◡ × (opposed to more frequent regular scansion ◡ ◡ – of this form after the caesura); and similarly but much more rarely in the *triṣṭubh* cadence, e.g., *jánāḥ* for – ×, e.g., RV 6.51.11b *pūṣā́ bhágo áditiḥ* *páñca jánāḥ* = ⏒ – ⏑ ⏑ ' ⏑ ⏑ – | – ⏑ ⁀ ×, as if we still had the old form **jánH-ās*.

Significantly these irregular scansions are most common in Arnold's 'Archaic' period of Vedic metre, continuously decreasing in later periods (Arnold 1905, §221), so it might well be called an archaism. Of course, Arnold's chronology is not proven (and partly based on exactly these scansions), but it would fit into our theory, and we might accept it for the time being.

Now before we proceed, we must bear in mind that what we are speaking about are metrical rules, not linguistic reality, as shown by the very special distribution. Most often, only one of a lexeme's possible prosodic structures displays the phenomenon. E.g., it is attested in disyllabic forms of *śáru-* and the plural of *jána-* but never in trisyllabic forms of these words nor even the singular of *jána-*. On the contrary, it is never found in disyllabic forms of *hári-*, *ávas-*, *kaví-* or the simple noun *háva-* while trisyllabic forms of these word or roots may show BIL. And while trisyllabic forms of *duhitár-* do show it (as against quadrisyllabic ones), structurally identical words of similar frequency do not, e.g., *janitár-*. It is far less frequent that we find a word or root that shows BIL in more than one position. The data for some important words may be summarized in this table:

Scansion of first syllable	**Disyllabic**	**Trisyllabic**	**Quadri-syllabic**
partly heavy	*śáru-*, *jána-* pl. *śávas*, *rathī́-*, *sákhi-*	*savitár-*, *duhitár-*, *hári-*, *ávas-*, *hávi̯ya-*, *kaví-* *śávas-*, *rathī́-*, *sakhi̯á-*	--
only light	*hári-*, *ávas*, *háva-*, *kaví-*, *jána-* sg.	*śáru-*, *harít-*, *hárita-* *janitár-*, *avitár-*	*savitár-*, *duhitár-*

We can conclude that normally BIL scansion is not a quality of the word or root itself but of some forms in metrically defined places. This behaviour is different from, e.g., genitive plural *-*aām* in all metrical positions (Arnold 1905, §143).

Already Oldenberg had noticed the main area of the phenomenon: The first syllables (second compound members included) of

a. trisyllabic forms of words beginning with two light syllables in the cadence of 8/12 syllable verses (Arnold 1905, §190 ii & §220 ii),

b. disyllabic forms of words with a light first syllable in the triṣṭubh cadence (Arnold 1905, §220 ii).

NB: It is important to note that from a metrical perspective we cannot assume *brevis in longo* <u>except</u> when the *brevis* follows a regular light syllable in the cadence, i.e., when the text gives ⏑ ⌢ × or ⏑ ⌢ ⏑ ×. When an irregularly long syllable precedes the *brevis*, i.e., in the cas̆e of – ⏑ ⏑ × for ⏑ – ⏑ × or – ⏑ × for ⏑ – × (see Arnold 1905, §190v & §220v), the phenomenon could rather be understood as a kind of *anaclasis* (⏑ – > – ⏑) and must be kept apart (pace Gippert).

Now, there are some other problems in this account of 'laryngealistic' metrics.

1. It is all about frequency or probability, not absolute rules: Is there really a difference in frequency between laryngeal cases and non-laryngeal cases? If there is, how to explain the non-laryngeal cases? Are they caused by secondary metrical analogy? Or could there be a third factor causing higher frequency of laryngeal cases?
2. The problem of metre itself: The rules would have to be inherited from Proto-Indo-Iranian, but was syllable quantity relevant in the metre then? As is well known, Old Avestan

metrics is syllable counting irrespective of quantity (some slight tendencies left aside). If this should be old, Indo-Iranian metrics could hardly have been different, and we would have to assume a special Indo-Aryan development before the loss of laryngeals – in spite of the fact that the loss of these in postconsonantal position seems to be a common or even Proto-Indo-Iranian process. Unfortunately, it is less than clear whether the nearly total neglect of quantity in Avestan is an archaism or an innovation.

3. Individual problems: Why do some 'laryngealic' words show irregular scansion, and others do not? Why is there not a single instance of a heavy first syllable of words as frequent as *prathamá-*, *janitár-* or the singular of *jána-*?

4. Relative chronology: The aspiration of preceding stops may presuppose (at least to my understanding of aspiration processes, pace Schindler as well as Gippert 1997: 63–64) the loss of segmental $*h_2$: $*Th_2 > *Th > *T^h$, at least in Proto-Indo-Iranian. So the metrical rule would have to be older than that.

5. Last but not least: What is our heuristic profit in concrete cases? Can Vedic metre prove or disprove original postconsonantal laryngeals in the absence of other evidence?

To answer these questions let us now have a more precise look at the data. I started from Arnold's collection of irregular cadences and collected the respective words, concentrating on those that occur rather frequently (more than once in the material). Details about these and some other cases may be found in the appendix at the end.

1.2. First we shall consider lexical distribution: Which words do show BIL scansion? We may divide them into four classes:

a. Words with a – fairly – certain postconsonantal laryngeal in PII, e.g., *á̲vas-*, *śá̲vas-*, *sa̲vitár-*, *du̲hitár-*, *sa̲khi̯yá-* / *sákhi-*, *átithi-*, *hári-*, *hávıya-*, *rátha-* / *rathiya-*, *jána-*, *kaví-* (rare) – in sandhi or compounds, the preservation of original laryngeals is less probable, as these combinations might be younger (e.g., *áditi-*, *úd V*, *duritá-*).

b. An equally large group of words that quite certainly did not exhibit a postconsonantal laryngeal, e.g., *ajára-*, *udára-*, *mánas-*, *apás-*, *bṛhat-*, *abhítas*, *-vacas-*, *uṣás-*, *ṛtú-*, *amṛ́ta-*, *bhṛ́gu-*, *namasıyà-*, *ap-*, *nár-*.

c. Words where a postconsonantal laryngeal in PII or its postconsonantal position is possible but uncertain, often without an assured etymology, e.g., *váruṇa-*, *ṛ́ṣi-*, *marút-*, *aruṣá-*, *-yaśas-*, *sanutár*, *mánuṣ-*, *áhan-*, suffix *-(t)ama-*, *-mahas-*.

d. Some cases where a heavy scansion might be explained by original vowel or consonantal length, thus not providing evidence at all, e.g., *gṛhápati-* (for **gṛhā́-pati-* < **°ó-poti-* with a residue of lengthening by Brugmann's law?), *ácidh$_u$vam* (< **áciddh$_u$vam*, Korn 1998: 178, n. 275), *dádṛśe* (< **dā́dṛś-*?), *vavṛmahe* (for **vu-vūr-m°*, see Gippert 1997: 75; Kümmel 2000: 459), *ruruhur* (<**Hru-Hrudh-*), *áraruṣ-* (**á-rā-r°* or **á-ra-rH-*?), *no ava* (< **nō (H)áu̯a* < **nas Háu̯a*).

Of course, the groups **a** and **b** are the most relevant, but on the whole, the picture looks rather like what Oldenberg said (1888: 12):

> Es ist kaum zu viel gesagt, dass es in häufigeren Worten keine Kürze giebt [– sofern natürlich ihre Umgebung zu den umgebenden Stellen des metrischen Schemas passt –], die nicht gelegentlich an drittletzter Stelle des achtsylbigen Pâda statt der Länge gebraucht würde,

i.e., every common word form with two successive short syllables might be used at the end of the cadence of 8 syllable verses (cf. Arnold 1905: 159). Indeed, in 'dimeter verse' BIL scansion is more than thrice as frequent as in trimeter verse; compare the counting of Gippert (1999: 107): 7.15% (8 syllables) against

1.64% (11 syllables) and 2.21% (12 syllables) in the trimeter verse. Why this difference?

2. THE METRICAL POSSIBILITIES

Here the constraints of the metre are crucial. They are quite different depending on the verse type.

2.1. Word forms beginning with two light syllables followed by a (potentially) heavy third syllable (i.e., with the structure ⏑ ⏑ –) are rather difficult to place, as can be inferred from the metrical schemata (unpreferred syllable weights are written above the preferred):

Dimeter verse (8 syllables)
  Regular anuṣṭubh, gāyatrī : × ⏓ ⏒ ⏓ | ⏑ – ⏑ × ||

Trimeter verse (11 syllables, triṣṭubh type)
  Early caesura: × ⏓ ⏒ ⏓ ' ⏑ ⏑ ⏓ | – ⏑ – × ||
  Late caesura: × ⏓ ⏒ ⏓ × ' ⏒ ⏑ | – ⏑ – × ||

Trimeter verse (12 syllables, *jagatī* type)
  Early caesura: × ⏓ ⏒ ⏓ ' ⏑ ⏑ ⏓ | – ⏑ – ⏑ × ||
  Late caesura: × ⏓ ⏒ ⏓ × ' ⏒ ⏑ | – ⏑ – ⏑ × ||

2.2. The relevant metrical constraints can be displayed in an Optimality Theory type table (cf. McCarthy & Prince 2001: 5ff.) which lists the constraints and their violations triggered by the 'candidates' (the possible placement of two light syllables followed by a heavy one). The constraints are ordered from left to right according to their decreasing rank (i.e. the frequency of their being violated increases from left to right).
The relevant constraints are indicated as follows: w = word boundary before the caesura; constraints as to syllable weight are indicated by the respective number of the syllable within the

verse followed by l = light or h = heavy. As elsewhere, * means violation of a constraint.

Trimeter verse with {early caesura} (late caesura)

	w	11l	9l	8h	10h	(7l)	6l	{5l}	2or3h	{7h}	4or5h	2h	4h
5–7	(*)					(*)							
1–3												*	
6–8										{*}			
2–4									*				
10–12					*								
8–10				*									
9–11		*			*								
7–9		*	*	*						*			
4–6	*										*		
3–5	{*}							{*}					*

Normal dimeter verse

	7l	5l	2or3h	6h	2h	4h
4-6						*
1-3					*	
6-8				*		
2-4			*			
3-5		*				*
5-7	*			*		

If we rank the constraints according to frequency of their violation in Arnold's collection, we see an important difference. While for all variants of trimeter verse the respective forms can easily be placed after the caesura, in dimeter verse there is no such place, so violation of a constraint is necessary.

But word forms like that are too frequent in the language to avoid them completely, and after the middle and the beginning of the line, the third best candidate for their placement would be the cadence. Thus, the metrical need for irregular scansion would be very much stronger in dimeter verse, and the respective scansions might be considered as artificial as 'metrical lengthening' in Homeric Greek.

2.3. As to the relative frequency of irregular scansion, different approaches are possible.

2.3.1. First, we may compare with a given word forms of identical prosodic structure. Here we see that words with or without laryngeals may show the same range from very high to very low percentages, e.g., from Groups **b** and **c**: *udára-* 66.7%; *ajára-* 30.8%; *nama̱s$_i$yà-* 30%; *áruṣī-* 21.4%; *abhítas* 12% – very similar to Group **a**: *yávasa-* 40%; *údita-/úditi-* 28.6%; *háv$_i$ya-* 20.5%; *ávas-* 19.4%; *átithi-* 18.6%; and we find some possible candidates for **a** without BIL: *avitár-*, *prathamá-*, *harít-* (or *hári-*, *kaví-* when disyllabic).

2.3.2. Second, we might compare the frequency of individual words relative to other words of the respective derivation type. Here we will immediately see that some types only comprise seṭ roots. This is because of what we might call the 'laryngeal bias': Derivation from seṭ roots (i.e., roots ending in postconsonantal laryngeal) produces more light syllables than from aniṭ roots, because of two special effects:

1. If a full grade root is combined with a consonantal suffix, seṭ roots become disyllabic, producing two successive short syllables, e.g., **°aCH-C° > °aCi-C°* ◡ ◡ ×: *savitár-*, *jánitár-*, *átithi-*, while aniṭ root derivatives will have one heavy syllable instead: **°aC-C° > °aC-C°* – ×: *sotári*, *bhartár-*. This increases the frequency of seṭ cases that might cause metrical problems.
2. The common type of simple thematic nouns or any other type with *o* grade of the root will have a short root syllable only with seṭ roots. This is because their laryngeals blocked Brugmann's Law in Proto-Indo-Iranian: whereas **°oC.H-o-* led to

*ăC(H)-a- ⌣ ×, in aniṭ roots *°o.C-o- the *o* stood in an open syllable and was lengthened, leading to *°āC-a- – ×, see, e.g., seṭ *svarā́-; gáya-, jána-, ráṇa-, vára-, háva-* vs. aniṭ *ghāsá-, tyāgá-, vāká-, vāsá-; mā́na-, śā́ka-*.

3. Compounds with prefixes like *úd* or *duṣ-* will only appear in the material when the root begins with a vowel where, normally, a laryngeal has been lost.

These facts additionally increase the statistical preponderance of seṭ roots in our material, as these cases were quite frequent in Indo-Iranian word formation.

2.3.3. So we must use the 'unbiased' formation types to compare seṭ and aniṭ roots. These would be vocalic suffixes after a zero or an *e*-grade root, and looking at these we arrive at the following relation between seṭ and aniṭ cases (percentage of BIL in brackets):

1. For *s*-stem nouns and adjectives, the seṭ cases *ávas-* (19.4) and *śávas-* (19.5) together with derived *yávasa-* (41.2) are clearly on top, but otherwise there is no difference in frequency: aniṭ *apás-* (8), *vácas-* (7.4) ≈ seṭ *tavás-* (6.4).

2. Non-*o*-grade thematic nouns (including derived *ī*-stems) and adjectives are not a very common type, so we should not be surprised that there is no relevant evidence.

3. As to thematic verb forms, we can see that seṭ and aniṭ roots show nearly the same figures in trisyllabic forms, and disyllabic forms are attested in only three single aniṭ cases! However, the thematic suffix (at least in the subjunctive) has been reconstructed as *-h_1o/e-* (Tichy 2002: 202–204; 2004: 101–102).

4. *i/u*-stems, trisyllabic: the scarce evidence for trisyllabic forms shows no difference, see *bhṛ́gu-* (aniṭ, 13) vs. *hári-* (seṭ, 11.9); as to disyllabic *śáru-* (seṭ?, 25) and *sákhi-* (seṭ, 4), both might have *o*-grade and thus are not really 'unbiased'.

5. We find only two root nouns, both aniṭ *ap-* (trisyllabic 0.6, disyllabic 6.2) and *nar-* (2.5).

6. When we come to other vocalic suffixes, the most frequent is *-iya-*, where we find an apparent difference in *háv$_i$ya-* (seṭ, 20.5) vs. *gúh$_i$ya-* (aniṭ, 6.3), but *-a̱s$_i$yà-* (aniṭ, 25) is as frequent as *háv$_i$ya-*. Other suffixes are rarely found, we have *-u(-)ṣá-* in an unclear case (*aruṣá- / áruṣī*) and a probable aniṭ case in *udára-* (66.7); with *-aná- / -anā̃-* we meet *śaraṇá-* (seṭ, 12.5%) vs. four single aniṭ cases; otherwise there is no relevant evidence.

What remains are some cases that begin with a prefix rather than a root:

7. The negative prefix **ń̥- > *á-* is frequently measured long like that in *ajára-* (aniṭ, 30.8), *amŕ̥ta-* (3.9) and 5 other single cases (aniṭ); as a seṭ case we can only adduce *áditi-* (5.5).

8. The homophonous verbal augment *á-* seems to show long scansion in 5 single forms, the roots of which never begin with **CH°* (or, **HC°*).

2.4. If we summarize the 'unbiased' types, we find positive examples with a clearly high frequency of *brevis in longo* in four words containing *v* and two compounds of *i*, *yávasa-*, *ávas-*, *śávas-*; *háv$_i$ya-*, *údit°*, *duritá-*; on the other hand we also find examples of aniṭ roots with a similarly high frequency: *udára-*, *ajára-*, *yáśas-* (?), *bhŕ̥gu-*, and *-asíya-*; and we have to note that some seṭ words like *prathamá-*, *harít- / hárita-*, *páyas-* are negative examples. When we look at the 'biased' types, we find a similar quantity of good examples, e.g., *átithi-*, *sánitar-* and (disyllabic) *jána-* in the plural, *rátha- / rathī́-*, *sákhi-* – but as many counterexamples without heavy scansions: *avitár-*, *jánitár-*, *kaví-*, *háva-* or *jána-* in the singular.

3. CONCLUSION

There is no clear correlation of frequency for *°*aCHV*° as against *°*aCV*°, when we consider the overall frequency of seṭ root derivatives and their specific syllable structure. Clear cases of frequent irregularity are attested in both cases, and when counted by word, there is no difference at all. When counted by instance, the frequency of two words, *ávas-* and *śávas-*, leads to a slight preponderance of seṭ instances. This slight dominance of the type *ávas-* might be a residue of a more original distribution, but the figures do not prove that.

The evidence for the case of originally interconsonantal laryngeals *°*aCHC*° > *°*aCHьC*° is even slimmer – in spite of their overrepresentation within all words with two successive short syllables. Even the most frequent case of this type, namely *átithi-*, is clearly less frequent than aniṭ cases like *ajára-*, *namasíya-*. As for most other cases, for instance, the often cited scansion *duhitā́* = ⌒ ◡ – is too rare (and possibly rather late) to have any significance for the reconstruction of this kind of structure.

What is most clear, however, is that there is no heuristic benefit for the judgement of unclear cases: if a word shows a high percentage of Vedic *brevis in longo* scansions, it may contain an old laryngeal, or it may not. If it does not show the phenomenon, we still have both possibilities.

It cannot be excluded that the whole phenomenon of this licence in Vedic metre could be explained as a residue older than the loss of laryngeals. But it is only the licence itself, not its distribution in the RV, that can have such an explanation.

REFERENCES

ARNOLD, E. Vernon 1905. *Vedic Metre in its Historical Development*. Cambridge: Cambridge University Press.

GIPPERT, Jost 1997. Laryngeals and Vedic metre. In: Alexander Lubotsky (ed.), *Sound Law and Analogy. Papers in Honor of*

Robert S. P. Beekes on the Occasion of His 60th Birthday: 63–79. Amsterdam: Rodopi.

——— 1999. Neue Wege zur sprachwissenschaftlichen Analyse der vedischen Metrik. In: Heiner Eichner & Hans Christian Luschützky (eds.), *Compositiones indogermanicae in memoriam Jochem Schindler*: 97–125. Prague: Enigma corporation.

KORN, Agnes 1998. *Metrik und metrische Techniken im Ṛgveda. Streckformen in Trimeter-Versen*. Graz: Leykam.

KURYŁOWICZ, Jerzy. 1927. Les effets du ə en indoiranien. *Prace Filologiczne* 11: 201–243.

——— 1928. Quelques problèmes métriques du Rigvéda. *Rocznik Orientalistyczny* 4 (1926): 196-218.

KÜMMEL, Martin Joachim 2000. *Das Perfekt im Indoiranischen. Eine Untersuchung der Form und Funktion einer ererbten Kategorie des Verbums und ihrer Weiterentwicklung in den altindoiranischen Sprachen*. Wiesbaden: Dr. Ludwig Reichert.

MCCARTHY, John. J. & Alan PRINCE 2001. *Prosodic Morphology. Constraint Interaction and Satisfaction*. Rutgers Optimality Archive: http://roa.rutgers.edu/view.php3?roa=482 Rutgers University, New Jersey. (Originally circulated in April 1993 and available as Technical Report no. 3 of the Rutgers University Center for Cognitive Science).

LUBOTSKY, Alexander M. 1997. *A Ṛgvedic Word Concordance*, I–II. New Haven, Connecticut: American Oriental Society.

NOOTEN, Barend A. van & Gary B. Holland (eds.) 1994. *Rig Veda – metrically restored text with an introduction and notes*. Cambridge, Mass.: Harvard University Press.

OLDENBERG, Hermann 1888. *Die Hymnen des Ṛigveda*, I: *Metrische und textgeschichtliche Prolegomena*. Berlin: Verlag von Wilhelm Hertz.

TICHY, Eva 2002. Zur Funktion und Vorgeschichte der indogermanischen Modi. In: Heinrich Hettrich (ed.), *Indogermanische Syntax – Fragen und Perspektiven*: 189–206. Wiesbaden: Reichert.

——— 2004. *Indogermanistisches Grundwissen für Studierende sprachwissenschaftlicher Disziplinen*. 2., überarbeitete Auflage. Bremen: Hempen.

APPENDIX: Material

Metrical behaviour of words with potential *brevis in longo* ('BIL') scansion in the cadence

Symbols used in the first column:

+	postconsonantal laryngeal assured
–	postconsonantal laryngeal excluded
!	postconsonantal vocalized laryngeal
( )	an alternative explanation for 'BIL' may be available

Light antepaenultima before light paenultima in the RV (in brackets: trimeter verse)

*VCH	Stem(s)	Total	'BIL'	Fre-quency	Periods					Maṇḍalas									
					A	S	N	C	P	1	2	3	4	5	6	7	8	9	10
–	*u̱dára-*	6	4	66.7%	1	3	-	-	-	2	-	-	-	-	-	-	2	-	-
+!?	(-)**na̱yi-tár-*	6	4	66.7%	4	-	-	-	-	-	-	-	-	3	-	-	1	-	-
(+)?	*á-ra̱-r-uṣ-*	8	4	50.0%	-	2	2	-	-	2	-	-	-	-	-	1	-	1	-
+?	*yá̱v-asa-*	17	6	41.2%	5	1	-	-	-	1	-		-	3	1	-	-	-	1
–	*a̱-jára-*	65	20(8)	36.9%	16	1	-	3	-	7	-	-	-	2	5	-	4	-	2
+?	*tá̱ru-tár-*	6	2	33.3%	1	1	-			1	-	-	-	-	-	-	1	-	-
–?	*-ya̱śas-*	12	4	33.3%	4	-	-	-	-	1	-	-	-	1	-	-	1	1	-
+	*ú̱d-i-ta- + ú̱d-i-ti-*	21	6	28.6%	2	4	-	-	-	-	-	-	-	-	-	3	3	-	-
–	*-a̱s-ɩyà-*	20	5(2)	25.0%	2	-	3	-	-	-	2	1	-	1	-	-	1	-	-
+	*há̱v-ɩya-*	32	8(3)	25.0%	7	1	-	-	-	-	-	-	-	1	-	1	6	-	-
+	*áv-as-*	165	33(8)	20.0%	21	7	5	-	-	7	-	1	-	5	3	-	15	2	-
+	(-)*śá̱v-as-*	113	22(1)	19.5%	17	3	1	-	-	4	-	2	-	5	2	1	6	-	2
(–)	*gṛhá̱-pati-*	21	4	19.0%	1	2	-	1	-	1	-	-	-	1	1	-	-	-	1
–	*a̱p-$_{a}$ā́m*	17	3(1)	17.6%	2	1	-	-	-	1	-	-	-	-	-	-	1	1	-
+	*sá̱ni-tar- / sá̱ni-ti-*	24	4	16.7%	2	1	1	-	-	2	-	-	-	1	-	-	1	-	-
+	*du̱r-itá-*	37	6	16.2%	4	1	1	-	-	-	-	-	-	1	-	1	-	-	4

*VCH	Stem(s)	Total	'BIL'	Fre-quency	Periods					Maṇḍalas									
					A	S	N	C	P	1	2	3	4	5	6	7	8	9	10
+!	*ra̲th-y-*	33	5	15.2%	3	1	1	-	-	-	-	-	-	-	-	1	3	1	-
+!	*á̲ti-thi-*	43	6	14.0%	8	-	-	-	-	-	-	-	-	1	2	-	3	-	-
–?	*bhŕ̥g-u-*	23	3(2)	13.0%	3	-	-	-	-	2	-	-	-	-	-	-	-	1	-
+?	*śa̲r-aṇá-*	16	2	12.5%	1	-	1	-	-	-	-	-	-	-	1	-	1	-	-
–	*a̲bhí-tas*	25	3	12.0%	1	-	1	1	-	1	-	-	-	-	-	-	-	1	1
+	*vi̲dh-at-*	25	3	12.0%	3	-	-	-	-	-	-	-	-	1	-	-	2	-	-
+!	*tá̲vi-ṣī-*	25	3(2)	12.0%	3	-	-	-	-	2	-	-	-	-	-	-	1	-	-
+	*há̲r-i-*	59	7(1)	11.9%	1	3	3	-	-	1	-	1	1	-	-	-	2	2	-
?	*a̲ruṣá- + á̲ruṣī*	57	5	8.8%	2	-	3	-	-	2	-	1	-	-	-	-	2	-	-
+!	*sa̲kh-iyá-*	57	5(1)	8.8%	5	-	-	-	-	-	-	-	-	1	1	-	2	-	1
–	*a̲p̲-̲á̲s̲-̲*	25	2(1)	8.0%	1	-	-	1	-	1	-	1	-	-	-	-	[illegible]	-	-
+!	*sa̲vi-tár-*	144	11(1)	7.6%	5	3	1	-	1	2	-	-	-	4	-	-	-	2	3
–	*(-)vá̲c-as-*	27	2(1)	7.4%	1	1	-	-	-	1	-	-	-	-	-	-	1	-	-
+	*(-)tá̲v-as-, ta̲v-ás-*	49	3(1)	6.1%	1	-	1	1	-	1	-	-	-	-	-	1	-	1	-
+	*á̲-di-ti-*	165	9(2)	5.5%	7	2	-	-	-	-	-	-	-	-	-	1	7	-	1
–	*má̲n-as-*	147	7	4.8%	6	-	-	-	1	-	-	-	-	-	-	-	7	-	-
?	*ha̲v-íṣ-*	72	3	4.2%	-	-	-	-	3	-	-	-	-	-	-	-	-	-	3

*VCH	Stem(s)	Total	'BIL'	Fre-quency	Periods					Maṇḍalas									
					A	S	N	C	P	1	2	3	4	5	6	7	8	9	10
+	*hár-i-vant-*	49	2	4.1%	1	-	1	-	-	1	-	-	-	-	-	-	1	-	-
+!	*duhi-tár-*	54	2	3.7%	-	1	1	-	-	-	-	-	1	-	-	-	-	1	-
?	*váruṇa-*	287	13	3.5%	8	2	2	1	-	1	1	-	-	3	-	2	6	-	-
–	*nám-as-*	88	3(2)	3.4%	2	1	-	-	-	-	-	-	-	-	-	1	2	-	-
–	*a-mṛ́ta-*	102	3	2.9%	2	-	1	-	-	-	-	-	-	-	-	1	2	-	-
?	*marút-*	324	7(3)	2.2%	3	3	1	-	-	1	-	-	-	2	-	1	1	2	-
–	*uṣ-ás-*	205	3(1)	1.5%	-	3	-	-	-	3	-	-	-	-	-	-	-	-	-
–	*bṛh-at-*	134	2	1.5%	1	-	1	-	-	1	-	-	-	-	-	-	1	-	-
+!	*pṛthi-ví-*	241	2	0.8%	1	1	–	-	-	1	-	-	-	1	-	-	-	-	-
(–)	*gúh-ịya-*	16	1	6.3%	-	-	1	-	-	-	-	-	-	-	-	-	1	-	-
(–)	*pṛ́tanā-*	18	1	5.6%	-	-	1	-	-	-	-	1	-	-	-	-	-	-	-
(+)!	*path-í-*	29	1	3.4%	1	-	-	-	-	-	-	-	-	-	-	-	1	-	-
(+)!	*kav-í-*	53	1	1.9%	-	-	-	-	1	-	-	-	-	-	-	-	-	-	1
+!	*avi-tár-*	32	0	--	-	-	-	-	-	-	-	-	-	-	-	-	-	-	-
+	*prath-amá-*	185	0	--	-	-	-	-	-	-	-	-	-	-	-	-	-	-	-
+	*harít-*	27	0	--	-	-	-	-	-	-	-	-	-	-	-	-	-	-	-
+!	*jánitār- / janitár-*	34	0	--	-	-	-	-	-	-	-	-	-	-	-	-	-	-	-

*VCH	Stem(s)	Total	'BIL'	Frequency	Periods					Maṇḍalas									
					A	S	N	C	P	1	2	3	4	5	6	7	8	9	10
Verbs:																			
–	*áy-a-*[te]	4	3(2)	75.0%	2	1	-	-	-	3	-	-	-	-	-	-	-	-	-
–	*kṛ-ṇáv-a-*[te]	6	2	33.3%	1	-	-	-	1	-	-	-	-	-	1	-	1	-	-
–	*vás-a-*[ti]	3	1	33.3%	1	-	-	-	-	-	-	-	-	-	-	-	1	-	-
–	*rám-a-*[ti]	3	1	33.3%	1	-	-	-	-	-	-	-	-	-	-	-	1	-	-
+?	*dhám-a-*[ti]	4	1	1 = 25.0%	1	-	-	-	-	-	-	-	-	1	-	-	-	-	-
–?	*pát-a-*[ti]	11	2	18.2%	-	2	-	-	-	1	-	-	-	-	-	-	1	-	-
–	*sṛj-á-*[ti]	14	2(1)	14.3%	1	-	1	-	-	-	-	-	-	-	-	-	1	-	1
+	*náy-a-*[ti]	29	4(1)	13.8%	3	1	-	-	-	2	-	-	-	1	-	1	-	-	-
–	*yám-a-*[ti]	8	1	12.5%	1	-	-	-	-	-	-	-	-	-	1	-	-	-	-
+	*tár-a-*[ti]	10	1	10.0%	1	-	-	-	-	-	-	-	-	-	1	-	-	-	-
+	*áv-a-*[ti]	64	6	9.4%	4	1	1	-	-	-	-	-	1	2	1	-	2	-	-
–	*sád-a-*[t(i)]	13	1	7.7%	1	-	-	-	-	-	-	-	-	1	-	-	-	-	-
–	*d-áy-a-*[te]	18	1	5.6%	1	-	-	-	-	1	-	-	-	-	-	-	-	-	-
+	*dá(-)d-a-*[ti]	19	1	5.3%	-	-	1	-	-	-	-	-	-	-	1	-	-	-	-
+	*át-a-*[ti]	1	1	100.0%	-	1	-	-	-	1	-	-	-	-	-	-	-	-	-
–	*va-náv-a-*[te]	1	1	100.0%	1	-	-	-	-	-	-	-	-	-	1	-	-	-	-

Light paenultima syllables in the RV

*VCH	Stem(s)	Total	'BIL'	Fre-quency	Periods					Maṇḍalas									
					A	S	N	C	P	1	2	3	4	5	6	7	8	9	10
+?	*śár-u-*	8	2	25.0%	2	-	-	-	-	1	-	-	-	-	-	-	-	-	1
?	°V̆-*tama-*	99	21	20.2%	14	2	1	3	-	4	1	-	1	1	10	-	-	1	2
–	*iṣ(-)i(-)rá-*	28	5	17.9%	-	-	3	1	1	-	1	-	-	1	-	-	-	1	2
–	*riṣ-*	14	2	14.3%	2	-	-	-	-	-	-	-	-	-	2	-	-	-	-
?	-*(t)ama-* (sum)	197	23	11.7%	14	2	1	3	-	4	1	-	1	1	10	-	-	1	2
+!	*ján-a-* (plural)	147 (54)	13	8.9 (24.1)%	11	-	2	-	-	2	1	1	1	1	7	-	-	-	-
+	(-)*śáv-as-*	39	3	7.7%	3	-	-	-	-	1	-	-	-	-	1	-	-	-	1
–	*ap-*	129	8	6.2%	4	-	3	1	-	1	3	1	-	-	2	1	-	-	-
+!	(-)*sákh-i-*	100	4	4.0%	-	1	3	-	-	-	-	-	2	-	-	1	-	1	-
+!	(-)*ráth-a-* + (-)*rath-í-*	392	12	3.1%	7	1	2	2	-	4	1	0	1	2	2	0	0	0	2
–	*nár-*	161	4	2.5%	3	1	-	-	-	1	1	-	-	1	-	1	-	-	-
?	°V̆C-*amá-*	98	2	2.0%	2	-	-	-	-	1	-	-	-	-	1	-	-	-	-
–	*bṛh-at-*	134	2	1.5%	-	-	1	1	-	-	-	-	-	-	-	-	-	1	1
(–)	*uṣás-*	57	1	1.8%	-	1	-	-	-	-	-	-	-	-	-	1	-	-	-
(–)	(-)*mán-as-*	116	1	0.9%	1	-	-	-	-	1	-	-	-	-	-	-	-	-	-

*VCH	Stem(s)	Total	'BIL'	Fre-quency	Periods					Maṇḍalas									
					A	S	N	C	P	1	2	3	4	5	6	7	8	9	10
(–)	*br̥hán*	161	1	0.6%	1	-	-	-	-	-	-	-	-	-	1	-	-	-	-
+	*hár-i-*	82	0	--	-	-	-	-	-	-	-	-	-	-	-	-	-	-	-
+!	*kav-i-*	133	0	--	-	-	-	-	-	-	-	-	-	-	-	-	-	-	-
Verbs:																			
–	*yu-ná-j-a-*$^{t(i)}$	3	1	33.3%	1	-	-	-	-	-	-	-	-	-	1	-	-	-	-
–	*áy-a-*$^{t(i)}$	6	1	16.7%	-	-	-	-	1	-	-	-	-	-	-	-	-	-	1
–	*ás-a-*$^{t(i)}$	17	1	5.9%	1	-	-	-	-	-	-	-	-	1	-	-	-	-	-

Relevant nominal forms (sum of the above, without single instance cases)

	Total	'BIL'	=	A	S	N	C	P	1	2	3	4	5	6	7	8	9	10
+	2074	186	9.0%	126	32	23	3	2	27	1	5	5	28	18	10	56	10	15
–	1362	85	6.2%	51	11	13	8	2	22	7	3	-	6	9	4	22	6	6

Thematic verb forms in general

	Total	'BIL'	=	A	S	N	C	P	1	2	3	4	5	6	7	8	9	10
+	127	14(1)	11.0%	9	3	2	-	-	3	-	-	1	4	3	1	2	-	-
–	107	18(3)	16.8%	12	3	1	-	2	5	-	-	-	2	4	-	5	-	2

On Polymorphic Presents in the *Ṛgveda*: Reduplication and 'Aktionsart'*

J. L. GARCÍA RAMÓN

1. The existence of the so-called 'polymorphic' presents to an extent without parallel in other IE languages is a salient peculiarity of the Vedic verb. Although it may reasonably be assumed that these different present formations played a decisive role in signalling the 'Aktionsart' or *actionality* (i.e. the morphologically marked 'Aktionsart') of the verbs on which they occurred, the actual determination of this nuance is exceedingly difficult, as can be seen from the presentation by Ulrike Joachim (1978): some of them are artificial ('Augenblicksbildungen'), having no real existence outside of the passages in which they occur, and in other cases it is impossible to recognize a real difference in the semantics of presents from the same root even if they are built with different affixes. In the latter case we may assume either

---

* The present article has been written as a part of the DFG-Research Project 'Verbalcharakter, Suppletivismus und morphologische "Aktionsart" im Indogermanischen', in the Institut für Linguistik of the University of Cologne (2000–2005). A first version was presented in the meeting of the group 'Indogermanische Syntax' in Eichstätt (Nov. 2, 2000). The final version has benefited from the remarks of Jared Klein (Athens, Georgia), Arlo Griffiths (Leiden), Stephanie Jamison and Calvert Watkins (UCLA, Los Angeles) after the oral exposition, and by Heinrich Hettrich (Würzburg) and Daniel Kölligan (Oxford, now Cologne). The editors, Jared Klein and Elizabeth Tucker, greatly improved my English and the contents of the paper itself with a number of very valuable suggestions. It is a pleasant duty to express my gratitude to all of them. Final responsibility remains my own.

that the 'Aktionsart' of the affix(es) has faded and become unrecognizable, or that the affix has become secondarily productive as a simple allomorph without recognisable function. There are, however, cases in which one Vedic root has two or more present stems, of which one at least is marked, i.e. is built by means of an affix (infix, suffix, reduplication): these are obviously the cases in which an attempt may be made to recognize the function, i.e. the 'Aktionsart' of the affix.

An important point must be stressed here: the synchronic function of the different affix formations of the Vedic verb can be determined only on the basis of a contrastive study of the present stems in those roots which have *more than one of them*, for they are in fact the only ones to allow a contrastive analysis of the affix-marked formations as against the *one* which constitutes *the* present stem, i.e. the one which stands in opposition to the aorist stem in the framework of the inherited aspectual system which in part survives in Vedic. A logical corollary of this statement is crucial at this point. The 'aspectual' present is frequently an athematic or thematic root formation, and, in some cases an affixed one: but, even in the latter case, it does not inform by itself about the former morphological 'Aktionsart' of the affix it has, for it is grammaticalized in the system of aspectual opposition.

A third remark is in order: once the functions of a given affix in the different roots in which it occurs have been established, as far as possible, it is important that they be subsumed under a general label integrating all of them at a synchronic level. The basic assumption is that the different functions recognisable for one affix may be understood as the realizations of one basic function, which are conditioned by the type of the lexeme. This point must be developed for every affix separately.

The present contribution, which is part of a research project on 'Aktionsart' in Indo-European, will deal with the reduplicated present formations (i.e. the function of reduplication in non-aspectual stems), and with the '*intensive*' formations, if attested in Vedic roots. Its aim is to provide an interpretation of the function ('Aktionsart') of reduplication in present stems in the *Ṛgveda* at a synchronic level on the basis of the premises set forth above.[1] Accordingly, attention will be paid exclusively to reduplicated presents which stand in a given root beside (and in opposition to) other present(s), one of which is actually the present stem. Consequently, some reduplicated presents will remain out of consideration as being uninformative about 'Aktionsart'. On the one hand, reduplicated presents which are the *only* present of the verb and do not allow a contrastive analysis, e.g. *gā-* : *jígāti* 'steps, goes' as against aor. *gāt* (§ **2**); on the other, 'Augenblicksbildungen' and present forms which actually go back to perfect or aorists (§ **3**). No attempt will be made to explain the details of the processes which lead some reduplicated presents to become the only present of their roots. The process of grammaticalization is easily understandable in some cases, e.g. *jígāti* 'goes', *píbati* 'drinks' as a grammaticalization of former *"makes a step repeatedly' and *"takes a gulp repeatedly' (iterative 'Aktionsart') to respectively aor. *(á)gāt* 'made a step' and *(á)pāt* 'took a gulp'.[2] Other cases in which reduplication seems not to be semantically motivated are surely the result of a process of expansion in which several factors (synonymy, formal structure of the root, and others) may have been at work. A systematic interpretation of formal aspects, such as the choice of the

[1] Concerning reduplicated presents reference must be made to the study of the corresponding roots in Joachim 1978 and to the corresponding entries in Gotō 1987, in Kümmel 2000a on the perfect, in Schaefer 1994 on the intensive, and in Lubotsky 1997. On reduplication in general cf. the presentation by Kulikov 2005.

[2] This interpretation of *jígāti* goes back, as far as I know, to Delbrück 1897: 17 (*jígāti* 'den Fuss wiederholt aufsetzen'). Further examples of reduplicated presents with iterative 'Aktionsart' to momentative roots (or 'divisibility of ... situation into (elementary) micro-situations', as per Ul'yanov 1902, 'series (chains) of elementary micro-situations' as per Kulikov 2005: 442) are pres. *bábhas-*", 3pl. *bápsati* :: root aor. *bhas* to *bhas* 'chew', or *jakṣ* 'laugh' (part. *jákṣat-* RV, opt. *jákṣ(y)us Drāhyāyaṇaśrautasūtra*) :: *hasa-* to *has* 'laugh' (cf. Hoffmann 1969: 209ff. = Aufs. 1.305ff.).

reduplication vowel *-a-* vs. *-i-* or the possible existence of a mini-system of reduplicated presents of the structure *Cí-CaC-/Ci-CC-* (*íyar-^{ti}*, *bíbhar-^{ti}*, *vívak-^{ti}*, *síṣak-^{ti}*), will not be undertaken in this paper even for the present formations relevant for 'Aktionsart' (§§ 4ff.).[3]

An attempt to determine the 'Aktionsart' of reduplicated presents must integrate the different functions which have been proposed for different roots. Some of them were recognized long ago:[4] intensive, iterative or 'divisibility into micro-situations' in G. Ul'yanov's formulation;[5] also non-telic ('ziellose Aktivität'), recognized *avant la lettre* by Berthold Delbrück in such cases as Ved. *bíbharti* 'bear', but never 'bring' ('... wird von der nicht auf ein Ziel gerichteten Thätigkeit des Tragens gebraucht').[6] In any case, the question about the basic function ('Aktionsart') of reduplication remains open, in view of the diversity of realizations attested. In what follows an attempt will be made to determine a basic function underlying (and causing) the different realizations which have been recognized in those verbs (of different lexeme types) in which a contrastive approach is possible. My point may be set forth as follows: the basic function of reduplication is to focus iconically the most salient characteristics of the lexeme in which reduplicated present formations occur. In other words, the different functions attested may be understood as the realizations of one basic 'Aktionsart' of reduplicated presents which are conditioned by (and depend on) the type of lexeme ('Verbal-

---

[3] The reduplication vowel in these presents is *-i-* with the exception of *vavákṣi* besides *vivaṣṭi* (§ **5.1**). Both the root structure and the appurtenance or not to the aspectual system proper may have played a role in the choice of *-i*-reduplication in roots without *-i-*. For a short overview of the explanations cf. Kulikov 2005: 435f., 445f.

[4] Cf. the pioneering pages of Delbrück 1897: 16ff. and the recent overview by Kulikov (2005: 443, with bibliography).

[5] Ul'yanov 1902 (*non vidi*); *apud* Kulikov 2005: 442.

[6] Delbrück 1897: 18; Kulikov 2005: 443f.

charakter') of the verbs in which they occur, namely stative, durative-cursive, durative-iterative, momentative, telic or atelic:[7] the reduplicated present stresses (1) the *state* (and is realized as [intensive]) if the lexeme is stative, (2) *durativity* and *non-telicity* (and is realized as [atelic]) if the lexeme is durative non-telic, (3) *iteration* and/or *plurality* (and is realized as [iterative] and/or [intensive]) if the lexeme is iterative, (4) *iteration* and/or *plurality* (and is realized as [iterative] or [distributive-iterative]), if the lexeme is momentative. If a lexeme is polyactional, i.e. admits analysis into two types of 'Verbalcharakter', the reduplicated present stresses the realization expected for the one or the other 'Verbalcharakter'. If no semantic or collocational difference may be established between the reduplicated present and other presents, the possibility of an [intensive] or [iterative] realization, expressed iconically by the reduplication, may not be excluded, but remains undemonstrable.

2. Let us begin by noting the roots which will not be taken into account because of the reasons set forth above. A first group is that of roots with a reduplicated present as the only present formation:

[1]*ar* 'arise, get in motion': *íyar-[ti]*
(for *ṛṇò-[ti]* and intensive *álar-[ti]* cf. below).
gā 'step, go': *jígāti* :: aor. *gā-*
dā 'give': *dádāti* :: aor. *dā-*
dhā 'put': *dádhāti* :: aor. *dhā-*
par 'bring over': *píparti* :: no aorist
[1]*pā* 'drink': *píbati* :: aor. *pā-*
[3]*pā* 'move, draw': *ut-pipīte* :: aor. *pās-* ??, cf. below
bhas 'chew': *bábhasti* (3pl. *bápsati*) :: aor. *bhas-*

[7] Cf. the classification by García Ramón (2002: 110ff.). The differentiation between transformative and non-transformative lexemes does not seem to be relevant in the case of reduplication.

yas 'boil': **yayás-*[ti] (*yayastu*, part. *yeṣant-*)[8] :: no aorist
rā 'give': *rarī-*[te] (also 1x *rirīhi*) :: aor. *rās-*
śā/śī 'sharpen': *śíśā-*[ti], med. *śíśī-*[te] 'be sharp'[9] :: no aorist
sad 'sit down': *sī́da-*[ti] :: aor. *sad-a-*
sthā 'stay, stand': *tíṣṭha-*[ti/e] :: aor. *sthā-*
hav/hu 'pour': *juhó-*[ti] :: 'impv.' aor. *hoṣi*
has 'laugh': *jákṣ-*[ti] :: no early attested aorist.
hā 1) 'leave': *jáhāti*, 3pl. *jáhati* :: aor. *hā-* (also *hāsiṣ-*);
2) 'go forth': *jíhīte* :: aor. *hās-*[ta]

Two remarks on this list are in order. To [1]*ar* 'get in motion': the reduplicated formation *íyar-*[ti] 'sets in motion', med. *ī́r-*[te] (:: aor. *ar-*[ta])[10] is considered as the present of [1]*ar/ṛ* (IE **h₃er-/h₃ṛ-*, cf. Hom. ὦρτο), in opposition to aor. intrans. *ar-*[ta], although it actually overlaps with causative *ṛṇáv-*[ti]. Present *íyar-*[ti] (med. *ī́r-*[te]) does not allow us to recognize a concrete 'Aktionsart': iterative. The causative *īráya-*[ti] 'sets in motion' recapitulates the transitive sense of *íyar-*[ti]. The 'intensive' *álar-*[ti] is also attested twice as intransitive.[11] The factitive sense of almost all the instances of *íyar-*[ti] is expressed by means of the active voice, not by the reduplication. In some cases *íyar-*[ti] and *ṛṇáv-*[ti] (*ṛṇv-á-*[ti])[12] are synony-

---

[8] Also thematic *yéṣantī* (hapax RV 3.53.22). The present **yayás-*[ti] is replaced by *yás-ya-*[ti] (AV). Both presents have perfect correspondences in Avestan: for *yayás-*[ti] (*yayastu* RV 7.704.2, part. *yéṣant-* 3.53.22) compare YAv. 3pl. *yaēšəṇta*, part. *yaēšəṇt-*; for *yás-ya-*[ti], compare YAv. *yaēšiia-*, cf. Joachim 1978: 159f. Both formations may therefore be traced back to Indo-Iranian.

[9] The hapax *śya-*[ti] (once injunctive pres. *saṃ śyat* 1.130.4 'sharpens [the Vajra]') is a secondary 'Augenblicksbildung', cf. Joachim 1978: 159f. (The only parallel is *títrat-* beside *tūrya-*, cf. § **8.2**).

[10] Ved. *íyar-*[ti] is an Indoiranian creation, cf. the Avestan present *iiar-/ īr-* (Hoffmann & Forssman 1996: 84, 205, 243): *īratū* (Y. 53.8), *˚uzirəidiiāi* (Y. 43.12, 14).

[11] Cf. Joachim 1978: 53ff.; Schaefer 1994: 101f.

[12] The *-nu*-formation Ved. *ṛṇáv-*[ti] actually reflects both IE **h₃ṛ-néu̯-* (cf. Gr. ὄρνυμι 'set in motion', Ved. [1]*ar/ṛ*) and **h₁-néu̯-* (Hitt. *arnu-*[mi] "bring', *'let arrive', Ved. [2]*ar/ṛ*, cf. Kümmel 2000a: 104f; 2000b).

mous, for instance 10.45.7c *íyarti dhūmám aruṣám bháribhrad* '(Agni) sets the ruddy smoke in motion agitating it hither and thither'[13] and 7.2.1b *śócā bṛhád yajatáṃ dhūmám ṛṇván* 'shine high, stirring up your adorable smoke'. The competition between these two presents may be explained in the framework of the substitution of the inherited present of ¹*ar/ṛ* (IE **h_3r̥-néu̯-*: Ved. *ṛṇáv-^{ti}*) by the Indo-Iranian reduplicated present *íyar-^{ti}* (**h_3i-$h_3$ér-^{ti}/*h_3i-h_3r-^{toi}*). Most of the instances of *ṛṇáv-^{ti}* (also *ṛṇv-á-*) actually belong to another root, namely ²*ar/ṛ* 'arrive, get in contact' (pres. *ṛcchá-^{ti}* :: aor. *ár-a-*), and provide corresponding transitive forms (**h_1r̥-néu̯-*: Hitt. *arnu-^{mi}* 'bring' from *'let arrive'), together with *arpáya-*.

To ³*pā* 'move' (as definitively established by T. Burrow[14]): only the present *ut-pipīte* 'rises' (TS 3.2.10.2+), part. *ut-pipāná-* (AV+) is attested (there is no root-pres. *pā́-^{ti}* belonging to this root: forms of this type belong to ²*pā* 'protect'). However, the existence of an aor. *pās-*, conjectured on the basis of AV 12.3.43 *mā́ prá pāsta*, and interpreted by Burrow as 'may it not come here', is far from being assured.[15]

3. Artificial forms ('Kunst-, Anklangsformen') and/or presents secondarily built on perfect or aorists will also remain out of consideration in this paper. Given that both explanations are often possible for the reduplicated present forms included under this

---

[13] There is no iterative 'Aktionsart' (*pace* Delbrück 1897: 21f. 'nicht "in Bewegung setzen", sondern "bewegen, hin- und herbewegen"'. The whirling motion (Geldner: 'er treibt wirbelnd den rötlichen Rauch fort') is actually expressed by the intensive participle *bháribhrat*.

[14] Burrow 1973. K. Hoffmann (*apud* Oettinger 1979: 498) compared OHitt. *pippa-^{hhi}* 'move upward, turn up' (**peH-*). The root may actually be reconstructed as **(s)peh₂-* on the basis of comparison with Gr. σπάω 'draw violently' and Arm. *hanem* 'id.' (**pā-no/e-*), as suggested by constructions and collocations with Ved. ²*pā* which are comparable with those of Hitt. *pippa-^{hhi}*. This view will be developed extensively in García Ramón 2009.

[15] Burrow 1973: 9. The form belongs most probably to ¹*pā* 'drink' cf. Narten 1969: 168 (with reference to *pra-píbante* 10.114.7).

label, they are presented in alphabetical order: ^{1}*par^{i}/pr̥̄* 'fill', *parc* 'fill, mix', *bhay^{i}/bhī* 'fear, get frightened', ^{2}*may^{i}/mī* '(make) disappear', *myak/mikṣ* 'provide with, stick to, make firm, rest firmly', ^{2}*yav* 'go apart, keep apart', *sav/su* 'press', and *hav^{i}/hvā/hū* 'call, invoke'.

^{1}*par^{i}/pr̥̄* 'fill': The present stem *píparti* AV 13.3.4 'fills' must be considered an isolated post-R̥gvedic creation. The thematic 3sg. impf. *ápiprata* (5.34.2) points to a pres. *pípr-a-^{ti}* (of the type *tíṣṭha-^{ti}*), which is surely old, but is about to be replaced by the innovative present *pr̥ṇā́-^{ti}* as the normal present of this verb.[16]

parc/pr̥c 'fill, mix, join': The reduplicated present stems *piparc-* (2x impv. 2sg. *sám pipr̥gdhi* 10.10.11d; 2pl. *sám* ... *pipr̥kta* 3.54.21) and *papr̥c-* (opt. *papr̥cyām*, 10.10.12a, subj. *papr̥cāsi* 1.141.11) are synonymous in spite of the different reduplication vowel, cf. in 10.10.11d/12a *tanvā̀ me tanvàm̐ sám pipr̥gdhi* ǁ *ná vā́ u te tanvā̀ tanvàm̐ sám papr̥cyām* 'unite with my body (your) body!' 'I would in no case unite with your body (my) body'. The stems *piparc-/papr̥c-* do not allow us to recognize any difference as against the regular *n-* present *pr̥ṇák-$^{ti/te}$*.[17] Both forms are surely secondary: *piparc-* is analogical to other reduplicated presents (cf. *mimikṣ-* beside *myakṣ* or *bibhr̥-* beside *bhar*; Joachim 1978: 109) and especially to *pípar-^{ti}* (*par/pr̥*), while *papr̥c-* is built on the perfect.[18]

bhay^{i}/bhī 'fear, get frightened':[19] the present stem *bibhay-^{ti}*/ 3pl. *bíbhyati*, attested besides *bháy-a-^{te}*, goes back ultimately to the perf. *bibhāya*, 3pl. *bibhyuḥ*.[20]

---

[16] Cf. Narten 1969. The frequently attested pres. *pípar-^{ti}* belongs (with the exception of *ápiprata* 5.34.2 which is in fact a thematic 3sg. form) to *par/pr̥* 'bring over', whence 'protect', cf. Narten 1969: 140ff. (= Kl. Schr. 109ff.).

[17] Med. *pr̥ṅkté* 'fills itself' is synonymous with fientive *pr̥cyá-^{te}* 'fills itself, is filled'.

[18] Cf. Kümmel 2000a: 305f. (with bibliography).

[19] On the root cf. Kümmel 2000a: 336ff.

[20] Both present stems are actually synonymous with the perfect, which expresses the state reached after the momentaneous action 'get frightened'

[2]*may*^{i}*/mī* '(make) disappear, change': the two attestations of the reduplicated stem **mimay-/mimī-* (*mimītaḥ* 5.76. 2, *mimīyāt* 'would change' 10.10.9) do not allow us to recognize any difference as against the regular present *máy-a-*^{te}.[21] The iterative action is actually expressed by the 'intensive' (part. *mém*$_{i}$*yāna-*, cf. 1.96.5a *náktoṣā́sā várṇam āmém*$_{i}$*yāne* 'night and dawn, which successively alternate (their) colour').

myakṣ/mikṣ- 'provide with, make firm, rest firm' (like *parc*): the reduplicated present *mímikṣ-*^{ti} (*mímikṣan* 7.20.4, *mimikṣátuḥ* 8.61.18 has been secondarily created on the basis of perf. *mimikṣ-*.[22]

[2]*yav/yu* 'be/go apart', probably also 'keep apart'[23]: the root is momentative, cf. root aor. subj. *ví-yavanta* (5.2.5).[24] Two present stems are attested, which are in clear opposition: transitive redupl. pres. *yuyáv-*^{ti} 'keeps (someone, something) apart, makes keep away' (in RV once *yā̆v-áya-* 10.10.11, which replaces it later in TS+) beside intransitive *(pra-)yúccha-*^{ti} (and *-s*-aorist *yauṣ/*

(cf. root aorist *bhema* RV, part. *bhiyāná-* RV), cf. 6.23.2cd *yád vā dákṣasya bibhyúṣo ábibhyad* | *árandhayaḥ śárdhata indra dásyūn* 'or if you, not afraid at all, overcame the bold dasyus who were afraid of (thy) skill, O Indra' and 4.6.5d *bháyante víśvā bhúvanā yád ábhrāṭ* 'all creatures get frightened, when he has shined'.

[21] Cf. Joachim 1978: 125ff.; Gotō 1987: 240f. The appurtenance of *mimī*-forms to an *aniṭ-* root *may/mi* (cf. *apa-mítya-* AV+) is controversial, cf. the different views in Joachim *loc. cit.*

[22] Joachim 1978: 132ff; *aliter* Kümmel 2000a: 385ff.

[23] The main question concerns the verbal character of the root. The transitive aorist subj. *ví-yavanta* (RV 5.2.5), if it is not a present of [1]*yav* (Jamison 1983: 174), seems to speak for transitivity, *mā te vyoma* (YV) for intransitivity: 5.2.5a *ké me maryakám̐ ví yavanta góbhir* 'who may have separated my male from the cows?', YV *mā te vyoma saṃdṛśi* 'may we not be separated in your sight' (Hoffmann 1967: 90, n. 178). The isolated present form *vyùnoti* (5.31.1) is synonymous with *ví-yuyav-* and occurs in the same collocation, with object *dvéṣas* 'enmity' (RV 6.44.16; 1.39.8): The hapax *vyùnoti* may be understood as an 'Augenblicksform' created on the basis of pairs like *íyarti* : *ṛṇóti* or 3pl. *suṣvati* : *sunóti*. *Aliter* Gotō 1997: 1030, who refers the form to *av/u*.

[24] Narten 1969: 213f.; Gotō 1997: 1030ff.

yoṣ-) 'keeps (himself) apart' and 'intensive' *áyoyavīt* 'retired' (step by step),[25] which expresses the iterative 'Aktionsart'. Neither *yuyáv-*^{ti} nor (*pra-*) *yúccha-*^{ti} allows us to recognize any 'Aktionsart' by itself. The stem *yuyáv-*^{ti}, always with transitive sense, is actually attested only once in the indicative (*yuyóti* 2.33.1) as against 33 modal forms, as stressed by Karl Hoffmann.[26] This does not actually mean that reduplication reflects causativity. The stem *yuyáv-*^{ti} is based either on a causative aorist *yūyot* 10.95.12 (Hoffmann, *ibidem*), which explains its transitive value if one admits that the root is intransitive, or on a transitive perfect.[27]

sav/su 'press': the hapax 3pl. *suṣvati* (2.16.5d *vṛ́ṣaṇaṃ sómaṃ vṛṣabhā́ya suṣvati* 'they press out the bull Soma for the bull [Indra])' as against the regular present *sunóti* may be explained as based on the perfect *suṣáv-* and/or as an 'Anklangsform' to *suṣvāṇá-*.[28]

hav^{i}/hvā /hū 'call, invoke': the stem *juhū-* (*juhūmási* 2x: 1.41.1; 8.52.4) is a sporadic creation on the model of *áhūmahi*. The present *háv-a-*^{te} stands beside *hv-áya-*^{te}, which is basically iterative.[29] The full reduplication intensive *johavī-*^{mi} may express iconically repetition or intensity (Schaefer 1994: 205f.).

4. We are left with a reduced list of roots for which a reduplicated present is attested beside other present(s): these are the roots which may allow us to identify the 'Aktionsart'/'actionality'

---

[25] Schaefer 1994: 171 with n. 516.

[26] Only one exception: AV 7.68.3 *mā́ te yuyoma saṃdṛ́śaḥ* 'may we not be separated from your view' (Hoffmann 1967: 90 'Kunstbildung').

[27] Jamison 1983: 174; also Kümmel 2000a: 401ff.

[28] Cf. Joachim 1978: 168; Kümmel 2000a: 557. Gotō (1991: 690, n. 84) interprets *suṣvati* as a 3.sg. subjunctive of the perfect ('soll man ... ausgepresst haben').

[29] Both have correspondences in Avestan (YAv. *zauua-*^{ti} and *zbaiia-*^{ti} : OPers. *zbaya-*). On the distribution of both forms in both languages, cf. Kölligan 2002: 140ff.

of reduplication on the basis of a contrastive approach (minimal pairs, collocations).

aj 'drive': *ī́ja-*^{te}/*ája-*^{ti}
tar^{i}/*tṝ* 'cross, pass': **títar-*^{ti}/*tára-*^{ti}
nas 'come to, get in contact': *níṃs(a)-*^{te}/*násа-*^{te}
pad 'fall': participle *píbdamāna-* (*píbda*^{te} *)/*pádya-*^{te}
bhar/*bhṛ* 'carry': *bíbhar-*^{ti}/*bhára-*^{ti}
(and intensive *bháribhar-*^{ti}, *járbhar-*^{ti})
^{2}*yā* 'seek, wish, ask for': *iye, īmahe*/*yā-*^{ti}
vaś / *uś* 'wish': *vavákṣi, vivaṣṭi*/*vaṣṭi*
vah/*uh* 'convey': *ū́ha-*^{ti}/*váha-*^{ti}
sac 'follow, come together, reach': *síṣak-*^{ti}/*sáca-*^{te}
han 'hit repeatedly, kill': *jíghna-*^{te}/*hán-*^{ti} (and intensive *jaṅghan-*).

In what follows attention will be paid exclusively to the syntactic behaviour of the reduplicated present formations, i.e. to the semantic and collocational differences one may observe as against those of the other present(s) attested for each root, and to the realization of the reduplication according to the type of lexeme.

5. Let us turn to two roots which contain stative (and, in part, actional durative) lexemes, with a root present, *vaś*/*uś* 'wish' (: *váṣṭi*) and ^{2}*yā* 'wish, seek, ask for' (: *yā́ti*, with -s-aorist *yā-s-*). In such cases, the reduplication places emphasis iconically on the salient feature of the lexeme, namely *state* (i.e. no change in the state of affairs) and durativity. The realization of the reduplication is [intensive]. In another formulation (S: situation, S_1, S_2 'situation limits'):

$$S_1 \quad [S] \quad S_2$$

5.1. In the case of *vaś/uś* 'wish' the co-occurrence of *váṣṭi* and *vavákṣi* in [1] may be explained in these terms, and the same applies for the collocation *pūrṇā́ṃ vaṣṭy āsícam* [2a] and *pūrṇā́ṃ vivaṣṭy āsícam* [2b]:

[1]	8.45.6b	*yás te váṣṭi vavákṣi tát* 'Whoever wishes something from you, you wish/determine it'
[2a]	2.37.1ab	*mándasva hotrā́d ánu jóṣam ándhasó* *'dhvaryavaḥ sá pūrṇā́ṃ vaṣṭy āsícam* 'Rejoice at your pleasure with the drink of the plant from the Hotṛ's cup; O Adhvaryus, he (the Hotṛ) wishes full pouring'
[2b]	7.16.11ab	*devó vo draviṇodā́ḥ* *pūrṇā́ṃ vivaṣṭy āsícam* 'God Draviṇodas wishes from you full pouring'.

It is not fully excluded that *vavákṣi* (with its accent like the root present) and *vivaṣṭi* are simply 'Augenblicksbildungen' conditioned by metre (Joachim 1987: 150). But forms of an identical structure are attested in Hittite beside regular *u̯ēk-*^{mi} 'ask' (a durative lexeme), namely *u̯eu̯akk-*^{hhi} (with secondary 'Entgleisung' to the *-mi-* conjugation from Middle Hittite onwards), and a preterite *u̯eu̯akt(a)*. The Hittite reduplicated forms may certainly be interpreted as expressing 'Aktionsart', namely [iterative] [30] or [intensive], and the same may apply to the Vedic forms. Given that Ved. *vaś* is a stative lexeme 'wish', the realization as [intensive] is in order. Accordingly, the *-a*-reduplication must be old, and the *-i-* reduplication is to be understood as analogical with other reduplicated presents of the same structure.

[30] Cf. Oettinger 2006: 38f.; García Ramón 2006: 32f.; *pace* Jasanoff 2003: 36ff. (who assumes that Hitt. *u̯eu̯akk-* goes back to an IE perfect).

5.2. The root ²*yā* 'seek, ask for' (as per Schmidt 1956) has two presents: *yā́mi* is an athematic root present, which always occurs in the active voice; the second one is attested only in the plural, in middle voice: *ī́mahe*, and part. *iyānā́-*. The appurtenance of both forms (actually both stems, cf. below) to the same verb is obvious in the light of minimal pairs such as [3] and [4]:

[3a] 8.3.9ab *tát tvā yāmi suvī́ryaṃ*
tád bráhma pūrvácittaye
'I beseech you for that possession of heroes, for that formulation (as a reward) for the one having the first thought'

[3b] 2.32.3ab *mā́ no ví yauḥ sakhyā́ viddhí tásya naḥ*
sumnāyatā́ mánasā tát tvemahe
'Do not dissolve our friendship, recognize as ours this (word) with benevolent spirit, for this we this entreat you'

[4a] 7.38.6d *bhágam ánugro ádha yāti rátnam*
'The weak one entreats Bhaga for the treasure' (cf. also 1.58.7d).

The same construction is found in Avestan with present *yāsa-* (*-sa-* <*-*sḱo-*/*e-*), cf. OAv. Y. 49.8b *sarəm taṯ θβā mazdā yāsā ahurā* 'for that alliance I entreat Thee, O Wise Ahura' (cf. also Y. 49.12d 'entreating for what is best'). Compare:

[4b] 2.17.7b (to Indra) *samānā́d ā́ sádasas tvā́m iye bhágam*
'From a common residence I entreat you (*tvā́m*) for happiness'

[4c] 3.62.11c *bhágasya rātím ī́mahe*
'We entreat the donation of Bhaga'.

1pl. *īmahe* [4c] corresponds to 1sg. *iye* [4b] (and 3sg. **īte*, which is not attested) and *īmahe* goes back to **i̯i-ih$_{2}$-med^{h}ai̯*, *iye* to **i̯i-i̯h$_{2}$-ai̯*, participle *iyānā́-* to **i̯i-i̯h$_{2}$-m̥h$_{1}$nó-*. Ved. *īmahe* could also be interpreted as the medial plural form of athematic *yā́mi* (i.e. *ih_2-$med^hai̯$). But two arguments speak in favour of an interpretation as reduplicated: (1) the medial diathesis, whereas *yā́-*^{ti} is only active; (2) the existence of a present stem, also with medial flexion, in Avestan (OAv. °*iiōi*) which perfectly matches Ved. *iye*, cf. Y. 31.2b *at̰ vå vīspə̄ṇg āiiōi* 'I entreat (*ā-iiōi*) you all' (Kellens & Pirart: 'je vous demande à tous').[31]

The reduplicated present (middle voice!) may be assumed not only on the strength of the Avestan data, but also on the basis of the comparative evidence of Greek: Hom. δίζημαι 'I seek' goes back to a reduplicated form of PGr. *$d^z\bar{a}$- (< *$i̯eh_2$-) with anomalous reduplication (διζᾱ- instead of *ζιζᾱ-), as I have tried to show elsewhere.[32] The participle *iyānā́-* and Gr. διζήμενος show precise coincidence in the collocation with verbs of movement (García Ramón 1993: 80). The Greek forms make clear that Ved. and Av. *yā-* go back to *$i̯eh_2$-. Once we assume that *iye*, *īmahe* are forms of a reduplicated present, it is reasonable to suggest that its 'Aktionsart' is intensive or iterative. The latter is preferable in view of the meaning of the verb. Av. *yāsa-* and Toch. B *yāsk-* 'beggar' in fact continue forms built with IE iterative *-sḱ-o/e-*.[33]

6. When the verbal lexeme is durative, the reduplication focuses the durativity. In fact the non-reduplicated present stem, being durative, may also be telic: telicity is expressed by means of an indication of direction or goal. On the contrary, the reduplicated presents exclude telicity, as already observed by Berthold Delbrück in the case of *bhar* : *bíbhar-*^{ti}, which does not occur with

[31] Kellens & Pirart 1988–91. But Humbach (1991) translates 'I approach', and Insler (1975: 182) excludes a connection with *yā-* 'entreat' because the preverb *ā* does not appear with *yāsa-*. Cf. also 2pl. impv. *ā-idūm* (< *$i̯i$-$i̯h_2$-$d^hu̯am$) Y. 33.7a *ā mā āidūm vahištā ... mazdā* 'demandez-moi les meilleurs ..., ô Mazdā' (Kellens & Pirart). Even more controversial is the interpretation of Y. 34.14cd (cf. Kellens & Pirart 1988–91 and Humbach 1991 *ad loc.*)

[32] García Ramón 1993, esp. 76ff.; Kümmel in LIV^2, *s.v.* *$i̯eh_2$.

[33] For the data cf. García Ramón 1993: 78ff.

directive or goal indication.[34] The same applies to *ū́ha-^{ti}* : *vah* 'drive, convey', but not to *ī́ja-^{ti}* : *aj* 'drive', cf. below. The function of the reduplication is to focus the durativity and non-telicity:

S_1 [S] S_2

6.1. As for *bhára-* 'carry, bring' vs. *bíbhar-* 'carry' (non-telic) besides intensive *bháribar-*, *járbhar-* 'agitate', cf. the evident contrast in [5]:

[5] 10.30.13ab, d *práti yád ā́po ádr̥śram āyatī́r*
ghr̥tám páyāṃsi bíbhratīr mádhūni ...
índrāya sómaṃ ṣúṣutam bhárantīḥ
'When the waters coming hither, carrying ghee, milk and honey, ... bringing the well pressed Soma-juice to Indra, became visible'.

The synonymy of *bhár-a-* and *bíbhar-* in the non-telic sense 'bring, carry' may be seen in such minimal pairs as [6] and [7]:

[6a] 2.52.3c *gárbho bhārám bharati*
'The new born carries the burden of this (world)'

[6b] 7.34.7d *bíbharti bhārám pr̥thivī́ ná bhū́ma*
'He carries the burden just like the earth the land'
(cf. also 3.56.2a *ṣáḍ bhārā́m̐ éko ácaran bibharti*
'Without moving the One carries six burdens')

[7a] 2.16.2d *háste vájram bhárati śīrṣáṇi krátum*
'He bears his club in his hand, his thoughts in his head'

---

[34] Delbrück 1897: 18f.; Joachim 1978: 116f.; Gotō 1987: 226, especially n. 485; Kulikov 2005: 443f. (atelic 'ziellose Aktivität' ... and/or iterative).

[7b] 8.29.04ab *vájram éko bibharti hásta ā́hitaṃ*
téna vṛtrā́ṇi jighnate
'The One bears the club placed in his hand, with it he beats/slays the enemies'
(cf. 8.29.5a *tigmám éko bibharti hásta*
'The one bears the sharp weapon in his hand').

Common to both stems is the non-telic meaning 'carry '[8]:

[8a] 1.1.7a, c *úpa tvāgne divé-dive ...*
námo bháranta émasi
'To thee, o Agni, day-by-day ... we come bearing homage'

[8b] 9.67.29 *úpa priyám ... yúvānam ... áganma bíbhrato námaḥ*
'To the friendly ... young man ... we have come bearing homage'.

For its part, the repeated movement 'agitate, carry to and fro' is expressed by the intensive stem *bháribhar-* [9]:

[9] 10.45.7c *íyarti dhūmám aruṣám bháribhrat*
'(Agni) whirls the ruddy smoke agitating (it) hither and thither'.

6.2. The case of *áj-a-* 'drive' vs. *ī́ja-*[te] (**Hi-Hĝ-o/e-*) is not the same as that of *bhar*: the reduplicated present, in spite of the scarcity of its occurrences (3x: with *ápa* 5.48.2; 6.64.3, with *sám* 6.29.5, also MS 4.5.6[p]), shows the same constructions as *áj-a-*. Both are non-telic [10], but may also be telic, with indication of direction [11]:

[10a] 10.68.5ab *ápa jyótiṣā támo antárikṣād*
udnáḥ śī́pālam iva vā́ta ājat
'With light he drove the darkness away from the sky, from the water, like the wind the śīpāla plant'

[10b] 6.64.3cd *ápejate śū́ro ásteva śátrūn*
bā́dhate támo ajiró ná vóḷhā
'She (Dawn) drives (the darkness) away, like a brave defender (drives away) enemies, she expels the darkness like a swift dray-horse'.

The construction with indication of goal is well attested with *ája-*, e.g. with *ápa* and *dūrám* 'drive away far away' [11a], and may be assumed for *ī́j-a-*[te] with *áparā* 'to the West' [11b]:

[11a] 1.42.3 *ápa tyám paripanthínam*
muṣīvā́ṇaṃ huraścítaṃ
dūrám ádhi srutér aja
'Drive away that marauder, the robber, the one plotting evil, far away from the road'.

Cf. also, with accusative and postponed *ácha*, 9.91.1cd *dáśa svásāro ádhi sā́no ávyè | 'janti váhniṃ sádanāny ácha* 'the ten sisters drive the traveler on the back of the sheep to its place'.

[11b] 5.48.2cd *ápo ápācīr áparā ápejate*
prá pū́rvābhis tirate devayúr jánaḥ
'Der fromme Mann treibt vor die westlich strebenden nach Westen hin, dringt vorwärts mit den östlichen' (Grassmann).

In view of the fact that the constructions of *áj-a-* 'drive' and *ī́ja-*[te] coincide, a concrete 'Aktionsart' may not be recognized for the reduplicated present. It is not excluded that it is iterative or that it stresses plurality,[35] but this assumption relies only on the assumed iconic value of the reduplication.

---

[35] Strunk 1977: 971ff.; Joachim 1978: 36f.; Gotō 1987: 90.

6.3. The situation of *vah* 'drive, transport, convey' is similar to that of *aj*. Both *váh-a-* and reduplicated *ū́h-a-*^{ti} (5x in RV: with *ápa* 5.34.3; 10.61.5, with *práti* 1.164.29, with *sam* 1.131.3, *sám* 8.21.14), as well as the intensive (repetitive)[36] *ūhyá-* (2x), show the construction without [12] and with [13] an indication of direction or goal:

[12a] 10.33.1b *váhāmi sma pūṣáṇam ántareṇa*
'I drive Pūṣan along the way'

[12b] 10.61.5b *ánuṣṭhitaṃ nú náryo ápauhat*
'The manly one straightway removed (his) flaccid (member?)'

[12c] 4.56.6c *ūhyā́the sanā́d ṛtám*
'You (Aśvins) both drive repeatedly from of old the ordered Truth' (*ūhyā́the* for *ūhyéthe*)

[13a] 3.58.2a *suyúg vahanti práti vām ṛténa*
'With good yoking they drive towards you two (Aśvins) at the right time'

[13b] 1.164.29d *vidyúd bhávantī práti vavrím auhata*
'Becoming lightning, she rolled her dress up'

[13c] 1.120.11 *ayáṃ samaha mā tanu*
ūhyā́te jánām̐ ánu
somapéyaṃ sukhó ráthaḥ
'This light chariot will take me somehow over the lineages (repeatedly) to the drinking of Soma, O thin one (?)'.

The reduplicated present *ū́h-a-*^{ti} does not behave differently from the root present. It may be interpreted as stressing durativity (or iteration or intensity), even if this only relies on the presence of reduplication.[37]

---

[36] Cf. Schaefer 1994: 178 ('kontinuativ-repetitiv').

[37] Cf. Gotō 1987: 296f. ('mit dauernder, stufenartiger Bewegung etw. in eine Richtung schaffen').

7. When the lexeme is by its nature iterative, the reduplication focuses repetition: the reduplicated present may be understood as stressing iconically repetition, or even intensity. The schematic formulation is the same as in the case of stative and durative lexemes:

$$S_1 \quad [S] \quad S_2$$

The root *han* (with root present *hán-*[ti], and reduplicated *jíghna-*[te] of which there are 17 instances) has actually two meanings in Vedic (and in Indo-European): (1) 'beat repeatedly' (durative-iterative), as clearly indicated by the fact that the root has a root present *hán-*[ti] (and not a root-aorist, which would be expected for a momentative lexeme); and (2) 'kill' (telic), as the result of a semantic shift which is actually of IE date, as has been shown by C. Watkins (1987). For our purpose not only is (1) certainly of interest, but also (2), for *jíghna-*[te] may mean 'kill' when the object is plural, e.g. *vṛtrā́ṇi* 'enemies'. The 'Aktionsart' of the reduplicated present as against root present *hán-*[ti] and intensive *jaṅghan-* may hardly be recognized when they occur in identical collocations, for instance with *támāṃsi* 'darkness' (collective!) and with *vṛtrā́ṇi* 'enemies'. In the latter case the sense (2) 'kill' is not excluded. With *támāṃsi*:[38]

[14a]	6.72.1d	*víśvā támāṃsy ahataṃ nidáśca* 'You two have beaten the darkness and the revilers'
[14b]	8.43.32	*sá tvám agne vibhā́vasuḥ* *sṛján sū́ryo ná raśmíbhiḥ* *śárdhan támāṃsi jighnase* 'You, Agni, whose goods consist of radiance, shooting like the sun with rays, you beat arrogantly the darkness' (cf. 9.100.8)

[38] Also with the perfect, cf. 10.39.2d *kṛṣṇā́ támāṃsi tvíṣyā jaghāna* 'he has beaten the black darkness with his shine'.

[14c] 9.9.7bc *támāṃsi soma yódhyā*
tā́ni punāna jaṅghanaḥ
'This darkness, which is to be fought against,
O Soma, who are being purified, you should beat'
(cf. also 9.66.24, 25).

With *vṛtrā́ṇi*:

[15a] 8.90.5c *tváṃ vṛtrā́ṇi haṃsy apratī́ni*
'You smash the enemies, to whom none are equal'

[15b] 1.102.7d *ádhā vṛtrā́ṇi jighnase puraṃdara*
'Then you smash the enemies, O splitter of citadels'

[15c] 6.16.34ab *agnír vṛtrā́ṇi jaṅghanad*
draviṇasyúr vipanyáyā
'Agni will smash the enemies, eager for wealth, wondrously'.

We observe that *jíghna-*[te], being attested in the singular, normally has plural objects[39], cf. [16], where intensive and *jighnate* coexist:

[16] 6.75.13ab *ā́ jaṅghanti sā́nv eṣāṃ*
jaghánā̐m̐ úpa jighnate
'She strikes (violently) their backs, she whips over their buttocks'.

This is not a specific feature of the reduplicated present, for it is also normal with athematic *hán-*[ti], but the fact that *jíghna-*[te] occurs only exceptionally with a singular object is an essential peculiarity against the root present. This suggests that *jíghn-a-*[te] may express plurality, concretely object-distributive iteration,

---

[39] Only two exceptions: 1.80.5ab (*vṛtrásya. .. sā́num vájreṇa ... áva jighnate* 'Indra strikes down at Vṛtra's back with his club') and 1.80.6a (*ádhi sā́nau ní jighnate*).

which is not inherent in *han-* by itself, as well as intensity, as a specific feature iconically represented by reduplication.

The stem *jíghn-a-*^{te} may be explained as an old reduplicated present of the type *píba-*^{ti}, *tí-ṣṭh-a-*^{ti},[40] or as the reflex of a former reduplicated stem of the structure *Ce-CC-o/e-* with secondary *-i-*reduplication (García Ramón 1998: 147, 149ff.): the inherited form with *-e-*reduplication would denote originally 'Aktionsart', namely iterative, or intensive, or distributive iteration in terms of Dressler's 'Pluralität',[41] as shown by YAv. *ja-γn-a-* (*nijaγnəṇte*: Yt. 13.48 *tå̊ daŋ́hāuuō haθrajatå̊ nijaγnəṇte* 'they strike down those nations with one stroke' [object-distribution], also *nijaγnəṇti* in Mss K38 *et al.* (Hintze 1999: 107, n. 32); *auua.jaγnaṯ*: Yt. 13.105 *yō fraēštəm ... anaṣ̌aonąm ... auua.jaγnaṯ* 'he who struck down ... most ... of the false ones') and by Gr. Hom. πεφνο/ε-, which has been grammaticalized as the Aorist of θείνω.

8. Let us now turn to the momentative lexemes, i.e., those in which there is no interval between the beginning and the end of the action or situation:

$$[S_1 = S_2]$$

They imply the attainment of a goal or of a state and, eventually, a transformation of the state of the subject. The crucial point is whether the lexeme remains constantly a momentative one: in this case, the present stem may by itself only be realized as [iterative]. The same applies *a fortiori* to reduplication. Less transparent is the situation when the lexeme, being originally momentative, enters a system of opposition, in which the present stem expresses the action in its 'Verlaufsschau', either as a 'displexive' extension of the action in the present time ('*de conatu*')

---

[40] So recently Hintze 1999: 109.

[41] Dressler 1968; Strunk 1994: 427; García Ramón 1998: 150.

or in terms of plurality, i.e. of distributive iteration (one subject performs the action with several objects or several subjects each perform the action once). Both realizations may be stressed by reduplication: this is the case of *nas*, *tar^i/tṝ*, and *pad*. A similar picture is seen with the root *sac* / *śc* (§ **9**).

8.1. The root *nas* 'get in contact (with the desired goal)'[42] is a perfect example of this type: *nás-a-^te* 'come close, approach' [17] vs. aor. (*sáṃ*) *nasīmahi* 'mögen wir uns vereinen' [18] / *niṃs(a)-te* 'touch repeatedly' [19]:[43]

[17] 4.58.8cd *ghṛtásya dhā́rāḥ samídho nasanta*
tā́ juṣāṇó haryati jātávedāḥ
'die Ströme des Butterschmalzes nahen sich den Brennhölzern. Diese genießend freut sich der Jātavedas' (Hoffmann 1967: 130)

[18] 2.16.8cd *sakṛ́t sú te sumatíbhiḥ śatakrato*
sám pátnībhir ná vṛ́ṣaṇo nasīmahi
'At once we would come together with your good will, O you of a hundred determinations, like the bulls with their females ...'

[19] 1.144.1cd *abhí srúcaḥ kramate dakṣiṇāvṛ́to*
yā́ asya dhā́ma prathamáṃ ha níṃsate
'He strides to the sacrificial spoons on the right side which touch first his abode'.[44]

The same applies to the remaining attestations of *níṃs(a)-* [21]

The comparison of [17] and [19] is illustrative: in [17] *nasanta* 'come closer' is not iterative, but 'displexive': the present

---

[42] Or 'approach / get near in joyful anticipation' (cf. Malzahn 2007: 238ff.). On the semantics and paradigm of Ved. *nas* and of IE **nés-* cf. García Ramón 2004 (root aorist **n̥s-to*). *Aliter* Malzahn 2007 (aor. **nes-to* of Narten-type, cf. also **nés-sḱo/e-* : B *ñäsk-* 'desire').

[43] Cf. Gotō 1987: 200f.; Kulikov 2005: 444.

[44] *Aliter* Gotō 1987: 201, who operates with an extension of the action into the present: '([Opfer]löffel), die soeben seine Wohnstätte aufsuchen'.

stem expresses the 'Verlaufsschau', the duration of the getting in contact. For its part, [19] is specifically iterative, and expresses that the spoons repeatedly touch Agni's abode. The same interpretation applies to [20]:

[20] 8.43.10 *úd agne táva tád ghṛtā́d*
arcī́ rocata ā́hutam
nímsānaṃ juhvò múkhe
'That flame of yours, Agni, poured upon, shines from the ghee ... touching the spoons in (its) mouths' ('Deine Flamme, Agni, leuchtet aus der zerlassenen Butter auf ... indem sie die Opferlöffel an ihrem Munde aufsucht' Gotō 1987: 201; not 'auf den Mund küssend' as Geldner).

Cf. also 10.74.2ab *háva eṣām ásuro nakṣata dyā́ṃ* | *śravasyatā́ mánasā niṃsata kṣā́m* 'at their call the Asura reaches the heaven (and) touches the earth with fame-seeking mind'.[45]

8.2. The root *tar*^{i}/*tṝ* 'cross, traverse' has several presents: a Class I present *tár-a-*^{ti} coexists with *tū́rva-*^{ti} 'overcome, be superior' and with a *tudáti*-type present *tir-á-*^{ti} (always with preverbs),[46] which is actually the causative of the root, like *tār-áya-*^{ti} (AV) and *tur-áya-* (RV).[47] Moreover a reduplicated present **titár-*^{ti} is attested as a hapax in the participle nom. pl. *títrataḥ* (2.31.2) [21b].[48]

---

[45] Cf. further with athematic 3pl. 9.85.3d *rā́jānam asyá bhúvanasya niṃsate* 'they touch (repeatedly) the king of this world'. But with thematic 3.sg the obscure hemistich 10.92.2cd *aktúṃ ná yahvám uṣásaḥ puróhitaṃ tánūnápātam aruṣásya niṃsate* (cf. also 10.94.9a).

[46] Medial only with *prá-*, namely in formulaic *ā́yuṣ pra-tira-*^{te} cf. Gotō 1987: 162f.

[47] Ved. *°tirá-*^{ti} was replaced as the causative by *tāráyati*, *tur-áya-* (RV). Whether *°tirá-*^{ti} conceals a former reduplicated causative **prá-titirá-*^{ti} with secondary dereduplication for metrical reasons, as proposed by Tichy 2004, is irrelevant for our purposes.

[48] The *aniṭ*-like form is analogical to *píprat-* 'bringing across', cf. Gotō 1987: 165.

For its part, the intensive *tartárīti* (*tartūrya-*), *tari-tr-* expresses iteration ('crosses *again and again*') [21c].[49] The root may be considered as originally momentative (cf. aorist passive *átāri*), but in Vedic synchrony, pres. *tár-a-ti* :: aor. *átārīt* may also designate a continuous crossing, or a crossing referring to different objects. As to the function of the reduplicated present, cf. the minimal pair [21a] and [21b] with *rájāṃsi* as the object:

[21a] 1.32.14cd *náva ca yán navatíṃ ca srávantīḥ*
śyenó ná bhītó átaro rájāṃsi
'When you crossed over ninety nine streams, like a frightened eagle the heavenly spaces'

[21b] 2.31.2cd *yád āśávaḥ pádyābhis títrato rájaḥ*
pṛthivyā́ḥ sā́nau jáṅghananta pāṇíbhiḥ
'When the swift ones, crossing the space with their kicks, beat on the back of the earth with their hooves'.

The comparison of [21a] and [21b] in their contexts does not allow us to recognize a clear-cut difference of meaning between *tár-a-*^{ti} and *titár-*^{ti}. One can, however, assume that the reduplicated form expresses iteration explicitly.[50] The same applies to the intensive, which expresses different variations of plurality, cf. [21c]:[51]

[21c] 4.40.3cd *śyenásyeva dhrájato aṅkasáṃ pári*
dadhikrā́vṇaḥ sahórjā́ táritrataḥ
'(The wind blows after) Dadhikrāvan, like after a darting eagle, (as he darts) around the curve with force, passing (other horses) again and again'

[49] On the different formations cf. Gotō 1987: 160ff.; Jamison 1983: 101; Schaefer 1994: 130ff.

[50] So Gotō 1987: 165 ('immer wieder durchdringend').

[51] Cf. Schaefer 1994: 130f.

The fact that the reduplicated stem is attested only once and does not show a significant difference as against the intensive may suggest that the part. *títrataḥ* is a 'Kunstform' without any real existence. But the existence of YAv. *titarat̰*, participle *titarəṇt-* points to an Indo-Iranian form[52], whatever its 'Aktionsart' may be.

To sum up: the reduplicated stem *títar-*, no matter whether it represents a living formation or an artificial one, fits into the pattern proposed above for a momentative root. It expresses iteration or, more precisely, plurality.

8.3. The part. *āpíbdamāna-* (once in RV 10.101.11; also ŚB 1.8.1.7; JB 2.75) points unmistakably to a reduplicated pres. **pí-bd-a-te* besides the regular present *pád-ya-te* (vs. aor. *apadran*), as convincingly argued by K. Strunk (1977: 417ff.): *āpíbdamāna-* 'fest auftretend' reflects the lexicalized iterative function of the reduplicated present **píbd-a-te* ('lässt sich hin und her [auf den einen und den anderen Fuß] fallen'), cf. the contrast between *pád-ya-te* and *āpíbdamāna* [22]:

[22a]	10.146.5d	*yathākā́mam ní padyate* 'One falls down (to rest) at wish' (cf. also *ánipadyamāna-* in 1.164.31ab [=10.177.3ab]: *ápaśyam gopā́m ánipadyamānam* | *ā́ ca párā ca pathíbhiś cárantam* 'I saw the shepherd not resting, going on the paths here and there')
[22b]	10.101.11ab	*ubhé dhúrau váhnir āpíbdamāno* *'ntár yóneva carati dvijā́niḥ* 'Between both poles runs the steed, putting its feet repeatedly/alternatively, like (one) who has two women in bed'.

---

[52] Gotō 1987: 165 (*aliter* Tichy 2004: 566, n. 5, who considers the Vedic form an artificial one)

9. The root *sac* occupies a special position, for it has two meanings which point to a polyactional lexeme, namely 'follow, go with' (durative) and 'reach' (momentative-telic), at least in Ṛgvedic synchrony. The paradigm includes a thematic root present *sác-a-*^{te} (which fits well with a durative lexeme) and a reduplicated present (cf. below), as well as a sigmatic aor. *sākṣ-* and a root aorist (attested only in the participle *sacāná-*), as well as a perf. *sasac-*. It is to be stressed that the thematic root-pres. *sác-a-*^{te} and root-aor. part. *sacāná-* point to a durative and to a momentative lexeme respectively: this fits into the pattern of polyactionality as mentioned above.

The construction pattern of *sac* includes the cases accusative and instrumental in the position of the actant, in the terms convincingly set forth by H. Hettrich (1990):[53] the accusative expresses the orientation towards the goal ('follow, come with', also 'strive', and 'arrive, reach') whereas the instrumental stresses the attainment of the goal and the remaining in touch with it [23]:

[23] 1.183.2cd *vápur vapuṣyā́ sacatām iyáṃ gī́r*
divó duhitróṣásā sacethe
'Let this spell follow (*sacatām*) (your) wondrous appearance with wonderment. You two consort (*sacethe*) with Dawn, Heaven's daughter'.

For the present research the main question is whether the reduplicated present, which shows two formal variants in complementary distribution,[54] namely *síṣac-*^{ti} (and once 3pl. *sáścati*) as

[53] Cf. Hettrich 1990: *sac* + acc. ('Ausrichtungs aufs Ziel hin'): a) 'zu etwas hinstreben', 'zu etwas hingelangen', b) 'begleiten, geleiten', 'folgen', as against *sac* + instr. ('Erreichen des Zieles' 'letzendliches Zusammensein'): a) 'etwas erreichen', b) 'verbunden sein mit'. *Aliter* Haudry 1977: 298ff.

[54] *síṣak-* occurs only before a consonant and *sáśc-* only before a vowel, (Gotō 1987: 320, n. 771).

against *saśc-*[te], them. *sá-śca-*[te],[55] allows us to recognize a concrete 'Aktionsart'. It is generally assumed that no semantic difference between *sác-a-*[te] and *síṣac-*[ti] (and *saśc-*[te], thematic *sá-śca-*[te]) may be recognized:[56] compare the minimal pairs of [24a] and [24b]:

[24a] 7.33.7c *tráyo gharmā́sa uṣásaṃ sacante*
'Three fire heats follow the Dawn'
(cf. also 8.5.2c *sácethe aśvinoṣásam* 'O Aśvins, you follow the Dawn')

[24b] 9.84.2cd *kṛṇván saṃcṛ́taṃ vicṛ́tam abhíṣṭaya*
índuḥ siṣakty uṣásaṃ ná sū́ryaḥ
'Making bound and unbound for superiority, the drop follows (them) like Sūrya (follows) the Dawn'.

There is, however, an essential difference between *sác-a-*[te] and *síṣac-*[ti] (and *sáśc(a)-*[te]), which has not been given the attention it deserves: thematic *sác-a-*[te] may be construed with both accusative and instrumental, whereas reduplicated *síṣac-*[ti] (and *sáśc(a)-*[te]) never has the instrumental as actant (one apparent exception of 1sg. *saśce* may be explained differently, see below). This statement of facts is a crucial one and speaks for the assumption that the reduplicated forms *sísac-*[ti], *sáśc(-a)-*[te] do not express the attainment of the goal, whence their non-telic meanings 'follow' and 'run for, strive for', but not 'attain, reach, join', for instance [25]:

[25] 1.66.2a *tákvā ná bhū́rṇir vánā siṣakti*
'Like an excited bird of prey he (Agni) strives for the forests'.

---

[55] These forms are commonly considered to belong to the present stem, although they originally belonged to the perfect stem (Kümmel 2000a: 540f. with references).

[56] Cf. Joachim 1978: 163; Gotō 1987: 318; Hettrich 1990: 94, n. 29. In any case, a difference of sense between both present stems in terms of *sácate* 'kommt zusammen' :: *síṣakti* 'sich an etw. hängen, zusammensein', as proposed by Gaedicke (1880: 87) and Delbrück (1888: 131), finds no support in the texts.

Two facts speak in favour of the assumption that the reduplicated present excludes telicity:

(1) The one alleged instance of the reduplicated present governing an instrumental (1sg. *saśce* with instr. *krátubhiḥ* in [26]) is only apparent:

[26] 5.33.8cd *váhantu mā dáśa śyétāso asya*
gairikṣitásya krátubhir nú saśce
'May his ten white horses carry me! I agree with the intentions of Gairikṣita' ('ich stimme mit den Absichten des G. überein' Geldner).

In fact the form *saśce* may be interpreted as a medial perfect (with zero grade of the root cf. *saścuḥ*, *saścire*), not necessarily as a middle present[57]: actually the sense 'I am coincident' (*'I am attached') fits perfectly into the pattern of a perfect which expresses the result of the action ('keep contact').[58]

(2) In spite of current translations, there is no instance of *síṣac-*^{ti} [27] or of the medial forms with *-e-* reduplication [28] where the sense 'attain, join' is certain. In all instances 'follow, go with' is also possible:[59]

[27] 8.75.13ab *anyám asmád bhiyā́ iyám*
ágne síṣaktu duchúnā
'May this calamity, o Agni, follow another one than us with its horror' ('nicht uns verfolge schreckensvoll o Agni dieses Ungemach', Grassmann)[60]

---

57 Both possibilities are assumed by Kümmel (2000a: 540). According to Gotō (1987: 320, n. 771) the medial forms go back to perfect forms.

58 Gotō 1987: 320, n. 771; Kümmel 2000a: 540f. ('sich jmdm. Akk. anschliessen, sich zusammenschliessen mit Instr.').

59 The same applies to 5.41.15cd *síṣaktu mātā́ mahī́ rasā́ naḥ smát sūríbhiḥ* ... 'may the great mother Rasā follow/accompany us, together with the Lords', 5.41.20a *síṣaktu na ūrjavyàsya puṣṭéḥ* 'may (the mother) of Ūrjavya's prosperity follow/accompany us'.

60 Cf. Geldner *ad loc.* ('einen anderen als uns soll zum Schrecken dieses Unheil heimsuchen'); Hettrich 1990: 94, n. 29.

[28] 7.26.4d *asmé bhadrā́ṇi saścata priyā́ṇi*
'May auspicious favors accompany us'
('dass ... lieber Segen freundlich uns geleite', Grassmann).[61]

To sum up, the situation in the *Ṛgveda* is fairly clear: reduplicated *síṣac-^{ti}* and *saśc(a)-^{te}* do not govern the instrumental, i.e. they do not express telicity. This is a restriction as against *sác-a-^{te}*, which, as the present stem, may be both telic and atelic. As against 'aspectual' *sác-a-^{te}* the reduplicated stem *síṣac-^{ti}* (and *saśc(a)-^{te}*), which is also attested in the Avesta,[62] expresses 'Aktionsart': it stresses the durativity and non-telicity of *sac* in the meaning 'go after, strive for', as strongly suggested by the absence of the construction with instrumental.

The prehistory of *sac*, although irrelevant for our purposes, may be reconstructed as follows: the lexeme *sac*, originally momentative and telic ('reach, attain, make contact with'),[63] as suggested by the residual existence of a root aorist (cf. part. *sacāná-*), had become polyactional in Ṛgvedic synchrony in the framework of an opposition pres. *sác-a-^{te}* :: aor. *sākṣ* - The present *sác-a-^{te}* expressed consequently (1) the 'Verlaufsschau' (i.e. the function of the present stem in the framework of the former aspectual opposition) of 'reach', 'get in contact with', i.e. 'is reaching', and

---

[61] For *sáśc(a)-* the sense 'go with' is clear with acc. *vāyúm* (7.90.3), *vŕ̥ṣaṇam* 'the bull' (1.64.12), *imám* (7.18.25 *et al.*), etc.

[62] The situation in Avestan basically confirms the picture resulting from the consideration of the Vedic synchrony. The paradigm of Av. *hac* is parallel to that of Ved. *sac*: thematic pres. *hac-a-*, reduplicated *hišc(a)-* (YAv. *hišhaxti*, OAv. *hiščamaidē*), root aorist (OAv. *hə̄c-/sc-*) and *-s*-aorist (OAv. *hāxš-*), as well as a perfect. The only essential difference is that *hišc(a)-* has instrumental rection, like *hac-a-^{te}* 'unite himself', cf. for instance Y. 40.4 *aθā xᵛaētūš aθā vərəzə̄nā aθā haxə̄mąm x́iiāt̰ yāiš hiščamaidē* ... '... ebenso Familien, ebenso Gemeinden. Möchten so die Genossenschaften sein, mit denen wir uns verbinden ...' (Narten 1986: 46, 284, cf. also p. 288).

[63] So rightly Kümmel (2000a: 540; also LIV² *s.v.* **sekᵘ̯-*). In this early phase the reduplicated stem **si-sekᵘ̯-* would have denoted an 'Aktionsart' [iteration], of which no recognizable trace remains in the *Ṛgveda*.

(2) the lexicalized sense 'follow, go after, strive for (i.e. *'be about to attain, be about to make contact with'), go with'.

10. Let us sum up. By taking into consideration the data from the few Vedic roots in which a semantic and/or collocational contrast between the reduplicated present and other present(s) may be observed, we have been able to gain insight into the semantics of the reduplicated presents, i.e. information about their 'Aktionsart'. Their basic function is to focus iconically the main semantic features of the lexeme in which they occur: their realizations depend on the nature of the lexeme.

If the lexeme is stative, the reduplicated present stresses the *state* and is realized as [intensive]: this is the case of *vavákṣi*, *vivaṣṭi* vs. *vaṣṭi* (*vaś* / *uś* 'wish') and *iye*, *īmahe* vs. *yāti* ([2]*yā* 'wish, search, ask for').

If the lexeme is durative and not telic, the reduplicated present stresses *durativity* and *non-telicity*, and is realized as [atelic]: this is the case *bíbhar-*^{ti} 'carry', not 'bring' vs. *bhára-*^{ti} (*bhar*/*bhṛ* 'carry'), *ū́ha-*^{ti} vs. *váha-*^{ti} (*vah*/*uh* 'convey'), and *síṣak-*^{ti} 'follow', not 'reach' vs. *sáca-*^{te} (*sac* 'follow', 'come together', 'reach').

If the lexeme is iterative, the reduplicated present stresses *iteration* and/or *plurality* and eventually [intensity] and is realized as [iterative] or [intensive]: this is the case of *jíghna-*^{te} beside *hán-*^{ti} (*han* 'hit repeatedly', 'kill').

If the lexeme is momentative, the reduplicated present stresses *iteration* and *plurality* and is realized as [iterative] or [distributive-iterative]: this is the case of *níṃs(a)-*^{te} 'get repeatedly in contact' vs. *nása-*^{te} (*nas* 'come to, get in contact'), **títar-*^{ti} 'pass through repeatedly' (1x) vs. *tára-*^{ti} (*tar*^{i}/*tṝ* 'cross, pass'), **píbda-*^{te} 'put the feet repeatedly' (part. *āpíbdamāna-*) vs. *pádya-*^{te} (*pad* 'fall').

If no semantic or collocational difference may be observed between the reduplicated present and other presents, as in the case of *ī́ja-*^{te} and *ája-*^{ti} (*aj* 'drive'), the possibility that the reduplicated formation is intensive or iterative remains open, but is not supported explicitly by the context.

REFERENCES

BURROW, T. 1973. Sanskrit *pā-* 'go, move, pass, traverse'. *Indo-Iranian Journal* 15: 81–108.

DELBRÜCK, B. 1888. *Altindische Syntax*. Halle: Buchhandlung des Waisenhauses.

——— 1897. *Vergleichende Syntax der indogermanischen Sprachen*, II. Straßburg: Karl J. Trübner.

DRESSLER, W. 1968. *Studien zur verbalen Pluralität*. Wien: Österreichische Akademie der Wissenschaften.

GAEDICKE, C. 1880. *Der Accusativ im Veda*. Breslau: W. Koebner.

GARCÍA RAMÓN, J. L. 1993: Griego ζητέω (: hom.-jon. δίζημαι), véd. *yā-*[2] 'pedir' e IE **i̯eh₂-* 'pedir, desear, buscar ansiosamente'. In: L. Isebaert (ed.), *Miscellanea Linguistica Graeco-Latina*: 71–84. Namur: Société des études classiques.

——— 1998. Idg. **gʷʰen-* 'wiederholt schlagen', 'töten'. In: J. Jasanoff, H. C. Melchert & L. Oliver (eds.), *Mír Curad. Studies Presented to Calvert Watkins* (Innsbrucker Beiträge zur Sprachwissenschaft, 92): 139–154. Innsbruck: Institut für Sprachwissenschaft der Universität Innsbruck.

——— 2002. Zu Verbalcharakter, morphologischen 'Aktionsart' und Aspekt in der indogermanischen Rekonstruktion. In: Heinrich Hettrich & J. S. Kim (eds.), *Indogermanische Syntax. Fragen und Perspektiven*: 105–136. Wiesbaden: Reichert.

——— 2004. Zum Paradigma von idg. **nes-*: homerisch ἀπενάσσατο, kausat. ἀπονάσσωσιν als Aoriste von (°)νέομαι und die Entstehung des Präs. ναίω. In: Th. von Krisch, Th. Lindener & U. Müller (eds.), *Analecta homini universali dicata. Arbeiten zur Indogermanistik, Linguistik, Philologie, Politik, Musik und Dichtung: Festschrift für Oswald Panagl zum 65. Geburtstag*, I: 33–47. Stuttgart: Heinz.

——— 2006. Review of Jasanoff 2003. *Kratylos* 51: 25–34.

——— 2009. Idg. **(s)peh₂-* 'in (heftige) Bewegung setzen, ziehen': Ved. *pā3*, heth. *pipp(a)-ḫḫi* und gr. σπάω, arm. *hanem*. *Protolanguage and Prehistory. Akten des XII. Fachtagung der indogermanischen gesellschaft vom 11. bis 15. Oktober 2004 in Krakau*: 134–148. Wiesbaden: Reichert.

GOTŌ, T. 1987. *Die 'I. Präsensklasse' im Vedischen*. Wien: Verlag der Österreichischen Akademie der Wissenschafte.

——— 1991. Materialien zu einer Liste altindischer Verbalformen: 4–7. *Bulletin of the National Museum of Ethnology* (Osaka) 16: 681–707 (5. *sav / su*, 6. [1]*savⁱ / sū*, 7. [2]*savⁱ / sū*, 688–701).

——— 1997. Materialien zu einer Liste altindischer Verbalformen: 16–28. *Bulletin of the National Museum of Ethnology* (Osaka) 22: 1001–1059 (25. [1]*yav / yu*, 26. [2]*yav / yu*, 1025–1033).

HAUDRY, J. 1977. *L'emploi des cas en védique. Introduction a l'étude des cas en indo-européen*. Lyon: L'Hermès.

HETTRICH, H. 1990. Rektionaler und autonomer Kasusgebrauch. In: H. Eichner & H. Rix (eds.), *Sprachwissenschaft und Philologie: Jacob Wackernagel und die Indogermanistik heute. Kolloquium der Indogermanischen Gesellschaft vom 13. bis 15. Oktober 1988 in Basel*: 82–99. Wiesbaden: Reichert.

HINTZE, A. 1999. Kategorienwechsel und funktionale Umdeutung im Präsens und Aorist. In: J. Habisreitinger, R. Plath & S. Ziegler (eds.), *Gering und doch vom Herzen: 25 indogermanistische Beiträge. Bernhard Forssman zum 65. Geburtstag*: 101–114. Wiesbaden: Reichert.

HOFFMANN, K. 1967. *Der Injunktiv im Veda*. Heidelberg: Carl Winter.

——— 1969. Materialien zum altindischen Verbum. *Zeitschrift für vergleichende Sprachforschung* 83: 193–214 (12. '*jakṣ*', 209–214) [= *Aufsätze zur Indoiranistik* I: 289–310 (305–310)].

HOFFMANN, K. & B. FORSSMAN 1996. *Avestische Laut- und Flexionslehre*. Innsbruck: Institut für Sprachwissenschaft der Universität Innsbruck.

HUMBACH, H. 1991. *The Gāthās of Zarathushtra and the Other Old Avestan Texts*, I–II. Heidelberg: C. Winter.

INSLER, S. 1975. *The Gāthās of Zarathustra*. Tehran: Bibliothèque Pahlavi – Leiden: E.J. Brill.

JAMISON, S. 1983. *Function and Form in the -áya-formations of the Rig Veda and Atharva Veda*. Göttingen: Vandenhoeck und Ruprecht.

JASANOFF, J. 2003. *Hittite and the Indo-European Verb*. Oxford: Oxford University Press.

JOACHIM, U. 1978. *Mehrfachpräsentien im Ṛgveda*. Frankfurt am Main: P. Lang.

KELLENS, J. & E. PIRART 1988–91. *Les Textes vieil-avestiques*, I–III. Wiesbaden: Reichert.

KÖLLIGAN, D. 2002. Zur Funktion schwundstufiger *-éje/o*-Präsentia im Indogermanischen. In: Heinrich Hettrich (ed.), *Indogermanische Syntax. Fragen und Perspektiven*: 137–156. Wiesbaden: Reichert.

KULIKOV, L. 2005. Reduplication in the Vedic verb: Indo-European inheritance, analogy and iconicity. In: B. Hurch (ed.), *Studies on Reduplication*: 431–447. Berlin: Mouton de Gruyter.

KÜMMEL, M. J. 2000a. *Das Perfekt im Indoiranischen*. Wiesbaden: Reichert.

——— 2000b. Der Aorist der Wurzel(n) *ar* im Vedischen. In: B. Forssman & R. Plath (eds.), *Indoarisch, Iranisch und die Indogermanistik. Arbeitstagung der Indogermanischen Gesellschaft vom 2. Bis 5. Oktober 1997 in Erlangen*: 253–266. Wiesbaden: Reichert.

LIV[2] = H. Rix (ed.), *Lexikon der indogermanischen Verben*. 2nd edition. Wiesbaden: Reichert, 2001.

LUBOTSKY, A. 1997. Remarks on the Vedic intensive. *Journal of the American Oriental Society* 117: 559–564.

MALZAHN, M. 2007. Tocharian desire. In. Alan J. Nussbaum (ed.), *Verba docenti. Studies in Historical and Indo-European Linguistics presented to Jay H. Jasanoff by Students, Colleagues, and Friends*: 237–249. Ann Arbor: Beech Stave Press.

NARTEN, J. 1969. Griech. πίμπλημι und RV. *Ápiprata*. In: *Studia Classica et Orientalia Antonio Pagliaro oblata*, III: 139–155. Roma: Herder [= Narten, *Kleine Schriften*, pp. 108–124, (1995)].

——— 1986. *Der Yasna Haptaŋhāiti*. Wiesbaden: Reichert.

OETTINGER, N. 1979. *Die Stammbildung des hethitischen Verbums*. (Erlanger Beiträge zur Sprach- und Kunstwissenschaft, 641.) Nürnberg: Hans Carl.

——— 2006. Review of Jasanoff 2003. *Kratylos* 51: 34–45.

SCHAEFER, C. 1994. *Das Intensivum im Vedischen*. Göttingen: Vandenhoeck und Ruprecht.

SCHMIDT, W. P. 1956. Vedisch *īmahe* und Verwandtes. *Indogermanische Forschungen* 62: 229–239.

STRUNK, K. 1977. Zwei latente Fälle des verbalen Präsensstammtyps *tíṣṭha-(ti)* im Veda. *Zeitschrift der Deutschen Morgenländischen Gesellschaft*, Suppl. III.2: XIX (Deutscher Orientalistentag, Freiburg 28.9.–4.10.1975): 971–983 [= Strunk, *Kleine Schriften*: 411–423].

——— 1994. Relative chronology and Indo-European verb-system: the case of present- and aorist-stems. *Journal of Indo-European Studies* 22: 417–434.

TICHY, E. 2004. Vedisch *tiráti*. In: A. Hyllested, A. R. Jørgensen, J. H. Larsson & T. Olender (eds.), *Per aspera ad asteriscos. Studia indogermanica in honorem Jens Elmegård Rasmussen sexagenarii idibus Martiis anno MMIV*: 565–571. Innsbruck: Institut für Sprachen und Literaturen der Universität Innsbruck.

UL'YANOV, G. 1902. Kratkoe znachenie udvoennykh osnov ('The divisible meaning of the reduplicated stems'). In: *Sbornik statei posvyashchennykh uchenikami i pochitatelyami akademiku i zasluzhennomu ordinarnomu professoru Filippu Fedorovichu Fortunatovu*: 235–249 Warsaw: Tipografiya Varshavskago uchebnago okruga [*non vidi*: quotations taken from Kulikov 2005].

WATKINS, C. 1987. How to kill a dragon in Indo-European. In: C. Watkins (ed.), *Studies in Memory of Warren Cowgill, 1929–1985*: 270–299. Berlin: W. de Gruyter.

The 'Competition' in the RV and AV between Stems in *-ín* and Stems in *-vant* Derived from Thematic Nouns

ELIZABETH TUCKER

1. INTRODUCTION

The most obvious difference between the Old Indo-Aryan suffixes *-ín* and *-vant* is in their derivational morphology: *-ín* builds derivatives in large numbers only from thematic stems, whereas *-vant*, and its phonologically conditioned variant *-mant*,[1] can be employed to create a secondary adjective on the basis of a primary substantive with any type of stem. In the case of thematic stems, however, according to Debrunner, the suffix *-ín* competes with *-vant*:

> Die mit *-ín-* gebildeten Stämme bedeuten meistens 'den Begriff des Grundworts an sich habend, damit versehen'; sie konkurrieren also mit denen auf *-vant- -mant-* ... (AiG II.2, p. 332, §213a).

The RV contains doublets such as:

aśvín- and *áśvavant-/áśvāvant-* 'having horses' from *áśva-* m. 'horse'
dyumnín- and *dyumnávant-* 'having splendour' from *dyumná-* n. 'splendour, majesty'
kṛśanín- and (once) *kṛśanāvant-* 'having pearls' from *kṛśana-* n. 'pearl'.

---

[1] AiG II.2, pp. 880–883, §708.

At the same time Debrunner observes a preference for secondary derivatives in *-ín* to describe living beings:

> Dagegen ist *-ín-* stets beliebt und wird es sogar z.T. vor *-vant-* bevorzugt bei Charakterisierung und Bezeichnung lebender Wesen (AiG II.2, p. 335, §215).

Well-known examples such as *vājín-* m. 'racer, race-horse', *Aśvínā* 'the two horsemen', AV+ *hastín-* 'elephant'[2] also illustrate how they are more likely than adjectives in *-vant* to develop into substantives themselves: '*-ín-* scheint leichter substantiviert zu werden als *-vant-* ' (AiG II.2, p. 333, §213).

In his review of volume II.2 of AiG Paul Thieme argued for a semantic difference between the formations in *-vant* and *-ín*:

> Was sich für *-vant-/-mant-* feststellen lässt, gilt zunächst auch für *-ín-*. Auch hier handelt es sich nicht nur um eine 'Ansichhaben', 'Damit Versehensein' (Debrunner §213a, §332) sondern um ein charakteristisches Besitz-verhältnis (Thieme 1955: 190, cf. 191).

Thus the two suffixes may indicate different sorts of possession: *-ín* indicates an essential characteristic of the possessor, hence in the RV Indra is invariably *vajrín-* even when he is not holding the *vájra-*, but **vajravant-* does not exist at any period;[3] similarly *kṣīríṇī-* 'having milk' designates a cow (AVŚ 7.50.9) because being full of milk is her defining characteristic, but the ritual pot (*carú-*) is *kṣīrávant-* because it can hold things other than milk (AVŚ 18.4.16–24). Such contrasts in meaning, Thieme believed, had great longevity in Sanskrit and are at the root of some of the prescriptions in the Indian grammatical tradition. A well-attested

---

[2] Cf. RV 4.16.4 *mr̥gó ná hastī́* 'like an animal with a hand'.

[3] The restrictions in distribution that are discussed throughout this paper only apply to secondary derivatives from thematic stems, not from stems of any other type. RV vocative *vajrivas* represents an unusual type of tertiary derivative **vajrivant-* from *vajrín-*, and it supports the hypothesis that **vajravant-* based on the thematic stem was not possible. AiG (II.2, p. 333, §213b) suggests that the absence of **vajravant-* can be attributed to an avoidance of *-vant* derivatives from nouns with initial *v-*, but RV *vayúnā-vant-* contradicts this.

later case is the difference between *daṇḍin-*, the Brahmin ascetic whose stick is his defining characteristic in the fourth stage of his life, and *daṇḍavant-*, the person who has a stick in his hand at a particular moment or for a particular purpose.

2. COMPETITION?

This paper will argue that there is also distributional evidence for an early distinction in function between derivatives from thematic stems built with the secondary suffixes *-ín* and *-vant*. The patterns of distribution that will be pointed out may result from an original difference in meaning along the lines suggested by Thieme, but I will concentrate on more formal features and try to avoid judgements about the meaning of individual formations in so far as possible. Debrunner's remarks, particularly his observation that formations in *-ín* are preferred for describing living beings, are substantiated by the following sort of distribution in the early RV:

- from *dyumná-* n. 'splendour': Soma is *dyumnín-* (RV 3.37.8; 9.109.7) but his juice (*páyas-* n., RV 9.66.30) and the sacred formula (*bráhman-* n., RV 3.29.15) are *dyumnávant-*;
- from *rátha-* m. 'chariot': humans and horses are *rathín-* (RV 5.83.3; 6.27.8, 47.31; 9.97.50) but generosity or a gift (*rā́dhas-* n., RV 5.57.7; 7.77.5) is *ráthavant-*;
- from **hiraṇa-/híraṇya-*[4] n. 'gold': horses are *hiraṇín-* (RV 5.33.8; 6.63.9), but wealth (*vásu-* n., RV 7.94.9) *híraṇyavant-*;
- from *rátna-* n. 'treasure': the Vasiṣṭhas hope to be *ratnín-* (RV 7.40.1), but the rite (*adhvará-* m., RV 3.28.5) is *rátnavant-*.

The first three of these examples appear to point to a contrast between the qualifiers for masculine and neuter nouns, but although this is how the distribution works out most of the time,

---

[4] A simple thematic stem in *-a-* beside the stem in *-ya-* seen in *híraṇya-* may be reconstructed for Indo-Iranian on the basis of the frequent Avestan adjective of material *zarənaēna-* 'made of gold'.

the last example shows a contrast between animate and inanimate masculine nouns. In other words it is the animacy or otherwise of the **referent** rather than the grammatical gender of the qualified noun or pronoun that is important.[5]

The pattern of distribution illustrated above is not so clear in cases where the formation with the suffix *-vant* only appears in the later parts of the RV, and several of Debrunner's examples of 'competing' doublets are of this sort (for instance, *kṛśanín-* and *kṛśanāvant-* 'having pearls'). It is an area of derivational morphology where it is important not to regard the RV monolithically since, as in other aspects of the language, the contents of RV 10 show a slightly different linguistic situation, which is closer to that of the AV. The data from RV 1 and 8 are mixed (as would be expected for these collections), and so in the following sections **3–10** the evidence is only taken from the Family Books RV 2–7, and also from RV 9, which shows a similar picture.

3. THE SUFFIX *-ín*

The use of the two suffixes will now be examined separately. 43 derivatives from thematic stems in *-ín* occur in RV 2–7, 9. Out of these 29 have obvious animate reference.[6] They are listed below with an indication of the sort of head nouns they qualify:

> Gods: *ṛjīṣín-*, *kabandhín-*, *dyumnín-*, *bhūripoṣín-*, *madín(tama-)*, *yakṣín-*, *rambhín-*, *rasín-*, *vajrín-*, *śiprín-*, *śuṣmín-*, *svānín-*, *sūyavasín-*
>
> Gods and humans: *áśvín-*, *ukthín-*
>
> Gods, humans and animals: *vājín-*

[5] It makes no difference whether the primary noun from which the secondary adjective is derived is animate (as in the case of *aśvín-* and *áśvavant-/áśvāvant-* from *áśva-* m. 'horse') or inanimate/abstract (*rathín-* and *ráthavant-* from *rátha-* m. 'chariot', or *dyumnín-* and *dyumnávant-* from *dyumná-* n. 'splendour').

[6] The case of *citríṇīṣu* (RV 4.32.2) is unclear, but as it is employed as a feminine substantive it is likely to be animate.

Humans: *arthín-*, *garbhín-* (f. subst.), *gharmín-*, *pakthín-*, *somín-*
Humans and animals: *rathín-*, *hastín-*
Animals: *r̥jipín-*, *keśín-*, *patatrín-*, *vrajín-*, *śr̥ṅgín-*, *hiraṇín-*

Six others refer to waters and plants, and sometimes also to deities. It is well-known that the conception of animacy is culture-specific, and there can be no doubt that waters and plants were animate in ancient Indo-Iranian culture as they themselves are frequently deified or are addressed directly by the poets as living beings:[7]

udrín- 'having water' qualifies *utsá-* 'spring' (RV 2.24.4), *divas-kávandha-* 'the cask of heaven' (RV 9.74.7)

purīṣín- 'having moisture (?)' qualifies the Maruts (RV 5.55.5) and River Sarayu (RV 5.53.9)

puṣkarín- is represented by f. substantive *puṣkaríṇī* 'lotus pond' (RV 5.78.7)

puṣpín- is represented by f.pl. substantive *puṣpíṇīs* 'flowering plants' (RV 2.13.7)

rukmín- 'having brilliance/gold' qualifies the *aṁśú-* 'shoots' of Soma (RV 9.15.5)

---

[7] For instance, RV 7.49 requests the help of all the different kinds of waters on earth with the refrain *tā́ ā́po devī́r ihá mā́m avantu* 'Let those divine waters help me here'. In Old Avestan the different kinds of waters are called collectively *ahurānīš* '(divine) ladies' (*Yasna Haptaŋhāiti* 38.3), and are invoked as mothers and milk-cows (Y 38.5). For plants the evidence is slightly different and later, but e.g. RV 10.97 (cf. AVP 11.6) is a eulogy of plants (*óṣadhīs*) which are addressed directly with vocatives such as *amba* 'mother', and the AV contains numerous hymns to individual herbs which are requested to make available their active medicinal qualities. The Younger Avestan *devatādvandva*-type compound *āpa uruuaire* 'waters and plants' and their protection by the Amesha Spentas *Hauruuatāt* and *Amərətāt* (who themselves appear in a dvandva in the Gāthās) may point to ancient parallelism in the Indo-Iranian conceptualization of these two elements.

On the other hand, as Thomas Krisch has observed to me, Indo-Iranian has some early neuter words for water(s), such as *udaká-* (RV 9.67.32, and RV 1 and 10), and RV *vā́r-*, Avestan *vāiri-*. Hence it is impossible to be certain whether the treatment of other words as animates is the result of their status as divinities or vice versa. However, none of the nouns which are qualified by *-ín* adjectives are neuter, and it is notable that when the *-ín* formations themselves become substantives they become feminines.

vanín- 'having wood' qualifies trees or functions as a substantive 'tree' (RV 3.40.7; 6.8.5, 13.1; 7.4.5, 34.25 = 7.56.25, 35.5, 43.1).

Four out of the seven remaining cases (*putrín-*, *śatín-*, *śatagvín-*, *sahasrín-*) qualify three very common masculine nouns, *rayí-* 'wealth', *vā́ja-* 'booty', and *póṣa-* 'prosperity', which at first sight do not appear to refer to animates. The same nouns are also sometimes qualified by *aśvín-*. The reason appears to be that the wealth, booty or prosperity consists of livestock and people, and indeed this is what *putrín-* 'having / consisting of sons' *śatagvín-* 'having a hundred cattle' and *aśvín-* 'having / consisting of horses' tell us. Compare the way that the masculine noun *yajñá-* is treated in a pāda about an offering to Agni which consists of three types of animals:

RV 4.2.5a *gómām̐ agne (á)vimām̐* ***aśvī́*** *yajñó*
'The offering, O Agni, **consists of** cows, sheep, **horses**'.

For 'consisting of cows', 'consisting of sheep' only an adjective in *-mant* is available, but for 'consisting of horses', the *-ín* derivative is preferred in this early book of the RV[8] even though it produces an unusual triṣṭubh cadence.

4. INFREQUENCY OF NEUTER FORMS FROM *-ín* ADJECTIVES

The remaining three adjectives in *-ín*, *kulāyín-*, *dhanín-* and *dhūmín-*, all attested only once in the early RV, will be discussed below. The evidence of the 40 others is consistent enough to establish their function as qualifiers of animates. The morphological consequence is that almost all the attested forms are masculine or, somewhat less frequently, feminine. However, neuter forms from the *-ín* paradigm, though very rare, are not totally

[8] Also in all its YV repetitions.

absent in the early RV since they are used to qualify animates which are grammatical neuters, e.g.

RV 6.13.6b *ágne tokám̩ tánayam̩ **vājí** no dāḥ*
'O Agni, give to us **prize-winning** offspring, progeny'

RV 3.54.8d *cárat **patatrí** víṣuṇam̩ ví jātám*
'What walks, **what has wings**, of various sorts, variously born'.

5. THE SUFFIX *-vant*

Books 1–7 and 9 of the RV also provide a fair amount of evidence which points to a polarization in the function of the suffix *-vant* so that it is employed to a large extent with reference to inanimates. Many inanimates are designated by neuters, and so with *-vant* adjectives, in contrast to *-ín* adjectives, it is the neuter forms which prevail. However, the distributional pattern is not so clear cut as for *-ín*. The formations in *-vant* may be grouped into the following categories:

a. *-vant-* derivatives which qualify only neuter substantives (8): *kṣaítavant-*, *candrávant-*, *tokávant-*, *nīlavant-*, *vayúnăvant-*, *ráthavant-*, *śaphávat-*[9], *sahásravant-*

b. *-vant-* derivatives where nom-acc. sg. neuter *-vat* is the most frequently attested form (5): *ámavant-*, *áśvāvant-*, *dyumnávant-*, *ghṛtávant-*, *vīrávant-*

c. *-vant-* derivatives which function as neuter substantives (4): *áśvavat*, *yávamat*, *híraṇyavat*, *vắjavat*

d. *-vant-* derivatives which qualify animates and inanimates, or inanimates that are masculine (3):

[9] *śaphávat-* means 'what has hoofs' at RV 5.83.5 and, although it is an obscure passage, RV 3.39.6 suggests that it may be an analogical formation modelled on *padvát*. Geldner translates '(alles) was Füsse und Klauen hat' and at RV 5.83.5 'alles was Hufe hat' presumably understanding an unexpressed neuter substantive 'all'.

vā́javant- (6x), *rásavant-* (2x), *apidhā́navant-* (1x)

e. *-vant-* derivatives which qualify only animates (11): *apūpávant-* (1x), *índravant-* (3x), *dátravant-* (1x), *devā́vant-* (3x), *pavítravant-* (2x), *bhágavant-* (3x), *matávant-* (1x), *matsarávant-* (1x), *yajñávant-* (1x), *śatā́vant-* (1x), *śípravant-* (1x, *śiprín-* 3x), *sutā́vant-* (2x).

The fact that forms such as *áśvavat*, *vā́javat* are employed as neuter abstract nouns meaning 'possession of horses', 'possession of booty' provides an additional indication that at a certain stage this formation became particularly associated with the neuter gender.[10] It can be observed that neuter nouns such as *vásu-* 'what is good, wealth' or *rā́dhas-* 'gift, generosity' are invariably qualified by adjectives in *-vant* even when the goods or the gift include livestock, e.g.

RV 3.13.7ab *nú no rāsva sahásravat*
tokávat *puṣṭimád vásu*
'Now give to us what is good a thousand-fold,
consisting of offspring, consisting of prosperity'.

The contrast with the treatment of masculine nouns such as *rayí-* suggests that we are dealing with a ranked hierarchy of animacy[11] where the grammatical gender of the qualified noun plays some part. In other words, a masculine noun is ranked higher on the animacy scale than a neuter of similar meaning, and so may be qualified by a type of adjective that is not possible in the case of the neuter. Some additional evidence for a hierarchy rather than a simple animate: non-animate opposition will be discussed below in section **7**.

---

[10] I am indebted to Georges-Jean Pinault for this observation.

[11] The basic studies which dealt with animacy hierarchies (Silverstein 1976; Dixon 1979) concern their role in determining case-marking in ergative languages; but their relevance to a large variety of cross-linguistic features is gradually being recognized.

It cannot be claimed that even in the early RV the suffixes *-ín* and *-vant* are in exact complementary distribution, since there is a considerable number of *-vant* formations which appear in masculine and feminine forms and qualify only animates (group **e** above). Why do the secondary adjectives belonging to group **e** behave differently, and also why are groups **b** and **d** out of step in only some of their occurrences with the general trend towards the specialisation of *-vant* for neuters and inanimates? The exceptions are not random and fall into some clear categories.

6. MULTIPLE QUALIFIERS INVOLVING *-ín* AND *-vant*

Any attempt to work out a rationale for the choice between the two 'competing' suffixes meets an obstacle in the lists of qualifiers referring to a single noun where the two types of secondary derivative alternate, e.g.

RV 5.4.11cd ***aśvínaṃ*** *sá* ***putríṇaṃ vīrávantaṃ***
gómantaṃ ***rayíṃ*** *naśate svastí*
'With well-being he reaches **wealth consisting of horses, children, menfolk,** cattle'.

In such instances Thieme (1955: 192) was obliged to suggest that the contrast in sense was not always marked enough for it to matter, and it does look as if the poets had free rein to alternate the suffixes for the sake of variety or to suit their metre. However, it should be pointed out that the poets' licence is quite limited in the early RV and on the whole the distributional patterns according to animacy that have been outlined so far hold good in such lists too. If the head noun in question is a neuter and regularly qualified by *-vant* forms, there is never any variation, e.g.

RV 5.57.7ab *gómad* ***áśvāvad ráthavat*** *suvī́ram*
candrávad rā́dho *maruto dadā naḥ*
'You gave us, O Maruts, a **gift consisting** of cows, **horses, chariots**, good men, **gold**'.

Where there is variation, the head noun is always one which is frequently qualified by *-ín* formations, most often *rayí-* m., whose treatment as animate in the case of single qualifiers appears to be partially contradicted when the qualifiers are multiple. Compare with RV 5.4.11cd:

RV 4.49.4 *asmé indrābṛhaspatī*
rayíṃ *dhattaṃ* ***śatagvínam***
áśvāvantaṃ sahasríṇam
'Bestow on us, O Indra and Bṛhaspati, **wealth consisting of a hundred cows, consisting of horses, a thousandfold**'.

Here *áśvāvant-* is unexpected, all the more so as *aśvín-* is well-attested in the early RV. Yet this irregularity does not only occur in association with particular head nouns such as *rayí-* which might be regarded as borderline cases. Rather, the unexpected *-vant-* suffix is found in two very frequent secondary adjectives, *áśvāvant-*, and *vīrávant-*, not only in passages where there are multiple qualifiers of a single noun, but also where these two adjectives represents the only qualifiers, e.g.

RV 7.41.7ab ***áśvāvatīr*** *gómatīr na* ***uṣā́so***
(= 7.80.3ab) ***vīrávatīḥ*** *sádam uchantu bhadrā́ḥ*
'Let the kindly **dawns possessing horses**, cows, **possessing menfolk**, shine on us always'.

7. OLD *-vant* FORMATIONS

áśvāvant- and *vīrávant-* both pattern in the same way as a few other *-vant* adjectives which Avestan comparative evidence proves represent inheritances from Indo-Iranian. The latter category sometimes show a leaning towards inanimate function, though not always, and they are also freely employed to qualify animates. Compare:

áśvāvant- 'having horses'[12] (10x inanimate, 4x animate)
vīrávant- 'having menfolk' (12x inanimate, 11x animate)
ámavant- 'having force' (6x inanimate, 5x animate): cf. OAv. *əmauuaṇt-*, YAv. *amauuaṇt-*
devávant- 'having gods' (2x animate + 1x PN *devā́vant-*): cf. YAv. (Y 12.4) *daēuuauuaṇt-*
híraṇyavant- 'having gold' (9x inanimate, 1x animate): cf. YAv. *zaraniiāuuaṇt-*
śatā́vant- 'one hundred-fold' (1x animate, but in RV 8 and 10 *śatávant-* 4x inanimate, 1x animate): cf. YAv. *satauuaṇt-*.

In all such cases the explanation is probably the same: in the early RV these adjectives are still being employed by the poets in an inherited traditional manner, dating from a prehistoric period when there was no specialisation of **-u̯ent-*. All are secondary derivatives from inherited nominal stems. It is interesting that in the case of *vīrávant-* the 'competing' formation *vīrín-* only occurs in RV 10.86.9 where Indrāṇī is speaking in the first person and *vīríṇī* qualifies 1st person pronoun *ahám*. This is precisely the situation where a qualifier is most likely to be marked for animacy in languages which have some sort of animacy hierar-

---

[12] If *áśvāvant-* is in fact a derivative from *áśvā-* f. 'mare' and originally meant 'consisting of mares' with reference to herds of horses which were composed only of mares (Insler 1997: 106–107) it is not a derivative from a thematic stem and so its distribution is unproblematic. But the problem raised by the distribution of the other forms remains.

chy that applies to nominals.[13] Likewise, in the case of *bhága-vant-* (in the early RV only 7.41.4–5 to Bhaga, 3 times with animate reference), which arguably belongs to the same diachronic group as *vīrávant-* since it is based on an inherited noun, *bhagín-* is substituted in two Śaunaka AV compositions (6.129.1–3; 7.12.3) where a first person pronoun is qualified.[14]

8. RECENT *-vant* FORMATIONS

In addition to the sub-group of *-vant* forms which probably represent archaisms, there are two other categories which complicate the picture in the early RV. However, these are categories which become very productive in the later RV and AV. Firstly, there is the type of formation represented in the early RV only by *índra-vant-* (3x, always with animate reference) and some occurrences of *vā́javant-* (RV 3.52.6, 60.5–6; 8.35.15), which are derived from Proper Names (Indra, and the Ṛbhu PN Vā́ja). Here the suffix *-vant* has developed a specialized meaning 'accompanied by ..., associated with ...'.[15] *índravant-* must be a creation on the model of the more frequent *marútvant-* 'accompanied by the Maruts', or

---

[13] See, for example, the description by Dixon (1979: 85) where first and second person pronouns are at the top of the hierarchy and inanimate common nouns at the bottom. Croft (2003: 130) uses the term 'extended animacy hierarchy' as such a scale involves person and referentiality in addition to animacy; he also emphasizes that 'the extended animacy hierarchy is not an ordering of distinct categories, but rather a more or less continuous category ranging from most animate to least animate'.

The contrast between Indrāṇī in RV 10.86 and the dawns who are *vīrávatīḥ* in 7.41.7 is also in perfect accord with Thieme's semantic distinction: Indrāṇī's essential characteristic, as her name shows, is her husband, the *vīrá-* par excellence.

[14] However, at RV 7.41.4–5 *vayám bhagavantaḥ syāma* the *-vant* adjective may be preserved not only because it is traditional but also because it permits a double meaning 'we would be possessors of fortune' and 'we would be associated with (the god) Bhaga' (cf. *índravant-* discussed below).

[15] The suffix *-vant* in adjectives with this value is to be distinguished from the oxytone suffix *-vát* which forms adverbs, many derivatives from PNs, e.g. *aṅgirasvát* 'in the manner of Aṅgiras' (AiG II.2, p. 876, §706; III, p. 444).

ṛbhumánt- 'accompanied by the Ṛbhus', *áṅgirasvant-* 'accompanied by the Angirases', all of which describe Indra himself and are based on non-thematic stems.[16] This type was later extended to create derivatives with similar meaning from the names of gods and rishis regardless of stem type, cf. *mitrā́váruṇavant-* (RV 8.35.13), *káṇvamant-* (RV 8.2.22), and several more based on thematic stems in the list of nonce formations at AVŚ 19.18: *antárikṣavant-*, *rudrávant-*, *ādityávant-*, *dyā́vāpṛthivī́vant-*, *saptarṣívant-*, *viśvádevavant-*.

The second group qualify both animates and inanimates, and are loosely connected in meaning because they all belong to ritual vocabulary. *ghṛtávant-* 'possessing ghee' (11x inanimate, 2x animate) is applied most frequently to *havyá-* n. 'oblation', but the rarer *apūpávant-* (RV 3.52.1), *pavítravant-* (RV 9.73.3, 101.4), *yajñā́vant-* (RV 3.27.6), *sutā́vant-* (RV 3.25.4, 58.9[17]) all qualify animates. However, later this productive type also qualifies inanimates too, e.g. AVŚ 18.4 *apūpávant-*, *drapsávant-*, *kṣīrávant-*, *māṁsávant-*, *ánnavant-*, *sómavant-*, all of *carú-* m. 'pot'. Perhaps *ghṛtávant-* was the starting point for this group as in all these cases *-vant* indicates a temporary association[18] for the purposes of ritual, e.g. both the Soma priests and the drops of Soma are described as *pavítravantaḥ* 'having a strainer' during the Soma ritual in two RV 9 hymns.

9. PROBLEMATIC EXAMPLES OF *-ín* AND *-vant*

There remain 8 individual occurrences of forms in *-ín* or *-vant*, whose suffix appears to be out of line with the overall distribu-

[16] A variant *índrasvant-* occurs at RV 4.37.5.

[17] Also 11x in RV 1 and 8, 2x in RV 10.

[18] In other words, Thieme's semantic theory that *-vant* indicated temporary possession/association can account for the creation of this new group. *ghṛtá-* 'ghee' by its very nature cannot be a constant attribute, and **ghṛtín-* does not exist.

tional picture for the early RV and cannot be linked to any special category:

dhanín- 'possessing wealth' (RV 4.2.15) of a rock, but also at RV 1.33.4 and 1.150.2 of people.

dhūmín- 'possessing smoke' (RV 5.9.5) of flames.

kulāyín- 'possessing a nest, nesting' (RV 6.15.16) of the *yóni-* 'birthplace'of Agni.

śípravant- 'possessing a moustache' (RV 6.17.2) of Indra, but otherwise only *śiprín-*.

dyumnávant- 'possessing splendour' (RV 5.28.4) of a bull (= Agni) in a ritual hymn, but elsewhere *dyumnávant-* and *dyumnín-* are distributed as expected.

dátravant- 'possessing gifts'(RV 6.50.8) of Savitar, but in a simile involving a neuter noun (*prátīkam*).

matávant- (RV 9.86.13) of Soma, meaning and morphology unclear.

matsarávant- 'possessing intoxication' (RV 9.97.32) of Soma, but also *matsaríntama-* x3; *matsará-* is normally used as an adjective 'intoxicating'.

rásavant- 'possessing sap' (RV 6.47.1) of Soma, but at RV 9.113.5 Soma is *rasín-* and a cow's milk (*páyas-* n.) is *rásavant-* at RV 5.44.13.

10. STYLISTIC EXPLANATIONS?

There are some indications that such forms are employed by the poets for special effect. For example, two 'irregularly' employed *-ín* adjectives may help to impart an exceptional animate character to the noun which they describe:

RV 5.9.5ab *ádha sma yásy**ārcáyaḥ***
*samyák saṃyánti **dhūmínaḥ***
'Whose (Agni's) **flames** just then
go right together, **possessing smoke**'

RV 4.2.15d ***ádriṃ** rujema **dhanínaṃ** śucántaḥ*
'We would break in fervour **the rock containing riches**'

In the first passage Agni's flames[19] are portrayed as living because they *saṃyánti* 'go together', and in the second the rock, which is Vala and encloses the treasure (= cows), is portrayed as a rich person: compare RV 1.33.4 *dásyuṃ dhanínam* and contrast RV 5.29.12 *gávyaṃ cid ūrvám apidhā́navantam* 'cow-pen with a covering'.[20]

At least one of the irregular *-vant* forms, *rásavant-*, has an obvious stylistic use as it balances two equivalent pādas about Soma, who in another passage is *rasín-*:

RV 6.47.1ab *svādúṣ kílāyám mádhumām̐ utā́yám*
tīvráḥ kílāyáṃ ***rásavām̐*** *utā́yáṃ*
'This one is truly sweet and this one possesses honey
This one is truly pungent and this one **possesses sap**'

Attempts to provide stylistic justifications for the remaining *-vant* adjectives (all likewise nominative singular masculine forms) may run the risk of subjectivity and circularity of argument. However, the evidence for polarization in the distribution of *-ín* and *-vant* is so plentiful that it indicates the choice of suffix may sometimes have importance for our appreciation of the RV Family books as poetry, and if we come across a form which does not have the 'regular' suffix we should always look for a reason why.

---

[19] *kulāyínam* 'having a nest' at RV 6.15.16c may indicate that the *yóni-* 'origin, birth-place' of Agni can also be treated as animate, but this is such an obscure passage that it remains doubtful. Here and elsewhere Agni's *yóni-* is described as *ghṛtávant-* 'possessing ghee', but we saw above that this is a ritualistic *-vant* derivative that can apply to both animates and inanimates.

[20] If at 4.27.4c the form is *patatrí* nominative sg. neuter agreeing with *parṇám* 'wing', this may be another example of the same phenomenon, but it is more likely, as Werner Knobl has suggested to me, that it is the nominative sg masculine form *patatrī́* which may refer to the animate *śyená-*.

11. THE LATE *ṚGVEDA* AND *ATHARVAVEDA*

Again it must be emphasized that these statements do not apply even to the late RV. In RV 10 and the AV *-vant* gains ground against *-ín*, e.g.

RV 10.34.9b *ahastā́so hástavantaṃ sahante*
'handless they (the dice) overpower the one with hands (the gambler)'

AVŚ 6.68.3d *gómān **áśvavān** ayám astu prajā́vān*
'Let this man be the possessor of cows, **a possessor of horses**, of offspring' (contrast RV 4.2.5a cited above, with ***aśvī́***).

Some hymns suggest equivalence between the two suffixes at this stage: RV 10.97.15b *apuṣpā́ yā́ś ca **puṣpíṇīḥ*** 'which are flowerless and **which have flowers**', but in RV 10.97.3b ***púṣpa-vatīḥ*** *prasū́varīḥ* 'having flowers, having shoots' (= AVP 11.6.3, *púṣpavatīḥ prasúmatīḥ* AVŚ 8.7.27); contrast RV 2.13.7 ***puṣpíṇīś*** *ca prasvàś ca*.

The overall picture shows that *-ín* became much less productive, and the newly attested formations are almost all of the type that replace 'irregularly employed' archaic *-vant* adjectives from the early RV, e.g. *vīrín-* , *bhagín-* mentioned above, also *devín-* first attested as 2nd compound member in AVŚ 4.38.1–2 *sādhu-devínīm*, AVP 7.11.3, 19.2 *mūradevínaḥ*.

12. DIACHRONIC PROBLEMS SURROUNDING *-in*

Can the distribution of *-ín* in the early RV that has been outlined in this paper suggest any answers to the diachronic problems surrounding the origin of the suffix with its very secondary looking pattern of inflection *-ī́*, *-ínam*, *-ínas*? The diachronic angle is complex in the extreme, not least because in the RV Family Books there is another class of forms which show the same suffix and inflection as the possessive adjectives in *-ín*, but which appear to be deverbative and to possess a participial value, e.g.

kāmín- (+ acc) 'loving'
vanín- 'winning'
mandín- 'rejoicing'
ánāmin- 'not bending'
prakrīḷín- 'leaping'
bhadravādín- 'speaking auspiciously'
vratacārín- 'practising a vow'.

The whole diachronic problem of this suffix cannot be discussed within the limits of this short paper, but I will conclude with two brief diachronic points which relate to the possessive adjectives in *-ín* that have been the subject so far.

13. AN OLD IRANIAN PARALLEL FOR THE CONTRAST BETWEEN *-ín* AND *-vant*?

The contrast in distribution between early Vedic *-vant* and *-ín* may be mirrored indirectly in Younger Avestan.

Consider the two following *Vidēvdād* passages:

Vd 3.2 *dātarə gaēϑanąm astuuaitinąm aṣ̌āum: kuua bitīm aŋ́hå zəmō ś́āištəm?*
āat̰ mraot̰ ahurō mazdå: yat̰ bā paiti nā aṣ̌auua ***nmānəm*** *uzdasta āϑrauuat̰ gaomauuat̰ nāiriuuat̰* ***puϑrauuat̰*** *huuąϑβauuat̰.*
'Creator of the material worlds, righteous one: where secondly on this earth is there the most happiness? Then Ahura Mazda said: "Truly, where a righteous man has built a **house which possesses** a priest, milk-offerings, a wife, **children**, good herds."'

Vd 4.47 *aδaēca uiti nāiriuuaite zī.tē ahmāt pourum framraomi spitama zaraϑuštra yaϑa maγauuō frauuāxšōit̰*
vīsāne ahmāt̰ yaϑa əuuīsāi
puϑrāne *ahmāt̰ yaϑa apuϑrāi*
šaētauuatō ahmāt̰ yaϑa ašaētāi

'Also I speak thus: I award first place to the man who possesses a wife, O Spitama Zarathushtra, (rather) than (to the one who) would grow old as a bachelor. To the one who possesses a house rather than to the one without a house. **To the one who possesses children** rather than to the one without children. To the one who possesses money (gen sg for dat sg: Bartholomae 1904: 1705) rather than to the one without money.'

In Vd 3.2 there is an adjective in *-uuaṇt-*, *puϑrauuat̰* 'possessing children' which qualifies an inanimate neuter noun *nmāna-* 'house'. In Vd 4.47 on the other hand, *puϑrāne*, dat. sg of the secondary derivative built by means of the 'Hoffmann suffix' refers to a **person** who has children. It is not suggested that Old Iranian had a fully worked out system of contrasts between secondary derivatives built with the 'Hoffmann suffix' and those built with **-vant.* This sort of contrast is not found in our limited Old Avestan corpus, and it is not upheld even by the final term in the list at Vd 4.47 when a 'person with money' is indicated by a derivative from a thematic stem *šaēta-* with a *-uuaṇt* suffix. But we may have some indications from the way *puϑrauuaṇt-* and *puϑrān-* are used that, if the latter type of form was available, it was preferred to a **-vant* form when reference to an animate was required. Since the 'Hoffmann suffix' forms were not very productive in Avestan, this pattern may go back to Indo-Iranian, and it could represent the kernel from which the early RV distributional pattern developed.

The Iranian derivative *puϑrān-* is well-known, and a comparison between Avestan *puϑrān-* and Vedic *putrín-* was accepted already by Bartholomae (1904: 911), but, of course, the form of the suffix raises problems. Since the generally accepted explanation of Old Avestan *mąϑrān-*, Younger Avestan *puϑrān-* by Hoffmann (1955), it has often been assumed that two diachronically distinct suffixes must have fallen together to produce the Vedic class, the 'Hoffmann' suffix *-H_3n-/*-H_3en-/*-H_3on- and a suffix *-i̯en-/*-i̯on-/*-in-.[21] Kuiper (1973: 190–194; 1976: 246–247) argued that in the possessive formations the origin of Old Indo-Aryan *-ín* is only *-H_3n- and the replacement of full-grade *-H_3en-/*-H_3on- by *-H_3n- in thematic stems may have started in Indo-Iranian. He identified a once attested accusative sg form *somā́nam* 'Soma priest' (RV 1.18.1, scanned *somáanam* by Grassmann) as a relic parallel to Avestan *puϑrān-*, explaining *somín-* as its regular replacement. On the other hand, because of the apparent word equation RV *parṇín-* : YAv *parənin-* 'feathered' Hoffmann and Forssman (1996: 146, §104) reconstruct an Indo-Iranian class with a suffix *-in-/*-i̯an-/*-i̯ān- (parallel to *-un-/*-u̯an-/*-u̯ān- which can have 'possessive' meaning). A complete solution depends on an evaluation of the fragmentary Avestan evidence for a comparable class of *-in* stems and this will not be attempted here.

14. THE EXTENSION OF THE SUFFIX *-ín* WITHIN INDO-ARYAN

On a descriptive level it seems possible that, whereas Avestan extended the thematic form (or full-grade form) of the 'Hoffmann' suffix to athematic stems (*vīsāne* 'for the one possessing a house', dative sg from a secondary derivative based on *vīs-* 'house, homestead', in Vidēvdād 4.47 quoted above), the converse process took place in Old Indo-Aryan and the weak form of the athematic suffix *-H_3n- was extended to thematic stems (Vedic *putrín-* from

[21] Cf., for instance, Thieme (1955: 191): 'Die wohl im Suffix *-ín-* zusammengefallen idg. *-jen-/-jon-/-in-* und *-əen-/-əon-/-ən-* stimmen dazu, besonders das letztere'.

putrá-). However, an explanation of the mechanism of such an extension within OIA is much more difficult. *-in-* could only have developed by regular sound change from **-H₃n-* in derivatives based on athematic stems. But the theory of an analogical extension encounters the problem that early Vedic derivatives from non-thematic stems are poorly attested: Hoffmann (1955: 380–381) identified only a pair of vocatives *sahasin*, *śavasin* (remodelling for **sahasan* < **seghes-Hen*), cf. YAv. nominative sg *hazaŋha* 'robber', genitive pl. *hazasnąm* < **seghes-Hn-ōm*. Moreover, it is not merely the extension of the weak form of the athematic suffix that requires explanation, it is also necessary to show how the derivational process came to involve the deletion of the thematic vowel in thematic bases.

However, at least two *-ín* adjectives found in the RV Family Books may be traced back to inherited 'Hoffmann suffix' derivatives from non-thematic stems: *vanín-* 'having wood, a tree' and *udrín-* 'having water'. *vanín-* could directly continue a derivative from the old root noun *ván-* 'wood, tree' which survives in RV *vánaspáti-*, and once attested *vanád-* 'consuming wood' (RV 2.4.5) according to Schindler (1972: 43). *udrín-* might be traced back indirectly to a prehistoric adjective based on the IE **-r/n-*stem 'water' (cf. Greek ὕδωρ -ατος, etc.), providing it can be assumed that there was an early remodelling of the paradigmatic alternation **udr-H₃en-/*udr̥-H₃n-* because it would have produced a very irregular pattern of inflection in Indo-Iranian. Both *vanín-* and *udrín-* are attested in the early RV only in forms based on the weak stem *-ín-*.[22]

These two formations are interesting because they could have supplied a starting point from which a suffix *-in* could have been more easily extended to thematic stems. The root noun **ván-* was probably already obsolescent in prehistoric Indo-Iranian as there

---

[22] *vanín-* does not possess any other stem in the RV and *udrí* nom sg masculine only occurs in the first two Vālakhilya hymns.

is no trace of it in Avestan.[23] From a synchronic point of view in the earliest stage of Old Indo-Aryan **vanin-* would have appeared to be derived from the frequent thematic noun *vána-*, and could have provided the model for deleting the thematic vowel before the suffix **-in* in new formations such as *somín-* from *sóma-*. In parallel fashion, since the heteroclitic *r*-stem of the IE *r/n* stem 'water' only survived in OIA in thematicized form in compounds such as RV *anudrá-* adj. 'waterless', *samudrá-* m. 'ocean', there would be reason to connect pre-existing **udrin-*, or to remodel an irregular paradigm **udran-/*udīrṇ-* so that its shape corresponded to that of thematic *-udrá-*.

Another sort of model for deleting the thematic vowel before the suffix **-ín* was doubtless provided by the deverbative class in *-ín* mentioned in section **12** above: the syntax of *kāmín-* + accusative proves that it is a deverbative formation from *kāmáyate*, e.g. RV 2.14.1 *kāmī́ hí vīráḥ sádam asya pītím* 'For the hero is always desiring a drink of it (of Soma)'. But, from a formal point of view and on the basis of its use in other early RV passages where there is no object in the accusative, *kāmín-* could also be interpreted as 'possessing *kā́ma-*' a secondary derivative in *-ín* from the thematic noun.[24] Other early Vedic examples where this sort of double interpretation is possible include *upamantríṇaḥ* (RV 9.112.4) where a deverbative formation from *upa-mantráyate* resulted in a formation *-mantrín-*. The latter appears formally identical to *mantrín-* (VS+) 'possessing *mantra*s' that is often compared to Old Avestan *mąϑrān-* 'prophet'. Although the history of the deverbative suffix *-ín* and its inflection in such formations is perhaps even more obscure, its inflectional pattern for masculine and feminine forms is equally well established in the early RV, and there is the syntactic and functional similarity

---

[23] Kellens (1974: 370) shows that it was replaced in Avestan by an *ā*-stem *vanā-*.

[24] I am grateful to Hans Henrich Hock for pointing out the possible role of such forms to me.

that deverbative forms with participial meaning invariably qualify animates just like the possessive adjectives in *-ín*. Mutual influence between the two groups becomes much easier to understand in the light of our findings that at a certain stage of OIA *-ín* only served to form qualifiers for nouns and pronouns which were high in the animacy hierarchy.

15. CONCLUSION

A partial diachronic explanation for the function and morphology of the Old Indo-Aryan possessive adjectives in *-ín* may be proposed along the following lines: OIA inherited secondary derivatives built with the 'Hoffmann suffix' on the basis of thematic stem nouns, such as **putrā́n-* from *putrá-*, *somā́n-* from *sóma-*. After the disappearance of laryngeals these derivatives would have had an anomalous pattern of inflection with suffix *-ān-* in both the strong and weak cases (with *-ān-* < **-e/o-H_3en-* and *-ān-* < **-e/o-H_3n-*). Their weak cases were remodelled on the analogy of athematic stem derivatives such as *vanín-* with *-ín-* < **-H_3n-*. Because in a case such as this the inherited root noun had been replaced by a thematic noun *vána-*, from a synchronic point of view *vanín-* appeared to be a derivative of thematic *vána-*. This new connection was supported by deverbative *kāmín-* beside *kā́ma-*, *upa-mantrín-* beside *mántra-*, which could also be interpreted as synchronic derivatives from thematic nouns and functioned as qualifiers for animates since their original value was participial. The inflectional pattern **putrā́* nominative / *putríṇas* genitive was then levelled to *putrī́* nominative / *putríṇas* genitive, possibly because this inflectional pattern already existed in some deverbative formations or perhaps simply on the analogy of other types of *n*-stem. New derivatives from thematic nouns with a weak stem *-ín-* were created and the whole class expanded greatly at an early Vedic stage because such adjectives acquired the regular function of qualifying animates and for a time took over part of the inherited territory of secondary derivatives in *-vant*.

REFERENCES

AiG = Jacob Wackernagel & Albert Debrunner, *Altindische Grammatik*. Göttingen: Vandenhoeck und Ruprecht, 1896–1930.

BARTHOLOMAE, C. 1904. *Altiranisches Wörterbuch*. Strassburg: K. J. Trübner.

CROFT, W. 2003. *Typology and Universals*. 2nd edition. Cambridge: Cambridge University Press.

DIXON, R. M. W. 1979. Ergativity. *Language* 55: 59–138.

GRASSMANN, H. 1873. *Wörterbuch zum Rig-Veda*. Leipzig: F. A. Brockhaus.

HOFFMANN, K. 1955. Ein grundsprachliches Possessivsuffix. *Münchener Studien zur Sprachwissenschaft* 6: 35–40. [= *Aufsätze zur Indoiranistik*, II: 378–383. Wiesbaden: L. Reichert, 1976.]

HOFFMANN, K. & B. FORSSMAN 1996. *Avestische Laut- und Flexionslehre*. Innsbruck: Institut für Sprachen und Literaturen der Universität Innsbruck.

INSLER, S. 1997. Vedic denominatives to thematic *a*-stems. In: A. Lubotsky (ed.), *Sound Law and Analogy. Papers in Honour of Robert S. P. Beekes*: 103–110. Amsterdam: Rodopi.

KELLENS, J. 1974. *Les noms-racines de l'Avesta*. Wiesbaden: L. Reichert.

KUIPER, F. B. J. 1973. Four word studies. *Indo-Iranian Journal* 15: 179–204.

——— 1976. Old East Iranian dialects. *Indo-Iranian Journal* 18: 241–253.

SCHINDLER, J. 1972. *Das Würzelnomen im Arischen und Griechischen*. Unpublished dissertation. Würzburg.

SILVERSTEIN, M. 1976. Hierarchy of features and ergativity. In: R. M. W. Dixon (ed.), *Grammatical Categories in Australian languages*: 112–171. Canberra: Australian Institute of Aboriginal Studies.

THIEME, P. 1955. Wackernagel, J.†: *Altindische Grammatik* II.2: Albert Debrunner: *Die Nominalsuffixe*. Göttingen 1954. *Göttingische Gelehrte Anzeigen* 209: 182–216. [= P. Thieme, *Kleine Schriften*, II, pp. 661–695. Wiesbaden: F. Steiner, 1971.]

On the Rise and Remaking of the Middle Voice in Anatolian and Indo-Iranian

VIT BUBENIK

1. MIDDLE VOICE AS A THEOREME?

It might seem that there is no reason to explicate the term 'middle voice' at a conference on Sanskrit linguistics: Pāṇini's category *ātmanepada* taken morphologically simply refers to a certain set of endings which are systematically different from their *parasmaipada* 'active' counterparts. Semantically, ātmanepada is interpreted in the sense of 'the fruit of the activity is such as generally goes to the agent' (Abhyankar & Shukla 1977: 58). In Western tradition this notion is directly comparable to Dionysius Thrax's *pathos* 'experiential disposition' (cf. Andersen 1994: 157). Modern Indo-European linguistics has accepted the term 'middle voice' but uses it in a variety of sometimes confusing ways. In the nineties there appeared several studies on the middle voice, most notably Kemmer 1993, Andersen 1994 and Perel'muter 1995 which helped to settle some of the misconceptions or misuses of this term.

A common theme in most of these studies is the problematic matching of the morphological exponents of the middle voice with their semantic counterparts. In Sanskrit one can pinpoint three paradoxical phenomena or mismatches between morphology and semantics in this respect:

i. The verbs of middle semantics (in the Fourth Class of presents) are conjugated actively (i.e. with parasmaipada endings), e.g. *kúp-ya-ti* 'is angry'.

ii. In the same class, the verbs of active semantics (= agentive verbs) form their stem by the same suffix *-ya-* which apparently marks middle semantics in group (i), e.g. *ás-ya-ti* 'throws', *náh-ya-ti* 'binds'.

iii. The later phenomenon (in Classical Sanskrit and Avestan) of conjugating the passive verbs by active endings is in need of proper diachronic explanation, e.g. *śrū-ya-ti* 'is heard', *bhr-iya-ti* 'is carried'.

In the confines of the present diachronically orientated paper I want to emphasize the status of the middle voice as a derivational (lexical) category in Anatolian and Indo-Iranian in section **2**. In section **3** I will outline the first attempts at the formal disassociation of the middle and the passive voice in Indo-Iranian by analytic means. In section **4** I will focus on the insufficiently appreciated phonetic reasons for the demise of the middle voice during the Middle Indo-Aryan period. The compensation for the loss of the synthetic middle voice by analytic formations will be sketched in section **5**.

2. MIDDLE VOICE AS A DERIVATIONAL CATEGORY IN ANATOLIAN AND INDO-IRANIAN

It is usually assumed that the Anatolian, Indo-Iranian and Hellenic ternary diathetic systems are a result of an evolution from a simpler binary system of Pre-PIE. According to Lehmann (2002) this earlier system was dichotomized into active and inactive. Exponents of the former category are the familiar (secondary) endings of the present-aorist system; those of the latter category are reconstructed on the basis of the perfect in Indo-Iranian and Hellenic, and the *hi*-conjugation in Anatolian.

As is shown in [1], the next historical step from the minimal system was the emancipation of the 'middle voice'. This was accomplished in two ways: either on the basis of inactive endings (in Anatolian) or the active endings (in Indo-Iranian and Hellenic). In Anatolian a major role in this process was played by qualitative ablaut which changed the inactive endings into their *o*-grade counterparts. In the other scenario, *-o* was added to the active endings:

[1] Emancipation of the middle voice in PIE

A			B		
Active	Inactive		Active	Inactive	
Active	Middle	Stative	Active	Middle	Stative
**-m*	*-h_2o[1]	*-h_2e	**-m*	**-(m)a*	*-h_2e
**-s*	*-th_2o	*-th_2e	**-s*	**-so*	*-th_2e
**-t*	**-o*	**-e*	**-t*	**-to*	**-e*
**-nt*	**-ro*	**-(ē)r*	**-nt*	**-nto*	**-(ē)r*

The scenario in A is ancestral to Anatolian. By the time of our earliest Hittite texts (17th century) the system is as shown in [2]:

[2] Diathetic system of Hittite

Active	Mediopassive	*hi*-verbs
-mi	*-ha* / *-hari*	*-hi*
-si	*-ta* / *-tati*	*-ti*
-zi	*-(t)a* / *-(t)ari*	*-i*
-anzi	*-anta* / *-antari*	*-anzi*

The second set of mediopassive endings shows that the earlier set was enlarged by *-ri* and *-ti*, with *-ri* found only in the pre-

[1] The evidence (especially of Greek) points to 1 sg *-h_2e (see Table 4 below), but the pattern shown by the other persons favours reconstructing *-h_2o for early PIE.

sent (in 1, 3 sg and 2, 3 pl). In other persons, and in all persons of the preterite, only *-ti* is found. Its source is the dative form of the 2nd pers. pronoun **toi*. In Hieroglyphic Luwian, it is *-si*, which is traceable back to the dative form of the reflexive pronoun **soi* (cf. most recently Rieken 2004). In the preterite, the *-i* of the medio-passive endings *-hati*, *-tati* (2, 3 sg), *-antati* was frequently omitted, since *-i* was used in the active system for marking the temporal contrast non-past vs. past (*-si*, *-zi*, *-weni*, *-teni* versus *-s*, *-t*, *-wen*, *-ten*). These matters are surveyed in [3]:

[3] Hittite present and preterite

Present Active	Pres Med Pass	Preterite Act	Pret Med Pass
-mi	*-ha / -hari*	*-(n)un*	*-hat(i)*
-ši	*-ta / -tati*	*-s*	*-tat(i)*
-zi	*-ta / -tari*	*-t*	*-tat(i)*
-anzi	*-anta / -antari*	*-ēr*	*-antat(i)*

The scenario in B (outlined in [1]) is ancestral to Indo-Iranian, Hellenic, and apparently Armenian. As shown in [4], in common with Anatolian the crucial event in its development was the introduction of the temporal contrast in both the active and middle voice categories by means of the deictic element **-i*:

[4] Establishment of the temporal contrast in the middle voice in Indo-Iranian and Hellenic

		Old Indo-Aryan		Hellenic	
Non-past	Past	Non-past	Past	Non-past	Past
**-(m)ai*	**-(m)ā*	*-e*	*-i*	*-mai*	*-mān*
**-soi*	**-so*	*-se*	*-thās*	*-sai / -soi*	*-so*
**-toi*	**-to*	*-e / -te*	*-ta*	*-tai / -toi*	*-to*
**-ntoi*	**-nto*	*-nte*	*-nta*	*-ntai / -ntoi*	*-nto*

Leaving Hellenic aside, we observe an interesting Anatolian-Indo-Iranian isogloss in the 1 sg. The endings *-e* and *-i* have to be traced back to the laryngeal endings **-h_2e* and **-h_2*, respectively, in Scenario A. The 2 sg past middle ending *-thās* appears to have arisen by combining the middle ending **-th$_2$o* in scenario A with the active ending **-s*. And finally, the original ending of the 3 sg non-past was *-e*, as in Vedic *śáye* 'lies', which goes back to the stative ending **-e* in both scenarios (the ending *-te* in *śéte*, and *-tai* in Greek *keî-tai* are apparently later).

In the confines of the present paper we will not have enough time to examine several controversial aspects of the development of the inflectional perfect and mediopassive from a common derivational category ('Proto-Middle') in Indo-Iranian and Anatolian languages. However, I want to mention one of them, namely Jasanoff's claim that the formal difference between the *mi-* and *hi-* conjugations is not correlated with any systemic difference in meaning (Jasanoff 2003: 2–3). Jasanoff maintains that both the *hi-* and *mi-*verbs may be transitive or intransitive, and both may denote an activity, process or state, as shown in [5]:

[5]

Hittite *hi*-verbs	*mi*-verbs
karāp-i 'eats, devours'	*ēzzaz-zi* 'eats'
ak-i 'dies'	*mer-zi* 'disappears'
dākk-i 'is like, resembles'	*ēs-zi* 'is'

Jasanoff concludes that the membership in these two classes is 'for no synchronically detectable reasons'. Diachronically, however, as outlined in Scenario A, in the Anatolian system we can identify the layer reflecting the early binary (Pre)-PIE system.

A closer look at 132 documented Hittite *hi*-verbs (Rose 2006) contains a number of prototypical active verbs (such as *slaughter*, *smite*, *slit*, *pierce*, *bite*, *build*, *crush*); on the other hand, there are many more verbs with prototypical middle semantics such as are shown in [6]:

[6] Hittite *hi*-verbs of middle semantics

i. psych verbs/emotions: *nāh*(*h*)- 'fear'[2], *dusk*- 'rejoice'[3], *wasta*- 'sin'
ii. verbs of speaking: *mema*- 'speak', *wai-/wiwa*- 'cry', *walla*- 'praise'
iii. verbs of perception: *au*(s)- 'see', *istamas*- 'hear'[4]
iv. verbs of translational motion: *huwai*- 'run'[5], *iyan*(*n*)*na*- 'go', *pidda*(*i*)- 'flee'
v. verbs of ingestion: *karāp*- 'eat up', *pass*- 'swallow', *sarap/sarep*- 'sip'
vi. verbs indicating body posture: *as-/es*- 'sit'
vii. verbs indicating spontaneous events associated with animate beings: *kis*- 'become', *mai-/miya*- 'grow', *parai*- 'appear', *dākk*- 'resemble'

Succintly, to quote Meid (1979: 174), the earliest layer of the verbs in the *hi*-conjugation consisted 'sicher aus Verben medialen Charakters'. In sections **3** and **4** I will argue that the gradual loss of its middle voice typology (the movement between the

---

[2] The verb *nāh*(*h*)- (< **neh₂*-) 'fear' is documented as a *mi*-verb in 1 sg (*na-ah-mi* in KBO V6 III 15) and as a *hi*-verb in 3 sg (*na-a-hi* in KUB XLIX 3 II 3). In the prohibitive (2 sg) both *le-e na-ah-ti* and *na-a-hi* 'don't be afraid' are found (Hattusilis and KBo XIII 131 vs. 14).

[3] Kronasser (1966: 521) lists *dusgai* 'rejoices' under *hi*-verbs (in the class of roots with 'gutturale Erweiterung'). The *hi*-forms of 3 sg *du-us-ga-i* and 2 sg *du-us-kat-ti* 'you will rejoice' versus *mi*-forms of 3 sg (*du-us-ki-iz-zi*, *du-us-ki-ya-zi*) are documented in KUB XVII 35 I 12.33, II 26, III 8.35, IV.13).

[4] *istamas*- 'hear', which is often classified as a *mi*-verb, displays 2 sg forms in *-ti*, typical of *hi*-verbs. For 2 sg Puhvel (1984: 452ff.) lists three examples with ending *-si* versus 12 with *-ti*, but for other persons only *-mi* endings are found (pres. 1 sg *-mi*, 3 sg *-zi*, 3 sg imp.*-du*, pret. 1 sg *-un*, 3 sg *-ta*).

[5] Documented *-hi* forms of *huwai*-'run, march (before), flee' are pres. 1 sg *hu-ih-hi* (KBo XI 19 Vs. 14), 3 sg *hu-wa-i* (KUB XIV 13 III 13) and pret. 3 sg *hu-wa-iš* (KUB XIX 39 II 11). The *mi*-form *hu-u-i-ya-mi* is marked with a Glossenkeil (Kronasser 1966: 501); the other documented *mi*-forms are 2 sg in *-si* (KUB XV 23.9, V 1 III 55) and 3 sg *-zi* (KBo X 20 22.41)

mi-conjugation and the *hi*-conjugation was so to say a two-way street) proceeded hand in hand with the formation of the synthetic mediopassive in *-ri* and the analytic *be*-passive. To strengthen Meid's stance it should suffice to glance at the situation in Sanskrit and Latin.

Typological comparisons with the verbs of 'non-active' morphology in Indic (Class 4 *dīv-*) and Latin (Second, *-ē*-Conjugation) reveal similar problems of the polysemy of a certain morphological type. Recall that diachronically these languages continue Scenario B, where the middle emancipated itself by differentiating the active endings (while the stative endings are reflected in the morphology of the perfect).

In Indo-Aryan, Class 4 presents (the *dīv*-class of the Hindu grammarians) are found for ca. 100 verbs, of which ca. 50 according to Whitney (1889: 761) 'signify a state of feeling, or condition of mind or body' versus about 40 which 'differ from the above in having an apparently original transitive or neuter meaning'. A finer analysis, along the lines of Kemmer (1993), allows one to establish a basic dichotomy: of typical active verbs on the one hand and the verbs of middle semantics on the other hand. As shown in [7], the latter group can be subdivided along similar lines as in Anatolian:

[7] Verbs of middle semantics in Class 4 (*dīv*-class) of Sanskrit

i. psych verbs/emotions: *kup-* 'be angry', *muh-* 'be confused', *lubh-* 'be lustful', *kliś-* 'be troubled', *tam-* 'be exhausted', *śam-* 'be quiet', *klam-* 'be weary', *dṛp-* 'become mad', etc.
ii. verbs of speaking: *hvā-* 'call', *gāi-* 'sing', *rāi-* 'bark'.
iii. verbs of perception/experience: *paś-* 'see', *kṣudh-* 'be hungry'.
iv. verbs of translational motion: *pad-* 'fall (down), go to', *bhram-* 'roam', *tṝ-* 'cross, transverse'.
vi. verbs indicating change of body posture: *bhraś-* 'drop, fall down'.

vii.a verbs indicating spontaneous events with animates: *jṛ-* 'grow old', *śram-* 'grow weary', *mlāi-* 'relax', *vāi-* ' be blown'
vii.b verbs indicating spontaneous events with inanimates: *śuṣ-* 'be dry', *klid-* 'become wet', *tap-* 'be heated'

On the other hand, among those 40 other verbs there are prototypical active verbs such as *as-* 'throw', *dīv-* 'play', *vyadh-* 'pierce', *nah-* 'bind', *kṣi-* 'destroy', *kṣā-* 'burn'.

Along the same lines, the verbs of the Second Conjugation in Latin (around 90 in number) can be dichotomized into typical active verbs (such as *dēleō/aboleō* 'destroy', *mordeō* 'bite', *tondeō* 'cut the hair', *torqueō* 'twist') on the one hand, and a much larger group of verbs with typical middle semantics on the other hand. The latter group can be subdivided as in Anatolian and Indo-Aryan into similar subgroups **i–vii**:

[8] Verbs of middle semantics in the Second Conjugation of Latin

i. psych verbs / emotions: *horreō*, *stupeō*, *timeō*, *lūgeō*, *fleō*, *caveō*, *faveō*
ii. verbs of speaking (or being silent): *cieō*, *suādeō*, *voveō*, *rideō* (*taceō*, *sileō*)
iii. verbs of perception/experience: *videō*, *doleō*, *algeō*, *frigeō*, *valeō*, *vigeō*, *egeō*
iv. verbs of translational motion: *moveō*
v. verbs of ingestion: *prandeō*, *sorbeō*
vi. verbs indicating body posture: *sedeō*, *iaceō*, *pendeō*, *maneō*, *haereō*, *lateō*
vii. verbs indicating spontaneous events: *placeō*, *appāreō*, *flōreō*, *vireō*, *madeō*

A closer look at the 50 or so verbs of middle semantics in the Sanskrit Class 4 reveals that many of them – not surprisingly –

display also middle voice (ātmanepada) endings; and then there are also *media tantum*. These are shown in [9a] and [9b], respectively:

[9a] (*P~A*):
tā́m-ya-ti/-te 'be exhausted', *múh-ya-ti/-te* 'be confused', *śúṣ-ya-ti/-te* 'be dry', *jī́r-ya-ti/-te* 'grow old', *bhráś-ya-ti/-te* 'fall down'.

[9b] (*A* only):
kṣam-ya-te 'have patience', *pád-ya-te* 'fall (down); go to (+ ACC), *búdh-ya-te* 'be awake', *mri-yá-te* 'die'.

As is well known, the accented suffix *-yá-* added to roots in the zero grade and equipped with ātmanepada endings derives passive counterparts to verbs of action (*kr-iyá-te* 'is made') and speaking (*uc-yá-te* 'is said'); then there are pseudo-passive or pseudo-reflexive counterparts to verbs of translational motion such as *gam-yá-te* lit. 'is gone', which are best translated by the Russian pseudo-relexive *идём-ся* or the Latin *verbum deponens it-ur* (as in *sīc itur ad astra* 'This is the way to the stars').

Given the existence of typical active presents in Class 4, one ends up with the verbs of middle semantics marked by parasmaipada or ātmanepada endings, and mediopassive forms of active verbs carrying accent either on the root or on the derivational suffix *-yá-*. (One also observes the prototypical middle verb *mri-yá-te* carrying paradoxically the passive accent on the derivational suffix *-yá-*). This rather delicate situation was limited to the present system and could be explained semantically, to judge by about 20 minimal pairs assembled by Kulikov (1998: 145); some of them are set out in [10]:

[10] Middle Semantics	Passive
múc-ya-te 'delivers oneself, escapes from bonds of existence'	*muc-yá-te* 'is released'
táp-ya-te 'burns, suffers, feels remorse'	*tap-yá-te* 'is purified'
pác-ya-te 'becomes ripe/mature, cooks for oneself', as in *Śatapathabrāhmaṇa* *lokáḥ pácyamānaḥ* 'the developing world'	*pac-yá-te* 'is cooked'

It should be observed that with other presents (e.g. Class 1) this contrast does not depend solely on the location of accent, as for example *páv-a-te* 'becomes clean; purifies oneself' versus *pū-yá-te* 'is purifed (by X)'.

3. EMANCIPATION OF THE PASSIVE

The situation in Vedic described in [10] could not be stable, and already during the OIA period we find the first signs of the formal emancipation of the passive. The formal dissociation of the middle and the passive was one of the cardinal events in the morphosyntactic history of IE languages. The best known is the case of Romance languages whose ancestral tongue, Latin, continued significant portions of the rhotic mediopassive morphology in its verba deponentia (compare *loquitur* 'speaks' with *laudatur* 'is praised'). But in modern Romance languages these two functions are separated morphologically in that most functions of middle semantics (especially direct and indirect reflexive and reciprocal) came to be expressed by personal clitics, while the passive is realized in analytic fashion by combining the past participle with the copula. In the Hellenic branch Modern Greek is unique in the IE phylum in its preservation of the mediopassive morphology of Ancient Greek in the imperfective aspect (e.g. with verbs of perception: *geúomai* 'I taste', *osphraínomai* 'I smell', etc.), but not in the perfective aspect (contrast Ancient Greek *egéneto* 'he became' with Modern Greek *égine*).

In Ancient Indo-Iranian the synthetic passive possessed a full paradigm in the present but was practically limited to the 3rd person in the aorist. In Indo-Aryan both relied on ablaut (zero-grade in the present and lengthened grade in the aorist e.g. *á-kār-i* 'was done', Vedic *śrā́vi*, Gathic Avestan *srāvi* 'was heard').

Already in the *Ṛgveda* we find the first occurrences of the analytic passive constructions in the aorist and the perfect. As shown in [11] they consisted in each instance of the past participle plus the copula (cf. Jamison 1990: 3), in the aorist *ábhūt*, and in the perfect *ā́sa*:

[11] Vedic

RV 3.31.20	*míhaḥ*	*pāvakā́ḥ*	*prátatā*	*abhūvan*
	mists	pure	extended	'become'+AOR+3PL

'The pure mists have become extended'

RV 10.92.3	*vayā́*	*asya*	*prā́hutā*	*āsur*	*áttave*
	branches	he+ GEN	offered	'be'+ PERF+3PL	eating+ DAT

'Branches were offered for him to eat'

Parallel analytic formations are not available from Gāthic Avestan, but those combining the passive participle with the auxiliaries *ah-* 'be' and *bav-* 'become' in the present are available from late Avestan. This is shown in [12]:

[12] Avestan

Visprad 9.3	*yōi*	*hənti*	*haoma* ...	*uzdāta* ...	*uzdahiiamna*
	which	are	haomas	up-set+PP	up-set+FUT+ MEDPASS

'The branches of haoma which ... have been set out ... [and which] are to be set out ...'

Yt 10.87	*yahmāi*	*xšnūtō*	*bauuaiti* ...	*yahmāi*	*ṯbištō*	*bauuaiti*
	who+ DAT	satisfied	become+3S	who+ DAT	offended	become+3S

'By whom he is satisfied ... by whom he (is) offended'

Another analytic formation which appeared in the Brāhmaṇas was that of the mediopassive periphrastic future. I suggest these forms represent an attempt to recreate the endangered synthetic middle voice on an analytic basis. In Whitney's words (1889: 337) 'a few isolated attempts are made in the Brāhmaṇas to form by analogy' middle voice counterparts to the periphrastic future, as shown in [13]:

[13] Mediopassive (analytic) future tense forms in the Brāhmaṇas

prayoktāse	'I will apply' (TS)
yaṣṭāhe	'I will make offering' (TA)
śayitāse	'you will lie' (ŚB)

On the basis of these forms the native grammarians could set up a complete paradigm for the analytic mediopassive future corresponding to the active periphrastic future:

[14]

Active periphrastic future		Mediopassive periphrastic future	
kartā=asmi	*=smaḥ*	*kartā=ahe* (~*=ase*)	*=smahe*
=asi	*=stha*	*=ase*	*=dhve*

The contrast active versus mediopassive was not available in the third person, which displays bare nominal forms (*kartā*, *kartārau*, and *kartāras*) without any clitic form of the copula. The mechanism governing these processes is rather transparent. The starting point was the agentive noun with the copula cliticized to it, *kartā=asi*; the resulting *kartāsi* was treated as the primary form *patasi*, i.e. as if consisting of the stem *kartā-* plus the ending *-si*; its middle voice counterpart was simply formed by replacing *-i* with *-e*, as in *patasi* versus *patase*:

[15] *patasi* : *patase* = *kartāsi* : X where X = *kartāse*

There is a remarkable parallel to these analytic mediopassive forms in Hellenic. Here the Ancient Geek formation combining the mediopassive participle with the copula has survived until the present day (cf. Bubenik 2001a: 100–103). During the late Medieval period the copula in the postverbal position started being treated as a middle voice suffix, a remarkable piece of evidence for the centrality of the middle voice in Greek morphosyntax. These matters are surveyed in [16]:

[16] Greek

	Ancient Gr copula	Modern Gr copula	Modern Gr Middle	Perfect Passive
			'I write', etc.	'I am written', etc.
Sg 1	*ei-mí*	*í-me*	*gráf-o-me*	*gramménos í-me*
2	*eî*	*í-se*	*gráf-e-se*	*gramménos í-se*
Pl 1	*es-mén*	*í-maste*	*graf-ó-maste*	*gramméni í-maste*
2	*es-té*	*ís-te*	*gráf-e-ste*	*gramméni í-ste*

Returning to Indo-Aryan, we may portray the whole diathetic system of late OIA consisting of both synthetic and analytic formations as shown in Table 1:

TABLE 1
Diathetic system of late Old Indo-Aryan

	Present	Aorist	Future	analytic	Perfect
Active	*karoti*	*akar* / *akārṣīt*	*kariṣyati*	*kartāsmi*	*cakāra*
Middle	*kurute*	*akṛta*	*kariṣyate*	*kartāh* / *se*	*cakre*
Passive	*kriyate*	*akāri*			*kṛtam*
(analytic)	*kṛtam asti*	*kṛtam abhūt*			*kṛtam āsa*

The late Avestan system could be reconstructed along similar lines according to the data in Kellens 1984; above all, one notices the existence of the mediopassive future, e.g. *vaxšiiete* (corresponding to Sanskrit *vak-ṣya-te*) and the mediopassive perfect, e.g. *vaoce* (corresponding to Sanskrit *ūcé*):

[17] Avestan

Visprad 15.3	*yauua*	*fraca*	*vaoce* ...	*fraca*	*vaxšiiete*
	ever	ADV forth	say+PERF+ MEDPASS	ADV forth	say+PERF+ MEDPASS

'[The best of these words which] has ever been said ... [and] will be said' (cf. Kellens 1984: 161–162)

Conservative MIA dialects – most notably Ardhamāgadhī – continued and further developed the OIA synthetic mediopassive morphology by adopting the stem of the passive (in *-ya* or *-ijja*) as a base for innovative temporal and participial forms. The present, aorist and future tense forms are shown in [18]:

[18] Ardhamāgadhī

	Present	Aorist	Future	Participles
Active	*kuvv-ai*	*kuvv-it(t)hā*	*kar-iss-ai*	*kar-anta*
Medio-passive	*kijj-ai*	*kijj-it(t)hā*	*kijj-ih-ii*	*kar-ijj-anta*
	< (**kr-iya-te*)	(**kr-iy-iṣṭa*)	(**kr-iy-iṣya-te*)	(**kar-iya-māṇa*)

Remarkably, also the OIA imperfective mediopassive participle in *-māna* was remodelled by means of the active suffix *-anta* (later on, in Apabhraṃśa, the form *kar-ijj-anta* was reduced to *k-ijj-anta*).

On the other hand, Pāli discontinued the mediopassive morphology of the perfect, aorist and future. A number of relic forms appear in the present (*bharate* 'carries for himself'). As in Ardhamāgadhī the OIA passive *kri-ya-te* is now conjugated with active endings; similar forms exist in Buddhist Sanskrit. Some examples are shown in [19]:

[19] Pāli & Buddhist Sanskrit

Pāli:	*kariyati* (also *kayirati*) 'is done', *dīyati* 'is given', *vuccati* 'is spoken' (< OIA *uc-ya-te*, cf. Mayrhofer 1951: 160).
Buddhist Skt:	*dṛśyatu* 'be it regarded', *vadhiṣyam* 'I will be slain', *vucyāmi* 'I am told' (cf. Edgerton 1953: 182).

In Pāli the passives in the preterite and the future tenses are now formed analytically by combining the participles, the PP *kata* and the gerundive *kātabba*, respectively, with the copula.

Returning to Anatolian, in Hittite there are also early analytic passive (or rather 'pseudo-passive') constructions whose rise can be brought into a causal nexus with the gradual attrition of the middle semantics of *hi*-verbs, on the one hand, and the rise of the analytic perfect, on the other. In the past they display the auxiliary *es-* 'to be' in the preterite form *es-ta* 'was'; in the present indicative the auxiliary (*es-zi*) is not used but it appears in its modal form *es-du* 'may he be / he should be'. The following examples are quoted after Friedrich 1960: 137.

[20] Hittite

KUB XXI 38 II 7 f.	*DUMU.SAL*	*piianza*	*ešta*
	girl	give +PART	was
	'the girl was given'		
A1. 2 B 6	*memiiaš*	*ištantanza*	
	matter	delay+PART	
	'the matter [is] delayed'		
KUB XIII 4 II 33	*lamniian*	*ešdu*	
	call+PART	be+3SG/IMP	
	'he should be called'		

These incipient passive constructions coexist with the inherited middle voice forms as shown in Table 2 portraying the overall diathetic system of Hittite. (There are no middle or passive counterparts to the innovative perfect forms.)

TABLE 2
Diathetic system of Hittite

	Active	Middle	**PASSIVE**
	'kill'	'stand'	'give'
Pres	*kwen-zi*	*ar-ta*(*ri*)	*pii-ants* 'is given'
Pret	*kwen-t*	*ar-tat*(*i*)	*pii-ants est* 'was given'
PERFECT			
Pres	dān har-zi 'has taken'		**(innovative ana-**
Pret	dān har-t 'had taken'		**lytic formations)**

4. THE DEMISE OF THE MIDDLE VOICE IN INDO-IRANIAN

While the rise and vicissitudes of the middle voice morphology in Anatolian, Indo-Iranian and Hellenic have always been studied with a great deal of interest, the same cannot be said about the other end of the process, namely, its demise. The demise of middle voice morphology, manifested by the loss of the fundamental distinction of the ātmanepada versus parasmaipada endings in favour of the latter set, has rather been considered as a 'corruption' of the former state of affairs in the classical language.

In the absence of Hittite texts from the first millennium we can create some hypotheses about the gradual demise of the synthetic middle voice morphology (and its consequence for semantics) on the basis of the rich Indo-Iranian corpora. For Indic it can be shown that the rapid decay of mediopassive synthetic forms was precipitated by the raising of mid vowels (*ē* > *e* > *i*; *ō* > *o* > *u*; cf. Bubenik 1996: 29–33). Our evidence comes from the spellings with grapheme I (i-kāra) and U (u-kāra) for short *ĕ* and *ŏ* found in Ardhamāgadhī, Śaurasenī, and Māhārāṣṭrī. The earliest examples are found in Pāli. Representative examples, taken from Pischel (1900: 73), are presented in [21].

[21]	A-Mg *miccha* 'barbarian'	versus Mg, J-Mah, Ś, Ap *mĕccha* (< OIA *mlēccha*)
	A-Mg *chitta/khitta* 'field'	versus Mah *chĕtta* (<OIA *kṣētra*)
	J-Mah *uṭṭha* 'lip'	versus A-Mg *ŏṭṭha* (< OIA *ōṣṭha*)

We may remind ourselves of an interesting typological parallel from the history of Latin. As is well known, the cardinal change separating Classical from Vulgar Latin was the merger of high short (lax) vowels (*i*, *u*) and mid long (tense) vowels (*ē*, *ō*); hence the identical reflexes for Classical Latin *i* and *ē* (and *u* and *ō*) in Modern French, e.g. *poir* [pwar] < **pirus* and *voile* [vwal] < **vēlum*).

During the MIA period the elimination of the crucial phonological contrast between *ē* and *i*, which was available in OIA, resulted in the elimination of the morphological contrast between the middle and the active diathesis (see Bubenik 1996: 29–33). Furthermore, even the contrast between the active and the synthetic passive was considerably weakened; given the identity of their inflectional endings, this contrast continued to be carried solely by the shape of the passive stem. As shown in [22], in Pāli this could be identical with its active counterpart (e.g. *chijjati* meant both 'is split' or 'splits'; but the latter transitive sense could also be realized by *chindati*); or it could be differentiated only by the geminate (*labbhati* 'is taken' vs. *labhati* 'takes'); or in the case of roots in nasals by the geminate palatal in the passive versus the dental nasal in the active (as in *haññante* 'they are killed' vs. *hananti* 'they kill'):

[22] Pāli

	'split'	'take'	'kill' (3 sg)	'kill' (3 pl)
Active	*chijjati* ~ *chindati*	*labhati*	*hanati*	*hananti*
Middle	*chijjati*	*labhati*	*hanati*	*hananti*
Passive	*chijjati*	*labbhati*	*haññati*	*haññante* ~ *haññare*

Late MIA (Apabhraṃśa) replaced the active preterite *akāsi* (< OIA aorist *akārṣīt*) by the ergative construction *tena kiyau*. The present passive is continued with further phonological development. In the preterite the copula *āsi* continued to be used in conjunction with the PP; in the perfect and the future tense, however, the copula was replaced by the verb 'to go'. The system of the synthetic passive of Ardhamāgadhī, the conservative MIA dialect, and the innovative system of late MIA are contrasted in [23]:

[23] Ardhamāgadhī & late Middle Indo-Aryan

	Present	Aorist	Future	Perfect
Ardhamāgadhī (Synthetic passive)	*k-ijj-ai*	*k-ijj-ithā̆*	*k-ijj-ih-ii*	
Late MIA (Analytic passive)	*kiyau* (PP)	*kiyau āsi*	*kiyau jāisai*	*kiyau gayau*

5. ANALYTIC FORMATIONS COMPENSATING FOR THE LOSS OF THE SYNTHETIC MIDDLE VOICE

During the late MIA and Middle Iranian periods we encounter the earliest attempts to compensate for the eliminated category of middle voice by analytic formations involving lexical auxiliaries (in Indic *jānā* 'go' and *lenā* 'take'; in Iranian *šodan* 'become' < Old Iranian *šyav-* 'move'). Given the uniform use of the ātmanepada endings in both middle and passive categories the choice of the auxiliary *jānā* for both the analytic morphologies of the middle and passive is understandable. Thus, an event such as 'he (has) died', expressed by the middle voice *amṛta* in Sanskrit, is realized by combining the PP *jāu* 'gone' (< OIA *yāta*) with the PP of the verb 'to die' in Apabhraṃśa; this is shown in [24]:

[24] Apabhraṃśa

Paumacariu 66.5.9	*so*	*jāu*	*jji*	*muu*
	he	go+PP	PRT	die+PP

'he (has) died' (8th c., quoted after Jain 1958)

On the other hand, the PP *gau* 'gone' (belonging to another OIA root) would be used to express the passive voice as shown in [25]:

[25] Apabhraṃśa

Paumacariu 19.17.5	*so*	*kālameha*	*vane*	*diṭṭhu*	*gau*
	that	Kālameha	forest+LOC	see+PP	go+PP

'That Kālameha was seen in the forest'

In Western Middle Iranian after the loss of synthetic middle voice morphology the main exponent of the mediopassive functions became the auxiliary *ēstādan* 'stand, be'. It corresponds to Indo-Aryan *sthā-* 'stand', which, however, was used as a temporal auxiliary; its functional counterpart in MIA was *jānā* 'go'. The following Middle Persian examples are taken from *Ardā Wirāz Nāmag* (ca. 8th century), ed. Vahman (1986):

[26] Middle Persian

Ardā Wirāz 9.1	*hu-rust*	*kū*	*pad*	*frārōnīh*	*rust*	*ēstād*
	well-grown	that	in	virtue	grow+PP	stand+PP

'Well-grown, that is she was grown in virtue'

Ardā Wirāz 38.15	*kē*	*tan*	*andar*	*dēg-ē*	*rōyēn*	*kard*	*ēstēd*
	whose	body	in	pot=GEN	copper	do+PP	stand+3SG

'Whose body has been put in a copper pot'

At the end of this line of evolution, in New Indo-Aryan, we witness the same verb *jānā*, whose PP is now the suppletive form *gayā*, functioning as the auxiliary in both the passive construction [27] as well as in a variety of constructions expressing most notably changes of state and completive events [28]:

[27] Hindi passive

vah	*dekhā*	*gayā*
he	see+PP	go+PP

'He was seen'

[28] Hindi

Inchoative	*vah*	*mar*	*gayā*	
	he	die	go+PP	
	'He (has) died'			
Completive	*ham*	*sṭeśan*	*pahuṃc*	*gae*
	we	station	arrive	go+PP+PL
	'We got to the station'			

Another function of the middle voice, such as the indirect reflexive, denoting an action done explicitly for one's own purpose (as in OIA *odanam pacate* 'he cooks rice for himself') can be expressed by the auxiliary *lenā* 'take', as demonstrated in [29]:

[29] Hindi indirect reflexive

laṛke=ne	*pūrā*	*pannā*	*paṛh*	*liyā*
boy+OBL=ERG	entire	page	read	take+PP

'The boy reads the entire page (silently for himself)'

With the auxiliary *denā* 'give' the meaning would be 'read for someone else's benefit'. In Hindi the auxiliary *lenā* 'take' is used above all with 'ingestive' verbs (*khānā* 'eat', *pīnā* 'drink', etc.) representing physical experience par excellence. In combination with abstract objects a number of 'allosemes' of the basic physical experience can be distinguished. Nespital (1997) characterized *lenā* as indicating that the actor performs the action himself, for his own benefit, or for his own pleasure (here the term 'experiencer' would be more appropriate). He listed several allosemes of the compound auxiliary *khāḷenā* 'take something as food' (Nespital 1997: 285):

[30] Hindi

mār khālenā	the experiencer 'allows himself to be beaten'
γam khālenā	the experiencer 'swallows his grief willingly / by restraining himself'
dhakke khālenā	the experiencer 'suffers indignities enduringly'

With verbs of mental experience (*verba sentiendi*), such as *samajhnā* 'understand', *sīkhnā* 'learn', *pahcānnā* 'recognize', etc., the use equivocates between the auxiliary *jānā* 'go' or *lenā* 'take'. According to Hook (1979: 65) the combination with *lenā* implies 'some measure of conscious effort' while *jānā* implies that 'the mental event occurs as if of itself':

[31] Hindi

maiṃ=ne pahcān liyā ki vah kaun hai
I=ERG recognize take+PP that he who is
'I figured out who he was'

vs.: *maiṃ pahcāñ gaī ki vah kaun hai*
I recognize go+PP/F that he who is
'I (Fem) realized who he was'

There is some evidence in our Apabhraṃśa texts that this state of affairs had already been reached by the end of the late MIA period. In addition to *le-* 'take' also *nī-* 'take' had a general reflexive sense heralding thus the NIA state of affairs. For instance, from the 8th century:

[32] Apabhraṃśa

Paumacariu 25.4.9 *vijjulaṅgu ṇiu āliṅgeppiṇu*
Vidyudaṅga take+PP embrace+GERUND
'(The king) embraced Vidyudaṅga'

Here the construction *ṇiu āliṅgeppiṇu* 'take+PP' 'embrace' achieves the same 'effect' as its OIA counterpart with the verb 'embrace' in the middle voice: *rājā vidyudaṅgam āliṅgata*.

6. CONCLUSIONS

The study of the middle voice in Indo-European linguistics has almost exclusively focused on its origins and its functioning in ancient IE languages. I suggest that a study of its demise – accompanying the emancipation of passive morphology during the later stages documented in the rich Indo-Iranian corpora – is of equal importance.

The main point here is the fact that morphology and semantics are NOT co-extensive (or rather morphology and semantics are not 'isomorphic'). Middle semantics can be expressed in a variety of ways ranging from derivational (lexical) classes (called traditionally conjugations) to various inflectional means (such as affixes and ablaut), but also analytically by various grammaticalized lexical verbs in verbal compounds. During the earliest stages of ancient IE languages there were lexical classes (conjugations) linked with middle semantics, such as the *hi*-conjugation in Hittite, the 4th *ya*-class presents in Vedic and the second *ē*-conjugation in Latin. The inflectional exponents of middle semantics are represented by *-ri* and *-ti* verb endings in Hittite, ātmanepada endings in Indo-Iranian and Hellenic, and rhotic endings in Latin. As we saw in sections **3** and **4**, their 'ambiguity', or rather, their polysemy, precipitated their replacement by analytic means featuring various grammaticalized lexical verbs. However, as shown in [16], Hellenic preserved its middle voice morphology until Modern Greek. On the other hand, it has to be emphasized that Indo-Iranian languages, by losing the mediopassive morphology of their earliest stages, did not lose the ability to express the whole range of meanings covered by the umbrella term 'middle semantics': what during their Old period used to be expressed synthetically came to be realized analytically during their Middle and New periods.

Thus, at the end of this development we encounter again the same type of morphology, the auxiliary *jānā* 'go' (in Hindi) and *šodan* 'become' < 'move' (in Farsi), realizing BOTH the middle and the passive voice whose exponents used to be the ātmanepada endings in Old Indo-Iranian:

[33]	Old Indo-Iranian	New Indo-Iranian
	a-mṛ-ta 'he died' (Vedic)	*vah mar gayā* 'he died' (Hindi)
	a-bhuṅk-ta 'he took his meal'	*vah sab roṭiyāṃ khā gayā* 'he ate all the rotis'
	us-zaiia-ta 'he was born' (Avestan)	*motavalled šod* 'he was born' (Farsi)

It should be emphasized that in New Indo-Iranian languages the expressions for a whole range of experiential meaning associated with the erstwhile ātmanepada morphology of Old Indo-Iranian have been highly systematized or rather 'paradigmatized' (see Bubenik 2001b). A new Indo-Aryan analytic descendant of the OIA predominantly synthetic system in Table 1 can be portrayed as shown in Table 3 (with V for the base of a verb):

TABLE 3
Diathetic system of New Indo-Aryan (Hindi)

	Imperfective	Perfective	Perfect
Active	*vah kartā hai*	*us=ne kiyā*	*us=ne kiyā hai*
Experiential	*vah* V *letā ha*	*us=ne* V *liyā*	*us=ne* V *liyā hai*
meaning	*vah* V *jātā hai*	*vah* V *gayā*	*vah* V *gayā hai*
Passive	*us=se kiyā jātā hai*	*us=se kiyā gayā*	*us=se kiyā gayāhai*

Along the same lines, in Modern Iranian (Farsi) the auxiliary *šodan* 'become' is used in BOTH the expressions of the passive voice (*karde mišavad* 'it is being done', *karde šod* 'it was done', *karde šode ast* 'it has been done') and in the expressions of experiential meaning (*esbâni šodan* 'become angry', *moztareb šodan* 'become agitated', *râm šodan* 'control oneself', etc.).

REFERENCES

ABHYANKAR, Kashinath V. & J. M. SHUKLA 1977. *A Dictionary of Sanskrit Grammar*. Baroda: Oriental Institute.

Al. = Alakšanduš Vertrag. In: J. Friedrich, *Staatsverträge des Ḫatti-Reiches in hethitischer Sprache*, I. Leipzig: J. C. Hinrichs 1926.

ANDERSEN, Paul Kent 1994. *Empirical Studies in Diathesis*. Münster: Nodus Publikationen.

BUBENIK, Vit 1996. *The Structure and Development of Middle Indo-Aryan Dialects*. Delhi: Motilal Banarsidass.

——— 2001a. *Morphological and Syntactic Change in Medieval Greek and South Slavic Languages*. Munich: LINCOM EUROPA.

——— 2001b. On the origins and evolution of the middle voice in Indo-Iranian languages. In: D. W. Lönne (ed.), *Toḥfa-e-Dil. Festschrift Helmut Nespital*: 67–86. Reinbek: Dr. Inge Wezler.

EDGERTON, Franklin 1953. *Buddhist Hybrid Sanskrit Grammar and Dictionary*. New Haven: Yale University Press.

FRIEDRICH, Johannes 1960. *Hethitisches Elementarbuch*, I: *Kurzgefaßte Grammatik*. Heidelberg: Carl Winter.

HOOK, Peter Edwin 1979. *Hindi Structures*. Ann Arbor: The University of Michigan.

JAIN, Devendra Kumār 1958. *Paumchriu of Kavirāja Svayambhūdeva*. Kāshī: Bhāratīya Jñānapīṭha.

JAMISON, Stephanie 1990. The tense of the predicated past participle in Vedic and beyond. *Indo-Iranian Journal* 33: 1–19.

JASANOFF, Jay 2003. *Hittite and the Indo-European Verb*. Cambridge: Cambridge University Press.

KBo = *Keilschrifttexte aus Boghazköy*. Leipzig: J. C. Hinrichs, 1916–23, Berlin: Mann, 1954–.

KELLENS, J. 1984. *Le verbe avestique*. Wiesbaden: Ludwig Reichert.

KEMMER, Suzanne E. 1993. *The Middle Voice*. Amsterdam: John Benjamins.

KRONASSER, Heinz 1966. *Etymologie der Hethitischen Sprache*, I. Wiesbaden: Otto Harrassowitz.

KUB = *Keilschrifturkunden aus Boghazköy*. Berlin: Akademie-Verlag, 1921–.

KULIKOV, Leonid 1998. Passive, anticausative and classification of verbs: the case of Vedic. In: Leonid Kulikov & Heinz Vater (eds.), *Typology of Verbal Categories. Papers Presented to Vladimir Nedjalkov on the Occasion of His 70th Birthday* (Linguistiche Arbeiten, 382): 139–153. Tübingen: Niemeyer.

LEHMANN, Winfred P. 2002. *Pre-Indo-European*. (Journal of Indo-European Studies, Monograph Number, 41.). Washington, DC: Institute for the Study of Man.

MAYRHOFER, Manfred 1951. *Handbuch des Pāli*. Heidelberg: Carl Winter.

MEID, Wolfgang 1979. Der Archaismus des Hethitischen. In: Erich Neu & Wolfgang Meid (eds.), *Hethitisch und Indogermanisch* (Innsbrucker Beiträge zur Sprachwissenschaft, 16): 239–254. Innsbruck: Institut für Sprachen und Literaturen der Universität.

NESPITAL, Helmut 1997. *Dictionary of Hindi Verbs*. Allahabad: Lokbharti prakashan.

PEREL'MUTER, Ilja Aronovič 1995. *Zalog drevnegrečeskogo glagola: teorija, genesis, istorija.* (English summary, pp. 248–262). Saint Petersburg: Izdatel'stvo Noach.

PISCHEL, Rudolf 1900. *Grammatik der Prakrit-Sprachen*. Strassburg: Trübner.

PUHVEL, Jaan 1984. *Hittite Etymological Dictionary*, I–II. Berlin: Mouton de Gruyter.

REICHELT, Hans 1909. *Awestisches Elementarbuch*. Heidelberg: Carl Winter.

RIEKEN, Elizabeth 2004. Das Präteritum des Medio-Passivs im Hieroglyphen-Luwischen. *Historische Sprachforschung* 117: 179–188.

ROSE, Sarah R. 2006. *The Hittite -hi/-mi Conjugations. Evidence for an Early Indo-European Voice Opposition.* (Innsbrucker Beiträge zur Sprachwissenschaft, 121.) Innsbruck.

VAHMAN, Fereydun (ed.) 1986. *Ardā Wirāz Nāmag. The Iranian "Divina Commedia"*. London: Curzon Press.

WHITNEY, William Dwight 1889. *Sanskrit Grammar*. 2nd edition. Cambridge, Mass. [2nd Indian Edition: Delhi: Motilal Banarsidass, 1969.]

Some Remarks on the Adverbal Genitive in Ṛgvedic Sanskrit

HEINRICH HETTRICH

1. The adverbal genitive[1] appears in the *Ṛgveda* in two variants: as possessive and partitive genitive. The possessive function of the genitive can be observed as a second complement either with the verbum substantivum or without a copula as in

[1] 10.108.5 (G_{poss}) *utā́smā́kam ā́yudhā santi tigmā́*
'And to us belong sharp weapons'.

On the other hand, the G_p[2] appears as a second complement after a verb of nourishing or consuming as in

[2] 9.51.3 (G_p) *táva tyá indo ándhaso*
devā́ mádhor vy àśnate
'(Of) your sweet sap, o drink, these gods consume'.

This paper concentrates on the G_p and asks the following questions:

---

[1] Abbreviations: A = accusative, D_{fin} = dativus finalis, G_p = genitivus partitivus, G_{poss} = genitivus possessivus, I = instrumental, L = locative, N = nominative. All Vedic text citations are from the *Ṛgveda* (RV).

[2] Most relevant previous work: Gaedicke 1880: 43ff.; Delbrück 1888: 158ff.; 1893: 308ff.; Brugmann 1911: 565ff.; Haudry 1977: 376ff.; Jamison 1983: 32f.; Gotō 2002: 25ff.

1. After which verbs can the G_p appear?
2. Which nouns can be used in the G_p?
3. With which other cases does the G_p compete, and in which syntactic functions?
4. Is there a semantic difference between the G_p and the competing cases or are relations desemanticized and only governed by the verb?

2.1. Question no. **1**: Gaedicke (1880: 43ff.) and Delbrück (1888: 158ff.; 1893: 308ff.) distinguish between the following semantic verbal classes:

a. verbs of nourishing or consuming (see example [2]),
b. verbs with the meaning 'to give, to supply with',
c. verbs of striving for, begging, reaching (for) something,
d. verbs meaning 'to rule over, to dispose of',
e. verbs of mental activity,
f. verbs of being glad of.

Each of these classes belongs to one or two higher level typological groups: the first group consists of classes **a**, **b** and **c**; **d**, **e**, and **f**[3] belong to the second group. The allocation to classes **c** and **f**, meanwhile, is not totally clear as there is some affinity to the respective other group.

Let us begin with a discussion of group 1. The following verbs belong to this group:

---

[3] Gaedicke (1880: 43ff.) included some instances which are scarcely to be viewed as partitive; Delbrück (1888: 158ff.) apparently considers only the genitives in classes a–c, not in classes d–f, as partitive.

Class **a**:

ad 'to eat'; *aś*^{i} 'to consume'; ^{2}*gar*^{i} 'to devour'; *ghas* 'to consume'; *joṣ* 'to enjoy'; ^{1}*pā* 'to drink'; *bhaj* (middle) 'to enjoy as a share'; *bhas* 'to devour, to crush'; *reh* 'to lick'.

Class **b**:

ā́-kar 'to construct, to get/bring here'; *ā́-cay* 'to load with'; *daśasy* 'to afford'; *dā* 'to give'; *dhā* 'to procure'; *pay*^{i} 'to (make) swell'; ^{1}*par*^{i} 'to fill'; ^{2}*par*^{i} 'to give'; *parc* 'to fill, to mix'; *bhar* 'to bring'; ^{2}*mā* 'to allot'; *yaj* 'to worship'; *yam* 'to grant'; ^{1}*yav* 'to connect, to arrest'; *rapś* 'to exuberate'; *van* 'to gain, to provide'; *vardh* 'to support'; *varṣ* 'to pour'; *vah* 'to carry, to bring'; *śak* 'to procure'; *san*^{i} 'to gain'.

Class **c**:

āp 'to reach'; *iṣaṇy/iṣudhy* 'to ask for'; *īḍ* 'to beg for'; *kā/kam*^{i} 'to desire, to strive for'; *krap*^{i} 'to long for'; *praś* 'to ask for, to request'; *yā* 'to beg for'; *vay*^{i} 'to strive for'.

2.2. Nouns which can take the G_p after these verbs are scarcely subject to any lexical constraint. But there is one condition, namely that the concept of a partitive relation must be possible. Most nouns are therefore mass nouns; abstract and concrete nouns are considerably less common. Some typical examples are:

Mass nouns:

sóma-, *mádhu-* 'sweetness'; *ándhas-* 'Soma plant' (and other metonymical designations of the soma); *páyas-* 'milk'; *havíṣ-* 'libation'; *rayí-* 'wealth'; *vásu-* 'good'; *yáva-* 'barley'; *vā́rya-* 'desirable'; *vā́ja-* 'booty'; *ū́rj-* 'nourishment, strength'.

Abstract nouns:

amṛ́ta- 'immortality'; *śávas-* 'power'; *sakhyá-* 'friendship'.

Concrete nouns and persons:

uṣás- 'dawn'; *márta-* 'human being'; *phála-* 'fruit'; *deṣṇá-* 'gift'; *gáv-* 'cow'; *bheṣajá-* 'medicament'.

2.3.1. Sentences of the first type show syntactic opposition of G_p and A. Compare example [2] with G_p and the following example belonging to class **a** with A:[4]

[3] 7.67.7 (A) *aśnántā havyám mā́nuṣīṣu vikṣú*
'consuming the libation among the human clans'.

The following two sentences with *dā* 'to give' and, respectively, G_p and/or A belong to class **b**:

[4] 7.28.5 (G_p) *mahó rāyó rā́dhaso yád dádan naḥ*
'in order that he should give us of the great wealth, of (his) gift'

[5] 2.32.5 (A) *yā́bhir dádāsi dāśúṣe vásūni*
'with whom you give goods to the sacrificer'.[5]

From class **c**, compare example [6] with G_p and example [7] with A:

[6] 7.27.1 (G_p) *śávasaś cakānáḥ*
'striving for strength'

[7] 5.44.15 (A) *agnír jāgāra tám ṛ́caḥ kāmayante*
'Agni is awake. Him desire the verses.'

2.3.2. Furthermore, the G_p can also compete with the I, namely with verbs of 'supplying with something' which exhibit the so-called 'ornative' construction. That is to say the addressee takes the A, and the substance referred to is represented in the I, as in the following two sentences:

[8] 1.76.5 (I) *yáthā ... havírbhir devā́n áyajaḥ*
'as you worshipped the gods with libations'

---

[4] For *aś*[i] 'to consume' cf. now Krisch 2006: 587f.

[5] Compare also from class **b** 6.44.20 with both cases: *prá túbhyam ... sutā́nām ... bharanti ... sómam*.

[9] 2.14.10 (I) *páyasódhar yáthā gó sómebhir īm pṛṇatā … índram*
'As with milk the udder of the cow, [in the same way] fill Indra with soma!'

Compare examples [10] and [8], also [11] and [9] which have the G_p in the same syntactic slot as the I:

[10] 3.53.2 (G_p) *sómasya nú tvā súṣutasya yakṣi*
'Now I will worship you with [some] well-pressed soma.'

[11] 6.69.7 (G_p) *sómasya dasrā jaṭháram pṛṇethām*
'With [some] soma, o masters, fill your belly!'

There are also intransitive sentences with ornative construction and G_p instead of I, for example:

[12] 1.37.5 (G_p) *jámbhe rásasya vāvṛdhe*
'I have strengthened myself with sap between the teeth.'

As a substitute for the I, the G_p is not affected by the difference between transitive and intransitive constructions.[6]

2.3.3. Finally, there is a third and extremely rare construction of the partitive genitive; I could only find the following two attestations in the RV:

[13] 2.19.1 (G_p) *ápāyy asyā́ndhaso mádāya*
'of this drink has been drunk for exhilaration'

[14] 6.63.3 (G_p) *ákāri vām ándhasaḥ*
'It was prepared for you of this drink.'

---

[6] See further 4.45.1 *madhúno ví rapśate*; 5.73.8 *mádhvaḥ … pipyúṣī*.

In these sentences, the G_p occupies the position of the subject in a passive construction,[7] corresponding to the direct object in active constructions and competing with the N, the normal case of the subject, as in the next example:

[15] 6.44.8 *ṛtásya pathí vedhā́ apāyi*
'In the path of truth, the master was drunk.'

2.3.4. Thus, on the whole there are three different types of constructions with the partitive genitive with verbs of classes **a–c**. However, these show a special semantic agreement.

In general linguistics a consensus has existed for some time concerning the complement connected most closely with the verb: with two-place verbs, it is the most patient-like complement; with three-place verbs, it is the complement which denotes the object transferred – not the addressee – regardless of the expression of this complement by the A or – in an ornative construction – by the I; and in one-place constructions in the passive, this complement surfaces as subject, as in examples [13] and [14].

Irrespective of the difference in construction, the complement connected most closely with the verb is itself designated 'internal argument', or 'erstzubindender Term'.[8] Accordingly, a simple rule emerges for the use of the G_p in verbal classes **a–c**: it is only the lexical concept underlying the internal argument (erstzubindender Term) which can surface as a G_p if it is affected only partially by the verbal process – irrespective of the three-, two- or one-place construction of the sentence. For the expression of other arguments, the G_p cannot be used.[9]

---

[7] The examples of other ancient IE languages with G_p as subject (adduced by Delbrück 1893: 332; Wackernagel 1909: 62 [= 1955: 1120] and Chantraine 1953: 50f.) are also intransitive or passive sentences.

[8] See e.g. Levin & Rappaport Hovav 1995, Chapters 1 and 4.1; and Zifonun *et al.* 1997: 956ff., 1020ff., 1300ff.

[9] As the data collected by Delbrück (1893: 308ff.) and Brugmann (1911: 565ff.) show, what is a rule in the Ṛgvedic language is only a tendency in

2.3.5. It should further be pointed out that there are no obvious morphosyntactical factors which restrict the use of the G_p or determine the choice between G_p and competing cases. Consider the following examples of G_p with opposing syntactic categories:

active	3.36.10	*prá yandhi rāyáḥ*
vs. middle	3.53.2	*sómasya ... tvā ... yakṣi*
present-	6.44.13	*prá ... sutā́nām ... bhara*
vs. aorist-	3.30.19	*ní te deṣṇásya dhīmahi*
vs. perfect-stem	2.11.10	*papivā́n sutásya*
affected	5.30.11	*púnar gávām adadāt*
vs. effected object	6.63.3	*ákāri ándhasaḥ* (passive with underlying effected object)
indefinite	8.71.9	*vásva úpa māsi*
vs. definite noun	10.8.9	*viśvárūpasya góṇām ācakrāṇáḥ*
singular	10.142.3	*bápsad ... úlapasya*
vs. plural noun	10.28.3	*átsi téṣām* [sc. *vṛṣabhā́nām*]

2.4. Besides its restriction to the internal argument (**2.3.4**), the use of G_p depends on semantic conditions only:

> Der Genitiv unterscheidet sich von dem Akkusativ [und ggf. dem I., H.H.] dadurch, dass bei dem Gen. der Verbalbegriff nicht auf den vollen Umfang des Substantivbegriffs zu beziehen ist. Er ist sozusagen ein verengerter Akkusativ. (Delbrück 1893: 308)[10]

This description is today as valid as ever but must be qualified in a somewhat different way for the two typological groups 1

---

other IE languages. Syntactically, the genitive of local or temporal determination (see Delbrück 1893: 356ff.; Brugmann 1911: 568f.) has to be classified as a satellite, but not as an argument or complement. In 3.16.3 *sá tvám̐ no rāyáḥ śiśīhi*, the G_p seems exceptionally be used as a substitute of a D_{fin} as satellite; cf. 7.18.2 *śiśīhi rāyé asmā́n*.

[10] Similarly Gotō 2002: 26.

(classes **a–c**) and 2 (classes **d–f**). The following characteristics apply to most verbs of the first group:

The verbal action refers from the beginning only to a part of the patientive nominal concept but affects this part completely:

Type 1:

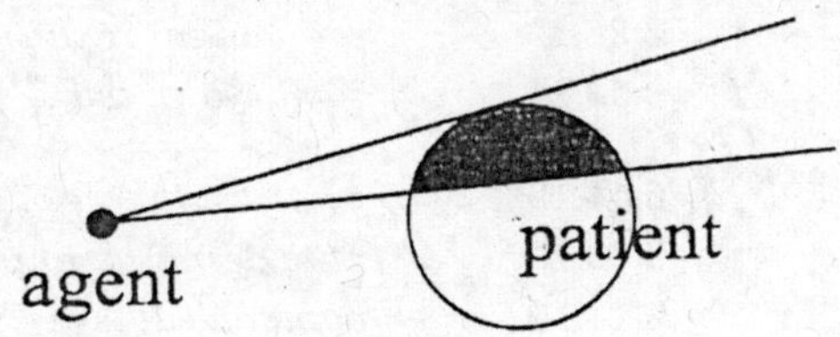

Fig. 1

Typical examples are, amongst others: 2.11.10 *papivā́n sutásya*; 3.36.10 *asmé prá yandhi ... rāyáḥ*; 5.62.7 *sanéma mádhvaḥ*. However, some examples of class **c** (such as 7.27.1 *śávasaś cakānáḥ*) are not confined to such a description but represent transitions between the first and second group (see below **3.3**).

2.5. It must be noted that with verbs of group 1, there are fewer instances of the G_p than of the competing cases A or I, respectively. Compare the number of instances with the following list of selected verbs:

ad	'to eat'	28 A	: 1 G
aś'	'to consume'	7 A	: 6 G
āp	'to reach'	18 A	: 1 G
kā/kam'	'to desire'	19 A	: 3 G
krap'	'to long for'	5 A	: 2 G
²*gar*'	'to devour'	6 A	: 1 G
ghas	'to consume'	12 A	: 1 G
joṣ	'to enjoy'	ca. 180 A	: 2 G
dā	'to give'	ca. 300 A	: 7 G
par'	'to fill'	ca. 20 I	: 3 G

parc	'to fill, to mix'	17	I	:	2	G
[1]*pā*	'to drink'	163	A	:	106	G
praś	'to ask for'	9	A	:	1	G
bhaj (middle)	'to enjoy as a share'	28	A	:	13	G
bhar	'to bring'	ca. 300	A	:	3	G
bhas	'to devour'	5	A	:	1	G
reh	'to lick'	26	A	:	1	G
vay[i]	'to strive for'	74	A	:	2	G
vah	'to carry, to bring'	ca. 240	A	:	1	G

The numerical relation alone suggests that the opposition between, respectively, A or I and G after these verbs is privative – with the G_p as the marked member. Careful examination of the data confirms this suggestion: A and I can both be used with neutral or complete inclusion as well as with only partial inclusion of the relevant concept into the state-of-affairs; the G_p is more restricted and can only be used with partial inclusion of this concept.[11] Compare the following instances:

[16] 8.77.4 (complete inclusion, A)[12]
ékayā pratidhā́pibat sākáṃ sárāṁsi triṁśátam
'In only one go he drank up thirty lakes together'.

[17] 7.74.2–3 (partial inclusion, A and G_p in parallel construction)[13]
píbataṃ sómyam mádhu ‖ 2 ‖
ā́ yātam úpa bhūṣatam
mádhvaḥ pibatam aśvinā

---

[11] See also Brugmann 1911: 568: 'Der Gegensatz zwischen dem Objektsgenitiv und dem Objektsakkusativ ist aber nicht etwa immer der gewesen, dass der Genitiv einen Teil, der Akkusativ das Ganze betonte, sondern der Akkusativ steht ganz gewöhnlich auch dann, wenn es nur auf die Gattung im Gegensatz zu anderen Gattungen ankommt und die Quantität dahingestellt bleibt.'

[12] Cf. also 10.102.4 *udnó hradám apibaj járhṛṣāṇaḥ*; 1.84.20 *víśvā ca na upamimīhí mānuṣa* | *vásūni carṣaṇíbhya ā́*; 4.27.2 *ná ghā sá mā́m ápa jóṣaṃ jabhāra*.

[13] See also with partial inclusion 4.18.3 *tváṣṭur gṛhé apibat sómam índra* | *śatadhanyàṃ camvòḥ sutásya*; 2.11.13 *rayíṃ rāsi*; 2.32.5 *dádāsi* ... *vásūni*.

'Drink ye the somic sweetness!
Come here, draw near!
Drink of the sweetness, o Aśvins!'

Similarly with I vs. G_p:

[18] 2.2.1 (complete inclusion, I)
agním yajadhvaṃ havíṣā tánā girā́
'worship Agni with a libation, with a continuous song!'

[19] 5.34.2 (partial inclusion, I)
ā́ yáḥ sómena jaṭháram apiprata
'who filled his belly with soma'

[20] 6.69.7 (partial inclusion, G_p)
sómasya dasrā jaṭháram pṛṇethām
'With soma, o masters, fill your belly!'[14]

2.6. As the examples above illustrate, with most relevant verbs, the G_p is rare. It can therefore not be excluded that this case could in principle also be used with other verbs; there simply happens to be no evidence for it. It is thus possible that Delbrück's classes do not define limits of use but only preferences. The following points would be in favour of this:

a. Class **b** in particular is semantically heterogeneous. Some verbs (e.g. *pay*^{i} 'to (make) swell', *yaj* 'to sacrifice, to worship', ^{1}*yav* 'to unite, to fasten') can be subsumed only with difficulty under the cover term 'to give, to supply with'.

b. In addition to the verbs mentioned so far, there are others with which the G_p can be observed but which do not belong to classes **a–c** (or **d–f**):[15]

---

[14] The same correspondence between (partial) I and G_p can be observed in 6.15.11 (I) *tám ít pṛṇakṣi śávasotá rāyā́* vs. 7.100.2 (G_p) *párcaḥ yáthā naḥ suvitásya ... rāyáḥ*.

[15] See Gaedicke 1880: 43ff.; Gotō 2002: 26f.

dar[i] 'to tear, to drag'

[21] 7.55.4 *tvám sūkarásya dardṛhi*
táva dardartu sūkaráḥ
'You should tear at the boar, and the boar should tear at you!'

jambh 'to snap, snatch'

[22] 10.86.4 *śvā́ nv àsya jambhiṣad ápi kárṇe*
'The dog should snap at him, at his ear.'

han 'to slay'

[23] 2.23.12 *yáḥ … śā́sām ugró mányamāno jíghāṁsati*
'whoever, thinking oneself powerful, wants to break some (of the) commandment(s) …'

In the end, classes **a–c** do not constitute precisely circumscribed verb classes but only semantically nuclear domains of the G_p, apart from which, however, in appropriate cases, the G_p is not excluded.[16]

In some cases of class **c**, the function of the G seems to be ambiguous. In part the scheme of 2.4 seems to apply (e.g. 7.24.5 *ī̈ṭṭe vásūnām*; 9.108.4 *āpire … amṛ́tasya*). However, there are some cases which can belong to a second type of partitivity, to be described in detail in 3.3; e.g. 7.27.1 *śávasaś cakānáḥ* 'striving for strength'; 1.93.7 *havíṣaḥ … vītám* 'strive for the libation!' In such cases, it is not impossible to view the state-of-affairs as referring to the patientive concept in its totality but affecting it only partially; cf. fig. 2 in **3.3**. Apparently, class **c** contains some cases bordering on group 2.

2.7. Let us now sum up the most important results concerning the first variant of the G_p:

---

[16] Some examples of G_p with other verbs from AV and Vedic prose, which also belong to group 1, are to be found in Delbrück 1888: 159ff. and Gotō 2002: 26.

a. The verbal action refers only to a part of the patientive concept but affects this part completely (**2.4**).

b. Among the nouns which take the G_p, mass nouns and abstract nouns prevail by far. However, nouns belonging to other semantic classes are not excluded (**2.2**).

c. Verbal predicates predominantly consist of verbs of nourishing/consuming, verbs of transfer and verbs of striving, begging, reaching for something (**2.1, 2.6**).

d. The G_p can exhibit a syntactic competition with A, I and N. It always designates the 'internal argument' (**2.3.1–4**).

e. The G_p is the marked member of a privative opposition with A or I, respectively. It is much rarer than the unmarked members A and I. The positive feature of the opposition is the only partial implication of the patientive concept, as described in **2.4**.

3.1. Now we shall consider the second group of G_p constructions with the following verb classes

d. 'to rule over, to dispose of',
e. verbs of mental activity,
f. 'to be glad of, to enjoy'.

In these classes, too, the G_p is restricted to the designation of the 'internal argument' and competes with the A, in some cases also with L and I. Here are some examples from class **e** with *man* 'to remember, to think up, to imagine':[17]

[24] 5.22.3 (G_p) *várenyasya té 'vasa*
iyānáso amanmahi
'Imploring we have remembered your desirable aid.'

---

[17] See Hettrich 2004: 75ff.

[25] 5.13.2 (A)

agné stómam manāmahe
sidhrám adyá divispŕ̥śaḥ
'Let's think out a hymn for/of Agni, a successful [song] today for/of [him, who] touches heaven.'

For further consideration of cases used with *man*, see **3.4.6** below.

3.2. The considerably varying distribution of both cases in classes **d–f** already indicates that the semantic relationship between G and A in these classes is different from that of group 1.

Compare the most important verbs of **d–f**:[18]

d. 'to rule over, to dispose of'

īś	'to dispose of, to rule over'	4 A	:	95 G
kṣā	'to rule over, to dispose of'	1 A	:	17 G
irajyá-	'to rule over, to dispose of, to straighten, to guide'	2 A	:	7 G
rāj	'to extend, to rule over'	10 A	:	28 G
[2]*pat*	'to possess, to rule over'	17 A	:	no G (besides 2 I, 3 L)

e. verbs of mental activity

ádhi-ay/ gam/gā	'to regard, to consider, to mind'	5 A	:	7 G
[1]*kar*[1]	'to mention, to celebrate'[19]	no A	:	8 G
cet	'to perceive, to comprehend'	ca. 50 A	:	16 G
bodh	'to be regardful of'	8 A	:	16 G
man	'to remember, to imagine'[20]	31 A	:	5 G

---

[18] Apart from the verbs arranged in the following survey, there are some others with very few attestations of the G_p: *pári-khyā* 'to forget, to ignore' (5.65.6 *maghónaḥ, asmā́kam*); *dhay*[1] 'to consider' (7.7.6 *asyá ... r̥tásya*); *śas* 'to rule over' (8.34.1 *divó amúṣya*).

[19] In the examples with passive construction 10.122.1; 10.105.4 (*cárkr̥ṣe*);10.50.2 (*carkŕ̥tyaḥ*) the subject nominative, however, can in principle be explained as a transformation of an accusative of the active source construction.

ved[21]	'to realize, to know'	ca. 130 A	:	ca. 60 G
śrav, á-ghoṣ	'to hear'			content of noise: A source of noise: G

f. 'to be glad of, to enjoy'

kan^i/can^i	'to be glad of'	3 A	:	5 G
		(besides, 2 I	:	11 L)
tarp	'to enjoy'	1 A	:	8 G
mad /mand	'to be intoxicated, to enjoy'	8 A	:	ca. 30 G (besides, ca. 15L, ca. 35 I)

3.3. These numbers suffice to show that the opposition between the two cases occurring with these verbs is not privative. In order to explain the great fluctuation between A and G_p with these verbs, we must first take into account their low degree of transitivity in terms of Hopper & Thompson.[22] Predominantly, in Vedic as in the other IE languages, the second complement of a verb takes the A. This holds, as a rule, when the degree of transitivity is high with a clear-cut difference between agent and patient. With decreasing levels of transitivity, vacillation occurs and other cases, such as the G, begin to compete with the A.

In this transitional sphere, the following principle holds: the more the referent of the second complement, that is to say the patient, is affected by or incorporated in the domain of the agent, the more the A prevails; the weaker this incorporation, the more the G_p prevails. This holds as a general rule; however, we have to accept some vacillation. The decisive factors for the degree of incorporation are, on the one hand, the degree of patient-orientated dynamicity of the verb caused by its lexical meaning or grammatical category (e.g. diathesis, aspect), on the other

[20] The instances with the present stem *mánya-* and the meaning 'to consider, think' are not to be taken into account here.

[21] The distribution of G_p and A with this verb is not yet fully understood; cf. Gaedicke 1880: 45ff.; Seebold 1973: 25ff.; Kümmel 2000: 493ff.; Hill 2004: 37ff.

[22] See Hopper & Thompson 1980 and also Lakoff 1987: 54.

hand, as an opposing factor, the degree of conceptual autonomy of the patient or patient-like concept, its individuality and ability to react. These factors operate against each other – the first in favour of the A, the second of the G_p – in a manner which differs from one verb to the next, and the scales turn the balance partly in favour of the A, partly of the G_p. In this way, the different distributions of A and G_p after various verbs of group 2 can be explained globally, but it remains difficult or in some cases even impossible to find out why in one given sentence the G_p is used and in another the A.

As a consequence, this result shows that the function of the G_p in sentences of group 2 is not the same as in those of type 1 (see **2.4** above). In type 2, the verbal action refers to the patientive nominal concept in its totality but affects it only partially:

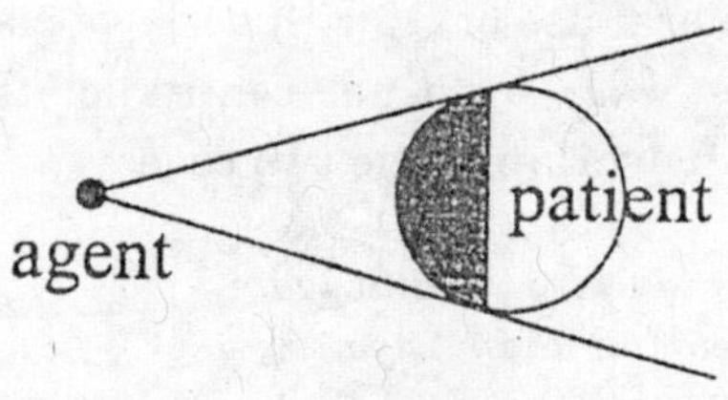

Fig. 2

3.4. The opposing factors just mentioned can be realized with different verbs in a different and not predictable manner. This can be illustrated with some selected verbs from classes **d–f**.

3.4.1. *īś* 'to dispose of, to rule over':

[26] 3.16.5 (G) *rāyá īśe svapatyásya gómata*
íśe vṛtrahátānām
'He [sc. Agni] disposes of wealth, consisting of good offspring, [and] of cows, he disposes of the killings of Vṛtra.'

[27] 8.25.20 (G) *váco dīrgháprasadmaní-*
-śe vā́jasya gómata
ī́śe hí pitvò 'viṣásya dāváne
'A word of/with Dīrghaprasadman disposes of wealth in the form of cows, disposes of non-toxic nourishment, for giving [it].'

As can be seen from the table in **3.2**, with *īś* we find 95 instances with G_p and only 4 with A. This distribution matches the observation that the precise lexical meaning of this verb, in Delbrück's words, is 'nicht bewältigen, sondern Gewalt haben an' (Delbrück 1893: 308; Brugmann 1911: 595). In other words only the subject's ability to dispose of the object or to have some control over it is expressed, but not yet an action already performed and affecting the object as a kind of patient. In the last example [27], such an action would only be realized through fulfillment of the dative action noun *dāváne*. In this respect, the use of G_p with *īś* corresponds to the general use of G_p with verbs of classes **d–f**.

The few instances with A do not contradict this rule. The next example shows an overlap of the two cases:

[28] 7.32.18 (G+A) *yád indra yā́vatas tvám*
etā́vad ahám īśīya
'if, o Indra, I myself disposed of so many [things] as you'

Here, it is understandable that the A takes part as well: because the second complement is constituted by a semantically empty neuter form of a pronoun, we have the weakest possible degree of conceptual autonomy.

The following example is very different:

[29] 7.37.7 *abhí yáṃ deví nírṛtiś cid ī́śe*
'even if the divine Nirṛti has power over him [sc. Indra]'.

Here the conceptual independence of Indra is out of the question and should require the G_p. However, the goal-oriented LP *abhí* indicates that this independence is restricted by Nirṛti. In such a special case, this leads to an accusative object.

3.4.2. *rāj* 'to extend, to rule over'

The following are typical examples with G_p and A, respectively:

[30] 5.63.2 (G_p) *samrā́jāv asyá bhúvanasya rājatho*
mítrāvaruṇā vidáthe svardṛ́śā
'As overall rulers, you rule over this world, Mitra and Varuṇa, sun-like, at the distribution.'

[31] 5.8.5 (A) *purū́ṇy ánnā sáhasā ví rājasi*
'You rule over much nourishment with power.'

The meaning of *rāj* has been much disputed.[23] In my opinion, Roesler's interpretation is right: the feature 'to shine' is not yet present in the RV as an autonomous component but at best as an implication. Rather, the meaning consists of the components 'to extend over' and 'to rule over' which are always present, even if according to the context one of the two dominates. Because of the component 'to extend over', the meaning of *rāj* exhibits a stronger patient-oriented dynamicity than *īś*; therefore the A is more frequent than with *īś*. Nevertheless, as the coexistence of A and G_p shows, that dynamicity exists in different gradations. It is also in accordance with the general result for the verbs of ruling that all 10 instances of the A after *rāj* have a direction- or goal-oriented local particle (*áti*, *ánu*, *prá*, *ví*), whereas the G_p exhibits such a particle (always *ví*) only in 4 of 28 instances.

3.4.3. Let us now have a look at the verb ²*pat* 'to rule, possess', which in spite of its semantic similarity to *īś* and *rāj* presents a

[23] See the overview in Roesler 1997: 173ff.

sharp syntactic contrast to these verbs because its object takes only the A.

A typical example is

[32] 6.2.1 *tvám̩ hí kṣáitavad yáśó*
'gne mitró ná pátyase
'You, o Agni, as [well as] Mitra surely possess magnificent splendor.'

As the meaning of the complement nouns – here as well as in other sentences – shows, the relation of [2]*pat* with these nouns is not the same as in the case of *īś* or *rāj*. The notions connected to *īś* and *rāj* possess in most cases an autonomous existence, as *rayí-* 'wealth', *bhúvana-* 'creature', *vásu-* 'good', *vā́ja-* 'prize, booty', whereas the notions combined with [2]*pat* predominantly denote personal attributes or qualities of the agent, as for example *śávas-* 'strength', *ójas-* 'power', *yáśas-* 'splendour', *táviṣī-* 'force', *śrī́-* 'splendour, excellence'. Concepts like these are scarcely autonomous; they rather pertain to the agent as a person and refer to his disposition. Thus, the use of the A conforms to the general rule.

3.4.4. We shall now comment on some verbs of mental activity, beginning with *cet* 'to perceive, to take care of, to comprehend':

[33] 4.45.6 (A) *víśvām̐ ánu svadháyā cetathas patháḥ*
'Through your own power you perceive all ways.'

[34] 1.128.4 (G_p) *agnír yajñásyādhvarásya cetati*
'Agni takes care of worshipping (and) of the sacrifice.'

A comparison of the attestations of *cet* with other verbs of seeing or optical perception shows that with *cet* the receptive component has considerable strength, compared with those of other verbs such as *darś*, *khyā*, *(s)paś*. With *cet*, the agent does not only concentrate on the perceived object but also reflects its perception. However, on the other hand, the use of local particles (*ánu*, *abhí*, *ā́*, *ví*) in combination with *cet* shows that there is also a relevant degree of agentivity. Thus with *cet* we have a coexistence of receptive and agentive features, and this concurrence of two semantic features corresponds to the concurrence of G_p and A as cases of the second argument. A sign of slightly differing degrees of agentivity vs. receptivity in the text's concrete instances is that with goal-oriented local particles only the A is used (see example [33]).

3.4.5. *bodh* 'to be regardful of' (act.)

[35] 6.23.7 (A) *sá no bodhi puroḷā́śaṃ rárāṇaḥ*
'Generously pay attention to our offering cake!'

[36] 2.16.7 (G) *kuvín no asyá vácaso nibódhiṣat*
'Will he not attend to this word of ours?'

The active instances of this verb, with the meaning 'to be regardful of', are more relevant than the middle which means 'to wake up'. As Gotō (1987: 220) and Kümmel (2000: 332) noticed, both of these meanings can be explained as exponents of a primary meaning 'to become attentive, observant'. This meaning illustrates that – in contrast to other verbs of perception – the receptive component is more prevailing than the agentive-dynamic component. Therefore, the use of the G_p cannot surprise – in contrast to, e.g. *khyā* 'to see, to catch sight of' or *(s)paś* 'to see, to look, to spy', which can only be construed with the accusative. Moreover, it is worth noting that with *bodh* the second complement, if it is animate, only appears in the G_p (3.14.7 *suráthasya*; 6.21.5 *avamásya*; 8.9.3 *kāṇvásya*), whereas inanimate second complements can be expressed in both the G_p and the A (see examples [35] and [36] above). This distribution, again, shows the relevance of conceptual autonomy or the second complement's capability of reaction, respectively. This capability is greater with animate than with inanimate concepts; therefore, only the former can be expressed in the G_p.

3.4.6. *man* 'to remember, to think up, to imagine'
The distribution of A (31 instances) vs. G_p (5 instances; see examples [24] and [25] in **3.1** above) allows the conclusion that with this verb the agentive-dynamic component is stronger than with *bodh* because the two cases are inversely distributed.

However, the fact that both cases are documented after all shows that we, nevertheless, have to distinguish between stronger and weaker dynamicity of the verb or – inversely – stronger and weaker conceptual autonomy of the second complement. Explicitly, this difference can be observed in the following distribution: With *man*, the A can designate affected as well as effected objects,[24] whereas only affected objects are encoded in the G. The concept of 'effected object' already entails that this type of object is more strongly incorporated in the dynamicity of the verb than an 'affected' object. However, in this case we must remain cautious: because there are only 5 attestations of G_p with *man*, it cannot be excluded that an effected object in the G_p is only lacking by chance, particularly since effected objects are generally rarer than affected ones.

3.4.7. We conclude this overview with two verbs of class **f** 'to be glad of, to enjoy'. First we will look at *kan^i/can^i* 'to be glad of':

[37] 8.31.1 (G_p) *brahméd índrasya cākanat*
'The brahmin will be glad of Indra.'

---

[24] See the effected object in ex. (25) and also in 5.35.8 *stómam* ; 5.66.3 *suṣṭutím*; 8.29.10 *sā́ma*.

[38] 3.28.5 (A) *ágne tṛtī́ye sávane hí kā́niṣaḥ*
puroḷā́śaṃ sahasaḥ sūnav ā́hutam
'At the third pressing, o Agni, you should be glad of the offered cake, o son of strength!'

This verb is admittedly an unequivocal example of class **f**, but because of the small number of examples for each case of the second complement (A, G, I, L; see the survey in **3.2**), it is not possible to work out reliable factors determining the second argument's choice of case.

3.4.8. *tarp* 'to enjoy'

[39] 4.46.2 (G_p) *vā́yo sutásya tṛmpatam*
'Vāyu [and Indra], enjoy [of] the pressed out (Soma)!'

[40] 8.70.10 (A) *tvānído ní tṛmpasi*
'You devour completely those mocking you.'

As can be seen from the basic meaning of this verb as well as its use in these sentences, it represents a borderline case between classes **a** and **f**, but the numerical relation of A and G (see the table in **3.2**) better fits class **f** than class **a**. Even if -similarly to *kan^i/can^i* – the few attestations of this verb in the RV cannot suffice to yield reliable results,[25] it is congruent with our general observation that the only attested example [40] with A, because of the metaphorical use of the verb, represents a very high degree of patient-oriented dynamicity, whereas this degree in the instances with G_p, as in [39], is relatively low; here the subject shows more features of an experiencer than of an agent.

[25] In post-Ṛgvedic Sanskrit also the stem *tṛ́pya-* is attested, which takes the I, G_p, and A (see Kulikov 2001: 407ff.).

3.5. At this point we shall summarize the most important results for the G_p in group 2-sentences:

a. In this group, the verbal action refers to the nominal concept in its totality but affects it only partially (**3.3**).

b. As in group 1, so also in group 2, the G_p designates only the 'internal argument'.

c. In contradistinction to group 1, the opposition between A and G_p with the verbs of group 2 is not privative. Rather, the use of the A or the G_p respectively depends on the balance between the patient-oriented dynamicity of the verb on the one hand and the patient-like concept's ability to react on the other hand (**3.3**). This balance changes heavily from one verb to the next and causes very different relations between both cases and the verbs in the classes **d–f** (**3.2**).[26]

[**Addendum:** After submitting this article, I recieved a manuscript by Eystein Dahl, entitled 'Semantic and pragmatic aspects of object alternation in Old Vedic', in which different conclusions are drawn about the alternation between accusative and genitive in Old Vedic. Any comment on the contents of this paper must be delayed to another occasion.]

REFERENCES

BRUGMANN, Karl 1911. *Vergleichende Laut-, Stammbildungs- und Flexionslehre nebst Lehre vom Gebrauch der Wortformen der indogermanischen Sprachen*, II.2: *Zahlwörter*. 2nd edition. Strassburg: Trübner.

CHANTRAINE, Pierre 1953. *Grammaire homérique*, II: *Syntaxe*. Paris: Klincksieck.

DELBRÜCK, Bertold 1888. *Altindische Syntax*. Halle: Verlag des Waisenhauses.

[26] I am indebted to Annick Payne for correcting my English text.

——— 1893. *Vergleichende Syntax der indogermanischen Sprachen*, I. Strassburg: Trübner.

GAEDICKE, Carl 1880. *Der Accusativ im Veda*. Breslau: Koebner.

GOTŌ, Toshifumi 1987. *Die "I Präsensklasse" im Vedischen. Untersuchungen der vollstufigen thematischen Wurzelpräsentia*. (Österreichische Akademie der Wissenschaften, Philosophisch-Historische Klasse, Sitzungsberichte, 489.) Wien: Verlag der Österreichischen Akademie der Wissenschaften.

——— 2002. Funktionen des Akkusativs und Rektionsarten des Verbums – anhand des Altindoarischen. In: H. Hettrich (ed.), *Indogermanische Syntax. Fragen und Perspektiven*: 21–42. Wiesbaden: Reichert.

HAUDRY, Jean 1977. *L'emploi des cas en védique*. PhD dissertation, Université de Lille III.

HETTRICH, Heinrich 2004. Zu Konstruktion und Bedeutung der Wurzel [1]*man* im Ṛgveda. In: Th. Krisch, Th. Lindner & U. Müller (eds.), *Analecta homini universali dicata. Arbeiten zur Indogermanistik, Linguistik, Philologie, Politik, Musik und Dichtung: Festschrift für Oswald Panagl zum 65. Geburtstag*, I: 75–83. Stuttgart: Heinz.

HILL, Eugen 2004. *Die Aorist-Präsentien des Indoiranischen. Untersuchungen zur Morphologie und Semantik einer Präsensklasse*. Habilitationsschrift, Ludwig-Maximilians-Universität München.

HOPPER, P. J., & S. A. THOMPSON 1980. Transitivity in grammar and discourse. *Language* 56: 251–299.

JAMISON, Stephanie W. 1983. *Function and Form in the* -áya-*Formations of the Rig Veda and the Atharva Veda*. Göttingen: Vandenhoeck & Ruprecht.

KRISCH, Thomas 2006. RIVELEX. *Rigveda-Lexikon*, I. (Grazer Vergleichende Arbeiten, 20.) Graz: Leykam.

KÜMMEL, Martin Joachim 2000. *Das Perfekt im Indoiranischen*. Wiesbaden: Reichert.

KULIKOV, Leonid 2001. *The Vedic -ya-presents*. PhD dissertation Universiteit Leiden.

LAKOFF, G. 1987. *Women, Fire and Dangerous Things. What Categories Reveal About The Mind*. Chicago: Chicago University Press.

LEVIN, Beth & Malka RAPPAPORT HOVAV 1995. *Unaccusativity. At the Syntax-Lexical Semantics Interface*. Cambridge/Mass.: MIT Press.

ROESLER, Ulrike 1997. *Licht und Leuchten im Ṛgveda. Untersuchungen zum Wortfeld des Leuchtens und zur Bedeutung des Lichts* Swisttal-Odendorf: Indica et Tibetica-Verlag.

SEEBOLD, Elmar 1973. Die Stammbildungen der idg. Wurzel **u̯eid-* und deren Bedeutungen. *Die Sprache* 19: 20–38 & 150–163.

WACKERNAGEL, Jacob 1909. Akzentstudien I. *Nachrichten der Akademie der Wissenschafen in Göttingen*, Philologisch-Historische Klasse: 50–63. [= J. Wackernagel, *Kleine Schriften*, II: 1108–1121. Göttingen: Vandenhoeck und Ruprecht, 1955.]

ZIFONUN, Gisela *et al.* 1997. *Grammatik der deutschen Sprache*, II. Berlin: W. de Gruyter.

Vedic Verb Accent Revisited*

HANS HENRICH HOCK

1. INTRODUCTION

As is well known, the general rule for the accentuation of (simple, non-prefixed) finite verbs in early Vedic is that dependent-clause (DC) verbs are accented, while main-clause (MC) verbs are unaccented; see [1a]. The main exception is initial MC position, which obeys a general rule that elements after a major prosodic break must be accented; hence [1b]. (Other exceptions, which are motivated by poetic prosody or by discourse considerations, are ignored. For fuller details see Klein 1992; Hock 1996.)

[1] a. [*tásmai víśaḥ svayám evā́* ***namante***]$_{MC}$
[*yásmin brahmā́ ... pū́rva* ***éti***]$_{DC}$ (RV 4.50.8)
'Even the common people bow to him for whom the brahmin goes first.'

b. ***áhann*** *áhim* (*ánv apás tatarda*) (RV 1.32.1cd)
'He slew the dragon (he bored out the waters after him).

So far, the most successful historical explanation of the accent difference between MCs and DCs has been that of Klein

* I am grateful to Jared Klein and Elizabeth Tucker for organizing the Linguistics Sessions at the 2006 World Sanskrit Conference and for dedicating them to the memory of Murray B. Emeneau. I have benefited from comments by Hassan Rezai Baghbidi, Stephanie Jamison, and Paul Kiparsky which have helped me sharpen some of my arguments.

(1992). In this paper I propose a further refinement of Klein's account. Instead of a prosodically conditioned accent loss in utterance-final MC verbs, I argue for accent retraction in the same context, with accent loss an indirect consequence of univerbation. Moreover, unlike earlier approaches (including Klein's), I account not only for the accentuation of simple, unprefixed verbs, but also of combinations of verbs and prefixes. The account is productive, in that it provides a simpler explanation of the commonly compared Ancient Greek accent retraction on finite verbs, as well as offering an explanation for the accentuation of augmented structures and certain Vedic forms of reduplicated presents.

Before discussing Klein's account and my proposed refinement, let me briefly examine earlier attempts to explain the difference between MC and DC verb accentuation. The major focus will be on the work of Delbrück, the most prolific writer on the subject.

2. EARLIER VIEWS

A number of accounts consider the DC verb accentuation marked, indicating that the DC proposition is incomplete and needs to be completed by the MC.

Delbrück (1871: 97–98) attributes DC accentuation to two factors applying in preposed DCs. First, the final DC verb expresses a 'Spannung' ('suspense'); and second, DC verbs, being more important than MC verbs, are more likely to be accented. MC verbs, by contrast, remain unaccented. He further claims that the contrast was exploited by the grammarians in lieu of what we achieve by punctuation. Delbrück even provided a presumed parallel for the 'Spannungs'-effect, namely the German expression in [2], with accent on DC-final *nützt*. (A similar argument is found in Hirt 1937: 124–125.)

[2] *Was man nicht **nützt**, ist eine schwere Last.*
'What one does not **use** is a heavy load.'

Although Delbrück repeated his 'Spannungs'-idea in 1878 (p. 77), he soon abandoned it, long before Whitney quite justifiably rejected Delbrück's claim that the DC : MC contrast is the work of the grammarians. More important for present purposes, Whitney also found fault with Delbrück's alleged parallel by pointing to German sentences like [3], where *ist*, the final verb of the DC, is not accented (Whitney 1892: 278–279).

[3] *Was uns nicht* ***nützlich*** *ist, belastet uns.*
'What is not **useful** for us, weighs us down.'

In fact, the problem is even greater, for unmarked German verb accentuation is not sensitive to clause type but to transitivity and to the nature of the verb's complements if any. In this sense, German is quite similar to English, in spite of its different clause structure. See the selected examples in [4]. Normal German sentence intonation, therefore, does not provide plausible parallels for the Vedic accent difference between MCs and DCs.

[4]	a.	*Wer nicht* ***lebt*** *...*	*Sie* ***leben*** *nicht*
		Who doesn't **live** ...	They don't **live**
	b.	*Wer nicht nach* ***Hause*** *geht ...*	*Sie gehen nicht nach* ***Hause***[1]
		Who doesn't go **home** ...	They don't go **home**
	c.	*Wer ein* ***Haus*** *baut ...*	*Sie bauen ein* ***Haus***
		Who builds a **house** ...	They build a **house**

[1] Manfred Krifka (personal communication 2004) has alerted me to the fact that German differs from English as regards transitive constructions. While the accentuation in [4c] is unmarked in German sentences with generic or indefinite direct objects, constructions with definite direct objects appear to allow two different patterns, as in [i] and [ii]. Of these, the type [i] seems to involve a reading of the direct object as given or old information, while [ii] seems appropriate as an out-of-the-blue utterance. This is an issue which deserves further investigation. Fortunately, it does not affect the present argument. (See also Krifka 2005.)

[i]	*Wer das Haus* ***sieht*** *...*	***Er sieht*** *das Haus*
[ii]	*Wer das* ***Haus*** *sieht...*	*Er sieht das* ***Haus***

A further problem, not addressed by Whitney, is the assumption that non-accentuation of MC verbs is basic or inherited. This view came to be advocated by Wackernagel (1892: 425–434, similarly e.g. Hirt 1937: 125–126) who argued that the MC verb was enclitic in Proto-Indo-European. Wackernagel further claimed that because of its enclitic nature, the MC verb regularly was in second position, although he felt the need for some reservations regarding forms of more than two syllables. Wackernagel's evidence for his claim includes examples of the type [5] and [6], as well as the view that verb-second position was inherited in Germanic.

[5] Gk. *Alkíbios anéthēken kitharōidòs* ... (CIA 1:357)
'Alkibios, the kithara-player, placed [me/this].'
[6] Ved. *sá hovāca gā́rgyaḥ* (ŚB 15.5.1.1 and similarly passim)
'Said Gārgya ...'

As shown by Delbrück (1900: 61–62) and Hock (1982b), structures of the type [5] and [6] are highly marked and do not furnish conclusive evidence for second position in PIE. In fact, the type [5] is an excellent example of Gonda's 'amplified sentence' (1959), with the appositive *kitharōidòs* postposed after the verb. Early Germanic evidence, likewise, is not in favor of the allegedly original, unmarked clitic verb-second position; see Hock 1982a with references and especially Pintzuk's work (e.g. Pintzuk & Kroch 1989; Pintzuk 1991). In fact, the evidence strongly suggests that Proto-Indo-European had SOV or verb-final constituent order; see e.g. Watkins 1976; Hock 1992 for recent discussions. Non-accentuation in main clauses, therefore, must be accounted for as secondary, not as inherited.

In 1878 Delbrück proposed a new explanation for MC non-accentuation; see [7].

[7] *Da* ***der Satzschluss stets schwach betont ist*** [my emphasis], *und das Verbum regelmässig im Satzschluss steht, so ist der häufigste Zustand des Verbums die Unbetontheit. Dieser häufigste Zustand nun wird so zu sagen zu seiner inhärirenden Eigenschaft und bleibt auch in Satzgestalten wie sá hovāca Prajā́patiḥ u.ähnl.* (Delbrück 1878: 77)

(Since sentence-final position always is prosodically weak and the verb regularly occurs in sentence-final position, the most common state of the verb is non-accentuation. This most common state becomes, as it were, its inherent property and remains even in structures such as *sá hovāca Prajā́patiḥ*, etc.)

A similar historical explanation of MC non-accentuation is found in Delbrück's next attempt (1888: 50); but he now also offers an account of DC accentuation that involves intonation; see the modern paraphrase in [8].[2] Similar accounts are found in Porzig 1923 and Hettrich 1988 (who mistakenly refers to Delbrück 1878, not 1888).

[8] In canonical order, the verb of the preposed DC has a middling intonational peak, from where the intonation falls toward the end of the MC, accounting for the non-prominence of its finite verb.

This hypothesis, too, was rejected by Whitney, in rather intemperate language and with arguments of disappointing quality (Whitney 1892: 280); see [9].

[9] The whole explanation ... appears to me not so much ingenious as artificial and forced, and altogether wanting in plausibility. As its author abandoned the 1871 form, so we may feel sure that he will hereafter abandon this of 1888. It is better to acknowledge that the law of verbal accentuation in

[2] The older 'Spannungs'-explanation of DC accentuation remains in the synchronic part of his account, renamed 'Erwartung'.

> Sanskrit is thus far an unexplained puzzle than to try to content our minds with any such unsatisfactory solutions as are offered us in these volumes.

Perhaps in light of Whitney's attack on his 1888 position, Delbrück abandoned his explanation in 1900; but curiously enough, he returned to a position quite similar to his 1878 one:

[10] Es ist klar, dass in diesen Fällen die Accentuierung des Verbums ein Zeichen dafür ist, dass noch **etwas zu erwarten** bleibt. Wäre die Äusserung zu Ende, so würde die Stimme am Schlusse (wo das Verbum steht) sinken, so aber ist die Betonung schwebend, **ähnlich wie im Fragesatz**. [my emphasis]
(It is clear that in these cases the accentuation of the verb is a sign that something still remains to be expected. If the utterance were finished, the voice would go down at the end (where the verb is found); but as it is, the intonation is suspended, similar to the question sentence.)

The significance of the 1900 account lies in its comparison of DC intonation with that of questions, a comparison which introduces another important element in the debate: are we to assume that the foundation for DC accentuation lay in a clause-final level intonation, or in a rising intonation? This issue is examined below, in the discussion of Klein's (1992) explanation.

Except for later reiterations of one or another of Delbrück's various claims and a very speculative account by Kuryłowicz (1958: 93), who gratuitously assumes that DC verbs were clause-initial in Proto-Indo-European,[3] the issue of Vedic verb accentuation was not taken up meaningfully again till Klein 1992.

To summarize: in spite of its many different, often mutually contradictory claims, Delbrück's work has introduced certain

[3] However, Kuryłowicz's suggestion that MC non-accentuation is connected with univerbation turns out to be fruitful; see section **5** below.

elements that are worthy of note and that anticipate much of Klein's account. One of these is the (implicit) assumption that DCs precede MCs in unmarked order and that both clauses are verb-final. A second one is the assumption of an intonational rise on the DC-final verb. The third element worthy of note is the claim that the MC verb typically occurs at the end of the complex sentence and that the prosodically weak nature of that position motivates the lack of MC verb accentuation.

Note, however, that in Delbrück's time, these assumptions were rather poorly motivated. The best-supported one concerns verb-finality and DC-MC clause order, for which Delbrück could refer to his study of the *Śatapathabrāhmaṇa* (1878) and his claim that the latter, being prose, has a less marked word and clause order than the earlier language of the mantras. As is well known, later researchers have questioned this claim; see e.g. Friedrich (1975); Lehmann (1974), and Miller (1975). However, recent research confirms Delbrück's perception (see Hock 1997 for word order and Hock 1993 concerning Ṛgvedic peculiarities in relative-clause syntax).

As we have seen in the preceding discussion, things are much more problematic as regards Delbrück's intonational claims. These are issues that are much more successfully addressed by Klein (1992).

3. KLEIN'S ACCOUNT

Klein proposes a prosodic explanation of the non-accentuation of MC verbs as arising in unmarked or 'canonical' constructions with the MC verb in sentence-final position, and with resolution of the conflict between the high pitch of the verb accent and the low pitch of sentence-final falling intonation through loss of verb accent; see [11].

[11] [The lack of accent on MC verbs] cannot be a Wackernagel's Law type enclisis, for nearly all the evidence available indicates that the Indo-European verb occurred in sentence or clause-final position. More likely, it is related to the fact that, as noted by Hock (1986: 105), the cross-linguistically unmarked, most common sentence-intonation pattern is characterized by a falling pitch at the end of the sentence. Because the word-class most frequently situated in sentence-final position ... may be presumed to have been the verb, its accent, which consisted of pitch elevation, may have come into conflict with the normal sentence-final falling pattern and have been lost, once again with the extension of this normal pattern to the minority of instances in which the verb was not sentence-final ... (Klein 1992: 96)

Klein further argues that the DC verb accent arose from an 'intonation rise' on clause-final verbs, 'a kind of anti-final contour indicating that the pronouncement is not finished' (Klein 1992: 21). This pattern, too, was grammaticalized and extended beyond its original context.

Making some allowances for differences in terminology, Klein's argument can be summarized as in [12] (where # indicates sentence-final position, ## utterance-final position, and ↑ intonation rise).

[12] a. Original canonical word order: S O V#
b. Original canonical clause order: DC MC
c. Accentual effects on V: [S O V↑]$_{DC}$ [S O V]$_{MC}$##
[anti-final acct.] [- acct]
d. Grammaticalization, extension to other contexts, such as [1a], where MC precedes DC.

While superficially similar to some of Delbrück's views, Klein's analysis has a better theoretical foundation. First, (implicitly) referring to recent scholarship, it affirms that Proto-Indo-European and early Sanskrit had unmarked SOV order.

Secondly (and again implicitly) it operates with the assumption of a canonical DC-MC clause order, based on the fact that this is cross-linguistically the normal order in SOV languages. Third, it anchors its account for MC verb accent loss in the fact that the cross-linguistically unmarked utterance-final intonation is falling and therefore would create potential conflicts with the high-pitch accent of utterance-final MC verbs. On the latter count, Hock (1986/1991: 105–106) actually provides empirical evidence in terms of Becker's (1977; 1979) explanation of Serbo-Croatian accent retraction. The first stage of this development was the shift of tonal prominence (high pitch) from the word-final mora to the one preceding it, limited to utterance-final position [13b]. This leftward migration of the accent then was extended to non-utterance-final elements, with the ultimate result of a generalized accent retraction. See the summary in [13]. For more recent, and more comprehensive discussion of such 'finality' effects in numerous languages, both on accent and on word-final vowels, see Hock 1999; 2005.

[13]	a.	Čakavian	*krãl*^{y}	=	[*kraál*^{y}]	'king'
	b.	Čakavian dial.	*krâl*^{y}	=	[*kráal*^{y}]	##
		vs.	*krãl*^{y}	=	[*kraál*^{y}]	elsewhere
	c.	Štokavian	*krâl*^{y}	=	[*kráal*^{y}]	
			vodá	>	*vòda*	'water'
			etc.			

4. SOME PROBLEMS WITH KLEIN'S ACCOUNT

Similar to Delbrück, Klein accounts for the accent on DC verbs as resulting from a clause-final intonational rise. Such a contour can indeed be observed in natural languages; see [14a]; and as Delbrück observed, it is indeed similar to the common rising intonation of yes/no questions [14b]. But depending on the nature of the preposed DC and/or the following MC, we may find instead a level intonation, or no noticeable special contour at all, as in [14c, d].

[14] a. In that they tear it up ↑ thereby they loosen it.
b. Do they tear it up? ↑
c. When they tear it up → they loosen it.
d. When they tear it up they loosen it.

Now, as is well known, especially since Strunk 1983, the rising intonation of yes/no questions has its Vedic counterpart in pluti, as in [15b]. Strunk's focus was mainly on yes/no questions; with an additional examination of vocatives, imperatives, and the like. What he did not consider in detail is another pattern, whose significance is discussed in Hock 1992. This pattern is found in certain *Aitareyabrāhmaṇa* passages, such as [15a], where the initial DC serves as something like a topic clause, and where rising intonation followed by a prosodic break would also be appropriate in modern languages such as English. Significantly, in the written version of passages such as [15a] the clause-final pluti-form is always followed by a daṇḍa, indicating a major prosodic break in the original oral tradition. Even within the *Aitareyabrāhmaṇa*, however, passages of the type [15a] are in the minority; normally, preposed DCs are not marked by final pluti and daṇḍa; see e.g. [15c], which may correspond to either [14c] or [14d].

[15] a. *taṃ yan* ***nabhayantī3m̐*** | *śrathayanty evainaṃ tat* (AB 6.24.2)
'In that they tear it up ↑ thereby they loosen it.'
(Other examples: AB 3.18.3, 5, 6; AB 6.23.9; 24.1, 2; 25.5 [2x], 7; 27.4; 28.6, 8; 32.3, 13; 33.9, 12; 36.15 [2x].)
b. *adháḥ svid* ***āsī́3d*** *upári svid* ***āsī3t*** (RV 10.129.5)
'Was there a below? ↑ Was there an above? ↑'
c. *sa yat prathamaṃ ṣaḍ vālakhilyānāṃ sūkthāni viharati prāṇaṃ ca tad vācaṃ ca viharati* (AB 6.24.10)
'In that he inverts the six hymns of the vālakhilyas for the first time thereby he reverses breath and speech.'

Put differently, the Vedic evidence suggests that DC-final rising intonation corresponds to pluti, not simply to verb accentuation, and that it is rare or marked, while the normal tonal or intonational characteristic of DCs is simple verb accentuation. Note moreover that, as accented texts show, the rising intonation of pluti optionally imposes a high-pitch accent on the last syllable of the word, as in the first instance of *āsī́3d* in [15b], while normal DC verb accentuation falls on the etymologically expected syllable (as in *ā́sīd* with accent on the first syllable).

Under the circumstances, the assumption that the DC verb accentuation preserves the etymologically underlying accent, inherited (in most cases) from Proto-Indo-European, is the simpler hypothesis.

As for Klein's assumption of utterance-final accent loss on the MC verb, I will in the rest of this paper argue for an alternative prosodic analysis which better accounts not just for Vedic MC verb accentuation, but also for word-initial default accent on certain verbs in Vedic, as well as the well-known recessive finite-verb accent of Ancient Greek.[4]

5. AN ALTERNATIVE, ACCENT-RETRACTION ACCOUNT

The starting point for this account is a different response to the conflict between intonation-final low pitch and the high pitch associated with word accent. Rather than assuming, with Klein, that the conflict was resolved by eliminating MC or utterance-final verb accent altogether, I hypothesize a resolution in terms of accent retraction. Moreover, following the preceding discussion I assume that the DC verb accent is simply a retention of the

---

[4] In all fairness, it must be stated that Klein's account constitutes just an appendix to a much broader study of the interesting and highly complex issue of finite verb accentuation conditioned by discourse considerations and/or poetic prosody.

original accent in canonical non-utterance-final position. See the summary in [16].

[16]			
a.	Original canonical word order:	S O V#	
b.	Original canonical clause order:	DC	MC ##
c.	Accentual effect:	$[S\ O\ V]_{DC}$	$[S\ O\ V]_{MC}$ ##
		[underlying acct.]	[acct. retraction]

Let us now turn to specific arguments in favor of the hypothesis that MC verb-finality at first resulted in accent retraction, not accent loss.

There is a well-known cross-linguistic tendency for verbs to receive less prominence in context than nouns or noun phrases in the same prosodic domain. The relevant prosodic domain typically is the Rheme or Comment, which complements the utterance-initial Theme or Topic. Thus in the examples in [4], the verb is relatively non-prominent in rheme structures with nominal goals [4b] or objects [4c]. For general discussion see Bing 1979; Ladd 1980; Schmerling 1976.[5]

There is a similar cross-linguistic tendency for utterance-final position to be prosodically the weakest, presumably because of the effect of the low, falling pitch of utterance-final intonation; see e.g. Ladd 1996.

In SOV languages, with canonical DC–MC clause order and canonical clause-final position of finite verbs, the combined effect of these two tendencies is that MC-final finite verbs are prosodically especially weak (see Ladd 1996: 192–193)[6] and may therefore be the target of a wide range of changes affecting both

[5] In structures like [4a], by contrast, with no nominal in the rheme domain, the verb is accented.

[6] Referring to Hayes & Lahari 1991, Ladd considers Bengali (Bangla) an exception to this tendency, but Dutta & Hock (2006) show that Bangla does conform to expectations. In fact, it avoids prominence on the verb even in intransitive constructions corresponding to the German and English structure in [4a].

suprasegmental aspects (accent etc.) and segmental ones (final vowel loss); see Hock 1999; 2005.

While this evidence would be compatible with either Klein's final deaccentuation or my accent retraction hypothesis, Becker's (1977; 1979) account of the Serbo-Croatian accent system shows that accent retraction is indeed a viable alternative.

An even more direct, and striking parallel for accent retraction, rather than accent loss, on utterance-final finite verbs is found in Modern Persian (Farsi)[7], a language with canonical verb-final order. In this language, MC/utterance-final finite verbs undergo accent retraction, thereby contrasting with the general default word-final accent of Farsi. See the simplified summary in [17], based on Lazard 1957; 1989; Windfuhr 1987, and interviews with Ali Darzi, a recent University of Illinois Ph.D. in linguistics.[8]

[17] a. Absolute-final verbs with 'normal intonation' have accent retraction; see [18a].
Note that the domain of retraction is the verb phrase, not just the verb.

b. MC verbs tend to generalize accent retraction (grammaticalization), even when preposed; see [18b].

c. MC verbs that are not utterance-final tend to have the normal, default word-final accent; e.g. colloquial [18c].

d. Rising intonation is found in preposed DCs, followed by noticeable intonational breaks, and also in questions, e.g. [18d, e].

---

[7] Similar phenomena seem to be found in other Iranian languages, see Blau 1989: 329 for Kurdish; Lecoq 1989: 346 for Sivandi; Payne 1989: 428 for Wakhi; a similar situation is suggested by Ruhlen's (1976) description of Tati. Unfortunately, these descriptions are not as detailed as those available for Farsi.

[8] I am grateful to Hassan Rezai Baghbidi for confirming the accentual and intonational observations. As he notes, some of the examples in [18] would be slightly different in a more colloquial variety of Farsi. However, I decided to retain the transcriptions given by Lazard and Windfuhr.

e. Preposed DC verbs exhibit variation. One tendency is to get an intonational break with rising intonation, and for rising intonation in this context to impose a final high tone on the DC verb, as in the first two DCs in [18d]. A second tendency is for the verb to have default word-final accent, as in [18f], presumably because the preposed DC is not utterance-final.

f. Utterance-final verbs in postposed DCs have accent retraction; e.g. [18b].

[18] a. ***ná***-*xāham raft*
'I will not go'

b. [*rast-aš **ín** ast*]MC [*ke **púl** nà-dār-am*]DC
'The truth (of it) is that I have no money.'

c. *mi**rám** Tehrún*
'I go to Tehran.'

d. *har vaqt mosāferát mi**rán*** ↑
*agar māl-i cīz-i dā**rán*** ↑,
*yā áhl-o a'yal-eṣun-ro miā**rán***
[*dáss-e mán mispāran*]MC
'Each time they leave for a trip, whatever they possess, something, or their family, they place confidently into my hand.'

e. *hanúz harekat **ná**kardi* ↑
'Haven't you gone yet?'

f. *àgar be-rav-**ád**, kàs-i digàr níst*[9]
'If he goes, there will be no-one left.'

As can be seen from [17] and [18], the state of Farsi verb accentuation is still in flux and has not been fully grammaticalized; but the observable tendencies are at least partly convergent with what we need to postulate for pre-Vedic. While MC verbs in canonical clause-final position do exhibit grammaticalized accent retraction, irrespective of whether the clause follows or precedes the DC ([18d] beside [18b]), postposed, hence utterance-final DCs have accent retraction, too [18b]. Preposed DC verbs, however,

---

[9] The lack of retraction in MC-final *níst* (= neg. *n*[*a*] + copula) reflects the fact that the negative particle normally blocks further accent retraction.

usually do not have accent retraction, but retain the normal word-final accent of Farsi [18d, f]. Interestingly, as in Vedic, they may optionally exhibit an additional intonational rise which, to judge by Lazard's description and what I have observed myself, is similar to Vedic pluti.

For the prehistory of Vedic, all we need to assume is that the grammaticalization has gone one step farther, with accent retraction on all MC verbs (except clause-initially), and with basic, underlying accent in all DC verbs, irrespective of whether they are preposed or postposed. (In addition, of course, DC-final verbs may optionally receive rising-pitch, pluti intonation.) The grammaticalization may be considered motivated by the same considerations as the grammaticalization of verb-second vs. verb-final order in German, Dutch, and Frisian MCs and DCs, namely as a means of further differentiating the clause types, beyond the differentiation in terms of DC conjunctions and/or relative pronouns and adverbs.

Following an idea of Kuryłowicz (1958), the more general Vedic distinction between MC and DC verb accentuation, with lack of accent on (non-initial) MC verbs, can then be explained as resulting from an interaction between MC accent retraction and the univerbation of verbs and prefixes.

The assumption of incipient (dialectal) Proto-Indo-European univerbation is, I believe, justified by the fact that even the earliest texts contain prefix-verb combinations whose meaning cannot be derived from the meanings of the component parts, such as Vedic *ā́* + *dā* (middle voice) 'take'.

The starting point is utterance-final accent retraction in canonical MC structures [19]. This retraction operates for both simple and prefixed verbs. In canonical DC structures, by contrast, no retraction takes place. The underlying accent remains in simple verbs. In prefixed verbs, possibly by polarization to the MC pattern, the original double accent on prefix and verb tends to be resolved in favor of accent only on the verb. In fact, traces of the original double accentuation of prefix and verb still remain in the *Ṛgveda*; see the examples in [20]. (The interaction of prefix and verb accent actually is more complex; see section **6** below.)

[19]	(Dialectal) Proto-Indo-European:	Without prefix	With prefix
	(Canonical) MC pattern:	**yú-n-g-enti*	*pró=yu-n-g-enti* (accent retraction)
	(Canonical) DC pattern:	**yu-n-g-énti*	*pro=yu-n-g-énti* (underlying accent)

[20] a. *yá ā́hutim pári véda námobhiḥ* (RV 6.1.9c)
'He who fully understands the oblation with signs of reverence ...'

b. *tváyā yáthā gṛtsamadā́so agne*
gúhā vanvánta úparām̐ abhí ṣyúḥ (RV 2.4.9ab)
'So that through you, Agni, the victorious Gṛtsamadas may secretly overcome the rivals ...'

On the way to Vedic, the MC : DC distinction was grammaticalized and, in the process, the MC and DC verb accentuations were polarized by extending the lack of accent on verbs preceded by prefix to the non-prefixed verbs in MCs; see [21]. No further change is required for DC verbs.

[21]	Development into Vedic:	Without prefix	With prefix
	MC pattern:	**yú-ñ-j-anti* → ***yu-ñ-j-anti*** (verb unaccented)	*prá=yu-ñ-j-anti*
vs.	DC pattern:	*yu-ñ-j-ánti* (verb accented)	*pra=yu-ñ-j-ánti*

Following a suggestion by Tista Bagchi (personal communication February 2005), we may hypothesize that this change in unprefixed verbs may have been helped by the synchronic version of tmesis, the (still) optional separation of prefix and verb.

What may have been especially important in this process were structures of the type [22], where simple verbs are fronted (for narrative or dramatic purposes) and where parallel prefixed verbs undergo partial fronting through tmesis. The 'stranded' verbs of structures of this type (such as the *adatta* in [22]) would provide surface instances of unaccented verbs which could be taken to legitimate the development in [21].

[22] *ā́ sā́yakam maghávādatta vájram*
áhann enam prathamajā́m áhīnām (RV 1.32.3ab)
'Indra took the weapon, the cudgel; he slew him, the first-born of dragons.'

6. FURTHER REMARKS ON THE INTERACTION OF PREFIX AND VERB ACCENTUATION

The account in the preceding section is based in large measure on the usual, idealized view of the interaction of prefix and verb accentuation, an account which in large measure reflects that of Pāṇini. As the examples in [20] show, however, one of the usual assumptions, namely that prefixes are always unaccented in DCs (while the verb is accented) is not entirely correct for the *Ṛgveda*. It is only in the late Vedic stage of the *Śatapathabrāhmaṇa* that we find the situation described by Pāṇini.[10] In this section I provide a preliminary, but more comprehensive discussion of the

---

[10] The relevant sūtras are as follows:
- *tiṅ atiṅaḥ* (8.1.28) 'a finite verb is unaccented unless initial (8.1.18), if not preceded by a finite verb.'
- *yadvṛttān nityam* (8.1.66) 'a finite verb always is not [8.1.29] unaccented in combination with a form of the pronoun yad.'
- *gatir gatau* (8.1.70) 'a prefix is unaccented [8.1.67] before another prefix.'
- *tiṅi codāttavati* (8.1.71) 'also before a verb that is accented [by 8.1.66 and other rules].'

Hence MC *abhyúddharati* (8.1.28 + 8.1.70) vs. DC *abhyuddhárati* (8.1.66 + 8.1.70 + 8.1.71)

accentuation of prefixes and verbs.[11] I intend to present a fuller investigation elsewhere.

So far, the most comprehensive account seems to be that of Delbrück (1888: 46–48).

Unfortunately, that account does not properly distinguish between the various relevant positions. Closer examination reveals that there are certain positions in which prefixes are always accented. These are tmesis (whether initial or embedded within the line or clause) and placement after the verb; see the examples in [23].

[23] a. Prefix in tmesis, line-initial:
ví ṣū́ cara svadhā́ ánu
kr̥ṣṭīnā́m ánv āhúvaḥ (RV 8.32.19ab)
'Go forth according to (your) desire,
according to the calls of the people.'

b. Prefix in tmesis, embedded:
(í)ndro asyā áva jabhāra (RV 1.32.9b)
'Indra brought down (his weapon) on her.

c. Prefix placed after the verb:
gámad vā́jebhir ā́ sá naḥ (RV 1.5.3c)
'Let him come to us with prizes.'

It is only in configurations where a prefix, or several prefixes (usually two) directly precede the verb that the question arises as to which element is accented – verb or prefix, or if more than one prefix, which ones.

For the *R̥gveda* the following generalizations hold. In MCs the norm is accent on the prefix or prefixes and non-accentuation of the verb; see [24a]. It is only in a few double-prefix combinations, where the second prefix is *ā́* (in one case *áva*), that only the

[11] I am grateful to Stephanie Jamison for alerting me to the need for this discussion.

second prefix is accented; see [24b].[12] We can distinguish the two types as (Ṕ) Ṕ V vs. P Ṕ V. While in the *Ṛgveda* the latter type is quite limited, it becomes the norm in the late Vedic *Śatapatha-brāhmaṇa* [24c].

[24] a. *dyumnaír abhí prá ṇonumaḥ* (RV 1.78.1c)
'We call forth to (you) with splendor.'
b. *tā́bhir no adyá sumánā upā́gahi* (RV 2.32.5c)
'... with these come up to us today with good intention.'
c. *tat svar evaitad ato'bhivipaśyati* (ŚB 1.1.1.21)
'So it is at the sun that he now looks from here.'

In DCs the situation is more complex yet. With single prefixes we find two patterns, with accent on both prefix and verb [25a] vs. accent only on the verb [25b]. Of these, the former type must be archaic (see section **5** above); the second type is the more productive. It is also the only one found in the late Vedic *Śatapathabrāhmaṇa*; see [25c].

[25] a. *tváyā yáthā gṛtsamadā́so agne*
gúhā vanvánta úparām̐ abhí ṣyúḥ (RV 2.4.9ab)
'So that through you, Agni, the victorious Gṛtsamadas may secretly overcome the rivals ...'
b. *yáṁ víśva íd abhiháryanti devā́ḥ* (RV 10.112.6d)
'... which all the Gods rejoice in.'
c. *tad yad apa upaspṛśaty* ... (ŚB 1.1.1.1)
'Now, in so far as he touches the waters ...'

In double-prefix configurations, we find three different patterns which might be characterized as Ṕ Ṕ V́ vs. Ṕ P V́ vs. P P V́; see [26a, b, c]. The pattern with accent on both prefixes is most

---

[12] Even in configurations with *ā́*, non-accentuation of the first prefix is not obligatory. Note for instance *sthaśó jánmāni savitā́ vyā́kaḥ* [Padapāṭha: *ví ā́ akar ity akaḥ*] (RV 2.38.8d) 'Savitṛ has divided the creatures according to their position'.

likely to be archaic, reflecting a time before MC : DC accent polarization. The third type is the norm in the late Vedic *Śatapatha-brāhmaṇa* [26d] and therefore no doubt represents the latest stage in the development.

[26] a. *yát sīm ánu prá mucó badbadhānā́ḥ* (RV 4.22.7c)
'… when you (Indra) released them (who were) hemmed in.'

b. *yátrābhí saṁnávāmahe* (RV 8.69.5c)
'… where we shout together with (them).'

c. *yáṁ víprāḥ … (a)bhipramandúḥ …* (RV 8.12.13ab)
'Whom the poets … have gladdened…'

d. *sa yān evopāva̱rttate …* (ŚB 1.1.1.11)
'Now, those to whom he turns …'

If we accept the assumption that the starting point lay in an interaction of MC accent retraction and univerbation, we can at least make a start at trying to account for the various patterns. The account which I present here is one of two competing, possibly complementary explanations that I can think of; I have chosen it for inclusion in this paper because of its formal 'elegance'.

As noted earlier, in configurations with single prefix, the MC pattern Ṕ V resulting from accent retraction led to a polarization of corresponding DC configurations, such that original Ṕ V́ (marginally preserved in examples such as [25a]) changed to P V́, as in [25b].

In multiple-prefix combinations, the developments are more complex. Let us start with the DC type Ṕ P V́ in [26b], which must be an innovation for the earlier type Ṕ Ṕ V́ in [26a], but does not survive into late Vedic. We can motivate this type as resulting from the effects of the 'Obligatory Contour Principle' (OCP), which seeks to avoid a succession of high tones or pitch accents within a given phonological or morphological domain (see Prince & Smolensky 2004 for a recent discussion). The change in

[27], then, would eliminate a violation of the OCP in the domain of prefix-verb combinations.

[27] Ṕ Ṕ V́ > Ṕ P V́

The incipient Ṛgvedic change from the MC type [24a] to [24b] can then be attributed to a parallel application of the OCP, as in [28].

[28] Ṕ Ṕ V > P Ṕ V

The final stage of the DC development (Ṕ P V́ > P P V́) can be explained as resulting from a combination of two factors. First, univerbation is complete, and the general rule that single words (normally) have only one accent becomes applicable. Second, the domain in which MC and DC accentuation can be expressed becomes limited to the verb and the immediately preceding prefix (if any).

7. FURTHER REMARKS AND CONCLUSIONS

Let us now see what the accent retraction hypothesis buys for us.

First, it makes it possible to account not only for the Vedic accentuation of simple finite verbs, but also of prefix-verb combinations, including multiple-prefix structures.

Second, postulating a dialectal PIE stage of verb-accent retraction in canonical MC/utterance-final position provides the most direct explanation for the well-known accent retraction on Greek finite verbs. The usual assumption (e.g. Schwyzer 1939: 389–390) is that there was first an accent loss comparable to what we find in Vedic and then re-accentuation with a 'dummy', retracting accent. The present hypothesis provides a simpler account: Greek accent retraction is simply a continuation of (dialectal) PIE accent retraction (within the limits imposed by the well-known Greek accent restriction to the last three syllables). See the summary in [29]. Under either analysis, of course, we need to assume an extension from MC-final position to all other occurrences of the finite verb.

[29] PIE **di / e-déO-mi* : Gk. *dí-dō-mi* 'I give'

a. Usual assumption: **didṓmi > *didōmi > dídōmi*
(with accent loss, followed by retracting dummy accent)

b. This proposal: **didṓmi > dídōmi*
(with generalized accent retraction, starting utterance-finally)

Third, the present hypothesis provides a historical explanation, rather than simply a description, of the fact that at least two classes of verb inflection exhibit a default accent on the first syllable of the word (see Kiparsky & Halle 1977 for a generative-phonological description which, however, extends beyond Vedic and Greek).

One of these classes consists of augmented past-tense forms, such as *áyajata* 'sacrificed for himself; was the yajamāna', which in accented contexts (DCs and clause-initially in MCs) consistently accent the first-syllable augment, rather than the syllable which, by the rules of Indo European ablaut and accent, should bear the accent (in this case, *yaj*).

The other class consists of Vedic verbs which, from the Indo-European perspective, lack a full-grade syllable for the accent to anchor to, and which have default accent on the first syllable, as in [30].[13] Both of these cases can be explained as continuations of MC verbs with accent retraction to the first syllable, which then were extended to DCs as well. (Ironically, of course, this pattern was subsequently eliminated in non-initial position in MCs as the result of the generalization of unaccented forms.)

---

[13] The present account presupposes that accent retraction took place quite early in the prehistory of Sanskrit and Greek, at a time when ablaut and accent were still strongly correlated. I am grateful to Paul Kiparsky for bringing up this issue of chronology.

[30] 3 pl. pres. *bí-bhr-ati* < **bi-bhr-n̥t-i* 'they carry'
(with zero-grade ending and zero-grade root)
vs. *yu-ñ-j-ánti* < **yu-n-g-ént-i* 'they yoke'
(with full-grade ending)
śé-re < **k̂éy-ro-y* 'they lie, sleep'
(with full-grade root)

The hypothesis that the Vedic opposition between accented DC and (non-initial) unaccented MC verbs started out as a contrast between DC verbs with underlying accent and (non-initial) MC verbs with accent retraction, thus, not only is paralleled by a similar development in Farsi; it is also productive, in that it provides a simpler historical account for Greek accent retraction as well as a historical explanation of initial accent in augmented forms and Vedic third-person plural forms of reduplicated presents.

REFERENCES

BECKER, Lee A. 1977. Leftward movement of high tone. Paper at the 1977 Annual Meeting of the Linguistic Society of America.

——— 1979. A contribution to an explanation of the Neo-Štokavian accent retraction. *Zbornik za filologiju i lingvistiku* 22.1: 87–94.

BING, Janet M. 1979. Up the noun phrase: another stress rule. In: Elisabet Engdahl & Mark J. Stein (eds.), *Papers Presented to Emmon Bach by His Students*: 14–31. Amherst: University of Massachusetts Graduate Linguistics Student Association.

BLAU, Joyce 1989. Le kurde. In: Rüdiger Schmitt (ed.), *Compendium linguarum iranicarum*: 327–335. Wiesbaden: Reichert.

DELBRÜCK, Bertold 1871. *Der Gebrauch des Conjunctivs und Optativs im Sanskrit und Griechischen.* (Syntaktische Forschungen, 1.) Halle: Waisenhaus.

——— 1878. *Die altindische Wortfolge aus dem Çatapathabrāhmaṇa dargestellt.* (Syntaktische Forschungen, 3.) Halle: Waisenhaus.

——— 1888. *Altindische Syntax.* (Syntaktische Forschungen, 5.) Halle: Waisenhaus.

——— 1900. *Vergleichende Syntax der indogermanischen Sprachen*, 3. (*Grundriß der vergleichenden Grammatik der indogermanischen Sprachen*, 5, by Karl Brugmann & Berthold Delbrück.) Strassburg: Trübner.

DUTTA, Indranil & Hans Henrich HOCK 2006. Interaction of verb accentuation and utterance finality in Bangla. In: Rüdiger Hoffmann & Hansjörg Mixdorff (eds.), *CD-ROM Proceedings of Speech Prosody. 3rd International Conference, Dresden, May 2–5, 2006*. (Studientexte zur Sprachkommunikation, 40.) Dresden: UD press.

FRIEDRICH, Paul 1975. *Proto-Indo-European Syntax. The Order of Meaningful Elements*. (Journal of Indo-European Studies, Monograph, 1.) Butte, Mont.: Journal of Indo-European Studies.

GONDA, Jan 1959. On amplified sentences and similar structures in the Veda. In: J. Gonda, *Four Studies in the Language of the Veda*: 1–70. The Hague: Mouton.

HAYES, Bruce & Aditi LAHIRI 1991. Bengali intonational phonology. *Natural Language and Linguistic Theory* 9: 47–96.

HETTRICH, Heinrich 1988. *Untersuchungen zur Hypotaxe im Vedischen*. Berlin: de Gruyter.

HIRT, Hermann 1937. *Indogermanische Grammatik*, VII: *Syntax* II. Heidelberg: Winter.

HOCK, Hans Henrich 1982a. AUX-cliticization as a motivation for word order change. *Studies in the Linguistic Sciences* 12.1: 91–101.

——— 1982b. Clitic verbs in PIE or discourse-based verb fronting? Sanskrit *sá hovāca gā́rgyaḥ* and congeners in Avestan and Homeric Greek. *Studies in the Linguistic Sciences* 12.2: 1–38.

——— 1986/1991. *Principles of historical linguistics*. 1st and 2nd edition. Berlin: Mouton de Gruyter.

——— 1992. Reconstruction and syntactic typology: a plea for a different approach. In: G. W. Davis & G. K. Iverson (eds.), *Explanation in Historical Linguistics*: 105–121. Amsterdam: Benjamins.

——— 1993. Some peculiarities of Vedic-Prose relative clauses. *Wiener Zeitschrift für die Kunde Südasiens* 35, Supplement 1993: 9–29.

——— 1996. Who's on first: toward a prosodic account of P2 clitics. In: A. Halpern & A. Zwicky (eds.), *Approaching Second. Second Position Clitics and Related Phenomena*: 199–270. Stanford: CSLI Publications.

——— 1997. Chronology or genre? Problems in Vedic syntax. In: Michael Witzel (ed.), *Inside the Texts – Beyond the Texts. New Approaches to the Study of the Vedas* (Harvard Oriental Series, Opera Minora, 2): 103–126. Cambridge, Mass.: Harvard University Press.

——— 1999. Finality, prosody, and change. In: O. Fujimura, B. D. Joseph & B. Palek (eds.), *Proceedings of LP '98*: 15–30. Prague: The Karolinum Press.

——— 2005. The Insular Celtic absolute: Conjunct distinction once again – A prosodic proposal. In: Karlene Jones-Bley *et al.* (eds.), *Proceedings of the Sixteenth UCLA Indo-European Conference. Los Angeles, Nov. 5–6, 2004* (Journal of Indo-European Studies Monograph, 50): 153–172. Washington: Institute for the Study of Man.

KIPARSKY, Paul, & Morris HALLE 1977. Toward the reconstruction of the Indo-European accent. In: Larry Hyman (ed.), *Studies in Stress and Accent* . (Southern California Occasional Papers in Linguistics, 1.): 209–238.

KLEIN, Jared S. 1992. *On Verbal Accentuation in the Rigveda*. (American Oriental Society Essay, 11.) New Haven, Conn.: American Oriental Society.

KRIFKA, Manfred 2005. Accentuating and deaccentuating arguments. Talk presented at 'Weak Words: Their Origins and Progress', 14–17 April 2005, Schloss Freudental near Konstanz. (Abstract at: http://ling.uni-konstanz.de/pages/home/a20_11/Weak_Words=Abstracts.pdf)

KURYŁOWICZ, Jerzy 1958. *L'accentuation des langues indo-européennes*. 2nd edition. Wrocław: Zakład Narodowy Imienia Ossolinskich, Wydawnictwo Polskiej Akademii Nauk.

LADD, D. Robert 1980. *The Structure of Intonational Meaning. Evidence from English*. Bloomington: Indiana University Press.

——— 1996. *Intonational Phonology*. Cambridge: Cambridge University Press.

LAZARD, Gilbert 1957. *Grammaire du persan contemporain*. Paris: Klincksieck.

——— 1989. Le persan. In: Rüdiger Schmitt (ed.), *Compendium linguarum iranicarum*: 263–293. Wiesbaden: Reichert.

LECOQ, Pierre 1989. Les dialects du sud-ouest. In: Rüdiger Schmitt (ed.), *Compendium linguarum iranicarum*: 341–349. Wiesbaden: Reichert.

LEHMANN, Winfred P. 1974. *Proto-Indo-European Syntax.* Austin: Univ. of Texas Press.

MILLER, D. Gary 1975. Indo-European: VSO, SOV, SVO, or all three? *Lingua* 37: 31–52.

PAYNE, John 1989. Pāmir languages In: Rüdiger Schmitt (ed.), *Compendium linguarum iranicarum*: 417–444. Wiesbaden: Reichert.

PINTZUK, Susan 1991. Phrase structures in competition: variation and change in Old English word order. Unpublished Ph.D. dissertation, Univ. of Pennsylvania.

PINTZUK, Susan & Anthony S. KROCH 1989. The rightward movement of complements and adjuncts in the Old English of Beowulf. *Language Variation and Change* 1: 115–143.

PORZIG, Walter 1923. Die Hypotaxe im Rigveda. Erstes Stück: Die durch das Pronomen *ya-* charakterisierten Sätze und syntaktischen Gruppen in den älteren Büchern des Rigveda. *Indogermanische Forschungen* 41: 210–303.

PRINCE, Alan & Paul SMOLENSKY 2004. *Optimality Theory. Constraint Interaction in Generative Grammar*. Malden, Mass.: Blackwell.

RUHLEN, Merritt 1976. *A Guide to the Languages of the World*. Stanford, Calif., Stanford University Press.

SCHMERLING, Susan 1976. *Aspects of English Sentence Stress*. Austin: University of Texas Press.

SCHWYZER, Eduard 1939. *Griechische Grammatik*, I. München: Beck.

STRUNK, Klaus 1983. Typische Merkmale von Fragesätzen und die altindische Pluti. *Sitzungsberichte der Bayerische Akademie der Wissenschaften, Phil.-hist. Klasse*, 1983: 8.

WACKERNAGEL, Jacob 1892. Über ein Gesetz der indogermanischen Wortstellung. *Indogermanische Forschungen* 1: 333–436.

WATKINS, Calvert 1976. Towards Proto-Indo-European syntax: problems and pseudo-problems. In: Sanford B. Steever, Carol A. Walker & Salikoko S. Mufwene (eds.), *Papers from the Parasession on Diachronic Syntax, April 22, 1976*: 305–326. Chicago: Linguistic Society.

WHITNEY, William Dwight 1892. On Delbrück's Vedic syntax. *American Journal of Philology* 13.3: 271–306.

WINDFUHR, Gernot 1987. Persian. In: Bernard Comrie (ed.), *The World's Major Languages*: 523–546. New York: Oxford University Press.

The Development of the Vedic Perfect: from Anterior Present to Inferential Past*

EYSTEIN DAHL

1. INTRODUCTION

This paper examines the semantic development of the Vedic Perfect Indicative. In Early Vedic, the language of the *Ṛgveda*, this inflectional category vacillates between a present anterior-resultative and a past perfective meaning in a sense to be defined below (cf. Kiparsky 1998; Kümmel 2000; Dahl 2008; 2009; 2010). In Late Vedic, the language of the later Vedic prose texts, the Perfect Indicative is mainly used in remote past contexts to denote situations which have not been directly witnessed by the speaker, but are reported on the basis of indirect or secondary evidence as for instance hearsay (cf. Cardona 2002; Dahl 2012). In the following, I shall refer to the broader semantic domain concerning the indication of information source as 'evidentiality'

* The present paper is a substantially revised version of my paper 'The relationship between lexical aspect and grammatical tense in the Vedic verbal system' presented at the Linguistics session at the 13th World Sanskrit Conference in Edinburgh July 14th 2006. I thank the audience for critical comments and suggestions after the presentation, in particular Stephanie Jamison, Hans Heinrich Hock, Vit Bubenik and Werner Knobl. I am also grateful to Eva Tichy and Martin Kümmel for discussions on some of the various topics which are dealt with in this paper and to Paul Kiparsky, Jared Klein and Elizabeth Tucker for reading and commenting on preliminary versions of the manuscript. I alone remain responsible for theoretical idiosyncracies and philological weaknesses.

and the particular type of evidentiality which involves indicating that the report is based on indirect evidence as 'inferential' or 'indirect evidential'. I have discussed some aspects of this development in a shorter and more formally oriented paper (Dahl 2009). Here I consider a broader range of data and attempt to refine some of the ideas developed in that paper. It should be noted from the outset that the results presented here are based on an examination of a limited set of sources from each period of the language and that I am currently planning a more careful and exhaustive evaluation of the data from the different stages of Vedic. Nevertheless, the tendencies I describe here seem to be fairly robust, even though they may have to be slightly revised when a larger set of data is taken into consideration.

The paper is organized as follows. Section **2** outlines the theoretical framework within which the analysis of the Vedic data is couched, defining basic notions such as tense, aspect and evidentiality. Section **3**, which constitutes the main part of the paper, contains a discussion of the data from the different linguistic stages of Vedic. Section **4** contains a summary and a conclusion.

2. SOME BASIC INGREDIENTS FOR THE SEMANTIC ANALYSIS OF GRAMMATICAL CATEGORIES IN DEAD LANGUAGES

As this paper aims at giving a principled account of the semantic development of the Vedic Perfect Indicative, an essential preliminary task consists in devising a method to evaluate the semantic properties of morphosyntactic categories in dead languages. In this section I introduce and define some key notions which enable a principled evaluation of the temporal, aspectual and modal value of a given category in a given language at a given time.[1]

---

[1] See Dahl 2008: 28–161 and 2010: 29–96 for a more thorough discussion of the theoretical and empirical basis for the claims made in this section.

The diachronic dimension of the present endeavour, on the other hand, mainly consists in comparing the behaviour of the Perfect Indicative at the various stages of Vedic, a task which presupposes that a synchronic analysis is in place, but does not in itself demand any special conjectures, apart from the intuitively rather reasonable assumption that an inflectional category maintains a basic identity through time which may be expected to be constant given no evidence to the contrary. The first part of this assumption is corroborated by the fact that the development of grammatical categories generally tends to follow certain patterns which are largely predictable from their semantic specification at an early stage in their history (cf. e.g. Bybee *et al.* 1994; Traugott & Dasher 2005). Semantic change often involves a process where an element of meaning which at an early stage represents one context-dependent reading in a cluster of readings associated with a given category in the course of time becomes more closely associated with that category, gradually eliminating its other readings and eventually becoming part of its semantic specification. Another frequent pattern of change consists in what has traditionally been called semantic bleaching, that is, the gradual erosion of a specific semantic feature, resulting in a more general category of a similar semantic type which is compatible with a broader range of discourse contexts. Note that there is a certain tension between these two types of semantic change, as the first represents a development from a general to a more specific category, whereas the second represents a development from a specific to a more general category. Nevertheless, both play an important role in the semantic evolution of verbal categories.

It is uncontroversial that tense markers are typically used to locate situations in time relative to a deictic point of reference (cf. Comrie 1985: 2–18). The default deictic centre of most tense systems is the time of speech, something which is motivated by the fact that linguistic communication is speaker-centred. Simple tense relations like past, present and future may simply be understood in binary terms, expressing that an event is located prior to, simultaneous with or after the moment of utterance. However, Reichenbach (1947: 287ff.) demonstrated that two points are not sufficient to account for more complex temporal relations and distinguished three temporal parameters which have points as their basic value, namely *speech time* or the time of the actual utterance, *event time* or the run time of the situation denoted by the verbal predicate and *reference time* or the time spoken about. In this paper I rely on a modified version of the Reichenbachian framework which distinguishes a separate perspective time parameter in addition to the three original temporal parameters and takes the parameters to refer to intervals, points being treated as minimal intervals (cf. Dowty 1979: 138–139; Kamp & Reyle 1993: 593–600; Kiparsky 1998: 37–39; Dahl 2008: 66–91; 2010: 46–96). Perspective time is understood as the temporal perspective of the speaker and thus typically coincides with speech time, but it can be shifted by morphosyntactic and contextual factors, for instance in constructions with shifted deixis, the historical present and so-called extended flashbacks (cf. Kamp & Reyle 1993: 593–600; Eberle & Kasper 1994: 156–160; Kiparsky 1998: 37–39; Smith 2004: 597–599). The hypothesis that four rather than three temporal parameters are involved in the analysis of temporal structure is able to account for a broader range of temporal relations and thus has an edge on the model originally proposed by Reichenbach.

Another tenet of this model is that different tense and aspect categories predicate different relations between the temporal parameters. Some important relations are precedence (A – B reads 'A precedes B'), overlap ($A \otimes B$ reads 'A overlaps with B') and inclusion ($A \subseteq B$ reads 'A is included in B', $A \subset B$ reads 'A is properly included in B'). Following Wolfgang Klein (1994; 1995) and Kratzer (1998) I understand *tense* as a set of possible relations holding between Reference Time (t_R) and Perspective Time (t_P) and *aspect* as a set of possible relations holding between

Event Time (t_E) and Reference Time. Some important tense and aspect relations are defined in Table 1 below:

TABLE 1
Some important tense and aspect relations

	Tense Categories			**AspectCategories**			
Name	Present	Past	Future	Neutral	Imperfective	Perfective	Perfect/ anterior
Temporal structure	$t_P \subseteq t_R$	$t_R - t_P$	$t_P - t_R$	$t_R \otimes t_E$	$t_R \subseteq t_E$	$t_E \subseteq t_R$	$t_E - t_R$

According to this theory, the four temporal parameters represent an obligatory part of the temporal interpretation of sentences in natural language. This assumption implies that sentences always have a temporal as well as an aspectual meaning.

I further assume that verbal predicates may be regarded as descriptions of different types of situations in somewhat the same manner as nouns may be regarded as descriptions of different types of individuals (cf. Parsons 1990: 6ff.). Elaborating on Vendler (1957), Dowty (1979), Verkuyl (1993), Dini & Bertinetto (1995), Olsen (1994), Smith (1997), Rothstein (2004) and others I distinguish six basic verb classes with different aspectual properties, namely States, Activities, Instantaneous Achievements, Semelfactives, Achievements and Accomplishments. These verb classes differ with regard to three different privative semantic features namely whether they denote a change of state or not [+Change of State], whether they are dynamic or not [+Dynamic] and whether they are punctual or not [+Punctual]. Accordingly, the semantic difference between the six situation types may be schematically represented as in Table 2 below (after Dahl 2008: 58; cf. also Dahl 2010: 40):

TABLE 2
The semantic features of the situation types

	[+Change of State]	[+Dynamic]	[+Punctual]
'States'			
'Activities'		+	
'Instantaneous Achievements'	+		+
'Semelfactives'		+	+
'Achievements'	+		
'Accomplishments'	+	+	

Although the lexical semantic properties of verbs clearly are central for the aspectual interpretation of sentences in natural language, there is a growing consensus that the quantificational properties of the verbal arguments also play an important role in this respect (cf. e.g. Krifka 1998). I therefore suggest that the six situation types on the verb level may be reduced to three situation types at verb phrase level, namely states, processes and telic events. State predicates are typically underspecified for dynamicity as they are exclusively derived from state verbs. They are compatible with a dynamic reading under given circumstances, for instance when they have a specifically quantified second argument. Process predicates, on the other hand, denote a dynamic process and are derived from activity verbs, semelfactive verbs, instantaneous achievement verbs, achievement verbs and accomplishment verbs. This group of predicates is characterized by the absence of the specific quantity feature and they are basically atelic. Some processes have an incremental theme which is not specifically quantified, e.g. *build houses*. Finally, there is a group of predicates I will label 'telic events' which are derived from instantaneous achievement verbs, achievement verbs, accomplishment verbs and from derived accomplishment predicates. They have a specifically quantitified internal argument and predicate an incremental relation between the situation and its internal argument. Some telic event predicates are inherently specified for dynamicity, others are not. Table 3 contains a summary of the semantic properties of the situation types at verb phrase level.

TABLE 3

The semantic features of the situation types at verb phrase level

	Dynamic	Incremental Theme	Specific Quantity
States			
Processes	+	(+)	
Telic events	(+)	+	+

Moreover, I assume that the temporal, aspectual and modal specification of a given verbal category at a given stage systematically determines its synchronic morphosyntactic behaviour, giving rise to a cluster of lexically and contextually conditioned readings and determining their compatibility with different types of adverbs. Cross-linguistic studies like Östen Dahl 1985 and Smith 1997 have established that there is a striking correspondence between the sets of readings associated with particular tense and aspect categories in genetically unrelated languages (cf. also Bybee & Dahl 1989). This may be taken as an indication that it is possible to identify a restricted universal inventory of tense and aspect categories which differ with regard to a limited number of lexically and contextually determined readings. On this assumption, the various readings associated with a given category in a given language provide important evidence as to its semantic properties and thus represent a crucial tool for the study of semantics and semantic change in dead languages like Vedic. Although two or more semantically distinct categories in many cases will have one or more readings in common, the present framework minimally presupposes that two typologically different categories differ with regard to the availability or non-availability of one reading. A reading which distinguishes two typologically distinct categories may accordingly be characterized as 'typologically relevant'. In some cases, a particular reading is peculiar to a language-specific realization of a given grammatical category, in the sense that the category is not normally associated with that reading. I shall refer to such readings as 'typologically significant'.

From what I have said so far, it remains unclear how the notion of inferentiality can be accounted for within this framework. To understand this notion we need a few additional assumptions, the most important of which is that assertive clauses implicitly refer to what may be called a world or modality argument in addition to a tense and an aspect argument. I understand a 'world' to be a set of propositions, 'context' to be the situation of the utterance and 'modality' to be a set of functions mediating between worlds and contexts (cf. e.g. Kratzer 1981: 41–51; Chierchia & McConnell-Ginet 2000: 330–331). The default world of evaluation in a given context will be referred to as the 'Common Ground' (cf. Stalnaker 2002).

At this point we need to distinguish two similar, but conceptually different dimensions of modality in the above sense. Epistemic modality is typically understood as a type of relation specifying the relative probability or possibility of the state of affairs to which the sentence refers. It is therefore tempting to understand inferentiality and evidentiality more generally as a special type of epistemic modality, but it is questionable whether this is correct. In her cross-linguistic study of evidentiality systems, Aikhenvald notes that evidential markers may co-occur with indicative as well as non-indicative markers of any type (Aikhenvald 2004: 257). This is a clear prima facie indication that realis/irrealis modality and evidentiality in the sense of indication of information source constitute two separate semantic dimensions. I take the notion of modality to include epistemic and deontic modality as well as indication of information source. This choice is motivated by the fact that some languages use the same set of forms to express irrealis modality and indirect information source. Consider for instance the Latin subjunctive, which is used as an irrealis marker and as a marker of indirect speech.

Simplifying matters slightly, I shall assume that different strategies for indicating that a given report is based on secondary or indirect evidence consist in binding the world argument of the sentence. In contrast, irrealis markers typically involve specifying to what extent the speaker considers a given proposition to be compatible with the Common Ground (cf. Kratzer 1981: 43–51). In this way, evidentiality and epistemic modality are ascribed different domains within the broader semantic field of modality.

3. THE DEVELOPMENT OF THE VEDIC PERFECT INDICATIVE

This section examines the semantic properties of the Vedic Perfect Indicative through the different stages of Vedic. It consists of five subsections. In section **3.1**, I outline a relative chronology of the Vedic texts which constitutes the diachronic frame of reference for the following investigation. Sections **3.2** through **3.5** discuss the morphosyntactic behaviour of the Perfect Indicative in Early Vedic, Early Middle Vedic, Middle Vedic and Late Vedic respectively.

3.1. The chronological stages of Vedic

The extant corpus of Vedic texts is rather voluminous and one may distinguish at least four distinct chronological stages of Vedic, namely *Early Vedic*, *Early Middle Vedic*, *Middle Vedic* and *Late Vedic*. I have chosen the term Early Vedic for the language of the oldest extant Vedic text, the *Ṛgveda* (RV). Early Vedic represents the oldest attested stage of Indo-Aryan and generally has an archaic character. Early Middle Vedic, on the other hand, is conceived of as the language of the youngest layers of the *Ṛgveda*, the Śaunakīya and Paippalāda versions of the *Atharvaveda* (AVŚ, AVP) and the mantra parts of the other Saṃhitās, most notably *Taittirīyasaṃhitā* (TS^{M}), *Maitrāyaṇīsaṃhitā* (MS^{M}) and *Kāṭhakasaṃhitā* (KS^{M}). Middle Vedic is represented by the language of the prose parts of the Saṃhitās, e.g. *Taittirīyasaṃhitā* (TS^{P}), *Maitrāyaṇīsaṃhitā* (MS^{P}), *Kāṭhakasaṃhitā* (KS^{P}) and of the older Brāhmaṇa prose, e.g. *Aitareyabrāhmaṇa* (AB 1–5) and *Śatapathabrāhmaṇa* (ŚBM 6.1–10.5). Finally, Late Vedic is understood as the language of the prose parts of the younger Brāhmaṇa prose, e.g. *Aitareyabrāhmaṇa* (AB 6–10), *Śatapathabrāhmaṇa* (ŚBM 1–5, 10.6–14.3) and *Kauṣītakibrāhmaṇa* (KB), of some Āraṇyakas, e.g. *Taittirīyāraṇyaka* (TĀ 7–9) and of some older Upaniṣads, e.g. *Bṛhadāraṇyaka-Upaniṣad* (BĀU = ŚBM 10.6.4.1–6.5.8, 14.4.1–9.4) and *Chāndogya-Upaniṣad* (ChU).

Although this relative chronology largely corresponds to the chronological framework developed in Witzel (1987; 1989; 1995a; 1995b), it differs from the latter in some details. First, I have generally chosen to regard the language of the *Ṛgveda* as one linguistic stage in spite of the fact that this text seems to consist of different chronological layers. In particular, the first and tenth book of the *Ṛgveda* are generally taken to represent a somewhat younger linguistic stage than the other books, but they nevertheless seem to contain material which is probably not any younger than that found in the other books (cf. e.g. Gonda 1975: 12; Witzel 1995b: 308–313). As the use of the Perfect Indicative is relatively consistent through the *Ṛgveda*, with some important exceptions which will be discussed below, the general discussion does not seem to lose much by simplifying the chronological framework slightly. In general, however, I consider the hymns and/or verses of the *Ṛgveda* which are also found in the *Atharvaveda* as relatively young and possibly belonging to Early Middle Vedic, apart from the hymns found in the twentieth book of the Śaunakīya version of the *Atharvaveda* (AVŚ) which is generally acknowledged to be a secondary addition to the other books in this collection (cf. Gonda 1975: 269).

Another point where the present framework differs from Witzel's chronology regards the status of the language of the Sūtras which he characterizes as Late Vedic (Witzel 1995a: 97). Although some of the texts belonging to this genre clearly are older than others and show a certain affinity to the younger Brāhmaṇa-texts, it is questionable whether the Sūtras in general should be considered as Vedic in a strict sense. Within the Indian tradition these texts are regarded as *smṛti*, i.e. as traditional (sacred) knowledge unlike the Vedas, Brāhmaṇas, Āraṇyakas and Upaniṣads which are regarded as *śruti*, i.e. as (divinely) revealed knowledge and these groups of texts should therefore be treated separately (cf. e.g. Gonda 1975: 34). Moreover, in most of the Sūtras it is the content and not the language which constitutes the link between these texts and the other Vedic texts (cf. Witzel 1989: 127). Finally, the Sūtras generally contain few finite forms, so that they do not constitute a fruitful set of sources for exploring the semantic properties of the Perfect Indicative. I therefore choose to exclude these texts from the present investigation, hence reserving the term 'Late Vedic' for the language of the younger Brāhmanas and the older Upaniṣads. Apart from these slight modifications, the following discussion is in accordance with Witzel's chronology.

3.2. The Perfect Indicative in Early Vedic

This section discusses the semantic properties of the Early Vedic Perfect Indicative. The present account draws heavily on previous works in this field (e.g. Kiparsky 1998; Kümmel 2000 and Mumm 2002), but differs from them in some important respects. I make two slightly controversial claims here. First, I argue that the Perfect Indicative is used as a proper past tense already in the *Ṛgveda* (pace Hoffmann 1967: 160; Kümmel 2000: 78), a property I regard as relatively young within this corpus. Second, I demonstrate that the Perfect Indicative is used with an inferential-like meaning in certain environments (*pace* Job 1994: 58; cf. also Dahl 2008: 350–379; 2009; 2010: 368–371). I have argued at considerable length elsewhere that the Early Vedic Aorist Indicative represents a past perfective category at this stage, whereas the Imperfect has a past neutral (or possibly imperfective) meaning and I cannot repeat the arguments here (cf. Dahl 2008: 221–251, 280–311; 2010, passim; Dahl, forthcoming (a) & (b)). Suffice it to say that the three past tenses compete in intricate ways, as there is considerable functional overlap between them, even though they clearly have distinct aspecto-temporal properties. Whereas the aspecto-temporal reference of the Imperfect remains fairly stable through the various stages of Vedic, the Aorist Indicative develops from a general past perfective category via an absolute perfective past category in Early Middle Vedic and a recent past category with a perfective aspectual character in Middle Vedic to a recent past category with a neutral aspectual character in Late Vedic (cf. Dahl 2013 for a detailed account of this development). Although the semantic development of the Perfect Indicative cannot be fully understood without considering its synchronic position within the verbal system in the various stages of Vedic, a full-scale investigation along these lines will have to be postponed to another occasion. I will, however, occasionally point out how the aspecto-temporal competition between the Perfect Indicative and the other two past tenses affects the synchronic behaviour of the former.

As regards the typologically relevant readings of the Early Vedic Perfect Indicative, it is commonly acknowledged that it can be used to express that a state resulting from the completion of an event of the type specified by the verb phrase holds at speech time, a reading I shall henceforth refer to as 'resultative'. The resultative reading gives rise to a recent past implicature when Perfect Indicative forms of the relevant type are modified by adverbs like *nūnám* 'now', *nú* 'now' or *adyá* 'today'. Consider the following examples:

[1] a. *alā́yyasya paraśúr* ***nanāśa***
tám ā́ pavasva deva soma ǀ
ākhúṃ cid evá deva soma (RV 9.67.30)
'Alāyya's axe has disappeared. O divine Soma, carry it hither by your flow, that which is (hidden) like a mole, divine Soma!'[2]

b. ***úpa*** *nūnáṃ* ***yuyuje*** *vṛ́ṣaṇā hárī*
ā́ *ca* ***jagāma*** *vṛtrahā́* (RV 8.4.11cd)
'Now the Vṛtrakiller has yoked his two bay horses and has come hither.'[3]

c. *vayáṃ te adyá* ***rarimā́*** *hí kā́mam*
uttānáhastā nämasā upasádya
yájiṣṭhena mánasā yakṣi devā́n
ásredhatā mánmanā vípro agne (RV 3.14.5)
'For having sat down extending our hands in homage we have granted you a wish today. You, the sage, will sacrifice to the gods with best-sacrificing mind, with unerring wisdom, Agni.'[4]

---

[2] Cf. Geldner (1951, III: 57): 'Die Axt des Alāya ist verschwunden; die läutere her, Gott Soma, die wie ein Maulwurf (versteckte), Gott Soma!'

[3] Cf. Geldner (1951, II: 289): 'Jetzt hat er sein Falbenpaar, das bullengleiche, angeschirrt und ist hergekommen, der Vṛtratöter.' Kümmel's translation is similar: '*Angeschirrt hat* jetzt seine falben Hengste und her *ist gekommen* der Vṛtratöter (Indra)' (Kümmel 2000: 75).

[4] Cf. Geldner (1951, I: 351): 'Wir haben dich ja heute deinen Wunsch gewährt, indem wir mit ausgestreckten Händen unter Verbeugung uns zu

The above definition of 'resultative' presupposes that this reading only arises with telic event predicates, as only predicates of this type can represent a situation as completed in the sense that it reaches an inherently specified endpoint. Perfect Indicative forms of instantaneous achievement verbs typically denote a state which holds at speech time and only implicitly refer to a causing event, thus having a simple present value (cf. e.g. Kiparsky 1998: 33; Kümmel 2000: 69–70). Perfect Indicative forms like *veda* 'I know, he knows' from *VED-* 'find out' and *ciketa* 'I am aware, he is aware' from *CET-* 'perceive, find out' represent paramount examples of this reading, which is commonly referred to as 'the present state reading'. This reading is peculiar to the Early Vedic Perfect Indicative and may be regarded as typologically significant (cf. also Kiparsky 2002: 113). Consider the following passages:

[2] a. ***vidmā́*** *hí tvā vásupatiṃ vásūnām* (RV 3.36.9b)
'For we know you as the good lord of riches.'[5]

b. *etā́ni dhī́ro niṇyā́* ***ciketa***
pṛ́śnir yád ū́dho mahī́ jabhā́ra (RV 7.56.4ab)
'The wise one knows (lit. 'has perceived') these secrets: that the great Pṛśni has borne an udder.'[6]

Third, Perfect Indicative forms of atelic predicates typically denote a situation which has extended from some indefinite time in the past and still holds at speech time, a reading which may be labelled 'universal'. It may be illustrated by the following examples:

---

dir setzen. Mit opfertätigsten Sinn opfere den Göttern, mit nie fehlendem Nachdenken als der beredte, o Agni.'

[5] Cf. Geldner (1951, I: 378): 'Wir kennen dich ja als den Herrn der Güter.'

[6] Cf. Geldner (1951, II: 231): 'Diese Geheimnisse kennt der Weise, dass die große Pṛśni (sie) im Euter getragen hat.' Kümmel's translation: 'Diese Geheimnisse kennt der Weise, daß die große Pṛśni ein Euter getragen hat.' (Kümmel 2000: 175).

[3] a. *śáśvad dhí vaḥ sudānava*
ā́dityā ūtíbhir vayám
purā́ nūnám ***bubhujmáhe*** (RV 8.67.16)
'For we have continuously enjoyed your refreshing favors, o munificent Ādityas, both earlier and now.'[7]

b. *satrā́ te ánu kṛṣṭáyo*
víśvā cakréva ***vāvṛtuḥ***
satrā́ mahā́m̐ asi śrutáḥ (RV 6.30.2)
'All races of men have always moved after you like wheels. You have always been known as the great one.'[8]

Finally, the Early Vedic Perfect Indicative is sometimes used to denote a situation which has happened once or more at some indefinite past time, a reading which may be labelled 'existential'. It is noteworthy that the Perfect Indicative is generally preferred to the Imperfect and Aorist Indicative in discourse contexts with a past reference time where existential quantifier adverbs like *bhū́ri* 'many times, often', *purudhā́* 'frequently, repeatedly' or *trís* 'thrice' induce a multiple event reading (cf. also Renou 1925: 23; Kiparsky 1998: 33; Dahl 2008: 364; 2010, passim)[9]:

[4] a. *prá va éko* ***mimaya*** *bhū́ry ā́go*
yán mā pitéva kitavám̐ śaśāsá (RV 2.29.5ab)
'I have repeatedly harmed you by offences, on account of which you have chastised me like a father (chastising) a gambling (son).'[10]

---

[7] Cf. Geldner (1951, II: 391): 'Denn immer wieder haben wir uns eurer Hilfen, ihr gütigen Āditya's, einst und jetzt gefreut.' Kümmel translates the passage as follows: 'Denn immerfort haben, ihr guten Geber, o Ādityas, durch eurer Hilfen w i r früher und jetzt Nutzen gehabt' (Kümmel 2000: 72).

[8] Cf. Geldner (1951, I: 457): 'Hinter dir liefen alle Völker insgesamt her wie die Räder (hinter dem Ross). Du bist mit einem Male als der Grosse bekannt.'

[9] Note, however, that the Imperfect as well as the Aorist Indicative are also occasionally modified by existential quantifier adverbs in Early Vedic (cf. Dahl 2008: 248, 310).

[10] Cf. Geldner (1951, I: 313): 'Ich allein habe viele Sünde gegen euch gefehlt, dass ihr mich gezüchtigt habt wie der Vater (den Sohn), der dem Spiele

b. *pravā́cyaṃ śaśvadhā́ vīryaṃ tád*
índrasya kárma yád áhiṃ vivṛścát
ví** vájreṇa pariṣádo **jaghāna
ā́yann ā́po áyanam ichámānāḥ (RV 3.33.7)
'This heroic deed shall always be praised, that deed of Indra, when he killed the dragon. With the mace he split the obstructions. The waters were flowing, searching a course.'[11]

Many scholars have noted that there is a close correspondence between the inventory of readings associated with the Early Vedic Perfect Indicative and the readings of the English Present Perfect (cf. e.g. Kiparsky 1998: 39–45; Kümmel 2000: 65–78; Dahl 2008: 350–378; 2010: 344–372). This is a strong prima facie indication that the Early Vedic Perfect Indicative represents a present anterior category, that is, that it denotes the aspecto-temporal relation 'event time prior to reference time, perspective time included in reference time' ($t_E - t_R$, $t_P \subseteq t_R$).

However, a more thorough examination of the Early Vedic data reveals that the Perfect Indicative has some additional readings which are not available for the English Present Perfect and thus create some problems for the above analysis. For instance, Perfect Indicative forms are sometimes used to denote a situation which has been terminated and/or completed prior to another situation located in the past, a reading commonly labelled 'relative past' and which may be illustrated by the following examples:

[5] a. *índraś ca yád yuyudhā́te áhiś*
*utá aparī́bhyo maghávā **ví jigye*** (RV 1.32.13cd)

---

fröhnt.' Kümmel's translates the passage in the following manner: 'Vermindert habe ich allein euch viel Unrecht, für das ihr mich wie der Vater den Spieler zurechtgewiesen habt' (Kümmel 2000: 368).

[11] Cf. Geldner (1951, I: 371): 'Diese Heldentat ist allezeit zu rühmen, das Werk des Indra, dass er den Drachen zerhieb. Mit der Keule zerschlug er die Schranken; es kamen die Gewasser einen Ausgang suchend.'

'When Indra and the dragon had/*have fought each other, then the bountiful one won completely for all future.'[12]

b. *áhann áhim párvate śiśriyāṇáṃ*
tváṣṭāsmai vájraṃ svaryàṃ ***tatakṣa*** (RV 1.32.2ab)
'He smote the dragon which was lying on the mountain, Tvaṣṭar had/?has fashioned the resounding mace for him.'[13]

c. *mātā́ pitáram ṛtá ā́ babhāja*
dhīty ágre mánasā sáṃ hí ***jagmé*** (RV 1.164.8ab)
'The mother let the father partake in his right share, for she had/*has first come to an agreement (with him) in thought and mind.'[14]

Although this reading is not typically associated with present anterior categories, the above definitions of present tense and anterior aspect do not exclude the possibility that categories with this aspecto-temporal specification may have a relative past reading. By distinguishing a perspective time parameter which is typically identified with, but in some cases independent of speech time, one could analyze the relative past reading of the Early Vedic Perfect Indicative as a shift in temporal perspective triggered by factors in the immediate discourse context. In example [5a] this shift is indicated by the temporal subjunction *yád* 'when'; in [5b] and [5c] it is signaled by a backflash in the narrative, i.e. the situation referred to by the first sentence is temporally posterior to the situation denoted by the second sentence. Although this explanation clearly represents a theoretically possible analysis, I am at present not aware of any other languages

---

[12] Cf. Geldner (1951, I: 38): 'Als Indra und der Drache kämpften, da blieb der Gabenreiche auch für alle Zukunft Sieger.'

[13] Cf. Geldner (1951, I: 36): 'Er erschlug den Drachen, der sich auf dem Berge gelagert hatte. Tvaṣṭṛ hatte ihm die sausende Keule geschmieden.' Note that this verse is also found in the *Atharvaveda* as AVŚ 2.5.6ab and AVP 12.12.2ab.

[14] Cf. Geldner (1951, I: 229): 'Die Mutter macht den Vater seines Rechtes teilhaft, denn sie hatte sich zuvor in ihrem Sinnen und Denken mit ihm geeinigt.' Note that this verse is also found in the *Atharvaveda* as AVŚ 9.9.8ab and AVP 16.66.8ab (the latter has *jajñe* instead of *jagmé*).

where a present anterior category can be used with a relative past value and it therefore suffers from the lack of empirical support. In contrast, past perfective categories are often used in this manner, as for instance the Early Vedic Aorist Indicative (cf. Dahl 2008: 113–114; forthcoming [a] & [b]). Although this fact does not underpin the analysis proposed here, it might indicate that we are faced with a language-specific peculiarity of Early Vedic which could be typologically significant and important for understanding the typology of present anterior constructions.

There is, however, a more severe challenge to the above analysis. In a few cases, Perfect Indicative forms are modified by frame adverbs and other modifiers specifying a definite past reference time, as illustrated by the following example:

[6] *adyā́ mamā́ra sá hyáḥ* ***sám āna*** (RV 10.55.5d)
'Today (the moon) has died. Yesterday he was/*has been alive.'[15]

This example clearly shows that the Early Vedic Perfect Indicative is compatible with an explicit definite past time reference, a temporal relation which is in direct conflict with the assumption that it is a present anterior category (cf. also Östen Dahl 1985: 137). On the basis of the readings which have been identified in the course of the previous discussion it is reasonable to suggest that the Perfect Indicative represents a past perfective category in this period, i.e. that it denotes the aspecto-temporal relation 'event time included in reference time, reference time prior to perspective time' ($t_E \subseteq t_R$, $t_R - t_P$).

However, this assumption likewise runs into a considerable difficulty, as past perfective categories are generally incompati-

[15] Cf. Geldner (1951, III: 219): 'Heute ist er gestorben, gestern hat er noch vollständig geatmet.' Cf. also Kümmel 2000: 96 (also p. 370): 'Heute ist er tot/gestorben – der hat gestern noch geatmet.' Note that this pāda is also found in the *Atharvaveda* as AVŚ 9.10.9d and AVP 16.68.8d.

ble with a universal interpretation (cf. e.g. Smith 1997: 67). Within the framework developed here, this follows from their aspecto-temporal specification which entails that the event time does not last longer than the reference time interval and that the reference time interval ends before speech time. The cluster of readings associated with the Early Vedic Perfect Indicative thus appears to reflect that it represents a basically polysemous category.

The observant reader will have noted that the passages I have cited as evidence for the simple past reading of the Early Vedic Perfect Indicative both belong to the 10th book and that one of them is also found in the *Atharvaveda*, something which indicates that they are relatively young within the Ṛgvedic corpus. Cross-linguistically, present anterior categories strongly tend to develop into past perfective categories (cf. e.g. Bybee *et al.* 1994: 81–87) and one might therefore be tempted to hypothesize that the apparent polysemy of the Perfect Indicative in the *Ṛgveda* in fact reflects two distinct stages of semantic development. At the first stage, Early Vedic proper, the Perfect Indicative represented a present anterior category. At the second stage, represented by the examples in [5] and [6], on the other hand, the Perfect Indicative represented a past perfective category. As most of these passages are also found in the *Atharvaveda*, it is likely that they belong to the Early Middle Vedic period and reflect the fact that the basic aspecto-temporal specification of the Perfect Indicative has changed in this period (cf. also Dahl 2009: 43). Although this explanation does seem to have a circular character, it is not clear to me that its circularity is of a vicious character. On the contrary, I show in section **3.3** below that the Early Middle Vedic Perfect Indicative in fact behaves like a past perfective category (cf. also Dahl 2009: 43).

Finally, I would like to draw attention to a fact which to my knowledge has not been observed earlier, namely that Perfect Indicative forms tend to be preferred when a sentence referring to a past situation is in the scope of a verbum dicendi or other type of direct or indirect attitude verb. The following examples show that *VI-VAC-* 'declare, explain, announce', *VED-* 'know', *PRAŚ-* 'ask' *VI-ŚRAV*$_{mid}$ 'be widely known, famous' all take a sentential complement with a Perfect Indicative form:

[7] a. *tán no ví voco yádi te purā́ cij*
jaritā́ra ***ānaśúḥ*** *sumnám indra* (RV 6.22.4ab)
'Tell us now, whether the singers of old in fact reached your benevolence.'[16]

b. *áthā kó veda yáta* ***ābabhū́va*** (RV 10.129.6d)
'And who knows whence it has arisen?' (J. Klein 1985: 76)[17]

c. *kím devéṣu tyája énaś* ***cakartha***
ágne pr̥chā́mi nú tvā́m ávidvān (RV 10.79.6ab)
'What harm, what sin have you done to the gods, I being ignorant now ask you, O Agni.' [18]

d. *té rāyā́ té suvī́ryaiḥ*
sasavā́ṃso ví śr̥ṇvire
yé agnā́ ***dadhiré*** *dúvaḥ* (RV 4.8.6)
'Enjoying riches and many sons they are widely known who have presented gifts to Agni.'[19]

It should be noted, however, that the Imperfect is also used in this type of environment, although it is much less frequently attested than the Perfect indicative. Consider the examples in [8].

---

[16] Cf. Geldner (1951, II: 121): 'Das sage uns bestimmt, ob auch schon vordem die Sänger deine Gunst erlangt haben, Indra?'

[17] Cf. Geldner (1951, III: 361): 'Wer weiß es dann, woraus sie sich entwickelt hat?'

[18] Cf. Geldner (1951, III: 261): 'Welche Feindseligkeit, welchen Frevel hast du an den Göttern begangen? Agni, ich frage dich nur, weil ich es nicht weiß.'

[19] Cf. Geldner (1951, I: 429): 'Die haben sich durch Reichtum, die durch gute Söhne reichbelohnt einen Namen gemacht, die für Agni Vorliebe hegen.'

[8] a. *víṣṇor nú kaṃ vīry ṇi prá vocaṃ*
yáḥ pā́rthivāni vimamé rájāṃsi |
yó ***áskabhāyad*** *úttaraṃ sadhásthaṃ*
vicakramāṇás trayidhórugāyáḥ (RV 1.154.1)
'I now proclaim the heroic deeds of Viṣṇu who meted out the earthly regions, who made the upper region firm having strode out widely thrice.'[20]

b. *yátrā samudrá skabhitó* ***ví aúnad***
ápāṃ napāt savitā́ tásya veda (RV 10.149.2)
'O Apām Napāt, only Savitṛ knows where the enclosed waters sprang forth.'[21]

From the overall perspective of this paper, it is significant that the Early Vedic Perfect Indicative is preferred in indirect sentences which refer to the semantic past. Intuitively, attitude verbs indirectly relate individuals and propositions, in the sense that they ascribe a certain attitude towards a propositional content to individuals. It is therefore hardly surprising that tense markers tend to be interpreted as bound variables when they are in the scope of attitude verbs, something which is particularly clear in sequence of tense constructions (cf. e.g. Ogihara 1995: 179–189; von Stechow 1995a: 5–6; Abush 1997: 16–20). On the other hand, it is clear that ascribing to someone a certain attitude towards a proposition involves relativizing the propositional content to his or her belief world, something which within the present framework may be understood as binding its world argument (cf. also von Stechow 1995b: 15; Abush 1997: 5–10).

If it is correct that attitude verbs bind the world argument of propositions within their scope, we may conclude that the Early Vedic Perfect Indicative is not only compatible with the semantic

[20] Cf. Geldner (1951, I: 212): 'Des Viṣṇu Heldentaten will ich nun verkünden, der die irdischen Räume durchmessen hat, der die obere Wohnstätte stützte, nachdem er dreimal ausgeschritten war, der Weitschreiter.' The verse is also attested in the *Atharvaveda* as AVŚ 7.26.1 and AVP 20.7.9.

[21] Cf. Geldner (1951, III: 382): 'Wo der befestigte Ozean herausquoll, das weiß nur Savitṛ, o Apām Napāt.'

boundedness of the world argument of a proposition, but even preferred. This is a clear indication that it represented an evidentiality strategy in Early Vedic (cf. Aikhenvald 2003: 18–20). However, this is not to say that the Perfect Indicative may be regarded as an inferential marker in a strict sense at this stage. A characteristic property of first person forms of indirect evidentials is that they tend to imply that the speaker acted non-intentionally or lacked control over what was happening (cf. Aikhenvald 2004: 220). The following examples show that first person Perfect Indicative forms are compatible with the implication that the speaker acted intentionally in Early Vedic, something which strongly suggests that this inflectional category did not represent an evidential marker at this stage (cf. also Job 1994: 45–58).

[9] a. *ihéha yád vāṃ samanā́* ***papṛkṣé***
sā́ iyám asmé sumatír vājaratnā |
uruṣyátaṃ jaritā́raṃ yuvā́ṃ ha
śritáḥ kā́mo nāsatyā yuvadrík (RV 4.43.7)
'As I have here and there bestowed richly upon you two equally, so (let) your favour (be) among us, you two who are rich in rewards: Protect the singer, you two! The wish contained (in this hymn) is directed towards you two, O Nāsatyas.'[22]

b. *víśvā matī́r* ***ā́ tatane*** *tvāyā́*
ádhā ma indra śṛṇavo hávā imā́ (RV 7.29.3cd)
'I have directed all prayers to you. Therefore you will listen to these callings of mine.'[23]

The use of present anterior categories to express that the source of the information is not first hand is well attested cross-

---

[22] Cf. Geldner (1951, I: 476): 'Da ich euch hier und dort in gleicher Weise gestärkt habe, so werde uns diese Gunst, ihr Reichbelohnende: Schützet doch ihr beide den Sänger! Dieser Wunsch ist an euch zwei gerichtet, ihr Nāsatyas.'

[23] Cf. Geldner (1951, II: 206): 'Alle Gedanken habe ich nach dir gespannt; darum höre auf diese Rufe von mir, Indra!'

linguistically and, moreover, represents one of the sources from which indirect evidentiality markers may develop (cf. Aikhenvald 2004: 276–287). The most important finding of this section is that the Early Vedic Perfect Indicative represents a present anterior category which is sometimes used with an inferential reading, but still cannot be regarded as an indirect evidential marker at this stage.

3.3. The Perfect Indicative in Early Middle Vedic

In this section I review the typologically most important readings of the Early Middle Vedic Perfect Indicative. I noted in the previous section that there are some indications in the *Ṛgveda* that the semantic properties of the Perfect Indicative are on the verge of changing from a present anterior to a past perfective aspecto-temporal reference (cf. also Dahl 2009: 41–43). The data discussed in this section corroborate this claim, showing that the Early Middle Vedic Perfect Indicative behaves like a past perfective category.

As regards the temporal reference of the Early Middle Vedic Perfect Indicative, we may note that it is occasionally modified by adverbial and adjectival constructions with a specific past time reference, as illustrated by the following examples:

[10] a. *prathamā́ ha vy ùvāsa sā́ dhenúr abhavad yamé*
(AVŚ 3.10.1ab)
'She first shone out; she became a milch-cow at Yama's.' (Whitney 1905: 99)[24]

---

[24] The assumption that the Perfect Indicative form *uvāsa* 'shone, has shone' has a simple past reading here is strenghtened by the fact that the parallel passage in the *Taittirīyasaṃhitā* has an imperfect form:

yā́ prathamā́ vyáuchat sā́ dhenúr abhavad yamé (TS 4.3.11.5)

'She who first shone forth hath become a cow with Yama.' (Keith 1914: 335)

Compare also the following pāda from another verse of the same mantra:

iyám evá sā́ yā́ prathamā́ vyáuchad

'This same is she that first shone out' (Whitney 1905: 100).

b. *yā́vantāv ágre prathamáṃ sam**eyáthus***
tád vāṃ váyo yamarā́jye samānám (AVŚ 12.3.1cd)
'Of what age ye two first came together in the beginning, let that be your same age in Yama's realm.' (Whitney 1905: 683)

c. *vā́jasya imám prasaváḥ **suṣuve** ágre sómaṁ rā́jānam óṣadhīṣv apsú* (TS^{M} 1.7.10.1)
'In the beginning, the impulse of strength extracted king soma from the herbs and plants.'

Passages like these make a strong case for ascribing the Early Middle Vedic Perfect Indicative a past time reference, something which would imply that it is not a present anterior category at this stage.

As regards its aspectual reference we may note that Perfect Indicative forms of telic event predicates invariably denote a situation which has been completed prior to speech time. In many cases forms of this type are used with a marked resultative meaning. In a few cases the resultative meaning gives rise to a recent past implicature, for instance when a Perfect Indicative form is modified by temporal adverbs like *nú* 'now'. Consider the following examples:

[11] a. *ulū́khale músale yáś ca cármaṇi yó*
vā śū́rpe taṇḍuláḥ káṇaḥ |
*yáṃ vā vā́to mātaríśvā pávamāno **mamā́tha***
agníṣ ṭád dhótā súhutaṃ kṛṇotu (AVŚ 10.9.26)
'What in the mortar, on the pestle, and on the hide, or what rice-grain kernel in the winnowing-basket, or what the wind, Mātariśvan, purifying himself, has taken away – let Agni as hotar make that a well-offered sacrifice.'[25]

---

[25] Cf. Whitney (1905: 604): 'What in the mortar, on the pestle, and on the hide, or what rice-grain [what] kernel in the winnowing-basket, or what the wind, Mātariśvan, blowing (*pū*), shook (*math*) – let Agni as *hótar* make that well-offered.' I follow Kümmel's (2000: 380) translation of the two last pādas: 'Oder den der Wind, Mātariśvan, der sich läuternde, geraubt hat, Agni soll das als Hotar gutgeopfert machen.'

b. *ihá evá sántaḥ práti dadma enaj*
jīvā́ jīvébhyo ní harāma enat |
apamítya dhānyàṃ yáj ***jaghása*** *ahám*
idáṃ tád agne anṛṇó bhavāmi (AVŚ 6.117.2)
'Being here, we give it back, we, the living, offer it to living beings. O Agni, now I become free from this debt for the grain which I have taken away and consumed.'[26]

c. *ā́ imáṃ yajñám ánumatir* ***jagāma***
sukṣetrátāyai suvīrátāyai sújātam |
bhadrā́ hy àsyāḥ prámatir babhū́va
sā́ imám yajñám avatu devágopā (AVŚ 7.20.5)
'Anumati has come unto this excellent sacrifice to grant us abundance of fields and heroes. For her providence has become prosperous (before). Let her, god-shepherded, promote this offering.'[27]

d. *vā́jasya nú prasavé sáṃ babhūvima*
imā́ ca víśvā bhúvanāni antáḥ (AVŚ 3.20.8ab)
'On the impulse of strength we have now come together and (so have) all these beings in the middle.'[28]

Moreover, Early Middle Vedic Perfect Indicative forms of atelic predicates are typically used to denote a single specific situation or a series of situations of the type specified by the predicate which have been terminated at some indefinite time prior to speech time. Consider for instance the following examples:

[12] a. *práty agnír uṣásām ágram akhyat*
práty áhāni prathamó jātávedāḥ |
práti sū́ryasya ***purudhā́*** *ca raśmī́n*
práti dyā́vāpṛthiví ***ā́ tatāna*** (AVŚ 7.82[87].5)

---

26 Cf. Whitney (1905: 367): 'Being just here, we give it back; living, we pay it in for the living; what grain I have devoured having borrowed (it), now, O Agni, I become guiltless as to that.'

27 Cf. Whitney (1905: 403): 'Anumati hath come unto this well-born offering, in order to [our] abounding in fields and in heroes; for her forethought hath been excellent; let her, god-shepherded, aid this offering.'

28 Cf. Whitney (1905: 122): 'In the impulse of vigor now have we come into being, and all these beings within.'

'Agni has seen the beginning of the dawns. Jātavedas is the first who (beholds) the days. He has frequently extended unto the rays of the sun and unto heaven and earth.'[29]

b. *tváyā pū́rvam átharvāṇo*
jaghnú *rákṣāṃsy oṣadhe* |
tváyā ***jaghāna*** *kaśyápas*
tváyā káṇvo agástyaḥ (AVŚ 4.37.1)

'In olden times the Atharvans killed demons with you, O herb. With you Kaśyapa killed, with you Kaṇva, Agastya'[30]

c. *yáś* ***cakā́ra*** *sá níṣ karat*
sá evá súbhiṣaktamaḥ |
sá evá túbhyaṃ bheṣajā́ni
kr̥ṇávad bhiṣájā śúciḥ (AVŚ 2.9.5)

'He who has caused (disease) will remove (it). He is indeed the most effective healer. He, the pure one, shall prepare antidotes for you together with the physician.'[31]

Just like its Early Vedic counterpart, the Early Middle Vedic Perfect Indicative is not infrequently modified by existential quantifier adverbs like *purudhā́* 'frequently, repeatedly', *bahudhā́* 'repeatedly' or *trís* 'thrice' in discourse contexts with a past reference time.[32]

---

[29] Cf. Whitney (1905: 449): 'Agni hath looked forth to meet the apex of the dawns, to meet the days, [he] first, Jātavedas, and to meet the rays of the sun in many places; to meet heaven and earth he stretched out.'

[30] Cf. Whitney (1905: 37): 'By thee of old the Atharvans slew the demons, O herb; by thee did Kaśyapa slay; by thee Kaṇva, Agastya.'

[31] Cf. Whitney (1905: 50): 'Whoso made, he shall unmake; he verily is the best of healers; he himself, clean, shall make for the remedies, with the healer.' Cf. also Bloomfield's translation (1897: 34): '(The god) that has caused (disease) shall perform the cure; he is himself the best physician. Let him indeed, the holy one, prepare remedies for thee, together with the (earthly) physician!'

[32] It should be noted, however, that Imperfect forms are also compatible with existential quantifier adverbs in Early Middle Vedic, as illustrated by the following example:

mugdhā́ devā́ utá śúnā́ 'yajanta
utá gór áṅgaiḥ purudhā́ 'yajanta | (AVŚ 7.5.5ab)

'The gods, confounded, both sacrificed with a dog and variously with limbs of a cow' (Whitney 1905: 392).

I noted in section **3.2** above that Perfect Indicative forms of atelic predicates often assume a universal reading in Early Vedic, i.e. they may denote a situation which has extended through the past and still holds at speech time. The universal reading is of considerable relevance for our present discussion, as it distinguishes present anterior from past perfective categories and hence represents a typologically relevant reading in the sense defined above. From this perspective, it is significant that there are extremely few unequivocal examples of Perfect Indicative forms of atelic predicates with a universal reading in Early Middle Vedic. In fact, I have only come across one isolated example, which is cited in [13].[33]

[13] *yad dhāvanti punate tad āpo*
yat tiṣṭhanti śuddhā it tad bhavanti |
na āsām avadyam avidaṃ na ripraṃ
sanād eva madhunā ***saṃ papṛchre*** (AVP 6.3.10)
'When they stream, then the waters cleanse themselves, when they stand still, then they become pure. I have not found any imperfection or vice of theirs. From olden times they have exchanged greetings with soma.'

---

[33] Kümmel (2000: 162–163) ascribes a universal interpretation to the Perfect Indicative forms in the following passages as well:
ā́po híraṇyaṃ ***jugupus*** *trivŕ̥dbhis*
tā́s tvā rakṣantu trivŕ̥tā trivŕ̥dbhiḥ (AVŚ 19.27.9ab)
'The waters have guarded the gold with triplets. The triplets shall guard thee with triplets.' [Cf. also Whitney's translation (1905: 939): 'The gold did the waters guard with triple ones; let those triple ones defend thee with triple ones.']
yama mṛtyo mā enaṃ hiṃsīr
yam ahaṃ hṛdā manasā ***jugopa*** (AVP 2.19.5ab)
'O Yama, O Death, do not injure him, whom I have guarded with heart and soul' [cf. Zehnder's translation (1999: 62): 'Yama, Tod, versehre ihn nicht, den ich mit dem Herzen, mit dem Sinn behütet habe']
Although a universal reading is not excluded in these cases, the discourse context is also compatible with an existential or even a simple past reading. It is therefore questionable whether these examples suffice to show that the universal reading was productive in Early Middle Vedic.

In contrast, Early Middle Vedic tends to use the Present Indicative with a durative adverbial modifier which denotes a past time interval, like *sanā́d* 'from of old', to express this temporal relation, as illustrated by the following examples:

[14] a. ***sanā́d*** *agne* ***mr̥ṇasi*** *yātudhā́nān*
ná tvā rákṣāṃsi pŕ̥tanāsu jigyuḥ | (AVŚ 5.29.11ab)
'From olden times you have been killing evil demons. Not (once) have the Rakṣasas defeated you in battle.'[34]

b. *tásya nā́kṣas tapyate bhū́ribhāraḥ*
sanā́d *evá ná* ***chidyate*** *sánābhiḥ* | (AVŚ 9.9.11cd)
'Its axle, much-burdened, is not heated; even from of old it is not severed with the nave.' (Whitney 1905: 554)[35]

These data suggest that constructions of the latter type were preferred to the Perfect Indicative in discourse contexts where a universal or present continuous reading was intended. This may be regarded as a classical case of morphosyntactic blocking where a semantically more specific construction blocks a semantically less specific construction from the environments where both are acceptable. From a more general perspective, this language-specific blocking process may be taken to have triggered the well-attested pattern of semantic change from present anterior to past perfective. If my interpretation of these data is correct, this is a neat illustration of how systemic factors may influence the semantic development of an inflectional category.[36]

---

[34] Cf. Whitney (1905: 275): 'From of old, O Agni, thou killest the sorcerers; the demons have not conquered thee in fights.' The half-verse is also found in the *R̥gveda* as RV 10.87.19ab.

[35] This verse is also found in the *R̥gveda* as RV 1.164.13. The latter has *śīryate* instead of *chidyate*.

[36] This explanation has another interesting corollary. Kümmel (2000: 59–61) notes that Perfect Indicative forms which primarily have a present state reading tend to be gradually assimilated to the Present Indicative, something which is partly reflected in their accentuation and partly in the fact that such forms are found with primary endings. From the perspective of the present work, this could be interpreted as the result of a paradigm

On the other hand, the assumption that the Early Middle Vedic Perfect Indicative represents a past perfective category is apparently contradicted by the following passage, where the form *cakā́ra* in the first pāda may be understood in a conative-like manner (cf. also Kümmel 2000: 510):

[15] *yáś* ***cakā́ra*** *ná śaśā́ka kártuṃ*
śaśré pā́dam aṅgúrim |
cakā́ra bhadrám asmábhyam
ātmáne tápanam tú sáḥ (AVŚ 4.18.6)
'He who created/tried to create, could not create, he crushed a foot (and) a finger. Nevertheless, he has created something auspicious for us which is causing pain for himself.'[37]

The so-called conative reading is typologically relevant in the sense that it distinguishes past imperfective and neutral categories from past perfective categories. Therefore, the fact that the Early Middle Vedic Perfect Indicative does appear to be compatible with this reading provides a strong argument against the assumption that it is a past perfective category. At this point I must emphasize that this is the only example of this sort I have come across in Early Middle Vedic. However, it is not clear to me that the passage in [15] represents a clear-cut case of the conative reading. For one thing, this reading typically expresses that

---

split where a lexically restricted set of Perfect Indicative forms, namely those derived from instantaneous achievement verbs, were incorporated in the present tense system, whereas other Perfect Indicative forms were incorporated in the past tense system. A paradigm split of this type would occur as a natural consequence of a semantic change of the type just discussed where the principal time reference of the Perfect Indicative was shifted from present to past, a change which was not implemented when a Perfect Indicative form had a salient present state reading.

[37] Cf. Whitney (1905: 182): 'He who hath made, hath not been able to make; he hath crushed a foot, a finger; he hath made what is excellent for us, but for himself a burning.' Bloomfield (1897: 70) translates the passage as follows: 'He that has undertaken them has not been able to accomplish them: he broke his foot, his toe. He performed a lucky act for us, but for himself an injury.'

a situation of the type denoted by the verbal predicate was terminated without being completed and thus primarily arises with telic predicates. In contrast, the verbal predicate underlying the Perfect Indicative form *cakā́ra* 'created, has created' represents an atelic process predicate as it does not have an overt object argument. Thus the above passage does not represent a prototypical instance of a conative construction. Nevertheless, the above passage clearly may be interpreted in a conative-like way, but it is not clear to me that an interpretation along these lines is necessary. In my opinion, the relevant form could equally well be used with an indefinite-existential reading here, so that the meaning of the pāda would be something like 'he who has (previously) created (successfully), has not been able to (successfully) finish creating (now)'. The immediately following discourse context might then be understood as specifying the actual results of a specific unsuccessful act of creation, where the Perfect Indicative forms are used with a resultative meaning.[38] I therefore do not regard this case as a genuine counterexample to the hypothesis I am developing here, that the Early Middle Vedic Perfect Indicative represents a past perfective category.

Before concluding this section, I would like to draw attention to the fact that the Early Middle Vedic Perfect Indicative is preferred to the other past tenses in sentences which are in the scope of a verb of attitude, as illustrated by the following examples:

[16] a. *ahaṃ veda yathā payaś*
cakāra ***cakāra*** removed

---

[38] A slightly different possibility, suggested to me by Jared Klein (p.c.) would be that the intended reading was 'he who has tried to create, has not been able to create (…), (however,) he has created something auspicious for us.'

[39] Cf. also the parallel passage in AVŚ:
védāhám páyasvantaṃ cakā́ra dhānyàm bahú (AVŚ 3.24.2ab)

b. *ahaṃ veda yathā* ***āsitha***
gurvikā nāma vā asi (AVP 1.59.3ab)
'I know how you have been, truly, Gurvikā is your name.'

c. *ácikitvāṃs cikitúṣaś cid átra*
kavī́n pṛchāmi vidváno ná vidvā́n ।
ví *yás* ***tastámbha*** *ṣáṭ imā́ rájāṃsy*
ajásya rūpé kím ápi svid ékam (AVŚ 9.9.7)
'Inexperienced I now ask the experienced poets, not knowing I now ask those who know. Did he who fixed asunder these six spaces do this alone in the shape of a goat?'[40]

These examples suffice to show that the Early Middle Vedic Perfect Indicative is compatible with a reading where the world argument of the sentence is bound by an attitude verb. I suggested in section **2** above that this essentially amounts to compatibility with an inferential interpretation. However, it is significant that first person Perfect Indicative forms do not necessarily imply that the speaker did not control the situation, something which rules out the possibility that it represents an indirect evidentiality marker at this stage. Consider the following examples:

[17] a. *ahám parástād ahám avástād*
aháṃ jyótiṣā ***ví*** *támo* ***vavāra*** । (TS^{M} 3.5.5.1ab)
'I from above, I from below, I revealed the darkness with the light.' (Keith 1914: 282)

b. *puṣṭíṃ paśūnā́m pári* ***jagrabha*** *ahám*
cátuṣpadāṃ dvipádāṃ yác ca dhānyàm । (AVŚ 19.31.5ab)
'I have seized all prosperity of cattle, of quadrupeds, of bipeds, and what grain [there is]' (Whitney 1905: 945)

'I know him that is rich in milk; he hath made the grain much' (Whitney 1905: 129).

[40] Cf. Whitney (1905: 553): 'I, not understanding, ask here the understanding poets, I unknowing them who know; he who propped asunder these six spaces, in the form of the goat – was that also alone?'

c. *ahám̐ rudrā́ya dhánur ā́ tanomi*
brahmadvíṣe śárave hántavā́ u |
ahám̐ jánāya samádam̐ kr̥ṇomi
ahám dyā́vāpr̥thivī́ ***ā́ viveśa*** (AVŚ 4.30.5)
'I stretch the bow for Rudra, for his shaft to slay the *bráhman*-hater; I make strife for the people; into heaven-and-earth have I entered.' (Whitney 1905: 201)

In these cases, the situations denoted by the first person Perfect Indicative forms *ví ... vavāra* 'revealed, have revealed', *pári jagrabha* 'seized, have seized' and *ā́ viveśa* 'entered, have entered' can hardly be understood as unintended on part of the speaker/subject. It should be noted, however, that first person Perfect Indicative forms are generally scarcely attested in Early Middle Vedic, something which could be due to the fact that forms of this type are roughly equivalent to the corresponding forms of the Aorist Indicative which represents a past perfective category with a strongly entrenched subjectively proximate past reading at this stage (cf. Dahl 2013). Hence, one might expect the Aorist Indicative to be preferred to the Perfect Indicative in contexts where the speaker refers to a situation in which he has played an active role.

The data discussed in this section indicate that the Early Middle Vedic Perfect Indicative is a past perfective category which is compatible with an inferential meaning, but does not represent a proper indirect evidentiality marker. The present proposal is corroborated by the fact that the use of past perfective categories as evidential strategies is well attested cross-linguistically (cf. Aikhenvald 2004: 212–214). The most important semantic difference between the Early Middle Vedic Perfect Indicative and its Early Vedic predecessor concerns their respective aspecto-temporal reference, the Early Vedic Perfect Indicative representing a present anterior category and the Early Middle Vedic representing a past perfective category.

3.4. The Perfect Indicative in Middle Vedic

In the Middle Vedic texts, Perfect Indicative forms are scarcely attested except for the forms with a stative present meaning which belong to instantaneous achievement verbs which are fairly frequent, as they are incorporated in the present system (cf. e.g. Kümmel 2000: 78). Discourse contexts with a past time reference strongly tend to prefer the Aorist Indicative or the Imperfect, depending on the relative subjective remoteness from the time of speech, the Aorist Indicative being used when a situation is regarded as subjectively proximate and the Imperfect being used to express that a situation is located at a past time which is not considered subjectively proximate (cf. e.g. Tichy 1997: 592 & fn. 8; Dahl 2013). Nevertheless, we do find a few examples of Perfect Indicative forms in discourse contexts referring to the non-immediate or remote past, as illustrated by the following examples:

[18] a. *ardhabhāg gha vā eṣa itareṣām ṛtvijām agra* ***āsa*** *yad brahmārdham eva brahmaṇa* ***āsa*** *ardham itareṣām ṛtvijāṃ* (AB 5.34)

'In the beginning, the Brahman was a sharer of half with the other priests; a half (of the holy power) was the Brahman's, a half the other priests.' (Keith 1920: 258)

b. *iyáṃ vā́ agnér atidāhā́d abibhet sā́ etā́ḥ apasyā̀ apaśyat tā́ úpādhatta táto vā́ imā́ṃ ná áty adahat yád apasyā̀ upadádhāty asyā́ ánatidāhāya* ***uvā́ca*** *ha iyám ádad ít sá brā́hmaṇā́nnaṃ yásya etā́ upadhīyā́ntai yá u ca enā evā́ṃ védad íti* (TS[P] 5.2.10.1–2)

'This (earth) was afraid of excessive burning by the fire; she saw these water bricks, she put them down, then (the fire) did not burn her excessively; in that he puts down the water bricks, (it is) to avoid excessive burning. She said, "He shall eat food with holy power, for whom these shall be put down, and he who shall know them thus."' (Keith 1914: 415)

These examples illustrate that the Middle Vedic Perfect Indicative is typically used to denote a single, specific situation which has been terminated at some point in the remote past. In fact, the Middle Vedic Perfect Indicative generally tends to be avoided in discourse contexts with a recent or immediate past reference time and is never modified by adverbs like *nūnám* 'now, just now', *nú* 'now, just now' or *adyá* 'today'. I have argued elsewhere that the Aorist Indicative represents a recent past category with a perfective meaning in the Middle Vedic period (cf. Dahl 2013). From this perspective, it is tempting to understand the apparent incompatibility of the Perfect Indicative with recent or immediate past reference times as the result of a blocking process where the semantically more specific Aorist Indicative is preferred to the semantically less specific Perfect Indicative in recent or immediate past contexts. Thus the temporal reference of the Middle Vedic Perfect Indicative is more restricted than it was shown to be in Early Vedic and Early Middle Vedic.

As regards the aspectual reference of the Middle Vedic Perfect Indicative, we may note a slight innovation. I noted in sections **3.2** and **3.3** above that the Perfect Indicative is sometimes used to denote a situation which has happened more than once prior to speech time in Early Vedic and Early Middle Vedic, a reading which typically arises when it is modified by existential quantifier adverbs like *bhū́ri* 'many times, often', *purudhā́* 'frequently, repeatedly', *bahudhā́* 'repeatedly' or *trís* 'thrice'. There are no unambiguous examples of Perfect Indicative forms modified by adverbs of this type in the Middle Vedic texts I have examined. Given that the Perfect Indicative is scarcely attested in this period, this might be due to an accidental gap in the corpus. On the other hand, there are several examples of Imperfect forms which are modified by existential quantifier adverbs in this period, as illustrated by the examples in [19]. It is therefore tempting to suggest that the fact that Perfect Indicative forms are not found in this type of environment in Middle Vedic should be taken at face value as an indication that it for some reason no longer was compatible with a multiple event reading.

[19] a. *índrāya tvā bṛhádvate váyasvata íty āha índrāya hí sá tám prā́yachat tásmai tvā víṣṇave tvéty āha yád evá víṣṇur anvá-tiṣṭhata jahī́ti tásmād víṣṇum anvā́bhajati trír nír gṛhṇāti trír hí sá táṃ tásmai* ***prā́yachat*** (TS[P] 6.5.1.2)

'To Indra thee, to him of the Bṛhat, the strong' he says, for to Indra he gave it; 'to him thee! To Viṣṇu thee!' he says. In that Viṣṇu supported him (saying) 'Strike', he gives Viṣṇu a share therein. Thrice he draws, for thrice he gave to him.' (Keith 1914: 538)

b. *prajāpatir akāmayata prajāyeya bhūyān syām iti sa tapo 'tapyata sa tapas taptvā imaṃ dvādaśāham apaśyad ātmana evāṅgeṣu ca prāṇeṣu ca tam ātmana eva aṅgebhyaś ca prāṇe-bhyaś ca dvādaśadhā* ***niramimīta*** (AB 4.23)

'Prajāpati felt desire 'May I be propagated, may I become greater.' He practiced fervour; he, having practiced fervor, saw the twelve-day (rite) in the limbs and the breaths of his self; he meted it out from the limbs and the breaths of his self twelve-fold.' (Keith 1920: 214)

As the Imperfect represents the unmarked past tense in Middle Vedic, it is questionable whether the apparent incompatibility of the Perfect Indicative with existential quantifiers may be understood as the result of a morphosyntactic blocking process. It rather indicates that the aspectual reference of the Perfect Indicative is slightly more restricted in Middle Vedic than in the previous two stages of the language and that it is now primarily used to denote a single, specific situation which has been terminated at some time remotely prior to speech time. From the overall perspective of this work, this may be hypothesized to represent a strengthening of the resultative implicature which typically picks out one situation of the type specified by the verbal predicate. This assumption is corroborated by the fact that Perfect Indicative forms of telic predicates tend to have a pronounced resultative meaning in Middle Vedic. Consider the following examples:

[20] a. *satyā́d vái sṛ́ñjayāḥ* ***párā babhūvur*** *íti ha uvāca yajñé vā́vá yajñā́ḥ pratiṣṭhā́pya ā̄ṣīd yájamānasya áparābhāvāya íti* (TS[P] 6.6.2.3)
'"But in truth the Sṛñjayas have perished", he said, "Indeed, the sacrifice was supposed to be placed upon a sacrifice, to prevent the death of the sacrifice."'[41]

b. *etā́ṁ ha vái yajñásenaś caitriyāyaṇáś cítiṃ vidā́ṃ* ***cakāra*** *táyā vái sá paśū́n ávārunddha* (TS[P] 5.3.8.1)
'Truly, Yajñasena Caitriyāyaṇa has made this layer known. By it he won cattle for himself.'[42]

The resultative reading of the Middle Vedic Perfect Indicative is often employed to denote a legendary mythical event which is invoked to explain the origin of a given sacrificial practice or the etymological origin of a given word, a reading which may be labelled 'etiological'. This reading is characteristic of the Middle Vedic Perfect Indicative and has been left out of the previous discussion as it is not particularly prominent in the earlier stages of Vedic. The following examples illustrate the etiological reading of the Middle Vedic Perfect Indicative:

[21] a. *yát kāmáyeta pāpavasīyasáṁ syād íti, gardabháṃ pū́rvaṃ nayeyur áparam áśvam. eténa vái vipū́janaḥ sáurākiḥ pāpavasīyasáṃ* ***cakāra****. tát pāpavasīyasam evá eténa karoti* (MS[P] 3.1.3)
'If he should wish "A pāpavasīyasa sacrifice shall it be!" one should first bring the donkey, then the horse. With this (don-

---

[41] Cf. Keith (1914: 548): '"But in truth the Sṛñjayas have been defeated", he said, "the sacrifice should have been made to rest on the sacrifice, to prevent the defeat of the sacrifice."'

[42] Cf. Keith (1914: 426): 'Yajñasena Caitriyāyaṇa taught this layer; by this he won the cattle.'

key) Vipūjana Saurāki made the pāpavasīyasa sacrifice. Therefore one makes the pāpavasīyasa sacrifice with it'[43]

b. *ṛṣayo vai sarasvatyāṃ satram āsata te kavaṣam ailūṣaṃ somād anayan dāsyāḥ putraḥ kitavo 'brāhmaṇaḥ kathaṃ no madhye 'dīkṣiṣṭa iti tam bahir dhanva udavahann atra enam pipāsā hantu sarasvatyā udakam mā pād īti sa bahir dhanva udūḷhaḥ pipāsayā vitta etad aponaptrīyam apaśyat pra devatrā brahmaṇe gātur etv iti tena apām priyaṃ dhāma upāgachat tam āpo 'nūdāyaṃs taṃ sarasvatī samantam paryadhāvat tasmād dha apy etarhi parisārakam ity ācakṣate yad enaṃ sarasvatī samantam* ***parisasāra*** (AB 2.19)

'The Ṛṣis were performing a sacrificial session at the (shores of the) Sarasvatī. They led Kavaṣa Ailūṣa away from the Soma (saying) "Has the child of a female slave, a rascal, a non-Brahmin been consecrated in our midst?" They sent him out in the desert (saying) "Let thirst kill him here! Let him not drink the waters of Sarasvatī." He, sent away into the desert, tormented by thirst saw the hymn to the child of the waters "Forth among the gods let there be a passage for the Brahman." With this (hymn) he reached the dear abode of the waters. The waters accumulated around him. Sarasvatī surrounded him on all sides. Thenceforth even today they call that place Parisāraka, because Sarasvatī surrounded him on all sides.'[44]

c. *áhar vā́ áśvasya jā́yamānasya mahimā́ purástāj jāyate rā́trir enam mahimā́ paścā́d ánu jāyate* | *etáu vái mahimā́nāv áśvam*

---

[43] Cf. Kümmel (2000: 138): 'Falls er wünschen sollte: "Ein Pāpavasīyasa-Opfer soll es sein!", soll man zuerst den Esel bringen, danach das Pferd. Mit diesem [Esel?] hat ja Vipūjana Saurāki das Pāpavasīyasa-Opfer durchgeführt. Daher führt man das Pāpavasīyasa mit diesem durch.'

[44] Cf. Keith (1920: 148): 'The seers performed a sacrificial season on the Sarasvatī; they drove away Kanvaṣa Ailūṣa from the soma, 'The child of a slave woman, a cheat, no Brahman; how has he been consecrated in our midst?' They sent him to the desert, (saying): 'There let thirst slay him; let him drink not the water of the Sarasvatī.' He sent away to the wilderness, afflicting by thirst, saw the 'child of the waters' hymn, 'forth among the gods let there be speeding for the Brahman.' Thereby he went to the dear abode of the waters; him the waters welled out after; all around him Sarasvatī hastened. Therefore they call it here Parisāraka, in that Sarasvatī went all around him.'

abhítaḥ ***sám babhūvatus*** *háyo devā́n avahad árvā́surān vājī́ gandharvā́n áśvo manuṣyā̀n* (TS[P] 7.5.25.2)
'Indeed the Mahiman cup is born before the birth of the horse as the day. The Mahiman cup is born after it as the night. On either side these two Mahiman cups surrounded the horse. As Haya it carried the gods, as Arvan the Asuras, as Vājin the Gandharvas, as Aśva the races of men.'[45]

Although the data from this period are rather scarce, it is significant that Perfect Indicative forms of telic verbal predicates invariably denote a single specific situation which has been completed prior to speech time. For instance, there are as far as I can see no examples where forms of this type denote an attempted situation which was terminated prior to completion. In principle, this could be due to an accidental gap in the corpus, but as there are a few passages where Imperfect forms of telic verbal predicates have a conative meaning, as illustrated by example [22] below, I think it is reasonable to assume that this reading was not available for the Middle Vedic Perfect Indicative.

[22] *tāṃ vāsantikābhyām māsābhyām* ***anvayuñjata*** *tāṃ vāsantikābhyām māsābhyāṃ na* ***udāpnuvaṃs*** *tāṃ graiṣmābhyāṃ tāṃ vārṣikābhyāṃ tāṃ śāradābhyāṃ tāṃ haimantikābhyām māsābhyām* ***anvayuñjata*** *tāṃ haimantikābhyām māsābhyāṃ na udāpnuvaṃs tāṃ śaiśirābhyām māsābhyām anvayuñjata tāṃ śaiśirābhyām māsābhyām āpnuvann* (AB 4.26)

---

[45] Keith (1914: 636–637) translates the form *sám babhūvatus* as a present: 'The Mahiman (cup) indeed is born before the birth of the horse as the day. The Mahiman (cup) is born after it as the night. These two Mahiman (cups) surround on either side the horse. As Haya (steed) it carried the gods, as Arvan (courser) the Asuras, as Vājin (racer) the Gandharvas, as Aśva (horse) men.' The present translation follows Kümmel (2000: 347–348): 'Als Tag wird der Mahiman-Becher geboren, bevor das Pferd geboren wird; als Nacht wird der Mahiman-Becher nach ihm geboren. Diese beiden Mahiman-Becher sind rings um das Pferd zusammengeflossen. Als Haya fuhr es die Götter, als Arvan die Asuras, als Vājin die Gandharven und als Pferd die Menschen.' As noted by Kümmel, the perfect indicative *sám babhūva* apparently never shows a present perfect reading.

'(Consecration departed from the gods;) it they sought to grasp with the two months of spring; it they could not grasp with the two months of spring. It they sought to grasp with the two months of summer, of the rainy season, of autumn, of winter; it they could not obtain with the months of winter. It they sought to grasp with the two months of the cool season; it they obtained with the two months of the cool season.' (Keith 1920: 216)

Again, it is dubious whether the preference for the Imperfect in this kind of discourse context should be analyzed as a case of morphosyntactic blocking, given that this inflectional category represents the default choice in remote past contexts at this stage. Therefore the fact that we do not find Perfect Indicative forms in such environments rather may be taken to reflect that it is incompatible with a conative reading. I suggested in section **3.3** above that the Early Middle Vedic Perfect Indicative represented a past perfective category and, as there is no compelling evidence to the contrary, it is reasonable to assume that the Middle Vedic Perfect Indicative has maintained a past perfective meaning as well, which might be taken to underlie its salient resultative reading as well as its incompatibility with discourse contexts presupposing a conative meaning.

Perfect Indicative forms of atelic verbal predicates, on the other hand, albeit exceedingly rare in Middle Vedic, are primarily used to denote a single, specific situation which has been terminated prior to speech time or prior to some other situation in the same discourse context, but they are also marginally compatible with a temporally overlapping reading. Consider the following examples:

[23] a. *etád dha sma vā́ āha nāradá idáṁ vā́va agnyupasthā́nam**āsa** íty* (MS 1.5.8)
'Nārada used to say 'This was indeed an *agnyupasthāna*.'

b. *tān etasminn uktha ābhajad atha ha ete tarhy ubhe eva niṣkevalye ukthe* ***āsatur*** (AB 3.20)
'He gave them a share in this litany; to that time, both litanies were his only.' (Keith 1920: 177)

c. *prajāpatir vā idam eka eva agra* ***āsa*** *so 'kāmayata prajāyeya bhūyān syām iti sa tapo 'tapyata sa vācam ayachat sa saṃvatsarasya parastād vyāharad dvādaśakṛtvo* (AB 2.33)
'Prajāpati was here being only one in the beginning. He desired "May I be propagated and become greater"; he practised fervour; he restrained speech; at the end of the year he uttered twelve times.' (Keith 1920: 158)

Unfortunately, the data are not as conclusive as one might wish, but they are nevertheless perfectly compatible with the hypothesis that the Middle Vedic Perfect Indicative represents a past perfective category just like the Early Middle Vedic Perfect Indicative.

Even though there are no examples of Perfect Indicative forms in the direct scope of attitude verbs in Middle Vedic, forms of this type sometimes do have an emphatic inferential meaning. Consider for instance the following passages:

[24] a. *tā uṣasam anvāgachatāṃ tām abrūtām apodihy āvāṃ vā idaṃ jeṣyāva iti sā tathā ity abravīt tasyai vai mama iha apy astv iti tathā iti tasyā apy atra akurutāṃ tasmād uṣasyam āśvine śasyate tāv indram anvāgachatāṃ tam abrūtām āvāṃ vā idam maghavañ jeṣyāva iti na ha taṃ* ***dadhṛṣatur*** *apodihi iti vaktuṃ sa tathā ity abravīt* (AB 4.8)
'They (the Aśvins) followed after Uṣas; to her they said "Give way; we two will win this." "Be it so", she replied, "Let me have a share here." "Be it so" (they said). For her they made a share therein. Therefore at the Āśvina (a litany) to Uṣas is recited. They followed after Indra; to him they said "We will win this, o generous one"; they did not dare to say to him "Give way". "Be it so", he replied.' (Keith 1920: 203)

b. *ādityā vā itas sarveṇa eva sahāmuṃ lokam āyaṁs. te 'muṃ lokaṃ gatvā vyatṛṣaṁs. te 'vidur: amutaḥ pradānād vā iha* ***ājagāma*** *iti. ta etaṃ punar ādadhata. tena ārdhnuvan* (KS[P] 9.3)
'The Ādityas went out from here with everything to yonder world. When they had come to yonder world, they were thirsty. Then they knew: "it (the thirst) has (surely) come hither from that gift." They put it (the gift) back (there). By that they succeeded.'[46]

In the first case, the Perfect Indicative form *dadhṛṣatur* 'have dared, dared' may be taken to express that the speaker bases his account of that particular situation on indirect evidence, namely the fact that the Aśvins did not say exactly the same to Indra as they had said to Uṣas. As Indra was generally known to be a fierce and violent god, it is reasonable to infer that they were afraid of him and therefore did not dare to say anything which could be taken as a token of disrespect. In the second case, the Perfect Indicative form *ājagāma* 'has come, came' may be taken in a similar manner, thus expressing that the Ādityas inferred that their present thirst was caused by a certain gift which they had brought with them from this world to yonder world. In this particular case, however, we may be faced with a resultative reading instead from which the inferential reading is notoriously difficult to disentangle and with which it is probably intimately related, at least from a synchronic perspective.

If my interpretation of the above data is correct, the Middle Vedic Perfect Indicative can be used to express that the world argument of a given sentence is bound in the sense that its validity is restricted relative to the indirect evidence on which the statement is based. This may be understood as a strength-

[46] Cf. Kümmel (2000: 157): 'Die Ādityas gingen von hier aus mit all dem zusammen in jene Welt. Als sie in jene Welt gekommen waren, bekamen sie Durst. Da wußten sie: "Von der Gabe von dort her ist es/er hierher gekommen." Sie legten ihn wieder [dort] hin. Dadurch hatten sie Erfolg.'

ening of an implicature which in the previous stages of Vedic was most transparent when Perfect Indicative forms were in the scope of attitude verbs. Given Pāṇini's definition of the Perfect Indicative as *bhūte paro'kṣe* 'in the past beyond the range of sight' it is tempting to generalize this finding and to assume that all tokens of the Perfect Indicative in Middle Vedic have an inferential meaning and that it represents an indirect evidentiality marker at this stage. I suggested in sections **3.2** and **3.3** above that first person forms constitute a fairly reliable environment for testing whether a given category has an inferential meaning or not, as first person forms of indirect evidential markers tend to imply that the subject acted non-intentionally or did not control the situation. I have come across only two examples of first person Perfect Indicative forms in the Middle Vedic texts I have examined, but it is significant that both of them have the relevant implications. Consider the following examples:

[25] a. *sò 'bravīd ŕ̥ṣayo vā́ imé puṇyamanyā́ agním ā́dadhate, tā́n párehī́ti sā́ párait tá imám ágrā ā́dadhata átha imám átha amúm̐ sā́ púnarait tā́m apr̥cchat kím abhyàgann íti sā́ abravīd imám evá ágrā ā́dhiṣata átha imám átha amúm íti sò 'bravīd ahám̐ vā́vá agnyādhéyam̐* ***vidā́ṃ cakāra****, sárveṣu vā́ eṣú lokéṣv ŕ̥ṣayaḥ prátyaṣṭhur íti* (MS[P] 1.6.13)

'He (Manu) said: "These blessed Ṛṣis are establishing a fire for themselves, go to them!" She went (to them). They first established this fire, then this one, then that one. She went back. He asked her: "How did it proceed?" She said: "They first established this fire, then this one and then that one." He said: "Indeed, (now) I have understood the true meaning of the Agnyādheya. Truly, the Ṛṣis have established themselves in all these worlds (just now)."'[47]

[47] Cf. Krick (1982: 369–370): 'Manu sagte: "Die Ṛṣis, die als glücklich gelten, gründen sich das Feuer. Geh fort zu ihnen!" Sie ging dorthin. Die (Ṛṣis) gründeten sich zuerst dieses Feuer, dann dieses, dann jenes. Sie kehrte wiederum heim. Er (Manu) fragte sie: "Wie sind sie vorgegangen?" Sie sagte: "sie haben sich zuerst dieses Feuer gegründet, dann dieses, dann

b. *etad dha vā Āruṇir uvāca: na tāvad rātrīṁ staryam* ***uvasa*** *yāvad etām ṛcam aśṛṇavam iti. na rātrīṁ staryaṃ vasati ya evaṃ veda.* (KS^{P} 7.9)

'Āruṇi spoke thus: "I have not spent nights in vain so long as I have heard this verse." He who knows thus, does not spend nights in vain.'[48]

In these cases, the Perfect Indicative forms *vidāṃ cakāra* 'I understood, have understood' and *(rātrīṁ staryam) uvasa* 'I spent, have spent (nights in vain)' clearly denote situations which are not within the subject's own sphere of control. The restriction of first person Perfect Indicative forms to cases where the situation is non-intentional or outside the control of the speaker constitutes a fairly strong argument for the view that the Middle Vedic Perfect Indicative represents an indirect evidentiality marker.

While the data reviewed in this section clearly indicate that the inferential reading of the Perfect Indicative has been strengthened, it is not equally clear that it represents an evidentiality marker at this stage. Most importantly, the Perfect Indicative is only rarely used in narrative discourse, where it might be expected to represent the default choice if it were a proper indirect evidentiality marker (cf. Aikhenvald 2004: 310–315 and section **3.5** below). Therefore I conclude from the data discussed in this section that the Middle Vedic Perfect Indicative represents a past perfective category which is strongly associated with an inferential reading, but does not represent a proper evidentiality marker. It has a slightly less general aspecto-temporal reference than its Early Middle Vedic counterpart in that it neither denotes multiple events in the past nor immediate past ref-

---

jenes." Er sagte:"Fürwahr, nun habe ich die (wahre) Feuergründung kennengelernt! Denn in allen Welten haben die Ṛṣis festen Fuß gefaßt."'

[48] Cf. Kümmel (2000: 483): 'Dies hat Āruṇi gesagt: "Ich habe solange keine Nacht fruchtlos verbracht, wie ich diesen Vers hörte." Keine Nacht verbringt fruchtlos, wer dieses Wissen hat.'

erence times. On the other hand, its resultative and inferential readings are more strongly entrenched at this stage. Although it is possible to understand all tokens of the Perfect Indicative as inferential and it passes the 'first person test' so that it might appear to be obligatorily associated with this semantic feature, the fact that it is scarcely attested in narrative discourse speaks against regarding it as an evidentiality marker.

3.5. The Perfect Indicative in Late Vedic

In this section I review some of the most important semantic and syntactic properties of the Late Vedic Perfect Indicative (cf. also Dahl 2012). A striking difference between the Middle Vedic and the Late Vedic sources concerns the relative frequency of Perfect Indicative forms in discourse contexts with a remote past reference time. Whereas the Perfect Indicative is relatively rare in this type of environment in Middle Vedic, it is well known that it becomes gradually more frequent in the Late Vedic prose texts (cf. e.g. Whitney 1892: 33; Kümmel 2000: 78–82). It is likely that this syntactic change reflects the fact that the semantic properties of the Perfect Indicative have somehow changed from Middle Vedic to Late Vedic. In the previous section I suggested that the Middle Vedic Perfect Indicative represents a past perfective category which under given circumstances may be used to express that the statement is based on indirect evidence, but that it is questionable whether it may be regarded as an evidential marker in a strict sense at that stage. This section aims at establishing in what respects the semantic properties of the Late Vedic Perfect Indicative differ from those of the Middle Vedic Perfect Indicative.

First, we may note that the Late Vedic Perfect Indicative is typically used to denote a single, specific situation which has been terminated prior to speech time. It is compatible with temporal adverbs denoting a temporal interval remotely prior to speech time, as illustrated by the following examples:

[26] a. *indre ha vā agre yajña* ***āsa*** *śrīr ha vā asmiṃs tad* ***āsa*** *yajña u ha vāva devānāṃ śrīḥ* (JB 2.139)

'In the beginning, the sacrifice was in Indra. Auspiciousness was in him. For the sacrifice is the auspiciousness of the gods.'

b. *púruṣaṃ ha vái devā́ḥ ágre paśum* ***ā́lebhire*** (ŚBM 1.2.3.6)

'In the beginning, the gods sacrificed Puruṣa as their sacrificial animal.'[49]

The Late Vedic Perfect Indicative is never modified by adverbs introducing a recent or immediate past reference time, like *nú* 'now, just now', *nūnám* 'now, just now' or *adyá* 'today'. These considerations suggest that the temporal reference of the Late Vedic Perfect Indicative largely corresponds to that of the Middle Vedic Perfect Indicative.

As regards the aspectual reference of the Perfect Indicative, on the other hand, we may note a significant difference between Middle and Late Vedic. It was noted above that Perfect Indicative forms of telic verbal predicates invariably denote a single, specific situation which has been completed prior to speech time in Middle Vedic. In Late Vedic, on the other hand, Perfect Indicative forms of telic verbal predicates may either denote a situation which has been terminated and completed prior to speech time or a past situation which has been terminated without being successfully completed. Consider the following examples:

[27] a. *kutso ha vā aurava indrasya ūror adhi nirmita* ***āsa*** *yādṛśa eva indras tādṛśa, yathā atmano nirmita syād evam taṃ ha saṃgrahītāraṃ* ***cakre*** *taṃ ha jāyayā* ***abhijagrāha*** *śacyā paulomyā tāṃ ha* ***uvāca*** *kathā ityam akar iti sā ha* ***uvāca*** *na vāṃ vyajñāsam iti sa ha* ***uvāca*** *khalatiṃ vā enaṃ kariṣyāmi, tathā vijānītād iti taṃ ha khalatiṃ* ***cakāra*** *sa ha uṣṇīṣaṃ parihṛtya* ***upanipede*** (JB 3.199)

---

[49] Cf. Eggeling (1882: 50): 'At first, namely, the gods offered up a man as the victim.'

'Kutsa Aurava was created from Indra's thigh. He resembled him so much as if he (Indra) should have been created from (Kutsa) himself. He (Indra) appointed him (Kutsa) as charioteer. He (Indra) caught him (Kutsa) in the act with his own wife, Śacī Paulomī. He said to her: "Why did you do it?" She said: "I could not discern you from one another." He said: "I will make him bald. In that manner you shall discern!" He made him bald. Having wrapped a turban round his head, he (Kutsa) went to bed with her again.'

b. *tau ha ādhāvayantau brāhmaṇakumāraṃ pathi krīḍantaṃ rathacakreṇa vicicchidatuḥ itaro ha ādhāvayann abhiprayuyāva* ***apa*** *itara* ***āyayāma*** *sa ha adhigatya na śaśāka apāyantum taṃ ha tad eva vicicchidatuḥ tasmin ha ūdāte tvaṃ hantā asi tvaṃ hantā asi iti sa ha vṛśo 'bhīśūn prakītyā avatiṣṭhann uvāca tvaṃ hantā asi iti na iti ha uvāca yo vai rathaṃ saṃgṛhṇāti sa rathasya īśe tvaṃ hantā asi na iti ha itara uvāca apa vā aham āyāṃsaṃ sa tvam abhiprāyauṣīs, tvam eva hantā asi iti* (JB 3.94)

'Once, when the two of them were driving fast they killed a Brahmin child who was playing in the road with the wheel of the wagon. One of them was speeding up, driving fast, while the other was steering away. Having come too close, he was not able to steer away and so they killed him. Then they started arguing: "You are the killer, you are the killer. Having laid down the bridles, Vṛśa said while stepping down: "You are the killer." "No", he said, "he who has hold on the wagon, he is the lord of the wagon. You are the killer." "No", said the other, "I was stopping, but you continued speeding up. Therefore you are the killer."'

From the perspective of the present paper it is significant that Perfect Indicative forms of telic verbal predicates are compatible with a properly conative reading in Late Vedic. As noted in section **3.3** above, the conative reading is typologically relevant as it distinguishes past imperfective and past neutral categories from past perfective categories. The conative reading predicates a proper inclusion relation between event time and reference time such that reference time is properly included in event time ($t_R \subset t_E$), a relation which is fundamentally incompatible with the aspectual relation predicated by the perfective aspect ($t_E \subseteq t_R$). The fact that the Late Vedic Perfect Indicative may assume this reading is an unambiguous indication that it does not represent a past perfective category, but rather a past imperfective or neutral category, i.e. it may either be taken to denote the aspectual relation 'event time included in reference time' ($t_R \subseteq t_E$) or the aspectual relation 'reference time overlaps with event time' ($t_R \otimes t_E$). Within the theoretical framework developed here, the perfective aspect and the imperfective aspect are understood as opposite inclusion relations between reference time and event time and it therefore remains unclear how a perfective category could develop into an imperfective category, as this would seem to violate the identity constraint mentioned in section **2** above. The neutral aspect, on the other hand, is understood as a general overlap relation between reference time and event time. As an inclusion relation represents a specific type of overlap relation, a development from past perfective to past neutral may be regarded as a development from a more specific to a more general category of roughly the same type. Thus I assume that the Late Vedic Perfect Indicative represents a past neutral category rather than a past imperfective category.

The examples in [26] and [27] illustrate that the Late Vedic Perfect Indicative is typically used in general narrative discourse, whereas the Aorist Indicative is used to denote situations which have occurred in the subjectively recent past. In some texts, however, there is a more or less systematic alternation between the Perfect Indicative and the Imperfect where the main narrative primarily selects the former, whereas the latter is preferred in sequences of direct discourse. Consider the following examples:

[28] a. *átha ha enam bhujyur lā́hyāyaniḥ* ***papracha*** *yā́jñavalkya íti ha* ***uvāca*** *madréṣu cárakāḥ* ***páryavrajāma*** *té patáñcalasya kā́pyasya gṛhān* ***aíma*** *tásya* ***āsīd*** *duhitā́ gandharvágṛhītā tám*

apṛchāma *kò'si íti* ***sò'bravīt*** *sudhanv àṅgirasa íti lokā́nām ántān* ***ápṛchāma*** *átha etám* ***abrūma*** *kvá pārikṣitā́ abhavan kvá pārikṣitā́ abhavann íti táttvā pṛchāmi yājñavalkya kvá pārikṣitā́* ***abhavann*** *íti sá hovāca* ***uvā́ca*** *vai sa tadágachan-vai te tátra yátrāśvamedhayājíno gáchantī́ti* (...) *evám iva vai sá vāyúmeva* ***práśaśaṃsa*** *tásmādvāyúreva vyáṣṭirvāyuḥ sám-aṣṭir ápa punarmṛtyúṃ jayati sárvamā́yureti yá evaṃ véda* (ŚBM 14.6.3.1 = BĀU 3.3.1)

'Then Bhujyu Lāhyāyani began to question him. "Yājñavalkya" he said, "once, while we were itinerant students traveling around in the land of the Madras, we visited the home of Patañcala Kāpya. He had a daughter possessed by a Gandharva. We asked him who he was and the Gandharva said that he was Sudhanavan Āṅgirasa. In the course of asking him about the ends of the worlds, we inquired: "Where in the worlds are the Pārikṣitas?" I put the same question to you Yājñavalkya, "where are the Pārikṣitas?" Yājñavalkya replied: "He no doubt told you: "They have gone to the place where those who offer sacrifices go" (...) What that Gandharva praised in that manner was clearly the wind. Both individual things and the totality of all things, therefore, are just the wind. Whosoever knows this averts repeated death"' (Olivelle 1996: 38)

b. *sa ha hāridrumataṃ gautamam etya* ***uvāca*** *brahmacaryaṃ bhagavati vatsyāmi upeyāṃ bhagavantam iti taṃ ha* ***uvāca*** *kiṃgotro nu somya asi iti sa ha* ***uvāca*** *na aham etad veda bho yadgotro'ham asmi* ***apṛcchaṃ*** *mātaram sā mā* ***pratyabravīt*** *bahv aham carantī paricariṇī yauvane tvām* ***alabhe*** *sāham etan na veda yadgotras tvam asi jabālā tu nāma aham asmi satyakāmo nāma tvam asi iti so'haṃ satyakāmo jābālo'smi bho iti taṃ ha* ***uvāca*** *na etad abrahmaṇo vivaktum arhati sam-idhaṃ somyāhara upa tvā neṣye na satyād agā iti* (...) ***prāpa*** *hācaryakulam tam ācaryo'bhyuvāda satyakāma3 iti bhagava iti ha* ***pratiśuśrāva*** *brahmavid iva vai somya bhāsiko nu tvā* ***anuśaśāsa*** *iti anye manuṣyebhya iti ha* ***pratijajñe*** *bhaga-vāṃs tv eva me kāme brūyāt śrutaṃ hy eva me bhagavad-dṛśebhya ācāryād dhaiva vidyā viditā sādhiṣṭhaṃ prāpatīti tasmai ha etad eva uvāca atra ha na kiṃcana vīyāyeti vīyāyeti* (ChU 4.4.3–9.3)

> 'He went to Hāridrumata Gautama then and said: "Sir, I want to live under you as a vedic student. I come to you, sir, as your student." Hāridrumata asked him: "Son, what is your lineage?" And he replied: "Sir, I don't know what my lineage is. When I asked my mother, she replied: "I was young when I had you. I was a maid then and had a lot of relationships. As such, it is impossible for me to say what your lineage is. But my name is Jabālā, and your name is Satyakāma." So I am Satyakāma Jābala, sir." Hāridrumata then told him: "Who but a Brahmin could speak like that! Fetch some firewood, son. I will perform your initiation. You have not strayed from truth." (...) He finally reached his teacher's house. The teacher called out to him: "Satyakāma!" He responded: "Sir?" "Son, you have the glow of a man who knows Brahman! Tell me – who taught you?" "Other than human beings", he acknowledged, "But if it pleases you, sir, you should teach it to me yourself, for I have heard from people of your eminence that knowledge leads one most securely to the goal only when it is learnt by a teacher." So he explained it to him, and, indeed, he did so without leaving anything out.' (Olivelle 1996: 130, 132–133)

These passages illustrate that the Perfect Indicative is mainly used in the frame story whereas the Imperfect primarily occurs in direct discourse. Observe, however, that we do in fact find three Perfect Indicative forms in direct discourse here, namely *uvā́ca* 'said, has said', *prā́śaśaṃsa* 'praised, has praised' and *anuśaśāsa* 'taught, has taught' which at first glance do not seem to differ from the Imperfect forms at the same level of discourse. Thus the question arises whether there is any semantic difference between the Imperfect and the Perfect Indicative forms in direct discourse and whether this difference could account for the fact that the Perfect Indicative is preferred to the Imperfect in the narrative frame story.

A closer look at the above passages suggests that the use of the Perfect Indicative and the Imperfect is not haphazard, after all. In example [28a], the Imperfect forms *páryavrajāma* 'we travelled around', *aíma* 'we visited', *āsīd* 'was', *apṛchāma* 'we asked', *abravīt* 'said', *áp̣rchāma* 'we asked' and *abrūma* 'we said' all refer to situations which are within the realm of the speaker's own experience. As the passage belongs to a story where various sages challenge Yājñavalkya's wisdom, it is dubious whether Bhujyu Lāhyāyani uses the first person plural in an inclusive manner here, for it would hardly be a challenge if Yājñavalkya were questioned about something he might be expected to know, as he would be if he had been present when Bhujyu Lāhyāyani asked the demon. From this perspective, it is likely that Yājñavalkya uses the Perfect Indicative forms *uvā́ca* 'said, has said', *prá́śaśaṃsa* 'praised, has praised' to denote situations which he has not witnessed himself, but which he infers from secondary evidence. Similarly, the Imperfect forms in [28b] all denote situations which are within the speaker's own experience, whereas the Perfect Indicative form *anuśaśāsa* 'taught, has taught' may be taken to refer to a situation which is inferred on the basis of secondary evidence, namely the fact that Satyakāma has the glow of a man who knows Brahman. On this assumption, the two characteristic patterns of use associated with the Late Vedic Perfect Indicative are both determined by a basic inferential meaning, i.e. it is obligatorily used to express that the information source on which the statement is based is not first hand, but based on secondary evidence.

However, the last sentence spoken by Bhujyu Lāhyāyani in example [28a] provides a possible counterexample to this analysis. If it is correct that the Perfect Indicative is a marker of indirect information source, it remains unclear why he uses an Imperfect form in his question addressed to the demon Sudhanu Āngirasa, namely *abhavan* 'became (> are)'. However, the immediate discourse context does not make it entirely clear whether his intention is to challenge the demon by asking a question to which he himself knows the answer or to acquire new information by asking the question. It is therefore questionable whether this case can count as a genuine counterexample to the general tendency of using the Imperfect to express that a statement is based on first hand information and the Perfect Indicative to express that it is based on some indirect information source.

A more serious difficulty for the present analysis arises from the fact that there is a considerable number of passages in Late Vedic where the immediate discourse context precludes that the speaker bases the statement on first hand knowledge, but nevertheless uses Imperfect and Perfect Indicative forms interchangeably. For example, in a number of narrative passages we find one or more Perfect Indicative forms at the beginning, followed by a number of Imperfect forms (cf. also Whitney 1892: 18, 25). Consider the following passages:

[29] a. *índro ha yátra vṛtrā́ya vájram* ***prajahā́ra*** *só 'balīyān mányamāno ná astṛṣi íti iva bíbhyan* ***nilayā́ṃ cakre*** *tád evá ápi devā́* ***apanyálayanta*** *té ha devā́* ***ūcuḥ*** *na vái hatáṃ vṛtráṃ vidma ná jīvaṃ hánta na éko véttu yádi ható vā vṛtro jī́vati véti té vāyúm* ***abruvan*** *ayaṃ vai vāyuryò 'yam pávate vā́yo tvám idaṃ viddhi yádi ható vā vṛtro jī́vati vā tvaṃ vai na ā́śiṣṭo 'si yádi jīviṣyáti tvámevá kṣipram púnar ā́gamiṣyasī́ti*
(ŚBM 4.1.3.1–3)
'When Indra had hurled the mace at Vṛtra thinking himself to be weaker he hid himself as if fearing not to have overthrown him (lit. fearing ("I have not overthrown (him)"). So the gods also hid themselves away. The gods said to themselves: "Verily, we do not know whether Vṛtra is dead or whether he is alive. Let one (of us) find out whether Vṛtra is dead or whether he lives." They said to Vāyu, Vāyu is the one, who purifies: "Vāyu, you find out whether Vṛtra is slain or is alive, for you are verily the swiftest among us. If he shall be alive, you shall come back quickly."'[50]

---

[50] Cf. Eggeling (1885: 265): 'Now Indra, when he had hurled the thunderbolt at Vritra, thinking himself to be the weaker, and fearing lest he had not laid him low, hid himself. The gods also hid themselves away in the same place. The gods then said, "Verily, we know not if Vritra be slain or alive: come, let one of us find out, if Vritra be slain or alive!" They said unto Vâyu-- Vâyu, forsooth, is he that blows yonder – "Find thou out, O Vâyu, if Vritra be

b. *bhṛgúr vaí vāruṇíḥ váruṇam pítaram* ***úpasasāra****. ádhīhi bhagavo bráhma iti tásmā etát* ***próvāca****. ánnaṃ prāṇaṃ cákṣuś śrótraṃ mánas vā́cam íti. tám* ***uvāca*** *yáto vā́ imā́ni bhūtā́ni jī́vante, yéna jātā́ni jī́vanti, yát práyanti abhisáṃviśanti, tád víjñāsasva, tád bráhma íti. sá tápo* ***'tapyata****. sá tápas taptvā́ ánnaṃ bráhma íti* ***vyàjānāt***. (TĀ 9.1–2)

'Bhṛgu, son of Varuṇa, visited his father Varuṇa. "Turn your mind towards Brahma" he (Varuṇa) said to him, "(He is) food, life, sight, hearing, mind and speech." He said to him "That by which these living things live, by which the creatures live, which they enter and surround, that shall thou perceive, that is Brahman." He (Bhṛgu) performed penance. Having performed penance, he understood that Brahman is food.'

Both these passages may be taken to refer to the mythical past, a remote past time outside the realm of the speaker's experience. It is significant that perfect and imperfect forms are used interchangeably, as this would seem to disprove or at least severely challenge the claim that the notion of inferentiality can be invoked to account for the distribution of these two inflectional categories.[51] On closer examination, however, it is far from clear whether passages like these provide compelling counterevidence against the assumption that inferentiality is a relevant dimension in the Late Middle Vedic past tense system. In her discussion of evidentiality and narrative conventions, Aikhenvald (2004: 314) notes that indirect evidential markers are not necessarily used throughout an entire narrative discourse, but may occur only at the beginning – to set the scene, so to speak. Along these lines, the Perfect Indicative forms in above examples could be understood as explicitly indicating that the following story is based on indirect evidence, whereas the Imperfect forms simply express that the situation happened at some time prior to speech

slain or alive; for thou art the swiftest among us: if he lives, thou indeed wilt quickly return hither."'

[51] A similar distribution pattern is found in many other prose texts, cf. for instance TĀ 2.7; ŚBM 11.5.5.1ff.; JB 1.163.

time. This would seem to suggest that the morphological opposition between the Late Vedic Perfect Indicative and the Imperfect is mapped onto a privative semantic opposition based on the notion of inferentiality [+INFERENTIAL]. On this analysis, the Perfect Indicative represented the semantically marked member of the opposition, being obligatorily associated with the inferentiality feature, whereas the Imperfect is underspecified in this respect and hence in principle compatible with the feature. This account would be consistent with Pāṇini's definition of the Perfect Indicative as *bhūte paro'kṣe* 'in the past beyond the range of sight' and the Imperfect as *bhūte anadyatane* 'in the past not pertaining to the present day' and would presuppose that the inferential reading associated with the Middle Vedic Perfect Indicative had developed into a fixed semantic feature of the Late Vedic Perfect Indicative (cf. also Dahl 2009).

This analysis would be perfectly feasible if all the Late Vedic passages where the Perfect Indicative alternates with the Imperfect invariably began with one or more Perfect Indicative forms, but this turns out not to be the case. A number of passages of this type begin with an Imperfect form, as illustrated by the following examples:

[30] a. *asurā eṣu lokeṣu puro* ***akurvata****. ayasmayīm asmin, rajatām antarikṣa loke, hariṇīm ha ado divi* ***cakrire*** *te devāḥ pariśriteṣv eṣu lokeṣv etam pañcadaśam vajram* ***apaśyan*** (...) *etena vai devāḥ pañcadaśena vajreṇa ebhyo lokebhyo asurān* ***anudanta*** (KB 8.8)

'The Asuras made fortresses in the (three) worlds. They made an iron (fortress) in this (world), a silver (fortress) in the world of the atmosphere and a golden (fortress) there in the sky. When these (three) worlds were fortified, the gods saw the fifteenfold thunderbolt (...) By means of the fifteenfold thunderbolt the gods drove away the Asuras from these worlds'[52]

[52] Cf. Keith (1920: 396): 'The Asuras made citadels in these worlds, iron in this, silver in the world of the atmosphere, golden yonder in the sky they

b. *mādhyamāḥ sarasvatyām satram* ***āsata*** *tad dha api kavaṣo madhye* ***niṣasāda*** *tam ha ima* ***upocuḥ*** *dāsvā vai tvam putro asi na vayam tvayā saha bhakṣayiṣyāma iti sa ha kruddhaḥ pradravant sarasvatīm etena sūktena* ***tuṣṭāva*** *tam ha iyam anviyāya tata u ha ime nirāgā iva* ***menire*** *tam ha anvādrutya ūcuḥ ṛṣe namas te astu mā no hāsīḥ tvam vai naḥ śreṣṭho asi yam tvā iyam anveti iti tam ha* ***jñāpayām cakruḥ*** *tasya ha krodham* ***vininyuḥ*** (KB 12.3)

'The Mādhyamas performed a session on the Sarasvatī. Then Kavaṣa sat down in the midst, they said to him, "Thou art the son of a female slave; we will not eat with you." He rushing on in anger praised the Sarasvatī with this hymn; she followed after him; thereupon they felt themselves free from passion; they went after him and said "O seer, homage be to thee; harm us not; thou art of us the best, seeing that she follows after thee." Thus they informed him; they removed his anger.' (Keith 1920: 414)

In both these cases, we find Imperfect forms at the beginning of the narrative which is followed by one or more Perfect Indicative forms. The discourse context clearly indicates that the situations referred to are located at a past time which is not within the sphere of the speaker's own experience. But why does the speaker use an Imperfect form to indicate that this is so, if the Imperfect is underspecified with regard to inferentiality?

One way of solving this apparent dilemma would be to assume that the semantic distinction between explicit inferentiality and compatibility with implicit inferentiality can be exploited to distinguish between statements which are generally known or taken for granted and statements which introduce new or surprising information. Aikhenvald (2004: 315–324) discusses various ways in which first-hand and indirect evidentiality markers are used to manipulate discourse and notes that indirect

made; the gods when these worlds were invested saw the fifteenfold thunderbolt (...) By means of this fifteenfold thunderbolt the gods pushed away the Asuras from these worlds.'

evidential markers are sometimes used to advance the narrative time (cf. Aikhenvald 2004: 317–318 with references and Johanson 2003: 287). Given that the Late Vedic Perfect Indicative in fact represents an inferential category whereas the Imperfect is neutral in this respect, passages like those cited in [28] might simply represent a different stylistic genre than passages like those cited in [29]. Although I shall adopt this solution here, more detailed research is needed in order to clarify whether the two patterns illustrated by the two sets of examples actually represent two different synchronically available stylistic possibilities arising from a privative inferentiality distinction or whether the two sets of texts belong to different chronological layers, one in which the Perfect Indicative and the Imperfect had different aspectual properties and one in which they had the same aspectual properties, but differed in their respective implications with regard to information source.[53]

Before concluding this section, I would like to draw attention to the fact that first person Perfect Indicative forms are extremely scarce in Late Vedic. I have only come across the following two examples:[54]

---

[53] For instance, the different discourse functions associated with the Perfect Indicative and the Imperfect in cases like those cited in [24] might in principle arise from an aspectual distinction between perfective and imperfective or neutral. As the Middle Vedic Perfect Indicative represents a past perfective category, whereas the Imperfect represents a past neutral category, passages of that type might simply belong to an older layer than passages like those cited in [28] and [29]. I will have to postpone a discussion of this possibility for another occasion.

[54] Another possible example is found in *Pañcav̥iṃśabrāhmaṇa*, the chronological status of which, however, remains problematic (cf. Whitney 1892: 7; Witzel 1989: 147–148; Kümmel 2000: 6):

dīrghajihvī vā idaṁ rakṣo yajñahā yajñiyān avalihaty acarat tām indraḥ kayā cana māyayā hantuṃ na ****aśaknot*** (text reads ***aśaṁsat***, but cf. JB 1.161: ***śaśāka***) *atha ha sumitraḥ kutsaḥ kalyāṇa āsa tam abravīd imām acchā brūṣveti tām acchābrūta. sā enam abravīn na aha etan na* ****śuśruve*** (text reads ***śuśruva***) *priyam iva tu me hṛdayasyeti* (PVB 13.6.9)

'That demon Dīrghajihvī was a sacrifice-slayer used to lick down the sacrifices. Indra could not kill her by means of any sorcery whatsoever. Now

[31] a. *sa hovāca* | *bŕhaspátirāṅgiraso yadvái* ***śuśrumá*** *devā́nām pariṣūtaṃ tádeṣá yajñó bhavati yáchṛtā́ni havī́ṃṣi kḷptā védisténāvamárśamacāriṣṭa tásmātpā́pīyāṃso 'bhūta tenā́navamarśa yajadhvaṃ táthā śréyāṃso bhaviṣyathetyā kíyata ityā́ barhíṣa stáraṇādíti* (ŚBM 1.2.5.26)

'Bṛhaspati Āṅgirasa then said, "What we have heard of as produced for the gods that is this sacrifice, that is to say, the cooked oblations and the prepared altar; therewith you have performed while touching: that is why you have become more sinful. Sacrifice therefore without touching, for thus you will become righteous!" "How long?" they asked. "Till the spreading of the sacrificial grass (on the altar)", he said.' (Eggeling 1882: 67)

b. *tádu sámevá nayet nanvatrā́ntareṇa* ***śuśruma*** *sómena nú mā yājayatátha ma etádāpyā́yanaṃ sáṃbhariṣyathétyabravīdíti na vái medáṃ dhinoti yánmā dhinavattánme kurutéti* (ŚBM 1.6.4.11)

'He may nevertheless offer the Sânnâyya; for have we not heard within this place that he (Indra) said, "Do ye now offer Soma to me, and then ye will prepare for me that invigorating draught (âpyâyana, viz. the Sânnâyya)! This does not satiate me, prepare for me what will satiate me!"' (Eggeling 1882: 179)

I noted in the previous sections that first person forms of evidentiality markers tend to assume specialized readings or be avoided altogether. If it is correct that the Late Vedic Perfect Indicative obligatorily expresses that the statement is based on secondary evidence, the fact that we find only a couple of examples of first person Perfect Indicative forms in Late Vedic can be straightforwardly accounted for as a consequence of the semantic incompatibility between the inferentiality feature and the first person feature. As the verb *ŚRAV-* 'hear, listen' does not necessarily imply that the situation is within the subject's own sphere

---

there was a handsome man, Sumitra Kutsa. He (Indra) said to him: "Invite her to come near (to you)!" He invited her. She said to him: "Such a thing have I never heard, but it is pleasing to my heart."'

of control, the fact that an evidential marker is used in the above cases seems unproblematic. Aikhenvald (2004: 324–329) notes that languages with a grammaticalized evidentiality system sometimes show rather idiosyncratic and surprising lexicalized combinations of evidentiality markers and various lexical items. A tempting, yet somewhat speculative explanation of the fact that we encounter two first person Perfect Indicative forms of one and the same verb would be that the Late Vedic evidentiality distinction is neutralized with this particular verb, as it indicates the type of primary sensory evidence on which the account of situations denoted by the Perfect Indicative is normally based, namely hearsay.

4. SUMMARY AND PROSPECTS

Having reviewed the data from the different stages of Vedic, we now have a relatively clear picture of the semantic development of the Perfect Indicative. In Early Vedic, the oldest stage of the language, the Perfect Indicative represents a present anterior category with more or less the same range of readings as the English Present Perfect. However, I noted that Perfect Indicative forms of instantaneous achievement verbs have a stative present meaning which is not among the readings of the English Present Perfect and may be regarded as a typologically significant reading of the Early Vedic Perfect Indicative. I also claimed that the Perfect Indicative has an inferential reading in Early Vedic, which, however, is particularly transparent in clauses bound by an attitude verb.

In the younger layers of the *Ṛgveda*, which may be taken to belong to the Early Middle Vedic period, the Perfect Indicative was shown to be compatible with a relative past reading and a simple past reading, two readings which were argued to indicate that it has developed into a past perfective category. In section **3.3** I attempted to show that the Perfect Indicative behaves like a past perfective category in the Early Middle Vedic texts, which among other things is reflected in the fact that it has lost or is on the verge of losing its universal reading. I noted that the Early Middle Vedic Perfect Indicative in one case appears to have a conative-like reading, which might be taken as counterevidence against the claim that it represents a past perfective category and to suggest rather that it should be understood as a past neutral or past imperfective category. I argued that the example does not represent a clear-cut case of a conative construction, as the underlying predicate is atelic and not telic, but this is clearly a point where a more careful evaluation of the data may reveal that the present analysis is not entirely correct. If future research should falsify this particular claim, a likely alternative would be that the Perfect Indicative represents a past neutral category already at this stage. In any case, the Early Middle Vedic Perfect Indicative is compatible with an inferential reading, for instance when it is in the direct scope of an attitude verb.

As regards the Middle Vedic Perfect Indicative, it has a more restricted range of readings than it was shown to have in Early Vedic and Early Middle Vedic. For one thing, it appears to be incompatible with a recent past reference time, probably being blocked from such discourse contexts by the semantically more specific Aorist Indicative. Moreover, it is no longer used with an iterative meaning in this period. I argued that this may reflect that it is more intimately associated with the resultative reading, which typically has a single-event presupposition. Although the Perfect Indicative does seem to be compatible with and perhaps even intimately associated with an inferential implicature at this stage, the fact that it is only rarely attested in narrative discourse speaks against the assumption that it represents a proper inferentiality marker or that the Middle Vedic past tense system may be characterized as an evidentiality system. I concluded that the Middle Vedic Perfect Indicative represents a past perfective category with a salient inferential reading. Again, future research may reveal that this conclusion must somehow be revised, but nevertheless I think it is basically sound, given the data I have taken into consideration.

Finally, the Late Vedic Perfect Indicative was argued to represent an inferential past category with a neutral aspectual character. At this stage the morphological opposition between the Perfect Indicative and the Imperfect appears to be mapped onto a semantic opposition based on a privative inferentiality feature, where the Perfect Indicative is inherently specified for the feature [INFERENTIAL], whereas the Imperfect is underspecified with regard to that feature and hence in principle compatible with it. This account corresponds quite well to Pāṇini's definition of the Perfect Indicative as *bhūte paro'kṣe* 'in the past beyond the range of sight' and might be taken to suggest that Pāṇini's account of the past tenses in fact described a system which corresponded more or less closely to the one we find in the Late Vedic prose texts, based on a distinction between proximate and nonproximate (*anadyatane*) past, on the one hand, and direct and indirect (*paro'kṣe*) evidentiality on the other.

REFERENCES

ABUSH, Dorit 1997. Sequence of tense and temporal de re. *Linguistics and Philosophy* 20: 1–50.

AIKHENVALD, Alexandra 2003. Evidentiality in typological perspective. In: A. Aikhenvald & R. M. W. Dixon (eds.), *Studies in Evidentiality*: 1–31. Amsterdam: Benjamins.

——— 2004. *Evidentiality*. Oxford: Oxford University Press.

BLOOMFIELD, Maurice 1897. *Hymns of the Atharva-Veda*. Oxford: Oxford University Press.

BYBEE, Joan & Östen DAHL 1989. The creation of tense and aspect systems in the languages of the world. *Studies in Language* 13: 51–103.

BYBEE, Joan, Revere PERKINS & William PAGLIUCA 1994. *The Evolution of Grammar*. Chicago: University of Chicago Press.

CARDONA, George 2002. The old Indo-Aryan tense system. In: J. P. Brereton & S. Insler (eds.), *Indic and Iranian Studies in Honor of Stanley Insler on His Sixty-Fifth Birthday* (Journal of the American Oriental Society, 122): 235–243.

CHIERCHIA, Gennaro & Sally MCCONNELL-GINET 2000. *Meaning and Grammar. An Introduction to Semantics*. Cambridge, Mass.: MIT Press.

COMRIE, Bernhard 1985. *Tense*. Cambridge: Cambridge University Press.

DAHL, Eystein 2008. *Time, Tense and Aspect in Early Vedic Grammar. A Time Relational Approach to the Morphosyntax-Semantics Interface*. Ph.D. thesis, University of Oslo.

——— 2009. Semantische und pragmatische Faktoren in der Entwicklung des altindoarischen Perfekts. Elisabeth Rieken & Paul Widmer (eds.), *Pragmatische Kategorien. Form, Funktion und Diachronie. Akten der Arbeitstagung der Indogermanischen Gesellschaft vom 24. bis 26. September 2007 in Marburg*: 35–50. Wiesbaden: Reichert.

——— 2010. *Time, Tense and Aspect in Early Vedic Grammar. Exploring Inflectional Semantics in the Rigveda*. Leiden: Brill.

——— 2012. Evidence for Evidentiality in Late Vedic. In: Jared Klein & Kazuhiko Yoshida (eds.), *Indic Across the Milennia: From the Rigveda to Modern Indo-Aryan. 14th World Sanskrit Conference, Kyoto, Japan, September 1st–5th, 2009. Proceedings of the Linguistics Section*. Bremen: Ute Hempen, 9–23.

——— 2013. Typological change in Vedic: tne development of the Aorist from a Perfective Past to an Immediate Past. In: Folke Josephson & Ingemar Söhrman (eds.), *Diachronic and Typological* Perspectives: 261–298. Amsterdam: Benjamins.

———, forthcoming (a). Zur Typologie des frühvedischen Tempus/Aspektsystems. In: Rosemarie Lühr & Suzanne Zeilfelder (eds.), *Struktur und Semantik der Verbalphrase. Akten der Arbeitstagung der Indogermanischen Gesellschaft in Jena* 2006. Wiesbaden: Reichert.

———, forthcoming (b). A note on the temporal semantics of the Early Vedic past tenses. In: Joel Brereton & Patrick Olivelle (eds.), *Selected Papers from the Fourth International Vedic Workshop, University of Texas at Austin, May 24th–27th, 2007*. New Delhi: Motilal Banarsidass.

DAHL, Östen 1985. *Tense and Aspect Systems*. Oxford: Blackwell.

DINI, Luca & Pier Marco BERTINETTO 1995. Punctual verbs and the linguistic ontology of events. In: *Quaderni del Laboratorio di Linguistica della Scuola Normale Superiore* 9: 123–160. Pisa: Scuola Normale Superiore.

DOWTY, David 1979. *Word Meaning and Montague Grammar*. Dordrecht: Kluwer.

EBERLE, Kurt & Walter KASPER 1994. French past tenses and temporal structure. In: Rolf Thieroff & Joachim Ballweg (eds.), *Tense System in European Languages*: 149–172. Tübingen: Niemeyer.

EGGELING, Julius (trans.) 1882. *The Satapatha-Brāhmaṇa according to the Mādhyandina School. Books I and II*. Oxford: Clarendon Press.

——— (trans.) 1885. *The Satapatha-Brāhmaṇa according to the Mādhyandina School. Books III and IV*. Oxford: Clarendon Press.

GELDNER, Karl F. (trans.) 1951. *Der Rig-Veda*, I–III. (Harvard Oriental Series, 33–35.) Cambridge, Mass.: Harvard University Press.

GONDA, Jan 1975. *Vedic Literature*. (A History of Indian Literature, I.1.) Wiesbaden: Harrassowitz.

HOFFMANN, Karl 1967. *Der Injunktiv im Veda. Eine synchronische Funktionsuntersuchung*. Heidelberg: Winter.

JOB, Michael 1994. Zur Funktion des Perfekts im Ṛgveda. In R. Bielmeier & Reinhard Stempel (eds.), *Indogermanica et Caucasica. Festschrift für Karl Horst Schmidt zum 65. Geburtstag*: 41–62. Berlin: De Gruyter.

JOHANSON, Lars 2003. Evidentiality in Turkic. In: A. Aikhenvald & R. M. W. Dixon (eds.), *Studies in Evidentiality*: 272–290. Amsterdam: Benjamins.

KAMP, Hans & Uwe REYLE 1993. *From Discourse to Logic. Introduction to Modeltheoretic Semantics of Natural Language, Formal Logic and Discourse Representation Theory*. Dordrecht: Kluwer.

KEITH, Arthur Berriedale (trans.) 1914. *The Veda of the Black Yajus School Entitled Taittirīya Sanhita*, I–II. (Harvard Oriental Series, 18–19.) Cambridge, Mass.: Harvard University Press.

——— (trans.) 1920. *Rigveda Brāhmaṇas. The Aitareya and Kauṣītaki Brāhmaṇas of the Rigveda*. (Harvard Oriental Series, 25.) Cambridge, Mass.: Harvard University Press.

KIPARSKY, Paul 1998. Aspect and event structure in Vedic. In: R. Singh (ed.), *The Yearbook of South Asian Languages and Linguistics 1, 1998*: 29–61. New Delhi: Sage Publications.

——— 2002. Event structure and the perfect. In: David I. Beaver *et al.* (eds.), *The Construction of Meaning*: 113–135. Stanford: CSLI Publications.

KLEIN, Jared 1985. *Toward a Discourse Grammar of the Rigveda*, I: *Coordinate Conjunction*, Part 2. Heidelberg: Carl Winter.

KLEIN, Wolfgang 1994. *Time in Language*. London: Routledge.

——— 1995. A time-relational analysis of Russian aspect. *Language* 71: 669–695.

KRATZER, Angelica 1981. The notional category of modality. In: H. J. Eikmeyer & H. Reiser (eds.), *Worlds, Words and Contexts. New Approaches in Word Semantics*: 38–74. Berlin: De Gruyter.

——— 1998. More structural analogies between pronouns and tenses. In: Devon Strolovitch & Aaron Lawson (eds.), *Proceedings of SALT VII*: 92–110. Ithaca: Cornell University.

KRICK, Hertha 1982. *Das Ritual der Feuergründung*. Wien: Österreichische Akademie der Wissenschaften.

KRIFKA, Mannfred 1998. The origins of telicity. In: Susan Rothstein (ed.), *Events and Grammar*: 197–235. Dordrecht: Kluwer.

KÜMMEL, Martin 2000. *Das Perfekt im Indoiranischen*. Wiesbaden: Reichert.

LUBOTSKY, Alexander 2002. *Atharvaveda-Paippalāda. Kāṇḍa Five.* Harvard, Mass.: Department of Sanskrit and Indian Studies.

MUMM, Peter Arnold 2002. Retrospektivität im Ṛgveda: Aorist und Perfect. In: Heinrich Hettrich (ed.), *Indogermanische Syntax – Fragen und Perspektiven*: 157–188. Wiesbaden: Reichert.

OGIHARA, Toshiyuki 1995. Double-access sentences and reference to states. *Natural Language Semantics* 3: 177–210.

OLIVELLE, Patrick 1996. *The Early Upanishads*. New York: Oxford University Press.

OLSEN, Mari Bromann 1994. The semantics and pragmatics of lexical aspect features. *Studies in the Linguistic Sciences* 24: 361–375.

PARSONS, Terrence 1990. *Events in the Semantics of English. A Study in Subatomic Semantics*. Cambridge, Mass.: MIT Press.

REICHENBACH, Hans 1947. *Elements of Symbolic Logic*. London: Macmillan.

RENOU, Louis 1925. *La valeur du parfait dans les hymnes védiques*. Paris: Librairie ancienne Édouard Champion.

ROTHSTEIN, Susan 2004. *Structuring Events*. Oxford: Blackwell.

SMITH, Carlota 1997. *The Parameter of Aspect*. Dordrecht: Kluwer.

——— 2004. The domain of tense. In: Jaqueline Guéron & Jaqueline Lecarme (eds.), *The Syntax of Time*: 589–619. Cambridge, Mass.: MIT Press.

STALNAKER, Robert 2002. Common ground. *Linguistics and Philosophy* 25: 701–721.

STECHOW, Arnim von 1995a. On the proper treatment of tense. Available at http://www2.sfs.uni-tuebingen.de/~arnim10/Aufsaetze/SALT95.pdf

——— 1995b. Tense in intensional contexts: two semantic accounts of Abusch's theory of tense. Available at: http://www2.sfs.uni-tuebingen.de/~arnim10/Aufsaetze/TenseAbusch.pdf

TICHY, Eva 1997. Vom indogermanischen Tempus/Aspekt-System zum vedischen Zeitstufensystem. In: E. Crespo & J. L. García Ramón (eds.), *Berthold Delbrück y la sintaxis indoeuropea hoy. Actas del Coloquio de la indogermanische Gesellschaft 21–24 septiembre de 1994*: 589–609. Madrid: Reichert.

TRAUGOTT, Elizabeth C. & Alan B. DASHER 2005. *Regularity in Semantic Change*. Cambridge: Cambridge University Press.

VENDLER, Zeno 1957. Verbs and times. *The Philosophical Review* 66: 143–160.

VERKUYL, Henk J. 1993. *A Theory of Aspectuality. The Interaction between Temporal and Atemporal Structure*. Cambridge: Cambridge University Press.

WHITNEY, William D. 1892. On the narrative use of imperfect and perfect in the Brahmanas. *Transactions of the American Philological Association* 23: 5–34.

——— (trans.) 1905. *Atharva-Veda Saṁhitā*, I–II. Edited by C. R. Lanman. (Harvard Oriental Series, 7–8.) Cambridge, Mass.: Harvard University Press.

WITZEL, Michael 1987. Localisation of Vedic texts. In: G. Pollet (ed.), *India and the Ancient World. History, Trade and Culture before A.D. 650. P. H. L. Eggermont Jubilee Volume, Presented on the Occasion of His Seventieth Birthday*: 173–213. Leuven: Departement oriëntalistiek.

——— 1989. Tracing the Vedic dialects. In: Colette Caillat (ed.), *Dialectes dans les langues indo-aryennes*: 97–265. Paris: College de France, Institut de Civilisation Indienne.

——— 1995a. Early Indian history: linguistic and textual parameters. In: G. Erdosy (ed.), *Language, Material Culture and Ethnicity. The Indo-Aryans of Ancient South Asia*: 85–125. New York: De Gruyter.

——— 1995b. Ṛgvedic history: poets, chieftains and polities. In: G. Erdosy (ed.), *Language, Material Culture and Ethnicity. The Indo-Aryans of Ancient South Asia*: 307–352. New York: De Gruyter.

ZEHNDER, Thomas 1999. *Atharvaveda-Paippalāda, Buch 2*. Idstein: Schulz-Kirchner Verlag.

RIVELEX – Presenting the First Volume of a New Dictionary of the *Ṛgveda*

THOMAS KRISCH

0. The *Ṛgveda* is one of the most important Vedic texts in many fields of research. While it is of central interest for Indologists, theologians and comparative philologists alike, it is also an essential corpus within linguistic studies and for people investigating culture.

As is well known, there already exists an admirable dictionary of the *Ṛgveda* composed by the great linguist and mathematician Hermann Grassmann (1873–75). This monumental and exemplary work remains the only Ṛgvedic dictionary to date. In 1996, the sixth edition of this dictionary, revised by Maria Kozianka, was published, which, essentially, introduced Grassmann's addenda into the main text and corrected misprints. As Vedic studies have made considerable progress since 1873, there is a need for a completely new dictionary of the *Ṛgveda*, which should focus on the current expertise and include the progress which has been made in the past 140 years – since Grassmann's work was first published. Our new dictionary (Krisch 2006, henceforth referred to as RIVELEX) tries to fulfil this need.[1] We

[1] This article is meant to give a short impression of the main features of this dictionary. It was written in 2007. This text has been left essentially unaltered. In the meantime the first volume of RIVELEX was published as an e-book (Krisch 2012a) with additions and corrections and the second volume was published in printed form (Krisch 2012b) and as an e-book (Krisch 2012c). Additional information about the structure of RIVELEX can

are currently in times that are optimal for writing a new dictionary of the *Rgveda*. In addition to a great deal of recent monographic research (e.g. Gotō 1987; Jamison 1983; Heenen 2006; Kümmel 1996; 2000; Kulikov 2001; 2012; Krisch 1996; Rix *et al.* 2001; Niederreiter 2001; Oberlies 1998; 1999; Sadovski 1996; 2001; Scarlata 1999; Schaefer 1994; Werba 1997, etc.) the following are also employed:

- a concordance (Lubotsky 1997),
- printed and electronic versions of the text of the *Ṛgveda* (van Nooten & Holland 1994, with disk; electronic versions including a 'Padapāṭha'-version on the internet:[2] http://titus.uni-frankfurt.de/indexd.htm),
- an excellent new etymological dictionary (Mayrhofer 1992–2001),
- various outstanding translations (Geldner 1951; Renou 1955–69; Elizarenkova 1999).

1.0. The following five points are particularly noteworthy when comparing Grassmann with RIVELEX:

1.1. The semantics of numerous lexical entries is interpreted differently today. One example is *arí-*, which now is held to mean

---

be obtained by reading the preface to the first published volume (Krisch 2006; with additional remarks in Krisch 2012b). My collaborators for the first volume have been Christina Katsikadeli (contributor), Stefan Niederreiter (contributor) and Thomas Kaltenbacher (English translations). Until 2007, RIVELEX has been supported by the following FWF (Austrian Science Fund) projects: P14411-SPR (2000–2002), P15833-G03 (2002–2004) and P17799-G03 (2004–2007). Thanks to Lucy Cripps for checking the English of this article from a native speaker's point of view. Registered trade marks are not marked as such. My thanks also go to Petteri Koskikallio for his careful editorial remarks and additions. I take full responsibility for the remaining faults, of course.

[2] June 3, 2013. Click on 'Textdatenbank' under 'Textus' and select 'Indic [Vedic]'.

something like 'a person exposed in Ṛgvedic society'. This paraphrase comprises meanings such as

a. socially and /or economically high-ranking person;
b. someone being different; a stranger or enemy;
c. someone who does not share his riches;
d. another sacrificer who does not sacrifice enough.

In Grassmann's dictionary, this lexical entry is interpreted as an adjective. His German meanings 'regsam, strebsam' can be rendered as something like 'lively, active'. From 'lively, active' Grassmann derives the meanings 'pious, greedy and hostile'. If it is assumed that Latin *alius* 'the other one' could be cognate to *arí-* and to ved. *anyá-* 'the other' and that ved. *aryá-* 'master' can be derived from *arí-*[3] then it is more difficult to match Grassmann's semantic interpretation with these semantics than is the case with the treatment in RIVELEX (exemplified above by the meanings **a–d**).

1.2. Grassmann has many good semantic insights which he presents in an intuitive way. An example is the word *anūcāná-* with the meaning learned, erudite'. Grassmann writes: '"recitierend" ... daher *gelehrt*'. The approach in RIVELEX tries to apply findings of diachronic linguistic research when these add to the understanding of the semantics of the lexical entry. It is well-known in historical semantics that one path for the change of meaning is the promotion of an implication to a primary meaning.[4] In this case the repetitive Brahmanic method of learning

[3] For a more detailed discussion cf. the respective lexical entries in RIVELEX.

[4] Cf. e.g. Panagl 1996. The RIVELEX also makes use of other semantic concepts. One of them is the 'incorporation' of meaning from arguments into the lexical meaning of the verb in order to link different shades of meaning of a verb (for diachronic investigations in this area cf. Krisch 1984, especially chapter 2). A Ṛgvedic example of this phenomenon is the verb *aj-* which

the ancient texts can account for *anūcāná-*, a middle perfect participle from *vac-* ‘speak’ and *ánu* ‘after’: ‘repeat something by speaking or singing after something’. The implication, that one gets ‘learned’ by doing that is promoted to primary meaning (cf. also RIVELEX, p. 222). This type of semantic change can be compared with the development of the German verb *kriegen*. This verb means ‘to get’ but it is a denominative weak verb formation from German *Krieg* ‘war’ and originally meant: ‘lead a war against’. For this original meaning cf. [1]:

[1] LENZ Schwabenkrieg 136b, (ca. 1500)
(cited after Grimm’s Deutsches Wörterbuch):[5]

vil	*ritter*	*und*	*menger*	*edelman,*
many a	knight	and	many a	nobleman

die	*wellen*	*die Swytzer*	*kriegen*
they.NOM.PL	want.to	the Swiss.ACC.PL	fight.INF

‘many a knight and many a nobleman, they want to fight the Swiss (Acc.)’

The modern German meaning of *kriegen*, ‘to get’, represents the promotion of an implication (i.e. a desired consequence when one leads a war) to a primary meaning.[6]

---

normally means ‘to drive, move someone/something forward in a certain direction’ (semantic roles: ACTOR, THEME, GOAL). But there is also a lexicalised meaning when the verb occurs with the preverbs *ā́* ‘here’ or *sám* ‘together’. Here the THEME in the meaning ‘booty’ is incorporated into the lexical meaning of the verb and the verb translates as ‘somebody drives booty here / together’. The overt THEME disappears and the meaning of the verb gets more specialised. An example of this meaning would be 1.100.11ab *sá jāmíbhir yát samájāti mīḷhé (á)jāmibhir vā puruhūtá évaiḥ* ‘When, with kinsmen or with strangers, he [scil. Indra] will drive booty together with zeal in the fight, invoked by many ...’

[5] http://woerterbuchnetz.de/DWB/ (June 1, 2013), under ‘kriegen, fehden, befehden’.

[6] In combination with preverbs the verb *kriegen* retains its old martial meaning, e.g.: *bekriegen* ‘wage war on’; *sich zerkriegen* (regionally used in Bavaria and in Austria) ‘behave in a hostile way towards one another’.

1.3. In Grassmann's dictionary, forms which belong to the same verbal paradigm are sometimes dealt with separately. Grassmann lists a lexical entry *īr* (containing e.g. *īrte*), which belongs to the verb *ar*[1]- 'to set (oneself) in motion', and in Grassmann there is no cross reference under *ar* to refer to *īr*. The RIVELEX aims at putting these forms together (thus, *īr*- may be found under *ar*[1]-) with cross-references to *ar*[1]- for the forms starting with *īr*-.

1.4. While Grassmann lists the individual forms, he often does not analyse them morphologically. Substantial progress has been made in this particular field of research, and the morphological definition of many forms has changed considerably.

Thus, Grassmann interprets the verbal form *arcase* as a 1st sg. middle of the aorist of *arc* 'sing, praise'. There is no comparable form of the aorist of this root attested in Vedic and Sanskrit. Consequently, this form is now interpreted in another way. Since Rasmussen's seminal article from 1985, it is known that this form belongs to a category of the Vedic verb which Rasmussen terms 'prospective' and probably has nothing to do with an aorist. There are 10 verbs, mostly those of saying, in the *Ṛgveda* which show forms of this 'prospective'; and there are about 50 attestations in the text.[7] RIVELEX offers this new interpretation.

1.5. Grassmann does not consistently provide all the references for more frequently used words – in the sense of 'tokens' nor does he comprehensively analyse them. RIVELEX aims at listing and analysing all the attestations of all the words of the *Ṛgveda*.

---

[7] E.g. *gāyiṣe* (1st person sg. from *gāyati* 'sing'), *yajase* (1st. person sg. from *yajati* 'make a sacrifice'), *stuṣe* (1st, 2nd and 3rd person sg. from *stauti* 'praise'), etc.

2. A linguistically oriented, up-to-date dictionary accompanying a large corpus should provide:

a. adaptable, individually modelled queries;
b. linguistically relevant information;
c. clarity;
d. international usability.

ad **a.** The first volume of RIVELEX came with a CD-ROM containing an abridged version of the text as a .pdf-file, as a .rtf-file, and as a Microsoft Word file to enhance search possibilities. The second volume and a second edition of volume one were published as e-books in pdf-format (see Krisch 2012a; 2012c).

ad **b.** Users should be able to retrieve a sort of 'minimal Ṛgvedic grammar' from RIVELEX, as detailed information is supplied concerning semantics, syntax and morphology.

ad **c.** The clear structure of this dictionary should be guaranteed by adopting the basic concept of Grassmann's well structured dictionary. However, RIVELEX does not include a characteristic often found with Grassmann, i.e. microcontext. This procedure would have stretched the new dictionary considerably. The lack of this feature is compensated by the fact, that the e-book versions (Krisch 2012a; 2012c) contain the whole Rigveda in electronic form in addition to the dictionary. Thus, one may always have a look at the context.

ad **d.** The main language of translation and of the commentaries is German. In order to adapt this dictionary for international users, English translations are provided in some parts. English translations are included for the main headline translation and everything that is linked with the 'grey box' (see below). (Addition 2013: Since this feature has been criticized by a number of colleagues in expert opinions and in reviews as being too clumsy and too confusing, from volume two onward, English will be present only in the e-book versions of the dictionary)

3.0. This section offers some examples for (abridged) lexical entries.

3.1. Starting with the noun *agní-* for 'fire' and 'god of fire'.

[2]

agní- (subst.) m. „FEUER; FEUERGOTT[1]"– 'FIRE; GOD OF FIRE[1]', Vaiśvānara*, Jātavedas**

I Feuer
▪ fire
II der Feuergott: N. pr., allgemein und mit verschiedenen Funktionen[2]
▪ the God of Fire: n. pr., in general and with various functions[2]
III Besondere Erscheinungen und Funktionen des Feuergottes
▪ specific appearances and functions of the God of Fire
als natürliches Feuer[3] – as natural fire[3]
1 Sonnen-, Lichtgott
▪ God of the sun, God of the light
2 Blitz-/Donner- u. Regengott
▪ God of lightning/thunder and rain
3 Feuer auf der Erde (meistens in Pflanzen und Gewässern)[4]
▪ fire on earth (mostly in plants and waters)[4]
als rituelles Feuer – as ritual fire
4 Opferfeuer
▪ sacrificial fire
4a Herdfeuer beim häuslichen Opfer (gṛhápati-agni)
▪ fire in the hearth during the domestic sacrifice (gṛhápati-agni)
4b Bote, Vermittler (Opferfahrer, Wagenlenker) zwischen Göttern und Menschen (Himmel und Erde) beim Opferritual
▪ messenger, mediator (driver at the sacrifice, chariot driver) between the Gods and man (heaven and earth) during the ritual of the sacrifice
4c Leichenfeuer
▪ funeral fire

Nom.Sg. *agnís* I 1.112.17; 1.161.9; 1.169.3; 6.18.10; 7.50.2; 10.78.2; 10.84.2; II 1.1.2; 1.1.5; 1.36.17abcd; 1.59.6*; 1.59.7*; 1.60.4 (auch zu 4a); ...

Vok.Sg. *ágne* II 1.1.6; 1.1.9; 1.14.7; 1.14.10; 1.36.12; 1.44.11; 1.58.8; 1.75.2; 1.75.3; 1.75.4; 1.79.4**; ...

Vok.Sg. *agne* **II** 1.1.7; 1.19.1; 1.19.2; 1.19.9; 1.23.24; 1.26.10; 1.27.7; 1.31.1; 1.31.2; 1.31.3; 1.31.5; ...

Akk.Sg. *agním* **I** 1.116.8; 2.12.3; 2.24.7; 3.31.15; 4.39.2; 8.73.8; 10.61.9; 10.64.8; 10.68.9; 10.136.1; 10.155.5; **II** 1.1.1; 1.12.7; 1.12.9; 1.14.3; ...

Akk.Sg. *agním-agnim*[5] **II** 1.12.2; 8.60.17; **III 4** 6.15.6

Instr. Sg. *agnínā* **II** 1.1.3; 1.36.18; 8.35.1; **III 4** 1.12.6; 1.162.11; 5.43.7; 8.43.14

Dat.Sg. *agnáye* **II** 1.74.1; 1.77.1; 1.78.5; 1.79.10; 1.127.10bc; 1.140.1; 1.143.1(auch zu 3); 3.2.1*; 3.6.1; 3.10.5; 3.13.1 (auch zu 4b); 4.5.1*; 5.5.11; 5.7.1; 5.12.1; 5.25.7; 6.3.2; 6.8.1* *; 6.10.3; 6.16.22; 6.48.1**; 7.4.1 (auch zu 4b); 7.5.1* (auch zu 4b); 7.8.6; 7.13.1*; 7.14.1**; 7.15.4; 7.62.2; 8.19.22; 8.23.15; 8.103.6; 10.80.7; 10.85.41; 10.91.14; 10.187.1; **III 4** 1.127.4; 4.8.5; 5.5.1** (auch zu II); 5.16.1; 7.3.7; 8.19.5; 8.23.23; 8.43.11(auch zu 4b); 8.103.8 (auch zu II); **4a** 8.23.24; **4b** 8.44.27

Abl.Sg. *agnés* **II** 10.62.5; 10.62.6; 10.76.5; 10.181.2; **III 4c** 10.16.7

Gen.Sg. *agnés* **I** 2.25.3; 2.38.5; 8.6.7; 8.73.9; 9.22.2; 10.34.11; **II** 1.24 ... ...

Gen.Pl. *agnīnā́m* **I** 10.78.3

Lok.Pl. *agníṣu* **III 4** 1.108.4; 5.6.6; 7.1.22

Iir.: jav. *Dāštāγni-*, akkad.-iran. *Ag-nu-par-nu* (nicht einmütig akzeptiert); idg.: lat. *ignis*, lit. *ugnìs*, aksl. *ognь* „Feuer" (die Ausgangsform dieser unstreitig zusammengehörigen Formen ist im Anlaut nicht geklärt), vgl. EWAia s.v.; Lubotsky 1988: 38 rekonstruiert *$(H_2)ng^{u}ni$-*. – Pā. *aggi-*, *aggini-*, *gini-* m., Pkt. *aggi-*, *aggini-*, *agaṇi-* 'fire', vgl. Tu. s.v.

[1] Die Übergänge zur Naturerscheinung sind fließend, s. auch Oldenberg 1894: 43ff. Zum Feuerritual allgemein vgl. Krick 1982.

· The transitions between the god and the natural phenomenon are floating, see also Oldenberg 1894: 43ff. For the fire ritual in general see Krick 1982.

[2] Als Hotṛ, Schutzpatron der Opferhandlung und der Familie (sorgt für Kinderreichtum), Vater und Freund des Menschen, kosmische Kraft.

· As Hotṛ, Patron Saint of sacrificing and the family (provides a large number of children).

[3] Auch im Sinne des Wasserkreislaufs (Verdampfen durch Hitze, lebensspendend durch Wärme und Wasser). Die Pluralformen können sich auf die unterschiedlichen Formen Agnis beziehen; Agni in den Gewässern: evtl. als Spiegelung der Sonne im Meer, in Flüssen und Seen zu interpretieren.

* Also in the sense of the water cycle (evaporation through heat, life giving through warmth and water). The plurals may relate to the different forms of Agni; Agni in the waters: may be interpreted as a reflection of the sun in the sea, rivers and lakes.

[4] vgl. z.B. Janda 2000: 194.

* Cf. e.g. Janda 2000: 194.

[6] verstärkend-iterativ.

The lemma in [2] starts with the stem form and is followed by the part of speech information – in this case a substantive/noun; then the gender is mentioned – in this case masculine – followed by the German translation and – after a hyphen – by the English translation. The next pieces of information 'Vaiśvānara' and 'Jātavedas' are marked by asterisks. These asterisks are repeated when the places of the individual attestations are cited, where Agni either gets the epithet Vaiśvānara (one asterisk, e.g. in 1.59.6) or Jātavedas (two asterisks, e.g. in 1.79.4).

Another feature of this dictionary can also be seen in the above example: there are footnotes which give additional information or comments on difficult passages. Footnotes are placed at the end of each lemma.

If the semantics of a lemma is more complex (as is the case with *agní-*), it is explained in the 'grey box' (so called because of its grey background). In the case of Agni one can find different shades of meaning where numbers refer to the morphology part in which all the individual attestations are listed. In this case, the 'grey box' contains information about the different manifestations of Agni, e.g. as fire in the hearth during the domestic sacrifice (**III 4a**) etc.

One point worth noting: every explanation and translation occurring in the part above the 'grey box' and inside the 'grey box' is given in German and in English, including the footnotes. For everything below the 'grey box', only German is used as a language of translation. Thus, footnote 5 is only in German.

Below the 'grey box' there is a morphological section where all the attestations for the individual case forms can be found. In [2], an extract of the morphological forms of Agni can be seen. Naturally, all the 1724 occurrences of Agni appearing in the *Ṛg-veda* are dealt with in RIVELEX. This dictionary aims at dealing with all the word forms appearing in the *Ṛgveda*, also with all the 'little' words' forms like pronouns, preverbs and conjunctions.

For the reader's guidance brief remarks on etymology and word formation in smaller characters have been included following the form block. We also name Middle Indian (Pāli and Prākrit) and sometimes also Modern Indian (Hindī, Marāṭhī) continuations (without further investigation) as supplementary information following Turner 1966. Using Agni, this information layout can be seen in example [2] above.

3.2. Taking now a verbal lemma: the very common word for 'to go', the root *ay*[1]-. The verbal roots in the RIVELEX are given in Guṇa, in the normal ablaut grade, as in Mayrhofer's etymological dictionary (Mayrhofer 1992–2001). Therefore this root may be found under the headletter *a* and not under *i*, as is the Indian tradition. There is, however, a cross reference under *i*- referring to *ay*-.

[3] (without footnotes)

ay[1]- (v.) facientiv-intransitiv „GEHEN, KOMMEN; WANDERN; FAHREN; GELANGEN"; – 'WALK/GO, COME; HIKE; DRIVE; REACH'; ácha, áchā prá (nahe hinzugehen – move close); **áchā párā** (weggehen – go away); **áchā sám** (nahe zusammenkommen – come close together); **áti** (hindurchlaufen; hinwegkommen, überwinden – run through; get over, overcome); **áti abhí** (hindurch hinzugehen – approach through); **áti prá** (vorüberschreiten an – march past s.th./s.o.); **ádhi** (denken an, erkennen, sich intensiv geistig beschäftigen mit – think of s.th., recognize s.th., to set one's mind strongly on s.th./s.o.); **ádhi ā́ niṣ** (herauskommen, vorantreten – come out, step ahead); **ádhi ví** (von einem Ort aus in verschiedene ...

prá sám (zusammen vorankommen – getting ahead together); **práti** (sich wenden an; zurückkehren – turn o.s. to, return); **ví** (durchlaufen; in verschiedene Richtungen gehen – run through; go into different directions); **sám** (hingelangen; zusammenkommen, sich vereinigen – reach; get together, unite); **húruk** (abseits gehen – go aside)
Tiefenkasus-Schemata (semantische Rollen):
▪ Deep Case Frames (Semantic Roles/Theta Roles):
1 [ACTOR =] THEME; 2 [ACTOR =] THEME – GOAL; 3 [ACTOR =] THEME – SOURCE – (GOAL); 4 [ACTOR =] THEME – PATH (–GOAL); 5 EXPERIENCER – (THEME); 6 [ACTOR =] THEME – $GOAL_1$ – $GOAL_2$; 7 [ACTOR =] THEME – INSTRUMENT

1 [ACTOR =] THEME „jmd./etwas geht/kommt" GOAL unspezifiziert
▪ [ACTOR =] THEME 's.b./s.th. goes/comes' GOAL not specified
1a [ACTOR =] THEME „jmd./etwas geht/kommt" [ACTOR =] THEME = Nom. +/-bel., +/-abstr. (**Simplex**); Aktiv
▪ [ACTOR =] THEME 's.b./s.th. goes/comes' [ACTOR =] THEME = Nom. +/-bel., +/-abstr. (**Simplex**); active
1aa [ACTOR =] THEME „jmd./etwas geht/kommt" [ACTOR =] THEME = Nom. +/-bel., -abstr. + in der Nähe des Verbums stehendes, eine Richtung angebendes prädikatives Adj. (**Simplex**); Aktiv
▪ [ACTOR =] THEME 's.b./s.th. goes/comes' [ACTOR =] THEME = Nom. +/-bel., -abstr. + predicative Adj. in the vicinity of the verb, specifying a direction (**Simplex**); active
2 [ACTOR =] THEME – GOAL „jmd./etwas geht/kommt in eine bestimmte Richtung"
▪ [ACTOR =] THEME – GOAL 's.b./s.th. goes /comes in/to a certain direction'
2a [ACTOR =] THEME „jmd./etwas geht/kommt in eine bestimmte Richtung" (Richtung ist vom jeweiligen Präverb/Adverb abhängig) [ACTOR =] THEME = Nom. +/-bel., -abstr.; GOAL = Präverbien/ Adverbien: **áchā prá; ánu; ápa; ápa ā́ párā; ápa párā; abhí; abhí ā́; abhí prá; áva; asmatrā́; ā́ ; ā́ úd; ā́ níṣ; ā́ nédīyas; (ā́) púnar; ā práti; ā́ sám; úd; úpa; úpa prá; úpa sám; kúha cit; kvà; dūrám; níṣ; párā; pári; pari pra; purás; pṛ́tak; prá-prā; prá purás; práti; ví; vi pra; sám; húruk**; Aktiv
▪ [ACTOR =] THEME 's.b./s.th. goes/comes in/to a certain direction' (the direction depends on the particular preverb/adverb) [ACTOR =] THEME = Nom. +/-bel., -abstr.; GOAL = preverbs/adverbs: **áchā prá; ánu; ápa; ápa ā́ párā; ápa párā; abhí; abhí ā́; abhí prá; áva; asmatrā́; ā́ ; ā́**

úd; ā́ níṣ; ā́ nédīyas; (ā́) púnar; ā práti; ā́ sám; úd; úpa; úpa prá; úpa sám; kúha cit; kvà; dūrám; níṣ; párā; pári; pari pra; purás; pṛ́tak; prá-prā; prá purás; práti; ví; vi pra; sám; húruk; active

2b [ACTOR =] THEME – GOAL „jmd./etwas geht/kommt in eine bestimmte Richtung“ (Richtung ist vom jeweiligen Präverb/Adverb abhängig); [ACTOR =] THEME = Nom. +/-bel., -abstr.; GOAL = **ácha; áchā prá; áchā párā; áchā sám; áti; áti abhí; áti prá; ánu; ánu párā; ánu; anu áva; ánu párā; ánu prá; ápi; ápi púnar; abhí; abhí ā́; abhí úd; abhí úpa; abhí ní; abhí prá; abhí ví; abhí sám; áva; áva ā́; ā́; ā́ úpa; ā́ úpa nédīyas; ā́ níṣ; ā́ nédīyas; ā́ púnar; ā́ sám; úd; úd práti; úpa; úpa prá; ní; pári; párā; párā púnar; párā ví; púnar; púras; prá; prá sám; práti; ví; sám;** mit appositiv dazugesetztem Akk. +/-bel.,+/-abstr.; *Lok. -bel., -abstr.; **Dat. +/-bel., +/-abstr.; Aktiv

▪ [ACTOR =] THEME – GOAL 's.b./s.th. goes/comes in/to a certain direction' (the direction depends on the particular preverb/adverb) [ACTOR =] THEME = Nom. +/-bel., -abstr.; GOAL = **ácha; áchā prá; áchā párā; áchā sám; áti; áti abhí; áti prá; ánu; ánu párā; ánu; anu áva; ánu párā; ánu prá; ápi; ápi púnar; abhí; abhí ā́; abhí úd; abhí úpa; abhí ní; abhí prá; abhí ví; abhí sám; áva; áva ā́ ; ā́ ; ā́ úpa; ā́ úpa nédīyas; ā́ níṣ; ā́ nédīyas; ā́ púnar; ā́ sám; úd; úd práti; úpa; úpa prá; ní; pári; párā; párā púnar; párā ví; púnar; púras; prá; prá sám; práti; ví; sám;** with appositively added Akk. +/-bel.,+/-abstr.; *Lok. -bel., -abstr.; **Dat. +/-bel., +/-abstr.; active ...

Präsensstamm athematisch II. Klasse (*e-*, *i-*)

**Aktiv

*Indikativ Präs. 1.Sg. *émi* 1a 7.89.2; 2c 10.34.5; *emi* 1a 8.100.1; 10.86.19; 2b 1.171.1 (**práti**, Tm.); 7.18.22 (**pári**); 7.86.3 (**úpa**); 10.13.3 (**ánu**); 10.66.13 (**ánu**); 2c 10.124.2b; 10.124.3; 3 10.17.10 (**úd; ā́**, Tm.); 10.124.2d*; 5 3.54.9 (**ádhi**)*; 6 8.48.10; 2.Sg. *éṣi* 1a 8.91.2; 10.8.4 (oder 2c) 2b 9.97.31 (**ati**); 10.142.5 (**anu**); 2c 1.123.10; 9.50.2*; 4a 10.86.21; *eṣi* 1a 9.97.14b; 9.97.14c; 2a 1.50.5 (**úd**); 1.53.7 (**úpa**, Tm.); 10.142.4 (**pṛ́tak**); 2b 1.50.7 (**ví**, Tm.); 1.52.12 (**ā́**, Tm.); 5.1.9 (**prá**, Tm.; **áti**); 8.93.1 (**úd, abhí**, Tm.); 9.82.2 (**pári**); 9.83.1 (**pári**); 9.97.55 (**sám**); 9.106.14 (**pári**);...

Präsensstamm thematisch IV. Klasse (Augenblicksbildung – momentary formation) (*-ya-*)

**Aktiv

*Indikativ Präs. 3.Sg. *íyati* 5 10.32.3 (**adhi**)*

Perfektstamm (*iye- / iyāy-, īy-*)
**Aktiv
*__Indikativ__ 2.Sg. *iyétha* **2b** 4.9.1 (**ā́**, Tm.); *iyatha* **2c** 8.1.7 (**kv...**); 3.Sg. *iyāya* **2b** 9.94.4 (**ā́ níṣ**)*; 3 4.4.11 (**ánu**); 7.33.13 (**úd**); 10.73.10a; 10.73.10c; 2.Du. *īyathus* **2b** 5.73.4 (**sám**, Tm.; **ā́**); 3.Du. *īyátus* **2a** 10.113.7 (**sam**); **2b** 8.68.3 (**pári**, Tm.); *īyatus* **2b** 3.2.9 (**úpa**, Tm.); 8.99.6 ...

-ta-Partizip
Nom.Sg.m. *itas* **2a** 10.83.5 (**ápa párā**); 10.121.6 (**úd**); 10.161.2a (**párā**); **2b** 10.161.2b (**ní**); Lok.Sg.m. *ite* **2a** 3.15.2 (**úd**); 5.54.10 (**úd**); 7.63.5 (**úd**); 7.65.1 (**úd**); 7.66.4 (**úd**); 7.66.7 (**úd**); 7.66.12 (**úd**); 8.1.29 (**úd**); 8.13.13 (**úd**); 8.27.21 (**úd**); Nom.Du.m. *itā* **2b** 3.39.3 (**ā́**)*; Nom.Pl.m. *itās* **2a** 7.83.7 (**sám**); *itāsas* 3 1.165.1 (**ā́**)

Absolutivum (Gerundium)
ítya **2b** 10.99.5 (**abhi**); 10.116.5 (**prati**); *ít(i)ya* **2a** 4.32.10 (**abhi**); 9.55.4 (**abhi**); **2b** 2.43.2 (**api**); 10.66.14 (**ā**)

Infinitiv (aus dativischen Verbalnomina)
étave **1a** 1.112.8; 8.69.17; 10.39.8; **2c** 1.46.11; 5.44.11; *etave* **2b** 7.33.8 (**ánu**); 8.24.21 (**pári**); 8.45.30 (**níṣ**); 3 1.37.9 (**níṣ**); *étavaí* **2c** 4.58.9; 10.108.6;

Infinitiv (aus dem Abl. eines *tu*-Verbalnomens)
étos **1a** 2.15.5; 2.38.3
Iir.: aav. *āitī* (*ā* + *aēitī*) „kommt heran", *idī* „komme!", *itē* „einzugehen", *aiienī* „ich soll gehen", jav. *aēiti* „geht", *yeiṇti* „sie gehen", *ite* „zu gehen", ap. *aitiy* „geht", *parīdiy* „befolge, respektiere!"; mp. *uz-īdan* „ausgehen, verschwinden"; idg. *h_1*ei̯*-, vgl. lat. *eō*, *īre* „gehen", gr. εἶμι „werde gehen", myk. *i-jo-te* „ἰόντες", heth. *i-it* „geh!", *e-hu* „herbei", luw. *i-ti* „er geht", *i-du* „soll gehen"; altlit. *eimì* „gehe", lit. *eĩti* „gehen", aksl. *iti* „gehen", vgl. VIA: 160f., EWAia s.v., Mayrhofer 2005: 12 und LIV s.v.

After the part of speech information and the rough translations into German and English, all the combinations of the verb with preverbs are listed with their translations into German and English.

The linguistic concept of deep case frames (/Theta Roles) is used to describe the interface between syntax and semantics. In [3] the semantic roles ACTOR (the animate or inanimate performer of an action), THEME (the person or thing that is affected or created by an action or an event/state) and GOAL (goal of a movement/action) are seen. As is possible in some versions of deep case theory, a concept of roles is used in which roles may be superimposed on each other. Somebody who goes is ACTOR and THEME (i.e. the one moved) at the same time. In the 'grey box' the deep case forms are assigned to the morphological case forms or to the preverbs here viewed as adverbs, e.g. THEME is assigned to the nominative, and GOAL is assigned to the respective preverbs or to the preverbs plus a morphological case like the accusative of direction (interpreted as a case form added appositively to the adverb). Below the 'grey box' the verb forms are analysed and assigned to their attestations. As is well known, the language of the *Ṛgveda* is a language which shows discontinuous constituents. This is immediately evident with the frequently dislocated positions of preverb and verb (tmesis). All these cases are marked in our dictionary with 'Tm.' meaning tmesis. An example is the first person singular *emi* in 1.171.1 (meaning **2b** with the preverb *práti* in tmesis).

The root *ay-* also contains examples which go beyond the semantic field of movement, and attach to another semantic field: with the preverb *ádhi* the semantics of *ay-* shifts to 'to know'. In RIVELEX this fact is presented in the following way:

The unmarked meaning and deep case frame with [ACTOR] = THEME and GOAL, is followed by the inclusion of an arrow to indicate word field change. In addition to that the change is explained in a footnote: 'Metaphoric transfer to the intellectual and promotion of an implication to the primary meaning. Thus the verb enters a new word field.' This part of the 'grey box' can be seen in [4]:

[4]

<u>5</u> [ACTOR =] THEME – (GOAL) „jmd. geht [scil. geistig] (an jmdn./etw.) heran" → EXPERIENCER – (THEME im Akk.) "jmd. erkennt jmdn./ kennt (etw. /jmdn.), jmd. ist im Zustand des Wissens"[1] EXPERIENCER = Nom. +bel., -abstr.; *(THEME = Akk. +/–bel., +/-abstr.) (ádhi); Aktiv
• [ACTOR =] THEME – (GOAL) 's.b. approaches (s.o./s.th.) [scil. mentally]' → EXPERIENCER – (THEME in the Akk.) 's.b. recognizes (s.o./s.th.), s.b. is in a state of knowing' EXPERIENCER = Nom. +bel., -abstr.; *(THEME = Akk. +/-bel., +/-abstr.) (ádhi); active

[1] Metaphorische Übetragung auf Geistiges und Aufrücken einer Implikation zur Hauptbedeutung. Das Verb ändert damit seine Wortfeldzugehörigkeit.
• Metaphoric transfer to the intellectual and promotion of an implication to the primary meaning. Thus the verb enters a new word field.

3.3. The following example illustrates the treatment of adjectives in RIVELEX. Apart from the usual information (word class, meanings, case, number, information in small print), every lexical entry for adjectives contains information about the syntactic status of the attestations. In this connection, information is given about attr(ibutive), pred(icative) and nominal use of adjectives (cf. also Krisch 2005). An example is (5):

[5] (there are no footnotes with this lemma)

ádridugdha- (adj.) „VON DEN PRESSSTEINEN GEMOLKEN" – 'MILKED BY THE PRESSING STONES'

<u>adj. Verwendung – adj. use</u>
<u>1a</u> attr.
<u>1b</u> präd. – pred.
<u>subst. Verwendung – nom. use</u>
<u>2</u> m. der von den Presssteinen Gemolkene
• he who has been milked by the pressing stones

Nom.Sg.m. *ádridugdhas* **<u>1b</u>** 9.97.11
Nom.Pl.m. *ádridugdhās* **<u>1a</u>** 4.50.3; <u>2</u> 1.54.9
Verbales Rektionskompositum aus *ádri-* „Stein, Fels, Pressstein" (s.d.) + *dugdhá-* „gemolken" (*-tá-*Partizip zur Wz. *dogh-* „melken", s.d.).

Components of 'split constituents' which are not immediately adjacent to each other are treated as relatively independent constituents. Adjectives not adjacent to 'their' noun are thus interpreted and translated nominally or predicatively. Adjectives are not considered split when they are – though not directly adjacent to 'their' noun – still within a homogenous group which is adjacent as a whole e.g. *asyá* (gen. sg. of *ayám* 'this') in RV 1.52.12 is interpreted as an attribute of *rájaso* : *asyá pāré rájaso*, 'on the other side (*pāré*) of this airspace'. Also, if a clitic stands between the 'adjective' and the rest of the nominal phrase then this clitic is not 'counted' as an intervening constituent and an attributive reading is considered.

3.4. The preverb *abhí* has been selected to display the treatment of a preverb in RIVELEX:

[6] (without footnotes)

abhí (Präverb, adv.) „HERBEI, HINZU, (ENT)GEGEN; WEGEN; ÜBER" – 'HERE, TO IT, AGAINST; BECAUSE OF; OVER'

1 Präverb oder GOAL (Adverb) von Verben (z.T. mit abgeschwächter Bedeutung des Präverbs): (ent)gegen, hinzu, herbei

▪ Preverb or GOAL (adverb) of verbs (partly with weakened meaning of the preverb): against, to it, here

1a bei Bewegungsverben als GOAL (fakultativ mit appositiv dazugesetztem Akk*. oder Lok.**): (ent)gegen gegenüber, hinzu, herbei

▪ with verbs of motion as GOAL (optionally with appositively added Akk.* or Lok.**): against, opposite, to it, here

1b Lexikalisierendes Präverb

▪ lexicalizing preverb

1c Verb elliptisch (bei Bewegungsverben fakultativ mit *abhí* + appositiv dazugesetztem GOAL im Akk.*)

▪ elliptical verb (with verbs of motion optionally with *abhí* + appositively added GOAL in the Akk.*)

2 Adverb in finaler Bedeutung (im Übergang zur Adposition) mit appositiv dazugesetztem Akk.*(/Lok.**) (nicht direkt vom Verb gefordert): für, wegen, zwecks, hinsichtlich, zu dem Zweck

▪ **Adverb in final meaning (in transition to apposition) with appositively added Akk.*(/Lok.**) (not directly demanded by the verb): for, because of, with regard to, with the purpose of**

abhí 1 1.5.1 (*gā*^{2}-, *prá*); 1.5.10 (*drogh-*); 1.10.4a (*svar-*); 1.10.4b (*gar*^{i1}-); 1.15.3 (*gar*^{i1}-); 1.24.3 (*yā*^{2}-); 1.33.9 (*dham*^{i}-); 1.37.1 (*gā*^{2}-, *prá*); 1.42.10 (*gar*^{i1}-); 1.48.14 (*gar*^{i1}-); 1.51.1a (*mad-*); ...

1a 1.11.2 (*nav-*, *prá*)*; 1.11.8 (*nav-*)*; 1.19.9 (*sarj*^{1}-)*; 1.22.11 (*sac*^{1}-)*; 1.25.11 (*spaś-*)*; 1.31.18 (*nay*^{i}-, *prá*)*; 1.33.13 (*gā*^{1}-)*; 1.35.9 (*ar*^{1}-); ...

1b 1.42.4 (*sthā-*; „bezwingen, bewältigen" – 'defeat, overcome'); 1.71.10 [*as*^{1}-; „jmd. ist besser/stärker als jmd./etw. (Akk.)" – 's.b. is better/ stronger than s.o./s.th. (Akk.)']; 1.74.8 (*sthā-*, *prá*; „sich die Spitzenposition erobern" – 'gain o.s. top position'); 1.94.8 [*as*^{1}-; „jmd. ist besser (stärker) als jmd./etw. (Akk.)" – 's.b. is better (stronger) than s.o./s.th. (Akk.)']; ...

1c 1.78.1; 1.86.5 (ellipt. *as*^{1}-; „besser/stärker sein" – ellipt. *as*^{1}-; 'be better/ stronger'); 1.135.4 (ellipt. *vah-*)*; 1.139.3 (ellipt. Transportverb, z.B. *vah-* – ellipt. verb of transport, e.g. *vah-*); ...

2 1.33.11; 1.45.8; 1.61.10; 1.119.1; 5.51.5; 5.51.6; 5.51.7; 7.18.10*; 9.6.2b*; 8.13.28 (oder 1c, ellipt. Bewegungsverb* – or 1c, ellipt. verb of motion); ...

abhī́ 1 1.35.4 (*var*^{2}-); 1.164.29 (*var*^{2}-); 3.44.5 (*var*^{2}-); 6.40.4 (*var*^{2}-); 8.39.5 (*var*^{2}-); 8.100.9 (*var*^{2}-); 10.73.2 (*var*^{2}-); 10.176.3 (*var*^{2}-)

abhí+ 1 1.140.13 (*gar*^{i1}-); 2.33.7 (*kṣam*^{i}-); 1a 4.31.4 (*vart-*, *ā́*)*; 9.97.49c (*arṣ*^{1}-)*; 9.100.1 (*nav-*, *sám*)*; 9.101.3 (*hay-*)*...

abhi 1 1.23.22 [(*drogh-*) = 10.9.8]; 1.54.7 (*gar*^{i1}-); 1.79.11 (*dā*^{5}-); 1.102.2 (*cakṣ-*); 1.113.6 (*cakṣ-*, *pra*); 1.115.5 (*cakṣ-*); 1.140.5d (*śvas-*); 1.163.5 ...

abhy-àbhi 1 9.110.5 (*tard-*)

Im Indischen dürften zwei Adverbialbildungen zusammengefallen sein: idg. **h₂m̥ bʰi* / **h₂embʰi* „von allen Seiten, ringsum", vgl. gr. ἀμφί „auf beiden Seiten, um", ai. *abhítas* „umher, ringsherum" und *(H)e/obʰi* „zuhin, entgegen", vgl. aksl. *o*, *ob*, *obĭ*, evtl. aav. *aibī*, jav. *aiβi*, ap. *abiy* „zuhin, gegen, über". Die Bedeutungen „herbei, hinzu, entgegen" können durch Desemantisierung von **h₂m̥bʰi* / **h₂embʰi* unter dem Einfluss von *(H)e/obʰi* oder als Fortsetzung vom letzteren entstanden sein. Die Bedeutung „über" in Bildungen wie *abhí-as*^{1}- „jmdm. überlegen sein", könnte aus *(H)e/obʰi* im Sinn von „(ent)gegen sein, Paroli bieten" entstanden sein, mit Aufrückung einer Implikation zur der Hauptbedeutung: „überlegen sein". Die finale Bedeutung „zwecks, hinsichtlich, wegen" könnte aus *h_2m̥ bʰi / *$h_2$embʰi stammen: vgl. gr. ἀμφί in der schon bei Homer bezeugten Bedeutung „für, wegen" und die Etymologie der dt. finalen Konjunktion „um". vgl. auch EWAia s.v. über weitere Verwandte.

Preverbs in Vedic, for the most part, behave as normal adverbs.[8] Therefore, the part of speech information on *abhí* [6] lists 'preverb' and 'adverb'. The 'grey box' contains syntactic and semantic properties of the preverb. The verb the preverb 'belongs' to is put in parentheses after the reference when listing the actual attestations (e.g. 1.5.10 (*drogh-*)). If there is a second preverb, this is put after the verb (e.g. *prá* in 1.5.1 (*gā²-*, *prá*) (1). Lexicalised formations (1c) are translated into German and into English.[9] In the case where the Padapāṭha shows auslauting short vowel whereas the Saṃhitā text has a long vowel a '+'-sign is written after the short vowel, e.g. *abhí+*.

4. The first part of RIVELEX, containing all the words beginning with *a* appeared in 2006. The next volume, containing further words in the *Ṛgveda* which start with a vowel has been published in 2012 (Krisch 2012b; 2012c).

RIVELEX reflects 'Western' scientific approaches. However, it is hoped that it will be of use to scientists internationally, specifically also to Indian scientists.

---

[8] This is a feature inherited from Proto-Indo-European, cf. also Krisch 1984, chapters 3.2.3.2 and 3.2.3.3.

[9] This is the only exception to the 'rule' that there are no English translations below the grey box.

REFERENCES

ELIZARENKOVA, Tatjana Ja. 1999. *Rigveda*, I–III: *Mandaly I–IV, Mandaly V–VIII, Mandaly IX–X*. 2nd edition. Moscow: Nauka.

EWAia = Mayrhofer 1992–2001.

GELDNER, Karl Friedrich 1951. *Der Rig-Veda. Aus dem Sanskrit ins Deutsche übersetzt und mit einem laufenden Kommentar versehen*, I–IV. Cambridge, Mass.: Harvard University Press.

GOTŌ, Toshifumi 1987. *Die "I Präsensklasse" im Vedischen. Untersuchungen der vollstufigen thematischen Wurzelpräsentia.* (Österreichische Akademie der Wissenschaften, Philosophisch-Historische Klasse, Sitzungsberichte, 489.) Wien: Verlag der Österreichischen Akademie der Wissenschaften.

GRASSMANN, Hermann 1996. *Wörterbuch zum Rigveda*. 6th edition, revised by Maria Kozianka. Wiesbaden: Otto Harrassowitz. [1st edition: 1873–75.]

HEENEN, François 2006. *Le désidératif védique*. (Leiden Studies in Indo-European, 13.) Amsterdam: Rodopi.

JAMISON, Stephanie 1983. *Function and Form in the -áya-Formations of the Rig Veda and Atharva Veda*. (Ergänzungshefte zur Zeitschrift für Vergleichende Sprachforschung, 31.) Göttingen: Vandenhoeck & Ruprecht.

JANDA, Michael 2000. *Eleusis. Das indogermanische Erbe der Mysterien*. (Innsbrucker Beiträge zur Sprachwissenschaft, 96.) Innsbruck: Institut für Sprachwissenschaft.

KRICK, Hertha 1982. *Das Ritual der Feuergründung*. Wien: Österreichische Akademie der Wissenschaften.

KRISCH, Thomas 1984. *Konstruktionsmuster und Bedeutungswandel indogermanischer Verben. Anwendungsversuche von Valenztheorie und Kasus grammatik auf Diachronie und Rekonstruktion.* (Europäische Hochschulschriften 21.35.) Frankfurt am Main: Peter Lang.

——— 1996. *Zur Genese und Funktion der altindischen Perfekta mit langem Reduplikationsvokal. Mit kommentierter Materialsammlung.* (Innsbrucker Beiträge zur Sprachwissenschaft, 87.) Innsbruck: Institut für Sprachwissenschaft.

——— 2005. Preliminaries to the study of adjectival syntax in Proto-Indo-European. In: Günter Schweiger (ed.), *Indogermanica. Festschrift Gert Klingenschmitt. Indische, iranische und indogermanische Studien dem verehrten Jubilar dargebracht zu seinem fünfundsechzigsten Geburtstag*: 303–320. Taimering: Schweiger VWT-Verlag.

——— 2006. *RIVELEX. Rigveda-Lexikon*, I: *Wörter beginnend mit "a" / words incipient with 'a'*. In collaboration with Christina Katsikadeli, Stefan Niederreiter & Thomas Kaltenbacher. (Grazer Vergleichende Arbeiten, 20.) Graz: Leykam.

——— 2012a. *RIVELEX. Rigveda-Lexikon*, I. *Wörter beginnend mit "a" / words incipient with "a"*. E-book Version. Zweite, verbesserte Auflage / 2nd edition with corrections. Graz: Leykam URL: http://www.leykamverlag.at/shop/advanced_search_result.php?XTCsid=dda4b1272bdb0c6239164c340c5761fe&XTCsid=dda4b1272bdb0c6239164c340c5761fe&keywords=Krisch&x=0&y=0 (June 3, 2013).

——— 2012b. *RIVELEX. Rigveda-Lexikon*, II: *Wörter beginnend mit anderen Vokalen als "a"*. Unter Mitarbeit von Christina Katsikadeli, Stefan Niederreiter, Konstantinos Sampanis & Sabine Ziegler. (Grazer Vergleichende Arbeiten, 26.) Graz: Leykam.

——— 2012c. *RIVELEX. Rigveda-Lexikon*, II: *Wörter beginnend mit anderen Vokalen als "a" / words incipient with other vowels than "a"*. E-book Version. Unter Mitarbeit von Christina Katsikadeli, Stefan Niederreiter, Konstantinos Sampanis, Sabine Ziegler, Alexandra Hörlberger & Thomas Kaltenbacher. Graz: Leykam. URL: http://www.leykamverlag.at/shop/advanced_search_result.php?XTCsid=dda4b1272bdb0c6239164c340c5761fe&XTCsid=dda4b1272bdb0c6239164c340c5761fe&keywords=Krisch&x=0&y=0 (June 3, 2013).

KÜMMEL, Martin 1996. *Stativ und Passivaorist im Indoiranischen*. (Historische Sprachforschung Ergänzungsheft, 39.) Göttingen: Vandenhoeck & Ruprecht.

——— 2000. *Das Perfekt im Indoarischen. Eine Untersuchung der Form und Funktion einer ererbten Kategorie des Verbums in den altindoiranischen Sprachen*. Wiesbaden: Reichert.

KULIKOV, Leonid 2001. *The Vedic -ya-presents*. PhD dissertation Universiteit Leiden.

——— 2012. *The Vedic -ya-presents. Passives and intransitivity in Old Indo-Aryan*. (Leiden Studies in Indo-European, 19.) Amsterdam: Rodopi.

LIV = Rix *et al*. 2001.

LUBOTSKY, Alexander M. 1988. *The System of Nominal Accentuation in Sanskrit and Proto-Indo-European*. Leiden: E.J. Brill.

—— 1997. *A Rigvedic Word Concordance*, I–II. (American Oriental Series, 82–83.) New Haven, Conn.: American Oriental Society.

MAYRHOFER, Manfred 1992–2001. *Etymologisches Wörterbuch des Altindoarischen*, I–III. Heidelberg: Carl Winter Universitätsverlag.

—— 2005. *Die Fortsetzung der indogermanischen Laryngale im Indo-Iranischen*. (Philosophisch-Historische Klasse, Sitzungsberichte, 730.) Wien: Verlag der Österreichischen Akademie der Wissenschaften.

NIEDERREITER, Stefan 2001. *Morphologische Varianz und semantische Konkurrenz. Verbalabstrakta im Rig-Veda*. (Arbeiten aus der Abteilung "Vergleichende Sprachwissenschaft" Graz, 16.) Graz: Leykam.

NOOTEN, Barend A. van & Gary B. HOLLAND 1994. *Rig Veda. A Metrically Restored Text with an Introduction and Notes*. Cambridge, Mass.: Harvard University Press.

OBERLIES, Thomas 1998. *Die Religion des Rig Veda*, I: *Das religiöse System des Ṛgveda*. (Publications of the De Nobili Research Library, 26.) Wien: Institut für Indologie.

—— 1999. *Die Religion des Veda*, II: *Kompositionsanalyse der Soma-Hymnen des Ṛgveda*. (Publications of the De Nobili Research Library, 27.) Wien: Institut für Indologie.

OLDENBERG, Hermann 1894. *Die Religion des Veda*. Berlin: Verlag von Wilhelm Hertz.

PANAGL, Oswald 1996. Implikationen und Präsuppositionen als Faktoren im lateinischen Bedeutungswandel. In: Hannah Rosén (ed.), *Aspects of Latin. Papers from the Seventh International Colloquium on Latin Linguistics. Jerusalem April 1993* (Innsbrucker Beiträge zur Sprachwissenschaft, 86): 619–634. Innsbruck: Institut für Sprachwissenschaft.

RASMUSSEN, Jens Elmegård 1985. Der Prospektiv – eine verkannte indogermanische Verbalkategorie? In: B. Schlerath, (ed.), *Grammatische Kategorien: Funktion und Geschichte. Akten der VII. Fachtagung der Indogermanischen Gesellschaft. Berlin, 20.–25. Februar 1983*: 384–399. Wiesbaden: Reichert.

RENOU, Louis 1955–69. *Études Védiques et Pāṇinéennes*, I–XVII. Paris: Éditions E. de Boccard.

RIVELEX = KRISCH 2006.

RIX, Helmut *et al.* 2001. *LIV. Lexikon der indogermanischen Verben: Die Wurzeln und ihre Primärstammbildungen*. In collaboration with Martin Kümmel, Thomas Zehnder, Reiner Lipp, Brigitte

Schirmer. 2nd extended edition by M. Kümmel & H. Rix. Wiesbaden: Reichert.

SADOVSKI, Velizar Savtchov 1996. *Die Entheos-Komposita und die präpositionalen Rektionskomposita (Hypostasen) im Ṛgveda*. MA thesis, Universität Wien.

——— 2001. *Untersuchungen zu den exozentrischen Nominalkomposita (bahuvrīhi- und Ableitungskomposita) im älteren Indoarischen (Veda und Avesta)*. PhD dissertation, Universität Wien.

SCARLATA, Salvatore 1999. *Die Wurzelkomposita im Ṛg-Veda*. Wiesbaden: Reichert.

SCHAEFER, Christiane 1994. *Das Intensivum im Vedischen*. (Historische Sprachforschung, Ergänzungsheft, 37.) Göttingen: Vandenhoeck & Ruprecht.

TURNER, Ralph Lilley 1966. *A Comparative Dictionary of the Indo-Aryan Languages*. London: Oxford University Press.

VIA = WERBA 1997.

WERBA, Chlodwig H. 1997. *Verba indoarica. Die primären und sekundären Wurzeln der Sanskrit-Sprache*. Wien: Verlag der Österreichischen Akademie der Wissenschaften.

Conjunctive Sequences in the *Ṛgveda**

JARED S. KLEIN

0. Having discussed the repetition of intrastanzaic nominals, verbs, NEGs, relatives, preverbs, interrogatives, numerals, adverbials, and *sá / tá*-demonstratives in the *Ṛgveda* (Klein 1999; 2004a; 2007a; 2007b; 2007c; 2008a; 2008b; 2008c; 2012a, respectively), I turn now to orthotonic conjunctions.[1] The data we will discuss here include 5 different forms appearing 79 times in iterative structures. In each case we shall arrange our presentation by the nature of the sequence relative to the verse structure of the Ṛgvedic stanza, first investigating line-internal sequences, then those extending into adjacent pādas, those within different distichs of four-line stanzas, patterns appearing in three-line stanzas, and ending with those instances where an item occurs in every pāda of its stanza.

---

* I have taken the liberty of substituting the present study for my paper 'Sequential Negation in the Rigveda' which I delivered orally at the 13th World Sanskrit Conference and which has since appeared as Klein 2007a. Like the latter, the current paper represents a chapter of my projected book, *Stylistic Repetition in the Rigveda*.

1 Sequences of enclitic conjunctions, such as *ca* and *vā*, will be treated elsewhere (see now Klein 2012b). In determining what forms to include in this study we have appealed to the criterion of whether a form can be analyzed in at least one of its occurrences as a simple word-level coordinator. By this standard *utá*, *ádha*, *ā́d*, and *átho* come into consideration. Our inclusion of a single passage involving *áthā* [22] is mainly for purposes of distinguishing this lexical item from the very different *átho*, with which it has been confounded by the entirety of the Sanskrit lexicographical tradition. For a demonstration of the fundamentally different employment of these two particles, cf. Klein 1997.

1. The orthotonic conjunction appearing, by a wide margin, most frequently in intrastanzaic sequential employment is *utá* 'and' (60x). As a pre-positional conjunction, *utá* occurs within the basic syntagms X *utá* Y (*utá* Z) and *utá* X *utá* Y (*utá* Z). An important difference between sequences involving *utá* and others we have studied, say of nouns, verbs, or preverbs, is that the sequence-types noted above are licensed by grammar rather than style. Nevertheless, it is still possible to consider these passages within an inquiry that investigates repetition as a stylistic feature of the *Ṛgveda* by focusing on the repetition types and comparing them to the types seen in other, purely stylistic instances of repetition. This will allow us ultimately to say that repetition in the *Ṛgveda*, whether stylistic or grammatical in nature, obeys certain rules. All the passages we shall discuss here are treated in Klein 1985 (Part 1) from the perspective of Ṛgvedic conjunction rather than as repetition types in general.

The occurrences of sequential *utá* include six that appear isolated within a single pāda of a stanza. Most are of the type *utá* X *utá* Y, the expected order for a repeated orthotonic, pre-positional conjunction (contrast X *ca* Y *ca*, with an enclitic, postpositional conjunction):

[1] a. 7.98.2cd ***utá*** *hṛd**ótá** mánasā juṣāṇá* |
uśánn indra prásthitān pāhi sómān
'Enjoying (them) with heart and with mind, desiring (them), O Indra, drink the offered soma drinks.'

b. 9.107.20ab ***utā́****hám náktam **utá** soma te dívā* |
sakhyā́ya babhru ū́dhani
'I am by night and by day at thy udder for friendship, O brown soma.'

c. 10.55.6d *vásu spārhám **utá** jét**otá** dā́tā*
'He conquers and gives desirable good.'

d. 10.88.14cd *yó mahimnā́ paribabhū́vorvī́ ।*
utā́vástād ***utá*** *deváḥ parástāt*
'Who with his greatness has encompassed the two wide (worlds) from below and from above, (he) the heavenly one.'

As we expect, the conjunction appears with parallel structures (in each case single words) sharing semantic features. Another passage of this sort is really of the type X *utá* Y *utá* Z, and the Y term has been truncated under metrical pressure from **prajā́su*:

[2] 1.67.9ab *ví yó vīrútsu ródhan mahitvā́ ।*
utá *prajā́* ***utá*** *prasū́ṣv antáḥ*
'Who with his greatness has spread out among the plants and the offspring and within the sprouting things.'

No doubt contributing to the truncation here is the fact that the locative plural ending *-su* is present on the adjacent conjunct *prasū́ṣu* within an easily parsable structure.

In the final passage showing repetition of *utá* within a single pāda the conjunction operates at a different level in each of its occurrences:

[3] 10.148.4cd *tébhir bhava sákratur yéṣu cākánn ।*
utá *trāyasva gṛṇatá* ***utá*** *stī́n*
'Become of single determination with those among whom thou hast found pleasure. And rescue the singers and (their) servants.'

In this instance the first occurrence of *utá* sententially conjoins pādas c and d (... *bhava* ... । *utá trāyasva*), while the second conjoins *gṛnatáḥ* and *stī́n*.

In a unique instance the type seen in [1]–[3] is expanded by a single occurrence of *utá* in an adjacent pāda: *utá* X ... | *utá* Y *utá* Z:

[4] 10.186.2ab ***utá*** *vāta pitā́si na* |
utá *bhrā́to**tá** naḥ sákhā*
'O Vāta, thou art our father and brother and our friend.'

Naturally, in cases such as this one must always consider whether the initial occurrence of *utá* functions within the structure of the stanza (*utá* X *utá* Y *utá* Z) or signals interstanzaic nexus. This is not always easy. But in this case the preceding stanza (10.186.1c) ends *prá ṇa ā́yūṃṣi tāriṣat* 'He will extend our lifetimes', which seems thematically remote from the structure of [4].

In fourteen passages *utá* appears once within each pāda of a distich of a four-line stanza. Eleven of these show the sequence in the opening distich. Of these, five show sentential conjunction, which is to be expected where longer discourse stretches are involved. With one exception, these are all of the type *utá* clause$_1$ *utá* clause$_2$. Examples are the following:

[5] a. 9.79.3ab ***utá*** *svásyā árātyā arír hí ṣá* |
utā́ *nyásyā árātyā vṛ́ko hí ṣáḥ*
'(Protect us) from the stinginess of one among us, for that one is (as) a stranger; and (protect us) from the stinginess of another, for that one is a wolf.'

b. 10.31.11ab ***utá*** *káṇvaṃ nṛṣádaḥ putrám āhur* |
utá *śyāvó dhánam ā́datta vājī́*
'And they say Kaṇva to be the son of Nṛṣad; and the dark courser has acquired the prize.'

c. 7.74.6 *prá yé yayúr avṛkā́so ráthā iva* |
nṛpātā́ro jánānām ||
utá *svéna śávasā śūśuvur nára* |
utá *kṣiyanti sukṣitím*

'The ones who have driven forth offering protection against enemies like chariots, the protectors of the heroes of the folk. (And) with their own power the heroes have swelled; and they dwell in secure dwelling.'

[5a] illustrates a feature which we shall see elsewhere among repeated *utá* sequences: the parallelism associated with coordinate conjunction is extended beyond the conjoined terms themselves to the entire clausal structure, producing responsion. This passage is in fact one of the most elaborate examples of perfect isosyllabic vertical responsion in the *Ṛgveda*: the frame *utá* ... *árātyāḥ* encompasses the antonymous *svásyāḥ* ... *anyásyāḥ*, but then in each case the explicative clause *arír /vṛ́ko hí ṣáḥ* is added. Whereas the parallel structure clarifies the role of the initial *utá* as sequence-internal in [5a], the situation is less clear in [5b]. A hint may be offered by the fact that this passage introduces the final stanza of its hymn, where one frequently finds in the *Ṛgveda* some demarcative device conveying a culminative or recapitulative value. If this is so here, then the role of the initial *utá* may be twofold, signaling both demarcational distance from what precedes as well as introducing an *utá* $clause_1$ *utá* $clause_2$ structure. A similar situation may obtain in [5c], this time relative to the opening distich. For once again, this is the concluding stanza of its hymn, and the demarcation may have been displaced to the final distich. Renou (1967: 52) suggests that the *utá* ... *utá* structure is meant to convey the contrast of ideas (*yoga* 'war' vs. *kṣema* 'peace').

The remaining sentential passage is a six-word parisyllabic responsion in which *utá* conjoins nominal clauses:

[6] 6.47.1ab *svādúṣ kílāyám mádhumām̐* ***utā́yám*** *|*
tīvráḥ kílāyáṃ rásavām̐ ***utā́yám***
'Sweet, indeed, is this, and full of honey is this; sharp, indeed, is this, and tasty is this.'

The conjunction here operates in each instance at the level of the nominal clause and *utá* is unusually positioned, almost certainly for metrical purposes. Moreover, we do not have here so much a continuous sequence as separate sequences, one in each pāda. We have ignored an additional occurrence of *utá* in pāda c of this stanza, which merely links the second distich with the first.

The second group of passages that we shall cite here is different from the above in that it represents either word or phrase-level conjunction [7a–d] or a combination of word and clause-level nexus [7e]:

[7] a. 2.28.8ab *námaḥ purā́ te varuṇ**otá** nūnám* |
utā́paráṃ tuvijāta bravāma
'Reverence to thee previously (have we spoken), O Varuṇa, and now, and in the future shall we speak, O thou born in might.'

b. 8.9.11ab *yātáṃ chardiṣpā́ **utá** naḥ paraspā́* |
*bhūtáṃ jagatpā́ **utá** nas tanūpā́*
'Drive as protectors of (our) roof and as our protectors from the distance. Become protectors of (our) moving possession and protectors of our bodies.'

c. 10.7.7ab *bhávā no agne (a)vit**ótá** gopā́* |
*bhávā vayaskṛ́d **utá** no vayodhā́ḥ*
'Become an aider and protector for us, O Agni. Become a maker of strength and a designator of strength for us.'

d. 10.81.3ab *viśvátaścakṣur **utá** viśvátomukho* |
*viśvátobāhur **utá** viśvátaspāt*
'Having eyes on all sides and having a mouth on all sides, having arms on all sides and having feet on all sides.'

e. 7.49.2ab *yā́ ā́po divyā́ **utá vā** srávanti* |
*khanítrimā **utá vā** yā́ḥ svayaṃjā́ḥ*
'Which waters are heavenly or flow (on earth), those found by digging or which are born of themselves.'

[7a] is the only one of these passages that shows a continuous sequence A *utá* B *utá* C. [7b–d] are like [6], both in the fact that they involve phrasal or lexical repetition and responsion and that they can be broken up into subsequences A *utá* B / C *utá* D. In [7b] the frame of the responsion is $\text{Verb}_{\text{impv}}$ A-*pā́ utá naḥ* B-*pā́*. In [7c] the responsion is not quite as precise, but the structure *bhávā* ... A *utá* B is maintained in each pāda with movable *naḥ* and paronomastic repetition of *vayas-*. This passage contains another occurrence of *utá* in pāda 7d, which is not relevant to the structure presented here. Aside from the fact that [7d] contains a distich with both jagatī and triṣṭubh lines, everything else conforms to the structure *viśváta*-X *utá viśváta*-Y. Finally, [7e], in addition to showing the compound alternative conjunction *utá vā* 'or', combines conjunction at three different phraseological levels: word-level (*khanítrimāḥ*), nominal relative clause (*yā́ ā́po divyā́ḥ, yā́ḥ svayaṃjā́ḥ*), and clause consisting of verb only which, however, falls under the scope of the relative (*srávanti*).

The remaining two passages in this group worth noting are the following:

[8] a. 2.9.6cd *ádabdho gopā́* ***utá*** *naḥ paraspā́* |
ágne dyumád ***utá*** *revád didīhi*
'As an undeceivable protector and our protector from the distance, shine brilliantly and richly, O Agni.'

b. 4.17.10ab *ayáṃ śṛṇve ádha jáyann* ***utá*** *ghnánn* |
ayám ***utá*** *prá kṛṇute yudhā́ gā́ḥ*
'This one is famed, therefore, as the conquering one and the smiting one. And this one drives forth the cows through battle.'

[8a] is remarkable in representing a single clause within which *utá* conjoins two separate compound constituents. In [8b], on the other hand, *utá* functions on two different levels, in pāda a conjoining the participles *jáyan* and *ghnán* and in pāda b occupying

a sentential role in relationship to the overarching anaphoric sequence *ayám* ... *ayám* ... .

Passages in which *utá* appears once in each distich of a four-line stanza are generally sentential in nature. Of twenty such passages, twelve show *utá* in pādas a and c. As usual, in these instances it is not always easy to determine whether initial *utá* signals nexus across a stanza boundary (clause$_1$ /// *utá* clause$_2$ // *utá* clause$_3$) or operates within the sequence *utá* clause$_1$ // *utá* clause$_2$. In three instances, however, it is clear that each occurrence of *utá* is sequence-internal:

[9] a. 10.137.1

utá *devā ávahitaṃ* ।
dévā ún nayathā púnaḥ ॥
utā́*gaś cakrúṣaṃ devā* ।
dévā jīváyathā púnaḥ

'The one placed down, O heavenly ones, do ye lead up again, O heavenly ones; and the one having committed a sin, O heavenly ones, do ye bring to life again, O heavenly ones.'

b. 10.142.3a–c

utá *vā́ u pári vr̥ṇakṣi bápsad* ।
bahór agna úlapasya svadhāvaḥ ॥
utá *khilyā́ urvárāṇām bhavanti.*

'(Sometimes,) indeed, O independent Agni, thou dost spare a thick bush, though (thou art) a consuming one. (At other times) wastelands come into being (in the midst) of sown fields.'

c. 1.153.4a–c

utá *vāṃ vikṣú mádyāsu ándho* ।
gā́va ā́paś ca pīpayanta devī́ḥ ॥
utó *no asyá pūrvyáḥ pátir dán*

'(Although) the cows and heavenly waters swell for you among the clans exhilarating themselves in the (soma) stalk, (nevertheless) (let) the master of this house of ours (be) first (in your eyes).'

In [9a], remarkable for the occurrence of the vocative *devāḥ* in each pāda, the sequence-internal role of *utá* is assured above all by the fact that this stanza appears at the beginning of its hymn.

But the parallel structures of its two distichs as well allows us to consider them bound tightly together, as if they formed the domain of an external operator BOTH. In [9b] and [9c] it is difficult not to read the two clauses as containing a structured opposition which is, admittedly, not normal for *utá*. We might then say, in each instance, that *utá* provides simple nexus, while the precise semantic nuance of the opposition is inherent in the context. Note in [9c] the opposition between clausal *utá* and word-level *ca* (*gā́va ā́paś ca ... devī́ḥ*).

In five remaining passages the structures conjoined by *utá* are in whole or in part word-level:

[10] a. 1.140.12 *ráthāya nā́vam* ***utá*** *no gṛhā́ya* ।
nítyāritrām padvátīṃ rāsy agne ॥
asmā́kaṃ vīrā́m̐ ***utá*** *no maghóno* ।
jánāṃś ca yā́ pāráyāc chárma yā́ ca
'O Agni, grant a ship for our chariot and our home, having its own rudder, possessing feet, which will cross our heroes and our liberal ones, and (our) folk over (dangers) and which (will be) protection.'

b. 7.104.22 *úlūkhayātuṃ śuśulū́kayātuṃ* ।
jahí śváyātum ***utá*** *kókayātum* ॥
suparṇáyātum ***utá*** *gṛ́dhrayātuṃ* ।
dṛṣádeva prá mṛṇa rákṣa indra
'The owl-sorcerer, the *śuśulūka*-sorcerer, smite the dog-sorcerer and the *koka*-sorcerer; the eagle-sorcerer and the vulture-sorcerer, like (grain) with a millstone, grind up the evil spirit, O Indra.'

c. 3.30.11a–c *éko dvé vásumatī samīcī́* ।
índra ā́ paprau pṛthivī́m ***utá*** *dyā́m* ॥
utā́*ntárikṣād abhí naḥ samīké*
'Indra alone has filled up the two conjoined possessors of good(s), heaven and earth. (And) also from the atmosphere (come) unto us in battle.'

d. 6.48.4 *mahó devā́n yájasi yákṣy ānuṣák* ǀ
*táva krátv**otá** daṃsánā* ǁ
arvā́caḥ sīṃ kr̥ṇuhy agne (á)vase ǀ
*rā́sva vā́j**otá** vaṃsva*
'When thou dost worship the great heavenly ones, worship without interruption through thy determination and wondrous skill. Bring them our way, O Agni, for aid. Grant booties and win (them).'

e. 10.61.14a–c *bhárgo ha nā́m**otá** yásya devā́ḥ* ǀ
svàr ṇá yé triṣadhasthé niṣedúḥ ǁ
*agnír ha nā́m**otá** jātávedāḥ*
'Splendor is his name, to whom also the heavenly ones (belong), who have set (him) down in the threefold seat like the sun. Agni is his name, and Jātavedas.'

In the first of these passages one cannot really speak of an *utá*-sequence. Rather, the phrasal *utá naḥ* belongs to a different level of structure in each of its occurrences (the first functions in the main clause, the second in the relative clause), despite its identical position in pādas a and c and the generally similar responsion-like structure of each of these pādas. This is one of the most convoluted syntactic structures in the *R̥gveda*. The real conjunctive sequence here (prior to various movement activity) is *nā́vam*$_x$ (A *utá* B) *yā́*$_x$ *ca* V (A *utá* B C) *yā́*$_x$ *ca* Pred. In [10b] the lexical repetition *-yātum* points to a sequential structure A B / C *utá* D // E *utá* F. *Rákṣaḥ* of the final pāda is then recapitulative. [10c] shows both word-level (*pr̥thivī́m utá dyā́m*) and sentential conjunction (*utā́ntárikṣād* ...). However, the frequent association of *antárikṣam* with heaven and earth as a place where the gods reside, as well as the immediate adjacency of *utā́ntárikṣād* to *pr̥thivī́m utá dyā́m* across a distich break is at least suggestive of a sequence, as is the apparent adverbial conjunctive value of *utá* here ('also'). [10d] is remarkable because of the vertical alignment of pādas b and d, which do not constitute a semantic responsion but show parisyllabic word-for-word equivalence heightened by a significant degree of assonance. Similar is [10e] where, however, the repeated stretch *ha nā́motá* makes it easy for the poet to align what is left. Note again the assonance and rhyme of the respective codas of these pādas, as well as the hypogram[2] *jātávedāḥ / devā́ḥ*.

In six passages *utá* occurs within three different pādas of a four-line stanza. Four of these involve sentential sequences:

[11] a. 5.81.5

***uté**śiṣe prasavásya tvám éka íd* ǀ
***utá** pūṣā́ bhavasi deva yā́mabhiḥ* ǁ
***uté**dáṃ víśvam bhúvanaṃ ví rājasi* ǀ
śyāvā́śvas te savita stómam ānaśe

'And thou alone art master of the impelling forth (of the creatures), and thou dost become Pūṣan, O heavenly one, along thy courses; and thou dost rule over all this world. Śyāvāśva has brought about a praise for thee, O Savitar.'

b. 10.71.4

***utá** tvaḥ páśyan ná dadarśa vā́cam* ǀ
***utá** tvaḥ śṛṇván ná śṛṇoty enām* ǁ
***utó** tvasmai tanvàṃ ví sasre* ǀ
jāyéva pátya uśatī́ suvā́sāḥ

'(And) many a one seeing has not perceived the speech, and many a one hearing does not hear her. And to many a one she has revealed herself like a desiring, well-clothed wife to her husband.'

c. 10.146.3

***utá** gā́va ivādanty* ǀ
***utá** véśmeva dṛśyate* ǁ
***utó** araṇyānī́ḥ sāyáṃ* ǀ
śakatī́r iva sarjati

'(And) it is as if cows are eating and as if a dwelling appears. And the forest maiden at evening creaks like a carriage.'

---

[2] For this term, see Klein 2006.

d. 10.117.1 *ná vā́ u devā́ḥ kṣúdham íd vadhám̐ dadur* ।
utā́*śitam úpa gachanti mṛtyávaḥ* ॥
utó *rayíḥ pṛṇató nópa dasyaty* । ***utā́****pṛṇan marḍitā́raṃ ná vindate*
'Indeed, the heavenly ones have not given hunger alone as a cause of death. Deaths come even to the sated one. (And) the wealth of the one granting in abundance does not become exhausted, but the one not granting in abundance does not find anyone to have mercy (on him).'

The first of these passages is part of a larger conjoined sequence which begins in the prior stanza (cf. [15a] below) and consists of seven straight pādas involving parallel second person verb forms all beginning with *utá*. The final pāda of 5.81.5 also marks the end of its hymn. [11b] is remarkable for its sequentially repeated *utá tva-* as well as the perfect vertical six-word responsion in the opening distich. The responsive parallelism is relaxed in pāda c, as the next clause spreads out over the entire second distich with appended simile occupying all of pāda d. The *utá tva-* sequence is continued by *utá tvam* at the beginning of the following stanza. In [11c] as well we find responsion in pādas ab (*utá* noun *iva* verb) with continuation of the sequence in relaxed form extending throughout the second distich and, once again, a simile in pāda d. The final passage shows antithetical parallelism (*utó rayíḥ pṛṇatáḥ* ... । *utā́pṛṇan* ...) in the second distich, imposing an adversative reading on *utá* in pāda d. But the initial occurrence of *utá* here in pāda b possesses an adverbial value ('even') and is therefore not sequentially linked to pādas c and d.

The remaining two passages of this sort show word-level conjunctive sequences:

[12] a. 1.114.7 *mā́ no mahā́ntam* ***utá*** *mā́ no arbhakám* ।
mā́ na úkṣantam ***utá*** *mā́ na ukṣitám* ॥
mā́ no vadhīḥ pitáram ***mótá*** *mātáram* ।
mā́ naḥ priyā́s tanvò rudra rīriṣaḥ

'Mayest thou not kill our great one nor our small one, not our growing one nor our grown one, not our father nor (our) mother. Do not injure our dear bodies, O Rudra.'

b. 7.41.4 ***uté**dā́nīm bhágavantaḥ syāma* I
***utá** prapitvá **utá** mádhye áhnām* II
***utó**ditā maghavan sū́ryasya* I
vayáṃ devā́nāṃ sumataú syāma
'(And) may we be fortunate now, and in the latter part and in the middle of the days. And at the rising of the sun, O liberal one, may we be in the favor of the heavenly ones.'

[12a] shows a continuous sequence broken up into three pairs which cohere not only metrically but also morphologically and semantically. Pādas a and b present a perfect seven-word parisyllabic responsion. This passage also illustrates the threefold structure associated pervasively with anaphora in the *Ṛgveda*: repetition itself, gapping of the verb in all but one of the anaphoric cola (*vadhīḥ* here only in pāda c), and parallelism of another (often the only other) argument or adjunct. What makes this passage so unusual is that the anaphora *sensu stricto* involves *mā́*, but the repetition encompasses also *naḥ* and *utá*. The inversion of *utá mā́* to *mótá* in c must be based on metrical considerations An independent structure with a new verb is seen in pāda d, but the anaphora of *mā́* (*naḥ*) continues there. [12b] illustrates twofold working of the conjunction in several of its occurrences. Thus, the first *utá* concatenates this stanza with the final pāda of its predecessor, to which it is lexically linked (7.41.3d *bhága prá nṛ́bhir nṛvántaḥ syāma* 'O Bhaga, may we be possessors of heroes, preeminent through heroes.') while at the same time initiating a temporal conjunctive series: now, late in the day, at midday, early in the day. The sequence is enhanced by two occurrences of *utá* in pāda b, both of which function solely within the sequence. However, the fourth occurrence of *utá*

stands at the beginning of a separate clause which occupies the entire second distich, albeit with the same verb (*syāma*) seen in the first clause, but with a separate predicate (*devā́nāṃ sumataú* rather than *bhágavantaḥ*). Consequently, this final occurrence of *utá* actually functions independently of its three predecessors on a syntactic level, while continuing the temporal sequence on a semantic level.

In addition to passages in which *utá* occurs three times within four-line stanzas, there are five passages in which the conjunction appears twice within a three-line stanza. Four of these show *utá* in pādas a and b and one in pādas b and c:

[13] a. 1.79.6 *kṣapó rājann* ***utá*** *tmánā* |
ágne vástor ***utóṣ****ásaḥ* |
sá tigmajambha rakṣáso daha práti
'O King Agni, do (thou) by thyself by night and by the lighting up of the dawn burn off the evil spirits, O thou having sharp teeth.'

b. 8.32.20 *píba svádhainavānām* |
utá *yás túgrye sácā* |
utā́*yám indra yás táva*
'Drink of those having their own milk-stream. (It is) both what resided with the offspring of Tugra and this which is thine, O Indra.'

c. 6.53.10 ***utá*** *no goṣáṇiṃ dhíyam* |
aśvasā́ṃ vājasā́m ***utá*** |
nṛvát kṛṇuhi vītáye
'And (make) our (poetic) thought cow-obtaining, horse-obtaining, and booty-obtaining; make (it be) enjoyed [i.e. greeted favorably] like a hero.'

d. 8.5.9 ***utá*** *no gómatīr íṣa* |
utá *sātī́r aharvidā* |
ví patháḥ sātáye sitam
'And (bring) us nourishments consisting of cows and attainments, O knowers of the day. Unbind our paths for winning.'

It is only in [13a] and (probably) [13b] that the two occurrences of *utá* are sequence-internal. This is manifestly the case in [13a], where the sequence is of the type *kṣapáḥ* ... *utá* ... *vástor utóṣásaḥ*: A *utá* B *utá* B', with the first occurrence of *utá* 'seeking out' *tmánā* to form a pāda-final sequence seen also at 1.41.6b and 8.84.3c. This is, admittedly, a nonce-sequence for *utá* based no doubt on the normal postpositional pattern of the enclitic conjunction *ca* (A *ca* B *ca*). In [13b], if our rendition (which follows Geldner 1951) is correct, the contextual semantics demands that both occurrences of *utá* must be sequence-internal with a strong break between pādas a and bc. The conjunction would then be basically word-level *utá* A *utá* B, a pattern occurring seven times with *utá*, with the first member expanded into a nominal relative clause. *yás táva* would then refer to the *utá* A *utá* B structure as a whole. In both [13c] and [13d] the first occurrence of *utá* is interstanzaic and therefore in neither instance are we dealing with a conjunctive sequence. In [13c] the structure is A / B C *utá*. The stanza is hymn-final and the initial occurrence of *utá* is, if anything, a distancing mechanism marking this finality. [13d] is the third stanza of a tercet whose structure is 78/9, with 8 representing a nonrestrictive relative clause expansion of 7, to which 9 is conjoined by *utá*. For a presentation of this entire structure see Klein 1985 (part 1): 405. A structure similar to [13d] is seen in stanza 21 of the same hymn, also a tercet-final stanza where, however, *utá* conjoins with its immediate predecessor.

In two passages *utá* appears initially in each verse of a three-line stanza (3 x 3 anaphora[3]). Both instances are from Maṇḍala 4:

[3] This term, which, together with the more common 4 x 4 anaphora (see below), I first used in Klein 2004a, is to be read '3 by 3 anaphora' (similarly, '4 by 4 anaphora').

[14] a. 4.9.4 ***utá*** *gnā́ agnír adhvaré* |
utó *gṛhápatir dáme* |
utá *brahmā́ ní ṣīdati*
'(And) Agni (leads) the women in the ceremony, and he is master of the dwelling in the home, and as a Brahmin he sits down.'

b. 4.52.3 ***utá*** *sákhāsy aśvínor* |
utá *mātā́ gávām asi* |
utóṣo *vásva īśiṣe*
'(And) thou art a friend of the Aśvins, and thou art mother of the cows. And, O dawn, thou art mistress of wealth.'

In both these passages we have placed in parentheses the translation 'and' of the first occurrence of *utá* as a means of signaling that each is an integral pāda-internal sequence (for discussion of the larger discourse contexts here, cf. Klein 1985 (part 1): 410–412). Pādas a and b of [14b] represent what I have elsewhere (Klein 2004b) termed a 4/2 responsion (a four-word responsion with two words repeated) with positional inversion of the last two words.

We come, finally, to cases of 4 x 4 repetition. There are two of these involving *utá*, both from the Fifth Maṇḍala:

[15] a. 5.81.4 ***utá*** *yāsi savitas trī́ṇi rocanā́* |
utá *sū́ryasya raśmíbhiḥ sám ucyasi* ||
utá *rā́trīm ubhayátaḥ párīyasa* |
utá *mitró bhavasi deva dhármabhiḥ*
'(And) thou dost drive, O Savitar, unto the three luminous spheres, and thou dost dwell together with the rays of the sun. And thou dost surround the night from both sides, and thou dost become Mitra, O heavenly one, after thy (own) nature.'

b. 5.46.4 ***utá*** *no víṣṇur* ***utá*** *vā́to asrídho* |
draviṇodā́ ***utá*** *sómo máyas karat* ||
utá *ṛbháva* ***utá*** *rāyé no aśvínā* |
utá *tváṣṭ****otá*** *víbhvā́nu maṃsate*

> '(And) Viṣṇu and Vāta, the unfailing ones, Draviṇodā and Soma will make refreshment for us; and the Ṛbhu's and Aśvins, and Tvaṣṭar and Vibhvan will have us in mind for wealth.'

[15a] is a classical case of 4 x 4 anaphora *sensu stricto*, with four separate second person clauses. The initial occurrence of *utá* seems to function within its own sequence rather than interstanzaically, since the prior stanza contains an internally resolved *yá- ... sá / tá*-sequence. This passage is, however, continued by [11a] above, the two together representing the longest continuous *utá*-sequence in the *Ṛgveda*. The independence of these hymn-concluding stanzas from their predecessors is also marked by the fact that they are the only instances in their hymn of second person discourse. [15b], from a Viśve Devāḥ hymn, is a more complex sequence involving extra occurrences of *utá* in pādas a, c, and d.[4] It is in fact the most densely structured subclausal *utá*-sequence in the *Ṛgveda*. 5.46.2–5 are all highly enumerative, with the two prior stanzas being essentially asyndetic. Stanza 4 is best analyzed into separate sequences of the types *utá* A *utá* B (a), A *utá* B (b), and *utá* A *utá* B *utá* C *utá* D (cd). The following stanza continues *utá tyán no mā́rutaṃ śárdha ā́ gamat* 'And that famous Marut-troop shall come hither to us' (5.46.5a), and 5c shows the sequence *bŕ̥haspátiḥ pūṣótá* (A B *utá*), completing the étalement of the three syntagms in which *utá* appears (A *utá* B, A B *utá* [rare], and *utá* A *utá* B). In each distich the final verb is singular in number, as if the subject were only the last of the conjoined terms in each instance.

2. Our survey of conjunctive repetition continues now with *ádha*. This form occurs sequentially on eight occasions, two of which appear isolated within a single pāda:

---

[4] I have elsewhere (Klein 2007) referred to this type as '4 x 4 (+3)'.

[16] a. 4.31.6 *sáṃ yát ta indra manyávaḥ* |
sáṃ cakrā́ṇi dadhanviré |
***ádha** tvé **ádha** sū́rye*
'When thy zeals and thy wheels run together,
O Indra, then (do I find my fortune) in thee and in the sun.'

b. 8.1.18ab ***ádha** jmó **ádha** vā divó* |
bṛható rocanā́d ádhi
'(Come hither,) therefore, from earth or from the lofty luminous sphere of heaven.'

The basic function of *ádha* is to signal temporal or logical nexus between clauses. In many instances, however, it is equivalent to *utá*, signaling a simple 'and' relationship between sentential units. Rarely, it appears to function as a subclausal conjunction. This value is reflected in the second occurrence of *ádha* in the passages just cited. In both instances, however, the first occurrence of *ádha* signals nexus with a preceding clause. This is illustrated in [16a], where the preceding material appears in pādas a and b. For the fuller discourse context of [16b], cf. Klein 1985 (part 2): 129. The structures *tvé ádha sū́rye* and *jmó ádha vā diváḥ* of [16a] and [16b] seem to be modeled on the constructions A *utá* B and A *utá vā* B, respectively. But the double-level employment of *ádha* gives the appearance of a sequence in each case.

Other sequences involving *ádha* show parallel structures across pāda-boundaries ([17a] & [17b]) or the sequence *ádha yád ... ádha* 'and when ... then' ([17c]):

[17] a. 5.52.11 ***ádhā** náro ny òhate* |
*(**á)dhā** niyúta ohate* ||
***ádhā** pā́rāvatā íti* |
citrā́ rūpā́ṇi dárśyā
'And the men proclaim (it) (as worthy), and (their) teams proclaim (it so); and wondrous (are their)

forms, worthy of being seen, (of whom they say,) "(They are) from the distance."'

b. 10.95.14 *sudevó adyá prapáted ánāvṛt* ।
parāvátam paramā́ṃ gántavā́ u ॥
ádhā *śáyīta nírṛter upásthe* ।
(*á*)*dhai***naṃ** *vṛ́kā rabhasā́so adyúḥ*
'(If) thy lover should today commit suicide, to go into the furthest distance, never to return; and should he lie in the lap of destruction, and should rapacious wolves eat him –'

c. 8.46.31 ***ádha*** *yác cā́rathe gaṇé* ।
śatám úṣṭrām̐ ácikradat ।
ádha *śvítneṣu viṃśatíṃ śatā́*
'And when in the wandering troop a hundred camels neighed, then (did I receive) twenty hundred among the Śvitnas.'

[17a] is the only three-term sequence involving *ádha*. The first occurrence of the conjunction possesses both an external and an internal role, conjoining also the prior pāda, 5.52.10d *yajñáṃ viṣṭārá ohate* 'in broad troop do they proclaim the worship (as worthy)' with stanza 11 (note the occurrence of *ohate* in three consecutive clauses). Similarly, the first *ádha* of 10.95.14 conjoins its clause with its predecessor, here across a distich boundary. The parallel three-clause sequence in this instance involves third person optatives. In [17c] the first occurrence of *ádha* links its stanza to the preceding *úpa mā́ yanti vádhrayaḥ* 'Up to me come the geldings' (8.46.30b) and shows a dual employment of *ádha* as both a simple sentential conjunction 'and' and a temporal conjunction 'then'.

3. The temporal value seen frequently in the syntax of *ádha* is paramount in the employment of *ā́d*. Roughly 85% of the occurrences of this particle signal temporal nexus; and in turn one half of these follow a subordinating conjunction, producing the diptych *yád* ... *ā́d* ... 'when ... then ...'. In over one half of its occurrences *ā́d* is followed by *íd*, which conveys a delimitative value, hence *ā́d íd* 'just then, then immediately'. *ā́d* appears six times in sequences, each time within four-line stanzas. Three of these show *ā́d* in pādas a and b, two in b and c, and the remaining case involves 4 x 4 anaphora. Two of the occurrences in a and b illustrate subclausal conjunction, a category seen less than 10% of the time with *ā́d*. The following are examples of sequential *ā́d* within the opening distich of a stanza:

[18] a. 4.1.18ab *__ā́d__ ít paścā́ bubudhānā́ vy àkhyann* |
__ā́d__ íd rátnaṃ dhārayanta dyúbhaktam
'Then immediately thereafter waking, they [viz. the Aṅgirases] looked out. Then straightway they held the jewel apportioned by the heavenly ones.'

b. 7.66.11 *ví yé dadhúḥ śarádam mā́sam* ***ā́d*** *áhar* |
yajñám aktúṃ ***cā́d*** *ŕ̥cam* ||
... | *kṣatrám ... āśata*
'The ones who have created the year [lit. autumn], the month, (and) then the day, the worship and night, (and) then the stanza ... they have attained the dominion.'

c. 10.88.8ab *sūktavākám prathamám* ***ā́d*** *íd agním* |
__ā́d__ íd dhavír ajanayanta devā́ḥ
'The heavenly ones begot first the utterance of the hymn, then straightway the fire, then immediately the oblation.'

In [18a] the first occurrence of *ā́d* links up temporally with the immediately preceding main clause 4.1.17c *ā́ sū́ryo br̥hatás tiṣṭhad ájrān* 'Sūrya mounted above the lofty fields' and is in turn followed in temporal sequence by the clause of b. In [18b] it is clear that we have a subclausal sequence, but its internal structure is uncertain. One would like to read AB *ā́d* C / (DE *ca*) *ā́d* F; however, the semantics of the sequence does not support this, *yajñám aktúṃ ca* not being a natural collocation (one would expect rather *áhar aktúṃ ca* 'day and night' or *yajñám ŕ̥caṃ ca* 'the worship and the stanza' (cf. 2.5.7cd *stómaṃ yajñáṃ cā́d áraṃ / vanémā* 'Praise and worship would we then fittingly win'). It may be, therefore, that this passage is to be taken as a continuous six-term sequence as it stands, with *cā́d* serving as a Behaghel-like device to create *wachsende Glieder* at sequence end and metrically fill out the pāda. In [18c] the unitary nature of the sequence is signaled at the outset by *prathamám*, following which *agním* and *havíḥ* represent direct, temporally contiguous creations.

The passages showing *ā́d* in pādas b and c both illustrate sentential conjunction. However, the two occurrences of *ā́d* in [19a] play slightly different roles:

[19] a. 1.32.4 *yád indrā́han prathamajā́m áhīnām* ǀ
ā́n māyínām áminā́ḥ prótá māyā́ḥ* ǁ
***ā́t** sū́ryaṃ janáyan dyā́m uṣā́saṃ* ǀ
tādī́tnā śátruṃ ná kílā vivitse
'When, O Indra, thou didst slay the first born of serpents (and) then moreover didst deceive the wiles of the wily ones, then begetting the sun, heaven, dawn, thou didst at that time find no rival.'

b. 1.148.4a–c *purū́ṇi dasmó ní riṇāti jámbhair* ǀ
***ā́d** rocate vána ā́ vibhā́vā* ǁ
***ā́d** asya vā́to ánu vāti śocíḥ*
'The wondrous one destroys many with his teeth; then the radiant one shines in the wood; then the wind blows behind his flame.'

The signal syntactic feature of [19a] is the accentuation of *áminā́ḥ* in pāda b. This means that *ā́d* which introduces this pāda functions like a conjoiner of parallel clauses, and *utá* must therefore here possess a strong sense 'moreover, also'. But *ā́d* in pāda c is clearly a temporal adverb in sequence with *yád* of pāda a. [19b] shows a straightforward temporal sequence clause$_1$ *ā́d* clause$_2$ *ā́d* clause$_3$.

The single instance of 4 x 4 anaphora involving *ā́d* is the following:

[20] 4.24.4cd–5 *sám̐ yád víśo (á)vavrtranta yudhmā́* |
ā́d *ín néma indrayante abhī́ke* ||
ā́d *íd dha néma indriyám̐ yajanta* |
ā́d *ít paktíḥ puroḷā́śam riricyāt* ||
ā́d *ít sómo ví paprcyād ásuṣvīn* |
ā́d *íj jujoṣa vr̥ṣabhám̐ yájadhyai*
'When the warring clans have come together (in battle), then straightway some seek (the help of) Indra in the encounter. / Then some immediately worship the (name) of Indra; then immediately may the cooked food outdo the rice cake, then straightway let soma leave the non-pressers bereft. Precisely then one enjoys sacrificing a bull.'

Note that this entire sequence depends on the subordinating temporal *yád*-clause of 4c, which is continued by five correlative temporal main clauses beginning with 4d. Remarkably, the conjoined *ā́d íd* clauses differ in tense and mood: present indicative in 4d, injunctive in 5a, optative in 5bc, and indicative perfect in 5d.

4. The forms *áthā* and *átho* both show an increasing distribution within the latter parts of the *R̥gveda* (cf. Klein 1985 [part 2]: 64–65). The former became shortened to *átha* already in the *Atharvaveda* and survives as such into Classical Sanskrit. It is in its origins a *-thā* adverbial to the anaphoric pronominal stem *a-* and therefore possesses temporal, logical, and modal value '(and) then, (and) therefore, (and) in this way', occasionally being employed as a simple 'and'. Its increasing use throughout the *R̥gveda* and beyond mirrors the obsolescence of the largely functionally equivalent *ádha* in the post-R̥gvedic period. *átho*, which must represent originally *áthā* + *u*, shows, on the other hand, a completely different syntax from *áthā* (cf. Klein 1997) and therefore must be accounted a separate lexical item. The critical facts are that *átho* appears as a subclausal conjunction in 16 of its 35 Ṛgvedic occurrences, whereas only two of the 96 occurrences of *áthā*[5] are subclausal. Moreover, *átho* shows no instance of temporal, logical, or modal conjunction. Finally, whether in sentential or subclausal conjunctive value, *átho* may appear multiply within sequences, whereas no such instances of *áthā* are found. The divergent syntaxes of these two particles are continued in the *Atharvaveda* (Klein 1985 [part 2]: 64–65).

We find four sequences involving *átho*. Three appear in pādas b and c of a four-line stanza and one appears in pādas b–d. Of these, one is subclausal [21a], the others sentential:

[21] a. 10.97.16a–c *muñcántu mā śapathyà̀d* I
átho *varuṇyà̀d utá* II
átho *yamásya páḍbīśāt*
'Let them release me from the consequence of a curse, and also from (the sling) of Varuṇa, and from the fetter of Yama.'

b. 1.113.13a–c *śáśvat puróṣā́ vy ùvāsa devy* I
átho *adyédáṃ vy à̀vo maghónī* II
átho *vy ùchād úttarām̐ ánu dyū́n*
'Repeatedly has the heavenly dawn shined out in the past, and today has the liberal one just dawned here; and she will shine out throughout later days.'

c. 1.157.6 *yuváṃ ha stho bhiṣájā bheṣajébhir* I
átho *ha stho rathyà̀ rā́thyebhiḥ* II
átho *ha kṣatrám ádhi dhattha ugrā* I
yó vām ... dadā́śa

---

[5] And both of these occur in consecutive stanzas of the same hymn (8.46.15–16) in the form *átha* and are exceedingly peculiar for other reasons as well, representing two of only three instances in which *átha* (never *áthā*) appears in verse-final position. For discussion and citation of these passages, cf. Klein 1996: 213–215.

'You two are healers with your healings and you are charioteers with your chariot skills. And you two create dominion, O powerful ones, (for him) who ... has worshipped you.'

d. 1.191.2 *adṛ́ṣṭān hanty āyaty* ।
***átho** hanti parāyatī́* ॥
***átho** avaghnatī́ hanty* ।
***átho** pinaṣṭi piṃṣatī́*
'Coming hither, she smites the invisible (serpents), and going forth, she smites (them). And she smites (them) smashing them down, and crushing (them), she crushes (them) (to death).'

In [21a] we find the subclausal sequence ... *śapathyà̀d* । *átho varuṇyà̀d utá* । *átho yamásya páḍbīśāt*, in which *utá* appears to reinforce the second conjunct ('and also'). [21b] shows the clausal sequence *vy ùvāsa* ... । *átho* ... *vy à̀vaḥ* ... ॥ *átho vy ùchād*, a textbook illustration of the remote temporal value of the perfect, the use of the aorist to indicate a past tense contiguous to the present, and a subjunctive qua future. [21c] shows perfect parisyllabic responsion in pādas a and b together with parallel clausal conjunction in c. [21d] is a stanza-long responsion with inversion of the position of finite verb and participle in pāda c.

By way of contrast, there is a single instance where *áthā* is repeated within a stanza. In line with our remarks above, however, it is not a single sequence, but rather two consecutive sequences of the temporal diptych *yadā́* ... *áthā* :

[22] 10.16.2 *śṛtáṃ yadā́ kárasi jātavedo* ।
*(**á**)**them** enam pári dattāt pitṛ́bhyaḥ* ॥
yadā́ gáchāty ásunītim etā́m ।
***áthā** devā́nāṃ vaśanī́r bhavāti*
'When thou wilt make (him) ready (viz. cooked), O Jātavedas, then thou shalt give him over to the fathers; when he will go along this (path of) conveyance of the souls, then he will become the leader (i.e. fulfiller) of the will of the heavenly ones.'

5. Having presented the entire range of sequentially-occurring orthotonic conjunctions in the *Ṛgveda*, we shall now summarize our findings. Four different forms come into consideration: *utá*, *ádha*, *ā́d*, and *átho* (cf. footnote 1). Of these the only form which is purely conjunctive is *utá*, whereas the remaining three items may be considered adverbial-conjunctive. The overwhelming majority of instances of sequential employment involve *utá*, a pre-positional conjunction whose major sequential syntagms are A *utá* B *utá* C and *utá* A *utá* B *utá* C. These syntagms are licensed by grammar rather than style. *utá* may appear as both a word-level and clause-level conjunction (cf. 7.98.2cd = [1a] and 5.81.4 = [15a], respectively), a fact that often renders structures of the sort *utá* A *utá* B, etc. ambiguous between a reading where the first occurrence of the conjunction (which is usually stanza-initial) signals clausal conjunction with a prior stanza and one in which *utá* functions internally within its own stanza (cf. 10.31.11ab = 5b). In some instances multiple occurrences of *utá* appear within different structures, and therefore the conjunction is not employed sequentially (cf. 4.17.10ab, 1.140.12 = [8b], [10a]). Because of its coordinating role *utá* is often associated with responsive structures in which it becomes itself a material part of the responsion (cf. 9.79.3ab = [5a]). Occasionally a stanza containing multiple occurrences of *utá* can be broken down into a series of shorter structures (cf. 5.46.4 = [15b]).

Unlike *utá*, *ádha* is an adverbial conjunction signaling temporal or logical nexus between clauses ('[and] then, [and] therefore'). However, in several instances it functions as a word-level conjunction, either by itself or in the collocation *ádha vā* 'or' (cf. the second occurrence of *ádha* at 4.31.6 and 8.1.18ab = 16a, b, respectively). Occasionally as well *ádha* may appear as a normal *utá*-like clausal conjunction in the structure (*ádha* A) *ádha* B *ádha* C with the same double or ambiguous role of initial *ádha* as both external and sequence-internal conjunction (cf. 5.52.11, 10.95.14 = [17a], [17b]).

Similar to *ádha* is *ā́d*. Primarily an exponent of temporal nexus following a relative pronoun (*yád* ... *ā́d* 'when ... then'), *ā́d* on occasion is employed in subclausal value, where the sense 'A (and) then B (and) then C' closely approaches, except for the temporal nuance, the value of *utá* (cf. 7.66.11, 10.88.8ab = [18b], [18c]). In the same way as the latter, *ā́d* may also appear in structures of the sort *ā́d* clause$_1$ *ā́d* clause$_2$, where the initial occurrence of the adverbial links up with a prior clause within or outside the stanza (cf. 1.148.4a–c, 4.1.18ab = [19b], [18a]).

Also echoing *utá* in its iterative employment is the late Ṛgvedic and Atharvavedic *átho*, which must be sharply distinguished from the externally similar *áthā*, to which it is originally built as *áthā* + *u*. Whereas *áthā* is a temporal-logical-modal adverbial '(and) then, (and) therefore, (and) so', *átho* has no such employment. Rather, it occurs in both sentential and subclausal conjunctive value in sequences of the type A *átho* B *átho* C (*átho* D), where there is never any ambiguity about the sequence-internal role of *átho* in each of its occurrences (cf. 10.97.16a–c, 1.113.13a–c, 1.157.6, 1.191.2 = [21a–d]).

REFERENCES

GELDNER, Karl F. 1951. *Der Rig-Veda. Aus dem Sanskrit ins Deutsche übersetzt und mit einem laufenden Kommentar versehen*, I–III. (Harvard Oriental Series, 33–35.) Cambridge, Mass.: Harvard University Press.

KLEIN, Jared S. 1985. *Toward a Discourse Grammar of The Rigveda*, I: *Coordinate Conjunction*. Parts 1 and 2. (Indogermanische Bibliothek. Erste Reihe: Lehr- und Handbücher.). Heidelberg: Carl Winter Universitätsverlag.

——— 1996. Rigvedic *áthā*: metrics, phonology, and etymology. *Studien zur Indologie und Iranistik* 20: 205–223.

——— 1997. Early Vedic *áthă* and *átho*. In: Douglas Q. Adams (ed.), *Festschrift for Eric P. Hamp*, II (Journal of Indo-European Studies Monograph, 25): 1–25. Washington, DC: Institute for the Study of Man.

——— 1999. A triadic structural feature of nominal anaphora in the *Rigveda*. In: J. Habisreitinger, R. Plath & S. Ziegler (eds.), *Gering und doch von Herzen. 25 indogermanistische Beiträge, Bernhard Forssman zum 65 Geburtstag*: 119–134. Wiesbaden: Reichert Verlag.

——— 2004a. Patterns of verb repetition in the Rigveda. *General Linguistics* 41 [2001]: 222–256.

——— 2004b. Phrasal repetition in the Rigveda. *Bulletin d'Études Indiennes* 21 [2003]: 7–45.

——— 2006. Categories and subtypes of phonological repetition in the Rigveda. In: Gerd Carling (ed.), *GIŠ.ḪURgul-za-at-ta-ra. Festschrift for Folke Josephson* (Meijerbergs Arkiv for Svensk Ordforskning, 32): 134–173. Goteborg: Meijerbergs institut for svensk etymologisk forskning.

——— 2007a. Sequential negation in the Rigveda. In: Alan Nussbaum (ed.), *Verba Docenti. Studies in Historical and Indo-European Linguistics Presented to Jay H. Jasanoff by Students, Colleagues, and Friends*: 213–229. Ann Arbor: Beech Stave Press.

——— 2007b. Relative pronoun sequences in the Rigveda: a syntactic, rhetorical-poetic, and discourse-level study. *Bulletin d'Études Indiennes* 22–23 [2004–05]: 495–536.

——— 2007c. On the nature and function of preverb repetition in the *Rigveda*. *Studien zur Indologie und Indoiranistik* 24: 91–103.

——— 2008a. Interrogative Sequences in the Rigveda. In: Alexander Lubotsky, Jos Schaeken & Jeroen Wiedenhof (eds.), *Evidence and Counter Evidence. Essays in Honour of F. Kortlandt*, I: *Balto-Slavic and Indo-European Linguistics*: 297–308. Amsterdam: Rodopi.

——— 2008b. Numeral repetition in the Rigveda. In: Karlene Jones-Bley *et al.* (eds.), *Proceedings of the Nineteenth Annual UCLA Indo-European Conference* (Journal of Indo-European Studies Monograph Series, 54): 171–191. Washington, DC: Institute for the Study of Man.

——— 2008c. Adverbial repetition in the Rigveda. In: L. Kulikov & M. Rusanov (eds.), *Indologica: T. Ya. Elizarenkova Memorial Volume*, I (Orientalia et Classica. Papers of the Institute of Oriental and Classical Studies, 20.): 167–182. Moscow: Russian State University for Humanities.

——— 2012a. *sá / tá*-Sequences in the Rigveda. In: Velizar Sadovski & David Stifter (eds.), *Iranistische und indogermanistische*

Beiträge in memoriam Jochem Schindler (1944–1994) (Sitzungsberichte der Österreichische Akademie der Wissenschaften, Philosophisch-Historische Klasse, 832; Veröffentlichungen zur Iranistik, 51): 45–76. Wien: Verlag der Österreichischen Akademie der Wissenschaften.

——— 2012b. Fashioning a coda: repetition of clitics and clitic-like elements in the Rigveda. In: Adam I. Cooper, Jeremy Rau, & Michael Weiss (eds.), *Multi Nominis Grammaticus: Studies in Classical and Indo-European Linguistics in Honor of Alan J. Nussbaum on the Occasion of his Sixty-fifth Birthday*: 143–158. Ann Arbor: Beech Stave Press.

RENOU, Louis. 1967. *Études védiques et pāṇinéennes*, XVI: *Notes sur le Ṛgveda, Hymnes aux Aśvin*. Paris: Éditions E. de Boccard.

Contributors

VIT BUBENIK
Department of Linguistics
Memorial University of Newfoundland

EYSTEIN DAHL
Department of Linguistic, Literary and Aesthetic Studies
University of Bergen

JOSE LUIS GARCÍA RAMÓN
Historisch-Vergleichende Sprachwissenschaft
Historisch-Institut für Linguistik
Universität zu Köln

HEINRICH HETTRICH
Lehrstuhl für vergleichende Sprachwissenschaft
Julius-Maximilians Universität, Würzburg

HANS HENRICH HOCK
Department of Linguistics
University of Illinois

JARED S. KLEIN
Department of Classics
University of Georgia

MASATO KOBAYASHI
Department of Linguistics
Graduate School of Humanities and Social Sciences
University of Tokyo

THOMAS KRISCH
Fachbereich Linguistik
Universität Salzburg

MARTIN JOACHIM KÜMMEL
Lehrstuhl für Indogermanistik
Friedrich-Schiller-Universität Jena

ELIZABETH TUCKER
Faculty of Oriental Studies
University of Oxford

Index

(of selected subjects and words)

(Superscript numbers after the page refer to footnotes)

abhí 144–145, 258–260
absolutive 3, 6
accent on augment 154, 174–175
accent retraction in verbs 154, 161, 163–168, 172–175
accentuation of preverbs 169–173
ácidh$_u$vam 30
ad 136
ā́d 265[1], 283–286, 289–290
ádha 57, 92, 265[1], 281–283, 286, 289–290
ádhāyi 8
adhi-ay 141
adjectives with suffix *-ín* 79–88, 91–101
adjectives with suffix *-vant* 79–82, 85–96
ádridugdha- 257
affected object 148
ā́-ghoṣ/-ghuṣ 142
agní- 249–251
aj 55, 60–62, 74–75, 245–246[4]
'Aktionsart' 45–50, 51[13], 54, 56, 58, 61, 63, 65, 69, 71, 73–74
anaclasis 28
analytic perfect passive (Modern Greek) 115
aneṣata 9
animacy 82–86, 89–91, 100–101
anūcāná- 245–246
āp 136
apāviṣur 15
[1]ar 48–51, 53[23], 247
áraruṣ- 30
arcase 247
arí- 244–245
aś[1] 136
aspect 180, 182–186, 190, 194–197, 201–202, 210, 212–213, 221, 223, 225, 233, 237
áśrāyi 8

atelic, see also non-telic(ity) 49, 59[34], 72–74
atelic predicates 184–185, 192, 203, 205, 208, 217, 236
áthā 265[1], 286–290
átho 265[1], 286–290
attitude verbs 197–199, 208–209, 218, 220, 235–236
'Augenblicksbildung(en)' 45, 47, 50[9], 56, 254
(ava-)dyáti 14
ay[1] / *i* 252–257
a-yiyam̐sam̐s 12

bhar / *bhr̥* 48, 52, 55, 58–60, 74, 131, 137, 175
bhas 47[2], 49, 131, 137
bhávuka- 15
bhay[i] / *bhī* 52
bháyya- 2, 5
bheya- 2
bodh / *budh* 141, 147–148
brávīti 15
brevis in longo 25–28, 35–36, 38

cet / *cit* 141, 146–147, 192
conative perfect 207–208, 216–217, 224, 236
converse of Sievers' Law 3

dā 49, 136
dádr̥śe 30
dar[i] / *dr̥̄* 139
dependent clause – main clause order 158, 161, 164–165, 175
deverbative forms with suffix *-ín* 95, 99–100
dhā 49
displexive 65–66
distributive-iterative/ iteration 49, 62, 64–66, 68–69, 73[63], 74
δίζημαι, διζήμενος 58
durative/durativity 49, 55–56, 58–59, 62, 70, 73–74
durative-cursive 49
durative-iterative 49, 63
durative adverbial modifier 206

effected object 135, 148
etiological perfect 214–216
evidentiality 179–180, 187, 200–201, 209–210, 220–222, 230, 237
existential perfect 193–194, 205[33], 208
existential qualifier adverb 204, 212–213

fortition of *i̯ (/y/) 13, 15–16, 19–20

gā 47, 49, 141
gam 141
[2]*gar*[i] / *gr̥̄* 136
gávya-, Avestan *gaoiia-* 18
gerundive 1–5, 10–11
ghas 136
gr̥hápati- 30

hā / *hī* 50
han 55, 63–65, 74, 139

has 47[2], 50
hav / hu 50
hav^i / hvā / hū 52, 54, 109
'Hoffmann suffix' 96–98, 100
Holtzmann's Law 15, 19

imperfect, alternating with perfect 198–199, 213, 225–233, 237
inferentiality / indirect evidentiality 180, 186–187, 200–201, 209–210, 219–222, 230–234, 235–237
intensive/intensivity 46, 48–50, 53–56, 58–60, 62–65, 68–69, 74–75
internal argument 134–135, 140, 150, 185
irajya- 141
īś 141, 143–146
iterative/iteration 47–50, 51[13], 53–54, 56, 58, 59[34], 61–69, 73[63], 74–75, 236
iyāya 8, 12, 255

jambh 139
jánāḥ 26–27
jáyya- 1–5
jeya- 1–2, 5
joṣ / juṣ 136

kā / kam^i 136
kan^i / can^i 142, 148–149
kar^i / kṝ 141
krap^i 136
kráyya- 1–2, 5, 10
kreya- 2, 11
kṣā 141

laryngeal offglide 7–8

mand / mad 142
man 140–141, 148
[2]may^i / mī 52–53
mediopassive periphrastic future (Sanskrit) 114
middle voice 103–127
modality 186–187
momentative 47[2], 49, 53, 63, 65–66, 68–70, 73–74
morphosyntactic blocking 206, 213, 217
myakṣ / mikṣ 52–53

nas 55, 66–67, 74
naiṣṭa 9, 15
náyiṣṭha-, -náyitum 9
nétar- 9, 11, 15
non-telic(ity) 48–49, 59–60, 71, 73–74, 236

ornative construction 132–134

[1]pā 'drink' 49, 51[15], 137–138
[2]pā 'protect' 51
[3]pā 'move, draw' 49, 51
pad 55, 66, 69, 74, 109, 111
par / pṛ 49, 52[16]
par^i / pṝ 52, 136, 138
parc / pṛc 52–53, 137
passive 111–113, 125–126, 134, 141[19]
past imperfective 207, 224–225, 236
past perfective 179, 190, 196–197, 201, 205–

208, 210, 217–218, 221, 224–225, 233[53], 235–236

[2]*pat* 141, 145–146

phonemicization of /y/ 12, 19

plurality 49, 61, 64, 66, 68–69, 74

pluti 162–163, 167

polyactional(ity) 49, 70, 73

praś / (pṛch) 137

pra-hāyyà- 5

pra-héya- 5, 11

present anterior 179, 195–196, 201–202, 205, 235

preverb–verb univerbation 167, 172–173

pṛthivī́ 14–15

rā / rī 50

raising of mid-vowels (Middle Indic) 119

rāj 141, 145–146

rayí- 6, 8, 10, 14–15, 84, 86, 88

rayyā́ 6–7

reh / rih 137

responsion 269, 271, 274–277, 288

resultative perfect 179, 191–192, 202, 208, 213–214, 217, 219, 222, 236

ruruhur 30

śā / śī 50

sac 48, 55, 66, 70–74

saceya 8

sav / su 52, 54

savitā́ 26–27, 29, 33

semantics of class 4 presents (Sanskrit) 109–112

semantics of *hi*-verbs 105, 107–108, 117

semantics of second conjugation (Latin) 110

Sievers' Law 2–3, 16–17, 20

śrav / śru 142

śréṣṭha- 9–10

śréyas- 9, 11

stative 49, 55–56, 63, 74

stative perfect 211, 235

substantives in *-vat* derived from secondary adjectives 85–86

syncope of /i/ before /y/ 3, 10–11, 17–20

tar[i] */ tṝ* 55, 66–67, 74

tarp / tṛp 142, 149

táviṣī- 15

telic(ity) 49, 58–60, 63, 70–74

telic predicates 184–185, 202, 208, 214, 216, 223–224

tense 181–186, 190, 199, 230, 236–237

THEME 246[4], 253–254, 256–257

threefold structure of anaphora 277

universal perfect / present-continuous 192, 197, 205–206, 236

utá 265[1], 266–281, 288–290

vac / uc 48
vah / uh 55, 59, 62, 74, 131, 137
vaś / uś 55–56, 74
vavṛmahe 30
ved / vid 142
'Verbalcharakter' 49
verb-second position 156, 167
vay̮ʻ / vī 15, 137

[2]*y̮ā* 55, 57–58, 74
yas 50
[2]*yav / yu* 52–54